ABOUT THE AUTHORS

Following the murder of his son in 1995, AZIM KHAMISA founded the Tariq Khamisa Foundation and the subsequent forgiveness movement that has reached millions. In 2002 he received Search for Common Ground's prestigious Award for Building Better Communities. In 2004 he participated in the Synthesis Dialogues with His Holiness the Dalai Lama. And in 2006 came the Spirit of Crazy Horse Award from the Reclaiming Youth Network. Azim is also the recipient of the California Peace Prize. A sought-after speaker, he has spoken in person to more than a half million children. He lives in La Jolla, California.

As an Associate Minister at the Interfaith Temple in New York City, host of her own weekly radio talk show, and a life and spiritual coach, JILLIAN QUINN has touched the lives of thousands of people around the country with her workshops, classes, and coaching. She is a member of Spiritual Directors International and the recipient of a grant from the National Endowment for the Humanities for scholarship in the area of Transcendental Philosophy. She lives in Millbrook, New York, with her husband and three young children.

4/10

OXFORD

JUAN DE LA ROSA

novels of the time—shortly thereafter it was recognized as a milestone of Bolivian literature. Considered a bearer of national values, it was soon incorporated into high school programs by the country's educational system. Also, it is as a direct consequence of this work that May 27 has been instituted in Bolivia as the Day of the Mother. This date corresponds to the historical event, described and emphasized in the novel, in which the women of Cochabamba came out to the streets with *macanas* to defend the city from the troops led by the Spanish officer Goyeneche.[1]

The first interpretations that were made of *Juan de la Rosa* treated it essentially as a historical novel and valued it to the extent that it recovers an "original" national model. I believe, however, that the virtue of this novel resides in the way that it registers in an allegorical manner—like few historical or literary works of the time—the contradictions associated with the process of modernization at the end of the last century in an Indo-American linguistic and cultural milieu, such as in Bolivia. And how, in this manner, it projects an intertextuality that opens up to the plurality and diversity of Latin American history and cultural traditions.

The Republic of Bolivia

Bolivia—known as Alto (Upper) Perú during the Colonial period—takes its name from the Liberator Simón Bolívar precisely at the moment it declares itself an independent republic. Upper Perú, which, in 1809, was an initiator in the uprising against the Spanish forces, was also one of the last countries in the region to gain its liberation from the Crown. The country was therefore in the war for Independence a very long time, and experienced a very particular situation during that struggle. Until 1816, the armies from the south, from what is now Argentina, sent reinforcements for the fight against the Spanish government; but after that, the patriotic fighters were forced to maintain an isolated fight because they lost complete contact with the other armies of the Independence Movement on the continent. It was only later, in 1824, with the arrival of the armies from the north, led by Grand Marshal Sucre, that the final victory over the Spaniards was accomplished[2] (see Map 1).

This meant, first of all, that during the last years of the Independence Movement the government of Upper Perú, which was still Spanish, maintained greater contact with Lima while the Viceroyalty still reigned there. Also, the patriotic forces, which had at first been strongly connected with the Independence Movement in Argentina, later remained quite isolated until Sucre's arrival. Furthermore, several delegates from Upper Perú, as representatives of their regions, which are today a part of Bolivia, signed the Independence Act of the United Provinces of South America in 1816.

These ties with the very new republics of Perú and Argentina were partially a continuation of those that existed during the Colonial period; but they also emerged, in part, with the spread of the Independence Movement against Spain. The territories of Upper Perú were included under the jurisdiction of the Audience of Charcas, which had at first corresponded to the Viceroyalty of Perú, with its capital in Lima. However, beginning in the last quarter of the eighteenth century, they were passed over to the jurisdiction of the newly established Viceroyalty of the Río de la Plata, with its capital in Buenos Aires.

The establishment of the Republic of Bolivia resolved a series of tensions implicit in the possibilities that were then being considered of annexing the newly liberated territories either to the Republic of Argentina or the Republic of Perú. It also played a role in a series of events that, at times, were considered an obstacle to Bolívar's project to create one single, large nation in South America. In reality, however, these events were only the moves necessary to help resolve the problems of predominance and confrontation that were emerging between the different nations.[3]

Nataniel Aguirre

Nataniel Aguirre (1843–1888) was a statesman and an intellectual in a republic that was already facing the challenges of consolidating its new institutions. In *Juan de la Rosa*, Aguirre focuses on the origins of the historical processes of these challenges from the perspective of the conflicts present at the end of the nineteenth century. In the last quarter of the nineteenth century, Bolivia entered a stage in which it sought to adapt the organization of the country to the international economy. This was achieved in such a manner that it set off large, violent forces against internal markets, as well as against indigenous organizations regarding access to land. The serious conflicts with the indigenous sectors of the country, which comprise a majority of the population, arose with the selling of community lands and the successive attempts to privatize property. Labeled as the "first agrarian reform," these would extend well into the twentieth century.[4] Furthermore, control over natural resources for which there was demand in international markets also produced tensions along the country's borders. This generated another form of external violence, one that led to the outbreak of the War of the Pacific, in which Bolivia and Perú fought against Chile.

Nataniel Aguirre actively participated in the major events that shaped the economy and the politics under which Bolivia entered the twentieth century. On the one hand, he was a protagonist in the discussion and the shaping of the laws that were meant to revert collective ownership of the land and modify the system of the Indian head tax (or Tribute) within the framework of a modern and supposedly "democratic" constitution. On the other, he participated in the War of the Pacific, in which Bolivia suffered an early and unfortunate defeat and lost an important stretch of land that represented its only access to the sea. It is important to note, especially in light of what will be seen later regarding *Juan de la Rosa*, that Aguirre was one of the main voices arguing in favor of democratic rights and for the establishment of an egalitarian political structure in the National Assembly of 1880. In economic matters, he formulated a policy that was not only based on modern liberal ideas, but also one that would strengthen small producers and energize internal markets that had already showed their virtues during the first decades of the republic. These proposals can be seen as part of a protectionist ideology. As an important leader of the Liberal Party, Aguirre argued for progress and modernization. However, proving the autonomy of his political thoughts, he also set forth proposals designed with the specifics of Bolivia in mind, sometimes going against fashionable "free market" ideas. In any case, these were set aside after the deliberations, and a crude, liberal economic policy whose character was based entirely on mining was adopted instead. Nataniel Aguirre spent the last years of his life distanced from political power and from the leaders of the country's economy.[5]

Aguirre wrote *Juan de la Rosa* immediately after these events, once Bolivia was already out of the War of the Pacific. The novel, however, goes back to the beginnings of a previous war, the one that led to the birth of the nation. Although he belongs to the time of the defeat in the War of the Pacific, the voice that conveys the story is that of a narrator who identifies himself as a witness of the first national struggles, and who defines himself as a spokesman of these in a time of chaos. Furthermore, in a move designed to focus the reader's attention and authorize his own statements, the narrator quotes several well-known historians who have dealt with the period of the Independence Movement (including Bartolomé Mitre, Mariano Torrente, and Eufronio Viscarra). This technique is common to the genre of the historical novel, to which *Juan de la Rosa* also belongs.

Nation and Narration

A National History

The novel *Juan de la Rosa* is written in the form of an autobiography. The retired Colonel Juan de la Rosa writes his "memoirs" in first person, recalling his childhood, the time during which he witnessed the events of the uprising of Cochabamba against the Spaniards. It is interesting to note that the narrator's own name, Juan de la Rosa, is not found written anywhere in the text—although in the first edition it did appear as the name of the author. This is a characteristic typical of the autobiographical genre; the effect it produces is one of creating the impression that the story is the testimony of a real, historical person.

The narrator presents his manuscripts in an introduction titled "Letter—Prologue." In it, he situates himself in a family setting: he is next to his wife Merceditas, on the occasion of celebrating with a group of friends the anniversary of the Triumph at Aroma, one of the first victories of the Independence Movement against the

Spaniards (see Map 2). From there, he addresses his writings to his readers, whom he calls the "youth of my beloved country," thus establishing a direct and familiar relationship with the "future" citizens of Bolivia.

The solemnity and formality of the qualifier "The Last Soldier of the Independence Movement," which brings the patriotic values to the forefront, are neutralized and relativized by a sense of humor and the tone of intimacy of the familiar anecdote. Alluding to his age, Colonel de la Rosa's wife uses an affectionate paraphrase, calling him "the last carrion of the times of the Independence Movement!" It is with this tone that the novel treats the national theme; a tone that is colloquial and familiar rather than official or formal, but that is not for this reason any less serious.

From this brief "Prologue" it is already possible to discern the three periods of the narrator's life. The period of his childhood will be covered by the story told in the novel. That of his youth, as a soldier in the Independence Movement, is referred to in the narrator's own characterizations: "lay heavily upon my heart, under my *officer's jacket of the Mounted Grenadiers of Buenos Aires*" (p. 12, italics added). Just as further on, when he mentions the titles belonging to the enemy of his homeland, he says: "quite smug with his title of Count of Huaqui—which I, my readers, would never exchange for mine, that of *Commander and Aide-de-Camp of the Grand Marshal of Ayacucho*" (p. 201, italics added). And, finally, the period of his mature, older years is that in which he carries out this narration. This can be seen in the instances when he reacts emotionally as he criticizes his contemporaries who are adulterating the values of the struggles of the Independence Movement and the institutions achieved through its victory:

> . . . today's soldiers . . . who break up congresses with the brute force of their weapons, who pitilessly murder the defenseless populace, who hand over Bolívar's blood-stained medal to a back-stabbing idiot, who laugh at the laws, mock the constitution, betray the country and sell themselves. . . . No, I cannot go on! . . . Mercedes! I'm choking! . . .
>
> As you can see, I have had to interrupt my story and scream out

for my Merceditas; the anger was suffocating me. But I am calm
again, and shall now continue. (p. 126)

This critical attitude toward the institutions of the narrator's time
underlies the novel's colloquial tone and lends a sense of commit-
ment with the nation's history that was very much pointed out by
the first readings made of the novel in Bolivia.

Thus, from a historical point of view, this narrator's "memories"
encompass almost the entirety of the history of Bolivia of the nineteenth century, focusing on three distinct periods. The story of the
narrator's childhood covers the period of the uprisings aimed at
obtaining independence from Spain (1810), which were linked
with the Independence Movement of the whole continent. Then,
the narrator's references to his youth correspond with the triumph
of these wars (1824), the direct effect of which was the foundation
of the Bolivian nation. Finally, the narrator's present, the time in
which the writing of the memoirs is carried out, is framed in the
life of the Republic, extending more or less from 1848—according
to the Note in Chapter I: "I began to write these memoirs in
1848"—to 1884, the date on the "Prologue." Thus, the narrator's
point of view is composed of a "memoir" that encompasses almost
an entire century of national history. It also projects itself toward
the twentieth century by addressing itself to the "youth of my
beloved country."

To construct a modern image of the nation, this voice legitimizes
itself by identifying with the original values of the country and the
history of the nation. But this legitimization is completed with another kind of identification, one more private than public, as the
voice also gains authority by being the father of a family. It was
mentioned above that the narrator situates himself in a familiar setting to present his story. This is a nuclear family, and it is contrast-
ed to the kind of family that is shown in the novel; that is, to Doña
Teresa's family, to which Juanito's father belongs, as the narrator
later finds out. The former is also proposed as an alternative to the
latter. The difference between the two families is primarily determined by the system of access to property. The family in the story is
a "primogeniture," a structure that held up a number of Colonial institutions. The *criollo*[6] "primogeniture" families were honored with

lands and Indians by the "*Encomienda*."[7] The oldest son of such a family, then, would inherit all the family's properties, including the lands and other assets. The other children, meanwhile, would serve in the army or take their vows in a religious order. The utopic family that appears in the writings of Brother Justo, or that from which Juan de la Rosa writes his story, on the other hand, imply a more "modern" social organization—although still within the patriarchal society of the nineteenth century—in which each citizen, thanks to his remunerated work, has the possibility of having access to property by purchasing it. Hence, the novel postulates an ideal national value, with the nuclear family as the basic unit of production.

Juan de la Rosa is the father. His wife, Merceditas, plays the role of the mother of that "youth of my beloved country," the implied reader of the novel, and the element on which the family structure of the novel rests. The nuclear family and the country are superimposed and assimilated, as the narrative function acquires authority and credibility by identifying with certain national values (the history of the *criollo* and mestizo struggles for Independence, their heroes, "justice"), and by resting on a paternal figure, one with whom any citizen can identify.

But in the opposition between the primogeniture family and the nuclear family, the indigenous community, because it coexisted with other Colonial institutions, is also aligned with the primogeniture family: "[From] the *encomiendas* . . . from the Apportionments . . . from the Tribute . . . from the *Comunidades* . . . arose the greatest degradation of the [Indians]"[8] (p. 96). Thus, in the utopia of the modern nation that the narration outlines as the result of civilization and progress, the nuclear family would have to substitute these institutions so as to leave behind the Colonial order. It is also important to remember that the debate regarding the lands of the indigenous *comunidades* was one of the central themes in Bolivian politics and economics during the second half of the nineteenth century, and that their "privatization" led to major confrontations.[9]

An Original Project

The narrative play of *Juan de la Rosa*, however, does not end there. The narrator Juan de la Rosa is complemented by another subordinate narrator, Brother Justo. This second narrator is Juanito's teacher, from whom the protagonist learns to read and write. It is through the teachings and writings of this character-narrator that the novel presents the original project of national identity. Furthermore, they lead to a resolution of the enigmas surrounding the identity of the protagonist. The writings of Brother Justo, which he leaves to Juanito at his death, complete and explain all the loose ends of the protagonist's life.

Brother Justo provides information to the past prior to 1810, to which Juan de la Rosa's personal life experiences do not extend. Thus, he explains the origins of the paternal side of the character's family in Spain, the story of Juanito's parents, and his own relationship with them. But he also explains the antecedents of the Independence Movement, and delineates the national project that drives it, as well as its basis on two fundamental characteristics: its inspiration from the Enlightenment and the important participation of the mestizos.

The readings that had fallen into Brother Justo's hands— Rousseau's *Social Contract*, pieces from the works of Charles-Louis Montesquieu (1689–1755), Guillermo Tomás Raynal (1713–1796), the *Encyclopedia* signed by Francisco Pazos Canqui, and, finally, the *Declaration of Independence* and the *Constitution* of the United States[10]—lead him to sympathize with, and to disseminate, a type of nation that begins to be postulated as a real alternative to the Colonial regime. This narrator is thus the bearer of the revolutionary ideas and of the project that Juan de la Rosa invokes.

Similarly, it is through Brother Justo's revelations that we learn that Rosita, the protagonist's mother, is a direct descendant of Alejo Calatayud, a historical personage who led one of the first mestizo uprisings against the Spanish government in 1730.[11] This is the first fact the boy comes across as he begins to construct that his identity is of mestizo origin. Brother Justo also postulates that the rebellion Cochabamba is currently experiencing (in 1812) is a continuation of Calatayud's struggles. At the same time, however, his voice effectively separates Calatayud's rebellion with the indigenous uprisings of the eighteenth century: "I will not exhaust your attention with . . . any of the bloody revolts in which the indigenous race insanely attempted to recover its independence" (p. 38). It is important to note the emphasis that Brother Justo lends to the figure of Calatayud in his discourse, and the distance he seeks to establish between Calatayud's uprising and others. This is especially interesting if we keep in mind that current historiography shows that there was not such distinctly outlined "mestizo" interests in the indigenous rebellions. Studies reveal, on the contrary, the wide range of factors that came into play, and the consequences of their impact on the Colonial government.[12]

This attempt to specifically exclude the indigenous factors from the national image is a common characteristic of modernization projects of the nineteenth century. These, because they were postulated by the dominant sectors, quite often ignored certain specific social conditions to maintain a privileged situation in relation to the sectors on which the Colonial regime had been traditionally based. This, in turn, necessarily produces a distorted view of the past. The image of *Juan de la Rosa's* modern national project contains the paradox of being made up of fragments of songs, icons, and indigenous languages—which were very much present during its time period, and even in the twentieth century—but at the same time affirming that these cultural forms were all but nonexistent in late nineteenth-century Bolivia.

The Figure of the Intellectual

Brother Justo, the "teacher," and Juan de la Rosa together compose a complex figure that carries out the function of the novel's narrator. Brother Justo, a member of the Catholic Church and a well-established *criollo* family, is part of the estates of Colonial power in America. He questions the Colonial system, however, and postulates a different system, thus committing himself to the struggles of the Independence Movement. Furthermore, Juan de la Rosa, the narrator of the period of the Republic, of the Bolivian nation, is a military man with liberal ideas. Even though he is proud of his link with the army, the institution that achieved national independence, he is able to be critical of it.

Both men of letters are critical of their respective institutions;

but, so long as they serve their proper functions, they also support them. Thus, Brother Justo finds "truths that derive from Christianity" (p. 294) in Rousseau; and Juan de la Rosa argues that if the army continued to follow the model of the Independence Movement, it would accomplish its goals. In short, Juan de la Rosa recovers Brother Justo's project for the homeland. In doing so, he has two objectives: to affirm the validity of the original project, and to denounce the fact that, in his own lifetime, it is being adulterated.

Both men are intellectuals who are disseminating the national project and "educating" others about it. Brother Justo expounds and explains it to Juanito, as well as to his parishioners; he also writes it down in a private space, his personal diary. Juan de la Rosa expounds and explains it publicly, through the story of his life, in his "memoirs," to the "youth" of Bolivia.

The image projected of both of the narrators in *Juan de la Rosa* is close to what Gramsci has defined in his writings as the "organic intellectual": both are educators and legitimating voices of a national project, the economic and political circumstances of which they are also capable of criticizing.[13] Although it is true that for Brother Justo there is still no "status quo" to legitimize, his figure, however, does legitimate the French and American Revolutions in South America. Further, it also gives Juan de la Rosa the function of legitimizing the nation he feels is having difficulties establishing itself. Hence, they both go a step further than their primary roles as "revolutionary intellectuals." For, after all, Brother Justo dies defending the entrance to the church from the Spanish enemy, and Juan de la Rosa is, above all else, a soldier of the Independence Movement.

As progressive, learned men, both formulate their projects with the exclusion of, or trying to negate, the indigenous cultural forms along with the Colonial past, for the model that they advocate tends toward a cultural homogenization. However, as we discuss in the next section, while Aguirre creates the public space in which the "organic intellectual" can be validated in this novel, he is unable to completely dispense with the indigenous cultural forms. In fact, he evokes them repeatedly.

We can see, then, that the global narrative strategy consists in seeking to recover the project of 1810, which is tacitly situated in opposition to the forgetting and betrayal of national values in the present lifetime of the narrator, Juan de la Rosa. This occurs in the same manner in which Brother Justo explicitly delineated the original project in opposition to the Colonial regime. Although the novel does not register the War of the Pacific in any way, it is impossible not to associate this silent accusation with Aguirre's great disillusionment following Bolivia's defeat in that war and the hurried signing of the Peace Treaty. As a representative, he opposed the Treaty, although he later found himself having to participate in the negotiations because of the majority's decision in the Bolivian Congress.

Juan de la Rosa reads and rewrites Brother Justo's ideas from the moment in time of his own life, just like the reader of the novel (the youth of Bolivia) will read and relive Juan de la Rosa's project. Therefore, this becomes a *mise-en-abime* reading contract that the novel proposes to its reader, for in each reading Aguirre would be put into effect as an organic intellectual of the national project. The expectation is for the reader to place the project in the perspective of his or her own historical reality.

National Representation

The insistence on the various visual images and the songs in Quechua recounted in the novel, and questioned by the narrator himself, reveal a pervasive preoccupation with the different modes of representation that can express the nation or the national ideal. A contraposition can be observed between the form of the novel and the other, nonwritten modes of representation present within it. These include the *Ollantay*, an important Colonial drama in Quechua; the *yaraví*, a pre-Colombian, poetic musical form; the very uses of the Quechua language; and the abundant descriptions of various visual images. The reflections made about these, and their placement within the story, seem designed to propose literature as the new mode of representation—a mode that corresponds to a modern period, and, above all, is able to surpass the other modes of representation.

From the very first lines of the novel, before establishing the relationships between the characters, the narrative voice stops to place emphasis on how words represent these relationships: "I always called her by the sweet name of 'mother'. . . . But she only referred to me as 'the child,' except for two or three times in which the word 'son' escaped her mouth" (p. 7). These are words or names that reveal how the Colonial order questions this family relationship, that of the "son," because Juanito is the product of the union between a *criollo* and a mestiza. But there is also a contrast here between the word "son" and the appellative "the child." According to uses in Spanish, and not just during the Colonial period, "the child" (*el niño*) is used by servants to address their master or owner. The blacksmith Alejo also addresses Rosita as "the child." During Colonial times, mestizos and Indians occupied the place of the servants, and the *criollos* that of the master. These categories, however, also appear to be relativized in the story, given the fact that Rosita is introduced as a "young *criolla*" with "a few drops . . . [of Indian blood] . . . in her veins" (p. 8), but that she is later characterized primarily as the sister, daughter, and descendent of mestizos.[14]

Similarly, at different times, the narrator stops to comment on Quechua songs or words, either praising the language when his mother speaks it ("in the most tender and affectionate language in the world" [p. 9]); devaluing it when he himself speaks it ("I asked him in Quechua, or rather in that awful dialect used by the brutish descendants of the sons of the sun" [p. 135]); or affirming, in a surprised tone, how foreign the language is ("But what am I doing? Can my young readers even understand that language, which is as foreign to them as Syrian or Chaldean?" [p. 118]). Quechua is currently the indigenous language spoken by the greatest number of people in the Americas; it is possible to infer that in the nineteenth century, at least in Bolivia, it was the mother tongue of a third of the country's population.[15]

Furthermore, the abundance of descriptions of visual images, such as paintings, engravings, images, and sculptures, presents us with yet another kind of representation, belonging to that of a visual language. I refer to this language, prominent in the novel's descriptions, as iconic. Within the visual category, pre-Colombian images occupy an especially relevant place in the case of countries like Bolivia.[16]

The love alliance between the protagonist's parents, although it is always latent and embodied by Juanito, is never actually realized. This alliance, however, is displaced onto, and reinforced by, the descriptions of the visual representations and the relationships established between them. The roles played by the images delineate a progression by which the indigenous mythical (the Death of Atahuallpa), and the Colonial religious (the Divine Shepherdess and the Virgin of Our Lady of Mercy) advance toward a secularization (literature, or the new artistic representations of the nation). The novel *Juan de la Rosa* becomes an emblem that projects the utopic image of a nation that is able to integrate the indigenous cultures—as long as, that is, it is able to dissolve them, along with other forms of Colonial culture, within modernity.

The Myths

The role played by the images begins to be constituted in the first pages of the novel, when two representations located in the room where Juanito lived with his mother are described. The first is presented in contradictory terms, similar to the manner in which the narrator refers to the Quechua language: "[An] original illustration stood out, a work by a hand that was as much clumsy as it was daring, depicting the Death of Atahuallpa" (p. 8). Then, immediately afterward, we read the following description: "In the place of honor, there was also an oil painting of the Divine Shepherdess, sitting with a blue mantle between two plain white sheep, the baby Jesus on her knees" (p. 8). These two images refer us to two myths of ritualistic characteristics. One is from the Christian tradition, widely disseminated throughout Europe and the Americas, and the other is of indigenous origin. Although with different cultural origins, these two myths resemble each other by both referring to a specific ritualistic practice.

In the Andean region, the Divine Shepherdess, or the Virgin Mary who brings the baby Jesus into the world, is associated with a series of festivities that commemorate either her Ascension to Heaven, the birth of her child, or her various apparitions. These are ritualistic celebrations that stand out from, and are intermixed with, the agrarian cycles in the calendar of community

Andean practices. The intermixing reaches such an extent, in fact, that the image of the Virgin is at times conceived as overlapping with the representation of the Pachamama, Mother Earth.

The Death of the Inca Atahuallpa is a widely utilized poetic, choreographic, and dramatic theme among the indigenous peoples of Perú and Bolivia. The tradition goes back to the sixteenth century, and its use has been documented into the second half of the twentieth century. This representation is also considered to express the vision of the defeated in the war implied by the Spanish Conquest, and simultaneously ritualize the resistance to the colonialization.[17] The ritualized representation of the Inca's death projects three basic ruptures: one referring to the confrontation between Spaniards and Indians; another to the division of the Inca from his subjects; and the third, at a cosmic level, between the earth and the sun. This last one is a conjunction that in Quechua culture appears as the base of agrarian production, as well as that of human reproduction, and is assimilated into the duality of the axiom defining the feminine and the masculine. This theme is also related to a myth that is quite widely disseminated today in the Andes: that of the Inkarrí, which predicts a "*pachacuti,*" or a radical change in the current order, with a return of the Inca who is now growing deep in the earth.[18]

Another detail that is important to mention, from our point of view today, is that these representations were always realized in the context of a celebration in the Catholic calendar. Further, the last ones that we know of took place during the Procession of the Virgin of Socavón.[19] Thus, the existence of both rituals—that of the representation of the Divine Shepherdess and of the Death of Atahuallpa—actually appears to overlap in space and time.

In *Juan de la Rosa*, the feelings of disjunction in cosmic harmony, combined with a messianic projection—represented in the indigenous inscription of the Death of Atahuallpa[20]—are complemented with the feelings of mediation projected by the representation of the Divine Shepherdess. These two images thus bring into play the feelings between a lost paternal filiation and a mediating maternal figure with messianic characteristics.

The Alliances

But the two images just discussed also enter into a relationship with two other representations. Chapter VI includes a description of the coat of arms of the Márquez y Altamira family at the entrance to the house and a painting of St. Michael inside. Let us consider the coat of arms first. The space that surrounds it is open and clearly depicted; this is not the case, however, with the representation itself, which is accompanied by a description that is very much unassertive (e.g., "what appeared to be," "something like"):

> We arrived at a large arcade with thick adobe and stucco pillars. It supported an arch that had painted on it a monogram of the Virgin and below it what appeared to be the family coat of arms, something like a bull grazing in a field of wheat. (p. 55)

The image of a bull in a field of wheat refers us to a series of ideas associated with agricultural societies. It is a symbol of concrete manifestations of power and strength. In Mediterranean cultures, it is associated with unbound virile forces, as the male counterpart to the conception of a "Mother Earth."[21] Zeus, in turn, takes on the shape of a bull in the rape of Europa.

The associations of strength, power, and virility that emerge from the representation of the coat of arms, and their relationship with the earth, appear to be opposing complements to the characteristics of charity, innocence, and motherhood projected by the image of the Divine Shepherdess. But the symmetrical complementation of the two images—in terms of motherhood/virility, feminine/masculine, charity and innocence/strength and power—is reinforced by another detail that makes this virtual alliance stand out. We only learn of it well into the story, when the protagonist receives that first "oil painting" of the Divine Shepherdess, after a long time, as part of his inheritance. At this point he observes two things: the similarity between the image and his mother, and the presence in the painting of the initials "C. A." These correspond to Carlos de Altamira, the primogeniture of the family (i.e., the oldest son, who was to inherit everything), who turns out to be Juanito's father. If we go back now to the description of the coat of arms, we find that the monogram of the Virgin is inscribed right above it (these would be the initials A. M., "Ave Maria," combined and interwoven in a painted design).

Therefore, we see that there is an exchange, a commutation, in these two cases: the letters—the signs of writing—that accompany one image refer to the other. In this manner, the complementation, or alliance, between the representation of the Divine Shepherdess and that of the coat of arms is strengthened by this link between letter and image. But the commutative relationship also projects a connection, or better yet a tension, between the two kinds of representation: the iconic and the written. A tension that, as I try to show here, turns out to be quite productive in *Juan de la Rosa*.

This complementation, or alliance, between the two images yields yet another result, for it refers us to that other tension existing in the narrative plane between the resolution of the story and the other possible outcome that is always latent, which I shall call the counterstory. The story will show the impossibility of the union between the protagonist's mestiza mother and his *criollo* father, which produces the unknowns surrounding the character's very identity. This suggested counterstory is precisely the affirmation of that union, which as such is never realized during the Colonial period but is produced as its consequence. In other words, it is the son of the primogeniture of the Altamira family and of Rosita: Juanito, who was able to become Colonel Juan de la Rosa and not Juan de Altamira, as should have been the case during Colonial times.

The fourth image, finally, is inside Doña Teresa's house: "On the wall, could be seen a large oil painting of the Archangel St. Michael, his foot on the chest of the rebel and the tip of his spear in the rebel's mouth" (p. 55). This image is related to that of the Death of Atahuallpa, in that both represent a rupture, or a disjunction, as opposed to that characterized by alliances, as we just discussed.

In the Christian tradition, the Archangel St. Michael is the leader of the forces of good that wage war against Satan, who is represented either as a dragon or a dark-skinned heretic; and, if a heretic, then either as an Indian or a Negro. In the image in *Juan de la Rosa*, he is fighting against a "rebel." The effect is to extend the representation as a projection of the fight of the Church against heresy—one of the banners the Spaniards raised in their aggressions against indigenous peoples during the Conquest, but that also overlapped into Colonial times. This battle is also present in the representation of the Death of Atahuallpa, as an indigenous, iconographic version of the war of the Conquest. The Christian image, on the other hand, is the Spanish version in terms of the evangelization of the indigenous peoples. The first image, therefore, is marked by loss and death, whereas that of St. Michael bears the traits of the victor and salvation.

It is important to point out that in the paintings portraying the Death of Atahuallpa in the Colonial period, and in theatrical representations performed in our century, the figure of "Santiago Matamoros"—also known in South America as "Santiago Mataindios"[22]—frequently appears next to the Inca, thus depicting the Conquest as a battle between good and evil, a battle against heresy. In this sense, the figure of St. Michael can be seen to merge into that of Santiago, fighting against that which is different—the rebel as the personification of evil. In other readings of this representation, however, the same image, because of the shining sword, is juxtaposed with the indigenous worship of the thunderbolt—Illapa—that even today warrants great respect and various forms of worship. We can therefore see how the conjunction of the representations of the Death of Atahuallpa and of St. Michael in *Juan de la Rosa*, and of Santiago in Colonial paintings and in nineteenth- and twentieth-century theatrical representations,[23] reveals the polysematic and intercultural value of these images. Hence, these two different perspectives indicate the tremendous difference between the Christian view of the Conquest as a battle between good and evil and the indigenous view of versatile and transformable forces, based on the confrontation of natural phenomena. In the first case, good and evil are expounded as polarized essences; in the second, these are dissolved among other complementary forces, which, although inevitable, are reversible, or at least capable of being transformed.

In Aguirre's novel, the four images discussed here as mythical representations from different traditions refer to the origins of a

confrontation, to a remote time prior to the Independence Movement. In this manner, they begin to give shape to an alliance based
on a background of the struggles for Independence that originated
at the time of the Conquest.

The alliance that the narrative proposes, however, goes beyond
the Independence Movement. It is embodied by the narrator as
the son of a mestiza and a *criollo*, of a tenant family and a proper-
ty-owning family. This is an alliance that wishes to leave behind
the previous struggles, represented by the images of the Death of
Atahuallpa, of Archangel St. Michael, or the coat of arms of the
Altamira family, which seem to embody the Conquest or Colonial
struggles.

In this landscape filled with all the contradictions regarding the
categories of *criollos*, mestizos, and Indians, *Juan de la Rosa* proposes an alliance between the ruling classes and a broad range of
Cochabamba mestizos, including artisans and the tenants of lands
owned by *criollos*. These last two sectors developed a large economic field of activity during the first years of the Republic, for
they had constituted and sustained quite an independent internal
market whose vigor and productivity surprises scholars to this
date. However, it is also evident that these sectors were the most
disdained by the ruling classes, which, precisely by installing these
"racial" categories, tried to preserve the hegemony inherited from
the Colonial system.[24]

Utopia

Throughout the narrative, however, another image of the Virgin
appears several times, and it does so in public spaces, where it no
longer connotes a familiar intimacy. It is the image of the Virgin of
Our Lady of Mercy, called "*la Patriota*," which was carried as their
only banner by the armies of the Independence Movement. We
come across two versions of this Virgin in the novel. The first, the
main one, is found in the Church of the Matriz in Cochabamba. It
is the one vested with the national values, even though, "Every
year, the most illustrious ladies tended to give very luxurious lamé
dresses and the most valuable jewels as offerings to her" (p. 126).
The second version, however, is a subaltern one. It is found in
Francisco Nina's place, a house in the country whose tenant resi-

dents are enthusiastic supporters of the Independence Movement, and who, furthermore, offer their kind hospitality to the protagonist—exactly the opposite of what the Altamira family does. But in this case the description reveals an image that is imperfect, with noticeably disproportionate features:

> an image of the Virgin Our Lady of Mercy, with eyes bigger than her mouth and cheeks redder than cherries, balancing a miniature of the child Jesus on the palm of her hand that was so small it looked like a toy with which she was playing. (p. 107)

This attitude of the narrator in pointing out an image's defects when he describes the representation was already suggested in his depiction of the Death of Atahuallpa: "A work by a hand that was as much clumsy as it was daring" (p. 8). But now the narrator explicitly emphasizes the defects in the making of this image of the Virgin. And because the ideals of the homeland are focused around her, these defects in turn extend to the capability that these peasants might have of realizing representations, specifically regarding the homeland, for which they are fighting next to the *criollo* patriots.

The identification of the patriotic ideal with representations of the Virgin is not specific to Aguirre's work. It was common for the troops of the Independence Movement to use it as a banner for their armies. General Belgrano,[25] among whose forces the narrator Juan de la Rosa says he fought, had as the patroness of his army this same Virgin of Our Lady of Mercy. This representation, incidentally, has occupied an important role in the symbology of identity in the Argentine army this century. In any case, the proposal contained in *Juan de la Rosa*, just as it intends to go beyond the indigenous representations, also proposes to go beyond these kinds of religious representations for the nation.

Toward the novel's end, when the protagonist already knows the story of his direct ancestors and finally finds the house where his father lives, he sees a series of strange drawings and sculptures:

> The whitewashed walls were covered with strange drawings, some of them done with charcoal, others with colored chalk. Among the drawings there were men with heads of animals, and animals with

human heads; fantastic trees; flowers with wings; and birds hanging from branches as if they were flowers. . . . All along the walls, at a level where they could be reached by a man of average height, boards were nailed up, serving as shelves. These held many clay, stucco, and stone figurines that were as strange and unpredictable as the drawings. I have one of them in front of me right now. . . . (p. 306)

These drawings have the distinctive quality of uniting or bringing together different beings, different natures: the human and the nonhuman, animals and plants. This mixed nature reveals changes and metamorphoses. Further, the place where they are found is the threshold that the protagonist must cross to meet his father. They therefore constitute a boundary, a point of transition, or a crossing over, from one state to another, and suggest the opening of something new, completely unknown, with a certain amount of augury and hope. In effect, these hybrid images, which indicate a transgression of nature and are the work of a repressed or crazy "artist"—as a result of the Colonial system—are constituted at the step, or the transition, toward something new. The narrator conceives this something new as a future national culture, represented by the image that transcends this space. Years later, it will occupy a privileged place in the narrator's space:

I have one of them in front of me right now; carved out of white stone, it is the figure of a woman dressed in a sheer tunic who is reclining back on one of her arms, resting against the back of a sleeping lion. (p. 306)

The image of the woman in the tunic is precisely an image, a neoclassical symbol, that even today carries the strength of the abstract notions of law, liberty, justice, and so on. Liberalism maintains that these values form the basis of modernity and shape the concept of the independent republic, which is what the intellectuals of the Independence Movement thought at the beginning of the nineteenth century. The origin of this manner of representing the nation is in the neoclassical imaginary utilized by the French Revolution. It can be seen in illustrations and statues. Even today, the image used to personify the nation is a woman in a tunic, with a laurel wreath around her head.

The image of the Virgin of Our Lady of Mercy, identified with the homeland during the times of the Independence Movement, has been substituted by this other image of a woman in a tunic, resting against the back of a lion. The major difference is that this latter representation is no longer inscribed within the mythical-religious associations. We are no longer dealing with a Virgin, or an angel, or another religious symbol, although this one is also ethereal.[26] Rather, it is a secular image that—although it does not eclipse the central place of that other feminine image, the Virgin, in the novel—projects more modern connotations. The lion, furthermore, is present in a number of Spanish emblems. Here, the sleeping lion could be thought of as replacing the bull that appears in the coat of arms. This icon would thus represent a national utopia as a result of the triumph of the homeland over the Spanish forces.

The two time periods of the protagonist-narrator run against each other in this fragment: the time of the story, when the boy finally goes to meet his father, and the time of the narration, when the narrator writes his "Memoirs of the Last Soldier of the Independence Movement" and has as his interlocutor and collaborator his wife Merceditas. Her name, furthermore, is also associated with the religious representation of the values of the homeland, the Virgin of Our Lady of Mercy.[27] Here, however, it is secularized, and it exists in a familiarized setting. She is thus also stripped of her religious inscription, both as the narrator's wife and collaborator.

That dividing line, or threshold, that the interaction between the images brings to the forefront, and which projects a national culture, also marks another change: the secularization of culture and art. *Juan de la Rosa* proposes to found a secular mode of representation that is different from—and surpasses—that constituted by the icons it describes and articulates. The novel proposes the beginnings of a Bolivian literature that would have, among others, the possibility of projecting and constituting an image of the nation. And it is precisely that secularizing impulse that articulates a national utopia aimed at dissolving the outdated Colonial institutions, such as the exacerbated religiousness, and the system of the primogeniture—the structure of family inheritance that made impossible any access to property by those who were not *criollos*. But in order to be able to leave behind these Colonial forms, this alle-

gory for the homeland also proposes leaving behind these indigenous forms of expression and languages that—although they
fought against them—the narrator finds as outdated as the Colonial institutions. He does, however, incorporate them in a conspic-
uous manner into the novel.

These different modes of representation exist in tension with
one another; the novel as representation constitutes itself on the
basis of these fragments, but does not strictly represent any one of
them. The topic of representation comes to the forefront and is
treated several times in the text. But it is also a topic of deeper reflection. *Juan de la Rosa* postulates itself as a representation that
problematizes representation. This makes it a novel that enters the
problematics of modernity, even when the form of the story and its
interweaving with history are so close to the cannon of the classic
romantic novel.

—*Alba María Paz-Soldán*
Translated by Sergio Gabriel Waisman

Notes

The original ideas for this essay first appeared in my doctoral thesis, "Una
articulación simbólica de lo nacional: *Juan de la Rosa* de Nataniel
Aguirre," presented at the University of Pittsburgh in 1986.

The present work is greatly indebted to the comments of my thesis advisor, Professor John Beverley; the invaluable observations of Professor
Edmond Cross (University Paul Valéry, Montpellier); and the later, detailed reading by Professor Antonio Cornejo-Polar (University of California, Berkeley).

1. Born in Arequipa, Perú, José Manuel Goyeneche (1755–1846) undertook his military education in Spain, where he received high honors.
Back in the Americas, he met with the Viceroy of the Río de la Plata,
Santiago de Liniers (1753–1810), in Buenos Aires, with whom he planned
the propagation and the war campaign on behalf of King Fernando VII
in the Americas. Upon the arrival of the Revolution of May in Buenos
Aires in 1810, the Viceroy of Perú appointed him to lead the army that
was to drive the rebellious provinces back into obedience. He fought the
rebels of the uprising of July 16, 1809, in La Paz with a large deployment

of troops, then condemned Murillo and three other revolutionaries to death and banished eighty-seven others. In 1811, he reached an armistice with Castelli and Balcárcel for forty days, but betrayed it when he attacked and defeated the armies of the Independence Movement in the Battle of Huaqui. After defeating Castelli in Sipe Sipe, in July 1811, he victoriously entered the city of Cochabamba. Most of these events, and Goyeneche's role in them, are dealt with extensively in *Juan de la Rosa*.

2. The victory was sealed by the Battle of Ayacucho on December 8, 1824, in which Marshall Antonio José de Sucre, then a General, defeated the Spanish army after several victories by the Independence fighters. See Alcides Arguedas, *Historia General de Bolivia* (La Paz: Juventud/reprint, 1980). See also Gunnar Mendoza, *Diario del Tambor Vargas, un combatiente de la Independencia* (Mexico: Siglo XXI, 1984).

3. See Herbert Klein, *Bolivia: The Evolution of a Multiethnic Society* (New York: Oxford University Press, 1982). For further information regarding this historical process, see also Charles Arnade, *The Emergence of the Republic of Bolivia* (Gainesville: University of Florida Press, 1957).

4. See Tristan Platt, *Estado boliviano y Ayllu andino* (Lima: Instituto de Estudios Peruanos, 1982) and Silvia Rivera, *Oprimidos pero no vencidos* (La Paz: Hisbol-CSUTCB, 1984).

5. See Porfirio Díaz Machicao, *Nataniel Aguirre* (Buenos Aires: Perlado, 1945) and Joaquín Aguirre Lavadenz, *Guerra del Pacífico. Pacto de tregua. 1884. Correspondencia privada de Nataniel Aguirre* (La Paz—Cochabamba: Los Amigos del Libro, 1987).

6. A *criollo* was a person born in the Americas to European parents; it does not have the same meaning as the contemporary term "Creole." (Trans.)

7. *Encomiendas* were the awards granted to conquistadors or Spaniards by the Spanish Crown in the form of a certain number of Indians who would then become workers or servants in one of the properties of that conquistador or Spaniard. Juridically, the *Encomienda* was based on the transfer from the King to his subjects (the *encomenderos*) of the Tribute, or the work of a group of indigenous people (the *encomendados*) in exchange for their protection and instruction in Christianity. In the first stages of the Conquest, trade and the flow of goods was regulated through the *encomienda*, by which the *encomendero* received the Tribute that the Indians supposedly owed to the Crown.

Several other aspects of the Colonial economic system are described below, including an explanation of the Tribute, or the Indian tax system. See also n. 8.

8. See n. 7 for an explanation of the *Encomiendas*. "Apportionments" (the *repartamiento*) was the name given to the distribution of the Indios de Mita (or Mita Indians) for work in general, but especially for working in the mines. It also refers to the action of determining the tax rate (the "Tribute") that the Indians had to pay. When the term *encomienda* is used, the emphasis falls on the responsibilities of the *encomendero* (the Spanish subject); when the term "Apportionment" is used, on the other hand, the emphasis falls on the distribution of the Indians and their lands.

The Mita system is mentioned in Chapter IV of the novel. The term is derived from the Quechua *mittani mittacuni*, meaning the time has come for one to do something. It refers to the system of work that organized Indians into various shifts for working the mines, farms, or estates of the Spaniards, all without any compensation. The "Tribute" comes from an old Spanish tradition. In the Americas, the obligation of paying the "Tribute," or tax, fell on the new, non-Spanish lower classes. In the Spanish juridical conception, the Indians were to pay the "Tribute" as part of their obligation as "subjects" to the Crown, in exchange for the supposed benefits of Spanish civilization. A large number of documents from the sixteenth century refer to the excesses of the *encomenderos* in the collecting of the "Tribute." By the nineteenth century, however, the Indians fulfilled their obligation of paying the "Tribute" on the basis of a juridical conception of reciprocity: they paid their tax in exchange for the right to work the land.

The *Comunidades* were a complex social and work system in the Andes based on the indigenous Aymaran and Quechuan institution of the *ayllu*. The Spaniards kept very strict records of the *comunarios* (the members of the *comunidades*) to collect the Tribute from them.

9. See n. 3.

10. The reference to these French writers and intellectuals from the Enlightenment (Rousseau, Montesquieu, and Raynal) through a text "signed" by Pazos Canqui is quite significant, for it alludes to an indigenous historical personage, of Aymara origin, who stood out among the ideologues who participated in the uprisings in Chuquisaca (1809) and Buenos Aires (May 25, 1810). Vicente Pazos Canqui, a journalist and a priest, became the editor of the newspaper *La Gazeta* in Buenos Aires in 1811 and translated the Declaration of Independence of the United Provinces of South America, drawn up by the Constituent Congress of Tucumán in 1816, into Aymara. He also published *An Outline of the History of the United States of America. Written in Spanish by an Aymara Indian from La Paz* [*Compendio de la historia de los Estados Unidos de América.*

Puesta en castellano por un indio aymara de La Paz] in Paris in 1825.

11. See Valentín Abecia, *Alejo Calatayud* (La Paz: Juventud, 1977). The uprising led by Alejo Calatayud, a silversmith artisan, occurred in Cochabamba in November 1730 following news of the arrival of the Collector Benero y Balero, who was supposedly trusted with undertaking a new registry (or Tribute list) to carry out the charging of a new Tribute from the Indians and new *Regalías* from the mestizos (*Regalías* was the head tax charged each mestizo, equivalent to the Tribute placed on each Indian).

12. Scarlett O'Phelan, *Un siglo de rebeliones anticoloniales. Perú y Bolivia 1700–1783* (Cuzco: Centro Bartolomé de Las Casas, 1988). Steve Stern, *Resistencia, rebelión y conciencia campesina en los Andes* (Lima: Instituto de Estudios Perúanos, 1990).

13. Antonio Gramsci, *The Modern Prince and Other Writings* (New York: International Publishers, 1959).

14. For a more thorough view of the category of mestizo in Bolivia in this time period, see Silvia Rivera, "La raíz: colonizadores y colonizados," in *Violencias encubiertas en Bolivia* (La Paz: Cipca-Aruwiyiri, 1993, 26–139). Also see Rossana Barragán, *Espacio urbano y dinámica étnica* (La Paz: Inst. de Historia Social Boliviana, 1990).

15. Xavier Albó, in *Lengua y sociedad en Bolivia (1976)* (La Paz: Instituto Nacional de Estadística, 1980), shows that currently, in the district of Cochabamba, 47.8% of the population is bilingual in Quechua and Spanish, 31.7% is monolingual in Quechua, and 16.7% is monolingual in Spanish. It is reasonable to infer that in Aguirre's time Quechua was even more widely spoken.

16. See the important work in this subject by Teresa Gisbert, *Iconografía y mitos indígenas en el arte* (La Paz: Gisbert y Cía S.A., 1980).

17. Jesús Lara, *La tragedia del fin de Atahuallpa* (Cochabamba: Imp. Universitaria, 1957); Mario Unzueta, *Valle* (Cochabamba: Edt. La época, 1945, 134–144); Hernando Balmori, *La conquista de los españoles y el teatro americano* (Tucumán: Facultad de Filosofía y Letras, Univ. de Tucumán, 1955); Nathan Wachtel, "La visión de los vencidos: la conquista española en el folklore indígena," in Juan Ossio's *Ideología mesiánica del mundo andina* (Lima: Bib. de Antropología, 1963, 37–75).

18. Juan Ossio, for example, in *Ideología mesiánica del mundo andino* (Lima: Bib. de Antropología, 1963) presents several versions of this myth.

19. See Luis Bredow, "La escena de la muerte de Atahuallpa," in *Hipótesis*, No. 23/24 (Primavera-Verano, 1987), 319–329.

20. See Hernando Balmori, op. cit., p. 52.

21. "El toro en las culturas mediterráneas" in *Gran Enciclopedia RIALP*

(Madrid, 1975), 588–591.

22. "Santiago Matamoros" literally means "St. James the Moor Killer," although "matamoros" is now used to refer to a bully or a braggart. Likewise with "Santiago Mataindios," which literally means "St. James the Indian Killer," but has the same connotations today as *matamoros*. In the first case, it is the Moor who functions as the "Other"; in the second, the Indian fulfills the same function. (Trans.)

23. See Teresa Gisbert, *Iconografía y mitos indígenas en el arte* (La Paz: Gisbert y Cía S.A., 1980) (op. cit.) and the works referred to in n. 17; Jesús Lara, *La tragedia del fin de Atahuallpa* (Cochabamba: Imp. Universitaria, 1957); Mario Unzueta, *Valle* (Cochabamba: Edt. La época, 1945, 134–144); Hernando Balmori, *La conquista de los españoles y el teatro americano* (Tucumán: Facultad de Filosofía y Letras, Univ. de Tucumán, 1955); Nathan Wachtel, "La visión de los vencidos: la conquista española en el folklore indígena," in Juan Ossio's *Ideología mesiánica del mundo andina* (Lima: Bib. de Antropología, 1963, 37–75).

24. See Gustavo Rodríguez and Humberto Solares, *Sociedad oligárquica, chicha y cultura popular* (Cochabamba: Serrano, 1990). And, for a study of another region, Roberto Laura, *La oligarquía de La Paz* (La Paz, Tesis de Sociología, Universidad de San Andrés, 1988), cited in Silvia Rivera, *Oprimidos pero no vencidos* (La Paz: Hisbol-CSUTCB, 1984).

25. Manuel Belgrano (1770–1820) was a general of the Independence Movement. He participated, from the beginning, in the Revolution of May 1810, and defeated the Spanish troops in Tucumán (1812) and Salta (1813). After his triumph in Tucumán, he handed over the command to the Virgin of Our Lady of Mercy, naming her the Generaless of the revolutionary army. He also designed what is still the national flag of Argentina.

26. These images somehow objectify what Marshall Berman characterizes as the ethereal project of modernity. See Marshall Berman, *All That is Solid Melts Into Air: The Experience of Modernity* (London: Verso, 1983).

27. The Virgin of Our Lady of Mercy in Spanish is "la Virgen de las Mercedes." Juan de la Rosa's wife, therefore, has literally the same name as the Virgin (i.e., "Mercedes"). (Trans.)

JUAN DE LA ROSA

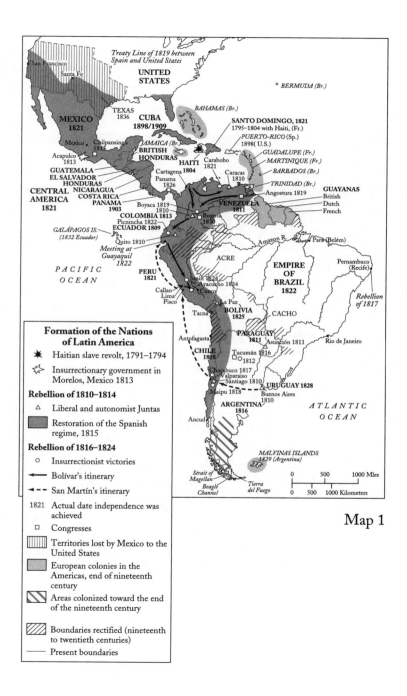

Treaty Line of 1819 between
Spain and United States

San Francisco
Santa Fe

UNITED
STATES

* BERMUDA (Br.)

BAHAMAS (Br.)

TEXAS
1836

MEXICO
1821

CUBA
1898/1909

SANTO DOMINGO, 1821
1795–1804 with Haiti, (Fr.)

PUERTO-RICO (Sp.)
1898(U.S.)

Mexico   Chilpansingo
1813

JAMAICA (Br.)

GUADALUPE (Fr.)

Acapulco
1813

BRITISH
HONDURAS

HAITI
1804

Carabobo
1821

MARTINIQUE (Fr.)

GUATEMALA
EL SALVADOR
HONDURAS

Cartagena 1804

Caracas
1810

BARBADOS (Br.)

Panama
1826

TRINIDAD (Br.)

CENTRAL
AMERICA
1821

NICARAGUA
COSTA RICA
PANAMA
1903

Boyaca 1819
1810

Angostura 1819

GUAYANAS
British
Dutch
French

VENEZUELA
1811

COLOMBIA 1813

Picincha 1822
ECUADOR 1809

Bogotá
1830

GALÁPAGOS IS.
(1832 Ecuador)

Quito 1810

Amazon R.

Pará (Belém)

Meeting at
Guayaquil
1822

ACRE

EMPIRE
OF
BRAZIL
1822

Pernambuco
(Recife)

PACIFIC
OCEAN

PERU
1821

Junín 1824
Ayacucho 1824

Rebellion
of 1817

Callao
Lima
Pisco

Cuzco

La Paz

Tacna

BOLIVIA
1825

CACHO

Antofagasta

PARAGUAY
1811

Asunción 1811

Rio de Janeiro

CHILE
1818

Tucumán 1816
1812

Chacabuco 1817
Valparaiso
Santiago 1810

Maipu 1818

URUGUAY 1828

Buenos Aires
1810

ATLANTIC
OCEAN

ARGENTINA
1816

Ancud

MALVINAS ISLANDS
1829 (Argentina)

Strait of
Magellan

Beagle
Channel

Tierra
del Fuego

0   500   1000 Mles

0   500   1000 Kilometers

Formation of the Nations
of Latin America

✳ Haitian slave revolt, 1791–1794

✵ Insurrectionary government in
Morelos, Mexico 1813

Rebellion of 1810–1814

△ Liberal and autonomist Juntas

▨ Restoration of the Spanish
regime, 1815

Rebellion of 1816–1824

○ Insurrectionist victories

◀— Bolívar's itinerary

◀- - San Martín's itinerary

1821 Actual date independence was
achieved

▢ Congresses

▨ Territories lost by Mexico to the
United States

▨ European colonies in the
Americas, end of nineteenth
century

▨ Areas colonized toward the end
of the nineteenth century

▨ Boundaries rectified (nineteenth
to twentieth centuries)

---- Present boundaries

Map 1

Cochabamba in the Republic of Bolivia
Important Dates of the Independence Movement

0   150 Miles
0   150 Kilometers

Battle of Junín, August 6, 1824

Battle of Ayacucho, December 9, 1824

BRAZIL

Cobija

PERU

BOLIVIA

Uprising in La Paz, July 16, 1809

Lake Titicaca

Caracato

AYOPAYA

Trinidad

COCHABAMBA

Uprising in Cochabamba, September 14, 1810

Ruins of Tiahuanaku

Defense of Cochabamba–La Coronilla, May 27, 1812

Battle of Aroma, November 14, 1812

Santa Cruz de la Sierra

Oruro

Battle of Amiraya–Sipe Sipe, August 12, 1811

Sucre (Audience of Charcas)

Potosí

PACIFIC OCEAN

Tarija

CHILE   ARGENTINA   PARAGUAY

Map 2

Prologue

Don N . . . N . . .

Caracato, November 14, 1884

Cochabamba

My Most Esteemed Sir and Master:

I have not had the honor of making your acquaintance, nor have I reason to believe that you know of my existence. However, I have been told that you are a correspondent for the "Society of September the 14th," and this is enough for me to beg you to deliver, if you might, the attached manuscript to the current president of this society.

I will also tell you what has finally encouraged me to take this step.

Just a moment ago, gathered round my table with several friends, celebrating the anniversary of the Triumph at Aroma, which I always remember on this date, an aged wine from my cellars rose to my head, and I tried to hug Merceditas, my beloved spouse.

She blushed, and said to me:

"Horrible monster! You are the last carrion from the times of the Independence Movement!"

"That is not so," I answered, "there must be others like me."

"No, sir!" she yelled, even angrier than before. "No one is as mean as you, to live so long."

"How about you, my love. . . ?"

"Be quiet, you drunk old man! I am talking about the men. . . . And I am not as tactless as you to go about speaking about a woman's age. You yourself told me that you read in *El Heraldo* that your compatriot Nicolás Monje died, and that was two years ago."

When I heard this, I became very serious. It set me thinking, and I have come here, to my room, to write this letter.

"With the title that my wife has given me," I said to myself, "I can already ask the youth of my beloved country to gather some profitable lessons now from the story of my life."

I believe, furthermore, that it will contain a number of interesting details, a reflection of old customs, and a few other little things, in short, with which serious historians never busy themselves.

That is all. May God bless you for many years to come,

Your humble servant,
J. de la R.

I

The First Memories of My Childhood

Rosita, the beautiful lacemaker whose memory is still preserved* by some of the old men and women in the Villa de Oropesa** who admired her unusual beauty, the kindness of her character, and the exquisite lacery that her hands produced, was the guardian angel of my blessed childhood. Her motherly affection, tenderness, and solicitude for me were endless, and I always called her by the sweet name of "mother" with pleasure and real pride. But she only referred to me as "the child," except for two or three times in which the word "son" escaped her mouth like an irresistible cry from nature that seemed to tear at her insides in a very cruel manner.

We lived alone in a room, or a shop rather, on the border of the Barrio de los Ricos, which today is Sucre, with only two doors: the one that opened out to the street and another little one, merely a half-door, in the corner to the left of the entrance. A wooden platform that was our dais, that we also converted into a bed at night; a long table on which Rosita ironed fine linen clothing, albs, and altar-cloths; a large coffer darkened by time; two small chairs with

---

*I began to write these memoirs in 1848.
**Old name of the city of Cochabamba.

armrests, their seats and backs made of tooled leather; a very low stool; and an iron brazier: these were the main items of furniture that made up the room. The walls, painted an earthen yellow, were decorated with barely illuminated prints, among which one original illustration stood out, a work by a hand that was as much clumsy as it was daring, depicting the Death of Atahuallpa. On the wall across from the door, in the place of honor, there was also an oil painting of the Divine Shepherdess, sitting with a blue mantle between two plain white sheep, the baby Jesus on her knees. The little door to the left led to a small patio completely surrounded by adobe walls, in which a shed served as a pantry and a kitchen.

Rosita—I do not believe that my memory deceives me, nor that my affection endows her now in my imagination with charms that she did not have—was a young *criolla* as beautiful as a perfect Andalusian woman, with a head full of long, plentiful curls; almond-shaped eyes, bright as stars; very fair features, except for a slightly pug nose; a mouth like the flower of a pomegranate tree; very white, small, tightly packed teeth, like those that are found only among Indian women, of whose blood a few drops must have flowed in her veins; hands and feet like a fairy's; and a graceful and pleasant figure that, without the reserve that accompanied her every movement and made her appear to be somewhat retiring, would have been the envy of the most presuming, svelte, and lively woman of the Peninsula.[1] Her voice, which easily took on all the inflections of passion, was usually sweet and harmonious like a lullaby. She had received, after all, the most meticulous education possible at that time.

She always wore a blue merino basquine down to about her ankles; a white doublet made of a simple, embroidered cotton cloth with wide sleeves exposing her arms as far as the elbows; and a darker-colored mantilla with black, soft cloth fringes, fastened with a thick silver pin. Her beautiful hair was pulled back in two braids that met again halfway down her back, tied together with a vicuña cloth ribbon with little colorful tassels. The only jewelry she wore consisted of large gold earrings on her delicate and petite ears and a ferruled ivory ring on the little finger of her left hand. Her feet, in the striped socks that were of the same preferred color as her dress, were hidden in small polished leather shoes with tan heels.

It seems to me that I can see and hear her now, as I used to then, enchanted when she would awake me from my peaceful sleep. Tidy and well kept, after having made up everything in our room, she is sitting by the door, in her little stool, with her lace pillow in front of her. Then her agile fingers move slower and slower until they languidly drop the bobbins, and she crosses her hands on one of her knees; her beautiful eyes look for I know not what in the part of the sky that can be seen beyond the roof of a large ugly house across the street. She sings softly to interrupt my sleep in the most tender and affectionate language in the world. It is the *yaraví*[2] of the farewell of the Inca Manco: the sorrowful lament from the last shelter in the heights of the mountains, addressed to his father—the sun—asking for death to take him so that he will not have to witness the eternal slavery of his race. Tears fall without her realizing it, dropping one after another down her pale cheeks. . . .

Few people approached our humble abode, and the number of those who entered it was even smaller. Servants from well-to-do families and errand boys from the convents stood at the door and handed materials across the threshold; they left the jobs they brought right there or took back those that were already finished without entering. Sometimes an old, venerable-looking gentleman, wrapped in a large, San Fernando wool cloak, his hat drawn down to his eyes and leaning on a walking stick with a thick handle and a long gold point, would arrive at dusk; addressing Rosita in a good-natured tone, he would hand her a small pouch or a little package. She would accept it kissing his hand, even though he tried to avoid it, taking his leave at once. Only once, on a hot afternoon in the month of October in which he seemed very tired from an excess of activity, did he agree to accept a chair, which we quickly placed in the cool breeze out on the sidewalk, laying a wool mantle at his feet. He spoke with Rosita a long time about the misery that the country had suffered two years before, in 1804, and then listened to her speak in a low voice without interrupting her except with a few questions. When she finished, he sat me on his knees; he let me admire his walking stick at my leisure, while he caressed my hair and mumbled two or three times:

"It is such infamy. . . . Poor Juanito!"

The night had become quite dark, the sky covered with clouds, when he decided to leave; Rosita insisted until he agreed to let us accompany him to his house.

"Your Worship will lean on my shoulder, and the boy will illuminate the way before us," she said, sending me right away to light a small paper lantern.

We went up a street further above ours in this manner and walked a long stretch to the left, between the fences and mud walls of orchards and sown fields, until we arrived at a very ample door that opened along a large thick wall beyond an irrigation ditch. A Negro servant of gigantic stature awaited on the bridge that crossed over the irrigation ditch.

The gentleman stopped there; giving me a gentle slap on the cheek, he said to my mother:

"Make him a good *mameluco*³ and buy him a doll for the festivities of All Saints' Day, but on the condition that he learn his reading primer."

"Sir," she answered, "I shall make the *mameluco* and the doll, too, as no one makes it better than I. As far as recommending the reading primer to him, your Worship is unaware that the child already knows how to read, almost fluently, from a very amusing book that his good teacher Brother Justo of the Holy Blessed Sacrament gave to him."

"Look here!" the old nobleman responded, "so this little rogue promises to be a man of high accomplishments? Good, my daughter; go with God and do not forget that this door will never be closed to you."

And having said these words, he entered through the blessed door preceded by the servant who had, in the meantime, run to fetch a light.

"Who is he?" I then asked Rosita. "Why does he love us like this, mother, and why do you not flee from him as you do from other gentlemen?" In the meantime she had taken me by the hand, and we were already returning with hurried steps.

"He is," she answered, "the father of the unfortunate ones, our Lord Governor." And immediately she told me his name, revered even today in spite of the hatred toward the Spanish domination.

He was Don Francisco de Viedma, who, when he died, wanted to found a home for orphans in that same manor.

My diligent reading teacher, Brother Justo, the Augustine priest, came two or three times a week, with his hood drawn over his eyes, his arms crossed on his chest, his hands hidden in the sleeves of his cassock, taking quick and silent steps like a ghost. He would let himself drop into the chair that was always next to the table, ready to receive him.

He was the most extraordinary man I have ever met in my life, and for a long time he was an impenetrable enigma for my coarse and rude understanding. Tall, dry, yellowed, with eyes like embers always flickering in their sockets—he was quite frightening at first sight. However, stepping back and looking at him—at his very fair, noble features, and his broad, protruding forehead crowned with premature gray hairs—he instilled respect. When one heard him talk, when one could penetrate at least part of his ideas and feelings, incomprehensible at that time to vulgar spirits, one loved him with veneration. Although habitually melancholy and distracted, he knew how to be jovial with lowly people, and he had outbursts in which he laughed like a fool, considering himself the most fortunate person in this vale of tears.

Already leaning back in his chair, he would stretch out his large bony hand to Rosita, who would approach to embrace it in hers and to kiss it (when he did not impede this, which was rare) with fraternal affection and religious submission. He would speak with her in a low voice. Then he would straighten up, the hood would fall on his back, and he would shout happily:

"Juanito, the *Quixote*! We are going to laugh, my lad, at the adventures of the Knight of the Sad Countenance and his Squire the Lord Governor of the Isle Barataria."

He would page through the book that I handed him and say things whose meaning I could not gather, such as, for example:

"Oh, the fantastic and unequaled adventure of those yokels! Could this be what happens to us with so many things that our imagination concocts and that we hold as truths in the thick darkness? And this Isle Barataria, so monotonous and submissive that it manages to have a good governor as a joke, could it not be said that it is an image of an entire world abducted for the benefit of distant masters? . . ."

His long thin finger pointed to one after another of the words that I read out loud, stopping on those that took me longer to decipher or that I mispronounced. A few times, satisfied with the lesson, he would repeat the words that he heard from Don Francisco de Viedma:

"He will be a man of high accomplishments."

But he would suddenly interrupt himself with a loud outburst of laughter, and continue:

"What will he be, my God? What can he do here? Be a priest? A cleric? Yes, you will be a priest, Juanito; and you will make the Indians dance and stagger in the processions. Masses will be sung; there will be *alferazgos*,[4] burials, and weddings. You will grow fat until you perhaps become—who knows?—a canon. Your poor mother will at least cease stooping over her lace pillow and the brazier, and . . . she will be able to live!"

He would then immediately become pensive, distracted, looking at the bricks out on the pavement or the black rafters on the ceiling, but without really seeing them. Meanwhile, Rosita, shaken up as she often was upon hearing his speeches, was now also absorbed in her own thoughts, pretending to be completely occupied in her lacery, or in sweetening a cold orange or pineapple drink for him that had been prepared beforehand in a small pitcher made of a fragrant clay. And all along I continued my reading; by then, neither one of them appreciated Cervantes' immortal novel.

Rosita's voice, or simply the sound of her steps as she approached to offer him the drink in a large glass decorated with flowers, exercised an irresistible fascination over the Father. He would come to as if from a sad dream, his yellowish face lighting up with an ineffable smile; and immediately he would try to dissipate any painful or unpleasant impressions so that he would not leave us with them when he departed. He would speak to Rosita about her lacery, or about a mysterious money box that I once saw her hide carefully at the bottom of the coffer; he would make paper boats or balloons for me, or, by folding a piece of paper and making just one cut, he would pull out a cross and all of the implements of the Passions of the Savior, Jesus Christ.

One day he wanted to evoke memories from a time that must undoubtedly have been better; but the results he obtained were entirely the opposite of those he intended.

"Do you know, Juanito," he began to say, "that your mother was once my sister?" And addressing her, he went on: "Don't you remember that you learned to read faster than this urchin?"

"How can I possibly have forgotten that? Do you know. . . . Father, you cannot forget," my mother stammered, "that at that time I might have believed in a happiness that is found in the Heavens."

And they both became quiet, but not before a doleful sigh from Brother Justo reached my ears.

Many years later, I understood the immense pain that they must have both suffered. One day, in Lima, I heard the admirable poet Olmedo[5] cite in the middle of a conversation a punishment that he said was found in a verse of Dante's *Inferno*: "There is no greater torture than to remember times of happiness during times of misery." And the memory of that scene, which touched me so much as a child, lay heavily upon my heart, under my officer's jacket of the Mounted Grenadiers of Buenos Aires.

Another loyal, more assiduous friend, one who visited us every day during the off-hours as his work permitted, was the master locksmith and blacksmith Alejo, a relative of my mother's—although I do not know to what degree. Cupreous, taller than most, robust, with wide shoulders and a broad upper back, a small head that looked as if it were on the end of a bull's neck, and enormous hands and feet, he looked like the personification of Strength—and in fact his strength in town was proverbial. But his face, usually peaceful, his eyes with their ingenuous and honest look, revealed a soul that was naturally gentle, unless they were enlivened by anger, in which case they would take on a terrible, savage expression.

His apparel was similar to that worn by the majority of mestizos, but better kept and of finer materials. He wore a hat with a round top and a wide brim; a wide-open, soft cloth jacket, so that underneath it one could see a *tocuyo*[6] shirt whose collar was never buttoned, as if it did not exist; twill trousers fastened with a wool belt with long fringes; and big, so-called Russian shoes that always seemed to bother him. He spoke Spanish without mutilating it too much; but if the person with whom he was speaking knew it, or if he was with one of his equals, he always preferred Quechua. He called Rosita "the child," and adored her like a saint. At times, his indulgence of me even managed to annoy that saint, my mother. Many times he told her:

"You are so beautiful, my child! If you wanted to have your portrait done, they would paint a picture like that of your Divine Shepherdess."

And referring to me he would add:

"Let him be. Let him run around and play out in the fields of the Lord! Let him frolic and shout and climb on trees! I don't know why you yourself don't go along with him in his games, when I, older than you, teach him antics and partake in them myself."

And if he heard Rosita sing, he would become transfixed, with his mouth open, like all simple people tend to do when they are fully concentrating on something. A thousand times he repeated to himself the lyrics of the Inca's farewell, or of some fragment of the *Ollantay*,[7] without ever being able to completely remember them. He would quite humbly admit that he was slow. He was not obstinate about his opinions; when someone dear to him would calmly and softly refute them, whether he understood his rival's reasoning or not, he would appear to be convinced, and say: "well . . . there you have it!" All of this does not mean, however, that he ceased to have, when it served his interest, the cunning and craftiness that tend to distinguish to a great extent even the most boorish of the native peoples.

My mother never wanted me to go out and never sent me on errands, but she would sometimes allow me to go on an outing with him. One afternoon he took me to see the bulls of the Patron St. Sebastian. After the event was over (an event I found amusing at the time, but since then it seems to me vulgar and even repugnant), we climbed the gentle grade of the small hill that rises above the plaza of the same name. He bought me a bag of sweets from one of the tents that were set up there at the time to sell refreshments. He led me up a few steps further, pointed out a thorny plant, and said these mysterious words to me:

"They put his right arm over there. Grandmother saw it on a pole and fainted. She loved him very much; that is why she had me take his name."

But seeing the amazement with which I was looking at him, he thought that he must have said something wrong; so he quickly took me by the hand to leave, and added:

"Don't tell the child Rosita what I just told you, and don't ask me anything else about it, either; I was only trying to frighten you."

Finally, a few plain women, dressed in thick, coarse, country wool, barefoot and unkempt, would come help Rosita to do simple tasks or clean the house. And they never left without blessing "the child"; they said she was as beautiful and good as the saint from Lima whose name she carried. I only remember the name of one of them: María Francisca. I later understood that as poor as we were, living from my mother's daily work, taught to read by the diligent teacher, we could consider ourselves, as far as material comforts and the development of our intellect were concerned, a thousand times more fortunate than the majority of the masses, made up of Indians and mestizos. The only ones who must have been happy, in their own way, were the Spaniards and a few *criollos*, who were satisfied living passively in their indolence during "the good times of our Lord, the King."

Rosita Is Taken Ill. A New Friend

In the memorable year of 1810, the eleventh of my life as I understand it, Rosita was paler and sadder than ever. I felt her lips and hands burning when she caressed me, her eyes were brighter than usual, and she coughed frequently. I noticed that she wanted to dedicate herself to her work with more zeal; so that when, at times, she was forced to lay down and rest on the bed, the suffering of her spirits was greater than that from her illness. Another observation that I made, one which could not have escaped me because I knew her habits, alarmed me most of all. She who was always so meticulous about her own personal cleanliness and about the neatness and tidiness of her house, had begun to allow some neglect in her attire, and would wait for María Francisca to come and sweep the room; she even allowed her to cook our frugal meals. The only thing that she never forgot about—my blessed mother!—was the well-being of her son, whom she tried to fool with soft smiles.

Don Francisco de Viedma,[1] who would have been our savior before anyone else, had died. Not even he had been able to overcome the loathing that the town felt toward the Spaniards known as the *chapetones*[2]; but his death was still lamented by the many lowly people whom he had aided. Our loyal friends Brother Justo and Alejo seemed to want to abandon us little by little. They visited less frequently; since the year before they were both very worried about something that I did not understand. When they ran into each other at our house, they would exchange mysterious words; sometimes they laughed, rubbing their hands together; other times they became gloomy and dejected, and one could see then the frightful transformation in Alejo's face.

One day I heard Brother Justo, beside himself, say:

"This time it has become truly serious. The affair on the 25th of May was bad enough; but Don Pedro Domingo Murillo,[3] now he really knows when the shoe has been tightened. Good God! Albeit from afar, I have finally seen a man!"

Another day he came in completely disheartened, to the point that he did not even extend his hand to Rosita, nor listen to the affectionate words with which she tried to pull him out of his painful dejection. I did not know what to do with the book I had in my hand; then, as if I had committed an error, he said to me severely:

"Get that out of here! . . . We can no longer read that."

And getting up right away, as if he were shot from a spring, he took a written scroll out of his sleeve, and added:

"This is what we must read, this and nothing else; and you must memorize it, young man. If you do not, you will lose my respect."

With my hand shaking, I took the paper (which I have presently before my eyes); I read with much difficulty, corrected and helped along at every step by my teacher, what I can now happily copy down:

Nuestra Señora de La Paz
February 5, 1810

"My Brother: I have been relating our disasters and our sufferings from Chacaltaya to you as they occur. Prepare yourself now to hear what our tyrants persist in calling, with apparent contempt and poorly hidden anxiety, 'the conclusion of the disturbance of the 16th of July.'

"On the morning of the 29th of January, by order of the authorities, we set out for the public jail where the prisoners were being held to give them their last rites and accompany them to the foot of the infamous gallows where, according to the sentence, 'they were to be hung as punishment for their abominable crimes and as a lesson to all rebels.' I was the one who heard Don Pedro Domingo Murillo's last confession. What a man, my God! What a soul, so superior to those of his common contemporaries! Whence did he manage to gather so much light in this night of heavy darkness in which we live? I will not—I cannot—tell you how he dazzled me with the sublime splendor that he then emitted—only to disappear into the abyss of eternity. There were even moments in which it seemed that I was the penitent and he the confessor. Shaken by his words, my faith wavered . . . it wavered, my brother, until he himself raised it and left it more radiant than it had been before!

"At noon we went to the place of execution, escorted by two tight files of soldiers, and followed by all the troops, armed in columns. The sentenced were visibly emotional, but they maintained an air of nobility and dignity that imposed respect even among the angriest of their enemies. If any of them had given in to weakness, their leader's example would have sufficed for them to regain their spirits and even inspire them with pride for dying at his side. For he walked calmly, his head held high above the crowd, as if instead of going to the scaffold, he was heading rather to a stage to pronounce the famous resolution that established the Junta Tuitiva.[4]

"When we reached the foot of the gallows, I still wanted to provide for him the comforts of our religion; but, with remarkable tranquility and sweetness, he said to me: 'That's enough, Father. I am well prepared to answer for my life before the Last Judgment. I have only one duty left to perform of my lofty mission.' And suddenly straightening up, growing more than a foot (or so it seemed to me from the admiration which he inspired in me), he shouted the following words with a vibrant voice, heard by all and forged forever in my memory: 'Fellow citizens! The fire that I have ignited will never be put out by the tyrants. Long live liberty!'

"And the sacrifice of the nine martyrs was consummated at once.

"I cannot conclude without relating to you an awful incident that will give you an idea of the wrath and fury of our enemies. When they were raising Don Juan Antonio Figueroa,[5] his hands tied behind his back, the rope broke, and this noble Spaniard who had enthusiastically embraced our cause fell heavily to the ground, face down. A sudden cry of horror and compassion arose from the crowd, imploring for mercy. But an officer stepped through the ranks of the soldiers and gave an unbelievable order to those presiding over the sacrifice, which was immediately carried out. The hangman, armed with a knife, beheaded the victim on the stones!

"All of this will bring you infinite pain, as it did me, or perhaps more, as I know the exaltation of your ideas and the exquisite sensibility of your being. Cry, my brother! But do not lose faith nor hope. The redeeming causes of humanity must overcome these tremendous trials of Providence. I believe I have previously warned you of this when I quoted Tertulian[6] to you: *Sanguis martirum semen christianorum!*"[7]

The paper had only a strange symbol as a signature, which was probably standard.

"He is right," Brother Justo exclaimed, pacing the room with large steps. "Murillo's fire will burn throughout the continent! This sacred fire will cleanse the pestilence from the foul air and. . . ."

A slight cough, to which I was accustomed, and a moan of pain, which I was hearing for the first time, drew our attention to the place occupied by my mother. We saw her sitting on her low stool, pressing one of her hands against her chest, while with the other she held a white cloth to her mouth—a cloth from which earlier that very day she had partially unraveled the edges so as to make a fringe and later decorate with fancy hemstitches.

When Brother Justo saw her and noticed a spot of blood on the cloth, he let out a kind of bellow; he ran toward her, lifted her in his arms, and carried her to the dais where he immediately placed her. All of this took only an instant—less, I am sure, than the time it has taken me to report it.

"I have told you not to work, not to kill yourself, woman!" he yelled angrily, and he threw the low stool, the lace pillow, and even the white cloth out to the street—all of which a confused María Francisca went out to retrieve.

"But I am not that sick," my mother answered, smiling softly like she always did. "Besides, what would become of us?"

This simple observation, before it was even completed, seemed to crush my teacher, who lowered his head to his chest. But it did not take him long to raise it triumphantly, asking:

"What about the money box? Haven't you yourself confessed to me that it is nearly full?"

"That is impossible," my mother answered, "that money is to send «him»[8] to study at the Universidad de San Francisco Javier and. . . ."

At that moment I could no longer contain myself. Crying, I ran to put my arms around the neck of the heroic mother who was dying silently for me, and I flooded her angelic face with kisses and tears.

Meanwhile, Brother Justo continued what he had been saying:

"I order it, I command it. As your brother, as the priest that I am, I cannot condone this, this kind of suicide; any reasonable man would try to prevent this with all of his strength."

"And I beg you," I added for my part. "Yes, I beg you mother, with these tears that you would not want your poor Juanito to continue spilling!"

Rosita—can you imagine how sacred and dear this name is to me when I use it now, on this occasion, instead of simply saying "my mother"?—had no recourse but to give in. The money box was solemnly taken out of the coffer, and Brother Justo anxiously broke it with his hands, spilling its contents on the table. It was not much; there were, however, a few very small gold coins among the silver ones.

From that day on, our affection and insistence forced her to take to her bed. She became a patient, surrounded by all the attention that the art of medicine could offer at the time, which consisted of the priests who were the practitioners of the Hospital of San Salvador. She was looked after not only with solicitude, but also with loving care by our good friends and the women who admired and aided her. I did not leave her side for a single moment. It was then—in the fondest and sweetest of voices that I compare with the cooing of a dove in her nest—that she revealed to me the treasures that she held hidden in her soul. I was able to feel her heavenly spirit, which had descended for some reason unbeknownst to me to one of the most somber places on earth, where it felt—in spite of its love and tenderness toward me—the nostalgia of its lost mansion. But never, ever did she want to reveal to me anything about my origin, nor how it came to be that she found herself lowered to trying to provide for our sustenance with her own hands.

After a month's time, she said she was so much better, and looked so handsome and lively, that we allowed her to return partially to her lacework. But when I happily told Brother Justo about seeing her so beautiful in the afternoons, he peremptorily repeated, his cheeks a bright crimson, his previous order. Apparently with more scientific knowledge than the Aragonese Father (a famous doctor of the time who was guided by the admirable collection of prescriptions by Doctor Mandouti*), Brother Justo prescribed: milk drawn each morning; a light walk in the sun, at noon; a long reading that I was to give to her in the afternoons of the forgotten *Don Quixote*; and another reading, a shorter one at night, that she would do herself instead of her long prayers and orations, of one page only from a small book that he himself brought, the *Imitation of Christ*.

Uncle Alejo heard him, and the next day he showed up at our door with a beautiful black cow.

"Here she is," he said to us triumphantly. "I have brought her. She is black, for although the Father did not say so, I know that this is the way it should be."

He had María Francisca fill the glass decorated with flowers with the foamy milk; then he offered it to my mother, and left with the cow, laughing, and returned with it every morning for many days afterward. I also performed my duties with the greatest of pleasure: I read entire chapters out loud and made comments on them, as best as I could, making the patient laugh. Things went so well that after twenty days' time we believed her to be completely recovered; she was happy and playful, like me.

---

*Editor's Note: Here is an example of one of them: "*For spitting blood.* Mix powdered mice dung, as much as will fit on a royal coin of silver, with half a cup of plantain juice, with sugar; drink first thing in the morning and before going to bed at night."

Calm and content, I went about the town and its outskirts with my mother on her mandatory outings. I began to recognize many notable people by sight, and I noticed strange things that were occurring in the town, which excited my curiosity.

Don Juan Bautista Oquendo, still a young clergyman then, especially drew my attention at first. He must have been endowed with tremendous stamina, for he could be seen everywhere and at all times. He visited the houses of many well-to-do *criollos* daily, he went to all the stores and marketplaces, and he would stop the most humble-looking people on the streets. He had some joke, or some affectionate words, to introduce himself with a tact which, as I later understood, is unusual in the human heart. And he would conclude by making the same request of everyone, including my mother, to whom he directed himself once, greeting her by the name of "the little nun":

"Pray, my daughter, for our generous King Don Fernando VII. Teach this rogue, this rascal (and here he gave me a little pat on the back) the love, the obedience, the respect—what am I saying!—the veneration that all of his subjects in these domains, all Christians, must have for him. The excommunicated Napoleon and the irreverent French heretics have stripped him of his throne; they hold him prisoner, martyrize him, and cruelly injure his paternal heart; they want to make us the slaves of the Devil."

He spoke Quechua with rare perfection (as it had already been much adulterated, tending to become a dialect mixed with Spanish, like today); his sermons in this language, which is so suggestive and persuasive, attracted immense crowds from the general populace to church. When he preached in Spanish, the Spaniards and *criollos* admired his eloquence, his religious fervor, his loyalty to the monarch; however, to tell the truth, it was already not liked very much for anyone to touch on this last point with any frequency, as it was said to be a delicate subject.

There were other inexhaustible *criollo* gentlemen and some mestizos who had the same tenacity to excite the loyalty of "the legitimate King, our rightful Lord." Among the mestizos, none equaled Alejo's enthusiasm, zeal, and abnegation.

My uncle now came by, very joyous, and shouted from the door:

"Long live the beloved King Fernando!"

To my mother he would say:

"Rosita child, if you do not shout 'Long live the king!' like this, like me, using up all the air in this room, you will never fully recover from the cough, which is the only thing that would make us happy."

Then, addressing me, after having lifted me up and holding me above his head by only one foot, which gave me a pleasant sensation of vertigo, he would continue:

"Let's go, young man! Long live the king! If not, I'll drop you to the ground or send you flying across the street to that house over there like a bird."

Meanwhile, he would be bouncing me up and down so that I thought my head would crash against the ceiling rafters, until I would shout a hundred times: "Long live the king!" And he did not leave in peace the poor María Francisca either, nor any of the simple women of which I have spoken, who looked at him with astonishment and said that he was either crazy or he must have regressed to being a child again.

He was incredibly extreme in his royalist fervor. On Good Friday he went out as a penitent, naked to the waist, with a heavy, enormous cross, a crown with carob thorns, and a horsehair rope or halter around his neck. He flagellated himself in such a way that his back looked like a burning sore, and he did not pass up the occasion to cry out that he was doing this as punishment for his own sins and to offer God this small sacrifice on behalf of the beloved king, who was being martyred even more than him by the sons of Satan. He edified the multitudes who cried loudly when they saw and heard him; all promised that they were willing to die at his side in order to be led to the doors of paradise. But the next day, when he came to see us, he was so healthy and recovered, and he laughed in such a way, that I am of the opinion that the cunning scoundrel performed his caper with cotton soaked in sheep's blood and that the thorns on the crown were very carefully rounded out.

One day—it must have been in the month of July, for the fields were almost entirely stripped of the abundant crops of the beautiful grains of the Altiplano of Upper Perú—as I accompanied my mother in one of her daily walks around the ravines of the Rocha River that border Calacala, I also witnessed a very curious scene. In the middle of a field of barley, which had been recently visited by the sickles of the *colonos* who worked for Mr. Cangas, whose manor was very close by, we saw respectable gentlemen, like Don Francisco del Rivero, Don Bartolomé Guzmán,[9] Don Juan Bautista Oquendo, and others whose names I only learned later, seemingly playing hide-and-seek. They were lying in ambush for I know not whom, and at times they made signs to each other to keep silent; at others, they laughed and covered their mouths with their hands. When they noticed our presence, Brother Justo, to my great surprise, came crawling out from among them on all fours.

"Do not tell anyone that you have seen us, and leave here right away," he told us—and went back into hiding just as he had come out.

Three days later we learned that the Lord Governor Don José González de Prada had placed Don Francisco del Rivero, Don Esteban Arze, and Don Melchor Guzmán Quitón[10] under arrest and sent them to the prison in Oruro. Our friends stopped coming by to visit and even forgot us for many days. Instead, but of course not at all preferable, I made a new friendship, one that displeased my mother very much. I shall tell now of how it came to be.

The street on which we lived was almost always deserted and did not have any paving; our street corner served, therefore, as a meeting place for the lazy and mischievous boys of the neighborhood to play *palama*. The name of this game must come from the pall-mall played in the Peninsula. It consists of setting up a tall rock on the ground, where a line has been drawn, and trying to knock it down by throwing other flat rocks, as heavy as possible, from a set distance. Every time the rock is knocked over, a point is scored; if none of the players knocks it over, the point is given to the boy whose stone is closest to the line. The game is played to twelve points, although it is often doubled to twenty-four, or even more, depending on the players' skills.

Among these boys there was one who was fair and blond, known as *El Overo*,[11] as mestizos of that complexion tended to be called. He was the most deft, the loudest, and the most cross of them all; he would get into a thousand quarrels from which he always emerged victorious if he was on equal footing, and from which he could escape with admirable speed if his enemy was considerably stronger. At a safe distance, as a last resort, he would make the most annoying gestures to his pursuers, like the one that consists, for example, of putting your thumb on your nose and waving your other fingers with your hand wide open.

He thought I was agreeable, or as he used to say, "I pleased him." Several times he circled around my street; he called me from afar to come out to play; he became exasperated trying to get me to participate or be a victim of one of his wild pranks. One morning, when my mother had gone to Mass, leaving me alone—which she seldom did—he took advantage of the long-awaited occasion and entered the house, "through the front door, like a king."

"Don't be silly, Don Little Saint," he said to me, "come have fun like us; leave that big, old book alone. . . . What good is reading for, anyway? I don't know why my father taught it to me along with other entirely useless things."

With amazing volubility, prying through everything, he kept rattling off a thousand different things—impossible to remember—without waiting for an answer, until he opened the door that led to the small patio and exclaimed:

"How beautiful! Long live the king! We don't even have to leave your haunt."

He set up the *palama* out there with rocks taken from the kitchen hearth, and he made me play for a while. He slowly taught me a thousand different games, one after the other, proper or improper for boys our age. He had, to this end, tops, balls, teetotums, and a dirty, filthy deck of cards in his pockets. When the both of us were tired, he said to me:

"Let's go rest in your room."

We went back in; but his rest consisted in disarranging and moving everything around, without sparing the prints nor the Divine Shepherdess. Suddenly, after looking behind the latter, he let out a scream; he separated the painting further from the wall and pointed to a small bundle that was in a recess in the wall.

"What is it?" he asked.

"I don't know; I've never seen it," I answered him.

"Well . . . let's see it," he replied.

And without waiting any further, he opened the bundle, which contained only a piece of esparto rope, about one vara long, of an indefinable color between suet and soot. He looked at the strange object with surprise and handed it to me right away.

At that moment my mother arrived; very angry, she said to me:

"Who has dared to rummage through all this? Who is this boy?"

I did not know how to lie; I fell to my knees and told her everything that had taken place. My new friend skipped out to the street, turned his head, and, before completing his escape, yelled:

"Carrasco, old friend!"

These words affected my mother very strongly.

III

What I Saw of the Uprising

I solemnly swore to my mother and to myself that I would not meet again with so dangerous a friend, thinking that I would certainly not go back on my word. But just three days later, *El Overo* came by again; tempting me, he dragged me along with his group; this caused my mother the greatest of sorrows, as my conscience still reminds me. All of this will be recounted in this chapter and in the one that follows it.

When dawn broke on the 14th of September, a day whose memory will not die in the memory of the native sons of Cochabamba, my mother had gone out to make a pressing delivery of lacery in the small town of Recoleta, leaving me still asleep and under the care of María Francisca, who was also in charge of the work in the kitchen. When I awoke, I heard some distant rifle and musket shots; then, shortly thereafter, the ringing of the bell from the tall tower of the Church of the Matriz, which was answered almost at once by the great bell of the Church of St. Francis and by all the others in the many bell towers in all the churches in town. I dressed quickly, and ran to the door. . . . There was such an uproar coming from the main plaza! Numerous groups of men and women were running in that direction, yelling:

"Long live Fernando VII! Death to the *chapetones!*"

I do not know if by design or accident, but my friend, who, last time, had left me with such strange words and seemingly so upset, appeared in the street. He was leading his group of companions, armed with sticks and reed canes; he was also shouting, like only he could, and the others were calling back, like only they could. When he saw me, he came toward me very brazenly, as if nothing had occurred; his troop halted and milled around the corner, waiting for their captain.

"I am not angry," he said to me. "What are you doing there, Don Open-Mouthed? Come with us, or we will take you as a recruit."

And without waiting for an answer, as was his custom, he grabbed me by the neck, dragged me out, and rushed me over to his companions; neither my screams, nor the threats of María Francisca who had come heroically out of the kitchen to my rescue, were of any use. All was in vain; the gang dragged me along toward the plaza.

Little by little I overcame my very justifiable indignation and the whole thing began to be fun, as was very normal for someone my age. I understood, furthermore, that the uproar might be related somehow to the "disturbance of the 16th of July"—the phrase that I knew thanks to the letter that my teacher had had me read. I had memorized the letter, as my teacher had requested of me, and I wanted to distinguish myself in my own way among the companions who had taken me by force.

"Stop, men!" I shouted, climbing onto a spur stone that may perhaps still exist today on the corner of the street that was later named Ingavi. "Fellow citizens! I will die for you." I continued with my hat in my hand: "Yes! I want to die even if I fall from the gallows and am beheaded on the stones; because the fire that we ignite will never be extinguished by the tyrants, and it will burn throughout the continent. Long live liberty!"

"Hurrah! Long live liberty!" the young band answered, electrified by Murillo's words, embellished in my style and augmented by those that I had heard from my teacher.

El Overo followed with: "Long live Juanito! He deserves to be the captain more than I do. Well, get down here! Take my stick and ... march on, men!"

Having said and carried this out, as was his manner, he pulled me down from the spur stone by my feet, placed his reed in my hand, pushed me to the front of the column, and situated himself respectfully behind me—all to the accompaniment of the swelling applause from our soldiers.

We thus arrived at the corner of the Church of the Matriz. The crowd already filled nearly the entire plaza, and it continued flowing in from all the streets. It surged in waves, currents, and eddies, the only steadfastness being that seen in the columns of the militiamen and of a strange troop, partially mounted and partially on foot, of robust and colossal peasants from the Valley of Cliza. The infantry of this troop wore leather caps embroidered with sequins, ponchos thrown diagonally over their left shoulders, trousers rolled up, and sandals on their feet. Few rifles and muskets shone in the sun among their files, the majority of their weapons being thick, wide cudgels called *macanas*. Furthermore, a noisy group of women from the marketplace roamed among them, distributing knives, daggers, and machetes that the men quickly snatched from their hands. The horsemen were better dressed and equipped, many with fine white and yellow wool hats, bright, colorful ponchos, spats, thick overcoats, and spurs; they were mounted on mares, nags, and jades, a few armed with lances or sables, and the majority with long sticks that had knives attached at the end in any way possible. At the front, a numerous group of *criollo* landowners could be seen on beautiful, gleaming colts donning armor with plentiful silver plating. Don Esteban Arze and the young Don Melchor Guzmán Quitón were in command of the troops, followed by many private assistants and friends, caracoling among the crowd on spirited horses covered with sweat and foam. The wide, spacious, carved wooden balconies of the side of the street opposite to where I was were filled with *criollo* families. The front rows were occupied by ladies in their best church clothes, with petticoats and mantillas; this was because the uproar had surprised them on their way to Mass, which, as was their custom, they attended every morning. On the upper gallery of the Cabildo,[*1] the notables of the town could be seen crowded together. At the doors

---

*I have been told that the building is now a beautiful, private house.

of the convent and atrium of the Church of St. Augustine,*[2] on the right-hand side of the street, circles formed; among them, one could distinguish completely white habits, and others with black, blue, or gray mantillas, and so on, depending on the different religious orders. Brother Justo—how could the presence of my dear teacher not especially draw my attention?—was speaking and gesturing like a man possessed. Amid the deafening noise from the bells, everyone was yelling at once, and a thousand different things; some: "Long live Fernando VII!"; others: "Death to the *chapetones*!"; those over there: "Long live the homeland!";[3] these: "We want the sons of our country!"; those closest to the Cabildo: "Long live Don Francisco del Rivero! Let Don Juan Bautista Oquendo speak!" The two latter figures were among the notables in the gallery of the Cabildo; they were shouting like everyone else and gesturing with their arms, although I do not know what they were saying. Those who were with these men waved their hats and handkerchiefs at the crowd. . . . All of this, of which I now give testimony, I saw better than anyone else, hoisted up by the arms of the most robust of my companions, oftentimes standing on their shoulders, able to balance myself thanks to the antics that Alejo claimed to have taught me.

Finally the noise from the ringing of the bells died down a little, as they had sent someone to quiet the bells of the Church of the Matriz (it was said that they had to tear the bell-ringer from his place by force, the ropes of the clapper still in his hands). With the popularity of Oquendo's name and the gesturing of the notables, they managed to get the attention of the crowd and quiet it down, at least at that end of the plaza. The orator then spoke for a few moments, but only the last three words reached me; they were hurled with all the strength of his powerful lungs, and were repeated everywhere at once:

"Open the Cabildo! Open the Cabildo!"

Shouting this new phrase, which replaced all the previous ones, the crowd pressed itself against the doors of the Cabildo to such an extent that, according to the observations of my adjutant *El Overo*,

---

*This is where the General Don José Ballivián had the praetorian house and palace of justice built with its galleries, which I am assured are very elegant and spacious.

it would have been possible for anyone, regardless of how slow and awkward they were, to walk on people's heads without fear of falling. Although we did not know why nor for what, we wanted to penetrate through that mass at all costs; but then a commotion and a frightening uproar drew our attention toward the street with the general stores.*

"Let's go! Let's go!" we said to each other. For where would we have gone with more enthusiasm than to the place with the loudest racket and the most confusion?

We therefore went in that direction, heading along the street opposite the main plaza, where it was very much possible to walk by then. On arriving at the corner of the above-mentioned street and Barrio Fuerte,** we found ourselves halted by the multitudes that had also been led there by their curiosity. There was no option other than to resort once again to my companion's services; I climbed onto the shoulders of the first ones who offered themselves in exchange for repeating out loud what I saw happening as it took place.

A gentleman who had obviously come out of the Church of St. Augustine with Brother Justo through the side door, and to the street with the general stores, was surrounded by a few individuals who were feverishly threatening to kill him. With his head already wounded and his clothes in complete disarray, he was desperately holding on to the Father's waist. The latter, meanwhile, was entreating and imploring them to stop; and also, when necessary, distributing vigorous blows to the necks and heads of those who were attempting to finish sacrificing the poor wretch.

"Let him die! Let the hypocrite who always served and flattered the *chapetones* die!" the enraged adversaries were yelling.

And I think that, in spite of my teacher's pleas and blows, they would have ended up tearing that man apart and dragging his limbs through the streets, if it had not been for the arrival of a troop from the Valley of Cliza that was led by Alejo, although this group at first seemed rather to augment the conflict.

When Alejo recognized the gentleman, his face underwent the

---

*This must be the street that has since been named after the Achá Theater.
**It was already referred to simply as the Street of St. Francis by then.

most bestial and savage transformation of which it was capable.

"Let him die! Let's kill him like a dog!" he yelled, wielding an iron bar as long and as thick as the *macanas* that his men carried, but which he brandished like a light reed.

Brother Justo knew Alejo's character in depth, and he took the only action that could have worked.

"Alejo, my dear Alejo," he said to him softly, falling to his knees. "Do not carry out this vengeance; or else kill me, too. . . . Shatter your friend's—your confessor's—head first!"

The Herculean locksmith stopped and hesitated a moment; then he said the words that he usually said in such situations:

"Well . . . there you have it!"

And he immediately turned his face toward the angry ones among the crowd. Leaning on his iron bar with both hands, he calmly added:

"No one will touch even one fiber of the Mayor's clothes in my presence."

The man was saved. Everyone knew that Alejo could bend a carline coin in half and then back as if it were made out of wax; everyone had seen him walking through the streets an entire day, laughing as he carried a donkey in his arms. Who would have wanted to expose themselves to even the slightest of blows from his iron bar?

As there was nothing further to do there, we went back to the Cabildo. The news of what was taking place within was spreading through the crowd by word of mouth and receiving the most enthusiastic of cheers.

"We have recognized," they were saying, "the Very Honorable Junta of Buenos Aires![4] Long live the Junta! Long live Don Fernando VII! Don Francisco del Rivero has been named Governor. Long live the Cabildo! Don Esteban Arze and Don Melchor Guzmán are to continue commanding the troops. They're brave and courageous! Long live Don Esteban! Long live Don Melchor! They say they are going to spare the *chapetones*. That's wrong! No, no, it's not . . . poor *chapetones*! No one should die! Long live the homeland!"

All along I was yelling and having my band yell "Hurrah!" more boisterously than all the people there. Inside, however, I kept asking myself: "What is this? What, after all, has happened here?" But I did not dare ask anyone these questions; I was afraid that being very well informed of these things, knowing exactly what was going on, they would laugh at my foolish ignorance or my naiveté.

Luckily my teacher, who had accompanied the man he had protected to his house, returned. Upon seeing me, he came up to me, and we had the following dialogue:

"You, too, around here, young man?"

"Yes, sir, they brought me . . . I did not want to come but. . . ."

"No, young man, it is not wrong. And what have you done?"

"I have yelled like everyone: 'Long live Fernando VII! Death to the *chapetones*!'"

"The first shout, we'll allow; the second is very wrong. No one should be killed if our homeland is to be brought to life."

"A few have recently said that very thing. I have also spoken like Murillo and finished with: 'Long live liberty!'"

"Excellent, my son."

"But . . . if you will allow me, Father; I don't really know what we have done here, nor how all of this has taken place since daybreak."

"That I can tell you with the greatest of pleasures, if you come with me to the monastery. There is time to talk while the Cabildo concludes its meeting; I believe I know, too, what will come of it."

My companions were not opposed to my going with him, out of their respect for the Father. Only *El Overo* made his normal mocking gesture, sticking his thumb on the end of his nose and waving his hand at me.

I Begin to Surmise
What Is Happening

There was nothing special about my teacher's cell that distinguished it from that of any other priest, nor do I believe that describing it would add very much to my simple story. He closed the door carefully behind us and had me sit on a bench next to the table, while he sat on the other side, on an armchair draped with beads, and began to speak as follows:

"Eventually, you will understand better than I what this uprising means. You will get to know many things thoroughly that I—in spite of the eager, clandestine studies I have undertaken these past twenty years—have barely caught a glimpse of. When this happens, when a brighter light fills your intelligence, remember me, the poor friar who taught you to read. And think, too, of how the rewards of science, which you will be able to enjoy, would have consoled me in my torturous life."

He stopped at this point for a moment. Then he quickly rubbed the palm of his hand hard against his broad forehead, as if he wanted to free himself from something that weighed upon it, and continued:

"The country where we were born, as well as many other countries in this part of the world, obey a king who is two thousand leagues away, on the other side of the ocean. It takes one year for our complaints to reach his feet, and we never know when—if at all—the resolutions that his Council dictates, or even his sovereign dispositions, will arrive here. His agents believe that they are demigods, high above us. His subjects who come from there consider themselves nothing more and nothing less than our masters and lords. Those of us who are their very children—the *criollos*—are looked upon with disdain; they think that we should never aspire to the honors and public positions that are reserved just for them. The mestizos, whose blood is half like their's, are scorned and condemned to suffer innumerable humiliations. The Indians, the poor, conquered race, find themselves reduced to being treated as beasts of labor—they are a flock that the *mita*[1] decimates every year in the depths of the mines.

"These reasons alone would suffice for us to wish to have our own government, of any kind, created right here, always within sight. But other reasons that are just as grave also exist, and these will make us choose to risk complete annihilation rather than continue living under the Colonial regime.

"A man destined to earn his bread, his material well-being, with his own sweat and toil, cannot freely satisfy even this decree of Providence. If he is a farmer, if he has been able to obtain a portion of land from the Crown, he is forbidden to grow anything that might compete with what is produced in the Peninsula. If he wants to exploit the rich mineral gold mines of our hills and our mountain range, he must know influential people so as to get laborers, or even the mercury needed in the smelting of ores. If he becomes a merchant, he discovers that all trade is in the hands of a few privileged individuals, from the large companies in Sevilla, Cádiz, and Cartagena, all the way down to the Spanish and Genovese storekeepers. If he dares to become a manufacturer, he discovers that the tools he needs for his industry will be brutally destroyed. I know of vineyards and olive groves that have been uprooted or burned down; I know *criollos* and mestizos who have discovered fabulously rich mines only to have to abandon them for Spaniards to exploit. This linen cloth with green stripes, which serves as my tablecloth, is *tocuyo* from Cochabamba, taken to Spain to be dyed, brought back as *angaripola*, and sold to its previous owners for unbelievable prices. The people from Cochabamba are not allowed to carry out such a simple operation themselves. I have seen, alas, the looms on which the *tocuyo* is relentlessly woven destroyed many times over.

"Education—the soul's nourishment, the internal light that, added to one's consciousness, raises man's control over Creation every day—can only be obtained by a limited few and in such a circumspect manner that it can barely be taken seriously. I have laughed so hard at times at what they taught me over the years at the Universidad de San Francisco Javier de Chuquisaca! There is a real effort to keep us ignorant; he who says the most foolish things in Latin among us is considered a wise man. And God have mercy on he who aspires to obtain any form of knowledge that is not permitted, as he exposes himself to be burned at the stake for being a philosophizing heretic! In Cochabamba, right here, for reasons which I will share with you in due time, it used to be a crime of the utmost severity to teach boys to read.

"Religion, which the priests themselves have allowed to grow dark—come closer to me, my son—no longer follows the doctrine of Jesus, nor any doctrine capable of moralizing man so as to lead him into eternity in glory. They tell people to repeat the Our Father, and they help maintain the social hierarchies and the division between the races, when it would have been so easy for them to show through the Dominical oration, taught by Christ himself, that all men are equal before our one Father and His judgment. They should strive for the faithful's love of God being 'in spirit and in truth'; instead, they foster superstitions, and even idolatry. In churches—come closer, my son—I see images that receive greater veneration than the Sacrament. I have been told of a certain parish where they worship the bull of St. Luke or the lion of St. Mark, and that they pray to them, holding candles in their hands! Maybe they are even doing the same in other parishes with the horse of St. James and the dog of St. Roque. Basically, in order to obtain more worldly goods, they increase the number of holidays and invent all kinds of devotions. And all under the intoxication of the sun's rays—the sun, that ancient Father-God that the poor Indian once adored with greater awareness and even with more purity, perhaps."*

He stopped again at this point, this time for a longer pause. I respected his silence; but I was unable to stop myself from bringing one of his large, thin hands to my lips.

He went on:

"It is necessary to stop all of this. In each of the population centers of these very vast domains there is a small group of men who have already committed themselves to this end, and they will achieve it. Today the multitudes do not understand them, and that is why they have searched for some pretext to bring them out to a glorious event: to avoid clashing with ideas that have been inveterated in the long night of the last three centuries. You should know that even slavery can become a difficult habit to abandon. I have heard of a man, imprisoned from a very early age, who was finally set free after many years. But then he asked to be returned to his beloved, dark, and silent dungeon because he said that it was the best place for the indolence and self-absorption in which he had fallen, and from which he never emerged.

"A grand genius of a ruler, sprung from the bosom of a tremendous upheaval in the French Kingdom, invaded Spain and saw the King Don Carlos IV and the Prince of Asturias Don Fernando fall to their knees at his feet. News of this event filled the American colonies with consternation. And the sense of freedom emerges from this consternation for the dethroned, natural king. Those 'Long live Don Fernando VII' that you hear actually indicate to the majority of the men in the Cabildo: 'Down with the King! Up with the people!'

"But the designs of these men—not yet revealed—is not new. It was not just conceived yesterday on this ground in which you were born, my son!"

At this point he stood up and raised his hands and became more and more animated as he proceeded:

---

*See the pastoral letters of the distinguished Don Fray Joseph Antonio de San Alberto, Archbishop of the Viceroyalty of the Río de la Plata.[2]

"I will not exhaust your attention with even the briefest account of any of the bloody revolts in which the indigenous race insanely attempted to recover its independence, proclaiming a war of the races—only inevitably to lose. But I will recount, at some length, a grand event: a heroic, yet premature effort that matches my objectives and has special interest for us both.

"In November 1730, the news that Don Manuel Venero y Valero was coming from the Viceroyalty of the Río de la Plata circulated through our town and the other towns of our lovely and fertile valleys. It was said that he had been named to the post of Collector by the King in order to register the mestizos, as the Indians were, to have them pay the individual Tribute—that disgraceful tax imposed upon the conquered race. The news was not quite accurate; they simply wanted to verify everyone's origin in order to clarify in the register who were really the indigenous ones. But even from this it was quite normal to expect and fear infinite troubles and abuses of all kinds.

"The mestizos, who already made up the majority of the population, responded to the news with pain, shame, and anger, and they directed it fearlessly toward the *guampos*, the name given to the *chapetones* back then. Resolved to raise a vigorous resistance, to spill their blood and that of their rulers before consenting to this new humiliation, they looked for a brave leader. They found one immediately.

"He was a young man, twenty-five years old, of mixed blood like theirs; a silver artisan, exceptionally well taught to read and write by his father—or perhaps, like you, by some generous friar. His name was Alejo Calatayud."

On hearing this name I became all ears.

"He lived," my teacher continued, "in a humble house, in the vicinity of the Hospital of St. John of God, with his mother Agustina Espíndola y Prado, his twenty-two-year-old wife, Teresa Zambrana y Villalobos, and a young girl named Rosa, the first fruit of their blessed matrimony. I must point out that the pompous surnames that I have just uttered do not necessarily imply a kinship to the families of the wealthy *criollos* to whom the names belonged (the Zambrana family was especially wealthy, having established a primogeniture[3]). It was common in those days, much more so than today, for servants born in their master's house to take on the surname of the master's family. That could have been the case with Agustina and Teresa; but it also would not have been strange for them to have some of the proud primogenitals' blood in their veins, spread by the dissipation that the lords entertained in their pursuits within the monotonous existence to which the blessed Colonial regime sentenced them.

"Alejo did not conceal his satisfaction when he heard the suggestions of his companions and friends, the artisans and workers of the town. In addition to the ill treatment that threatened everyone and that in and of itself would have been enough for him to decide to lead the uprising, there was a personal affront that he wanted to avenge. The arrogant Don Juan Matías Cardogue y Meseta, captain of the King's militia, unable to humble him in an argument, had resorted to drawing his sword, and had wounded one of Alejo's hands. The scar, which he always had in front of him, would often make Alejo stop his work and send him wandering off into somber thoughts.

"On the 29th of November of that year—it will soon be eighty years since then—the silversmith's family was happily eating dinner, when Esteban González, José Carreño, José de la Fuente, someone Prado, someone Cotrina (I have not been able to find out their first names), and a few other mestizos, arrived at their small house in a very agitated state. Immediately calling Alejo to the door, showing great anxiety in front of his mother and wife, one of them told him that the occasion had arrived: the town was almost completely disarmed because the Collector had asked the town of Caraza for an escort to enter there safely, and the garrison troop, captained by Cardogue, had marched away to that town. Then all the men asked Alejo for his help and leadership; they asked him to fulfill the promises that he had made to them earlier.

"'Let's go!' Alejo answered. 'Let's get our men together; we will seize the weapons from the guards of the Cabildo and the jail and raise a black flag against the *guampos*.'

"All of this was carried out that night and the following day. The multitudes, gathered together, yelling 'Long live the king! Death to the *guampos!'*—see, my son, how similar it is to what you heard today—took over the main plaza. They broke down the doors of the Cabildo and the jail and seized the few weapons that they found there; it turned out that there were barely ten of these, and not all of them functional. By sunrise on the 30th of November, there were four thousand men, armed with slings, sticks, and knives, on the small hill of San Sebastián; Calatayud waved his flag of death and yelled his delirious words of vengeance from its peak. In this manner, the young silver artisan challenged the greatest power that has ever existed or will ever exist on earth.

"When he heard about the uprising, the Collector became terrified and fled to Oruro. But Cardogue was not intimidated, and he retraced his steps with his small troop. The captain was audacious and arrogant, like the old conquistadors; he thought his firearms would suffice to instill respect among the populace—which, by the way, only felt the deepest and most cordial scorn toward him. The battle was dreadful; the victory went to the side with the greatest numbers, and everyone on the defeated side was sacrificed.

"As it often occurs in these cases—may God prevent it from happening this time around!—the multitudes felt that horrible, insatiable thirst for blood and plundering that extends dark shadows and indelible stains over the glory of their most just sacrifices and worthy triumphs. Overrunning the town, they immolated the Spaniards who were unable to follow Valero in his escape; they pillaged their houses and did not even stop outside the doors of some of the houses of the *criollos*. I don't know if Calatayud authorized these excesses, but he must have at least given his consent or tolerated them. I do believe that he himself did not participate in the plundering, because he continued to live and later died a poor man; neither his mother nor his wife ever saw him in possession of any money nor of any other object that he had not earned through his honest work.

"In order to bring these criminal excesses to an end, the *criollo* notables proposed a capitulation, which was later discussed in an open meeting in the Cabildo. Still recognizing the authority of the King, it was agreed—among other things which we don't know today—that public positions would only be conferred upon the native sons of our country, as long as they protected and sheltered all their brothers. New Mayors were named, among them Don José Mariscal and Don Francisco Rodríguez Carrasco. And until the King of Spain confirmed the capitulation, the leader of the movement, Calatayud, was given the right to attend the Cabildo and veto decisions as he thought necessary.

"Only God knows what consequences this great event might have had, had the darkest of betrayals not brought it to an atrocious end—an end much bloodier than its beginning. I can assure you, without a doubt, that it alarmed the Viceroy of Perú beyond measure and that it resonated in Buenos Aires and in the General Captainship of Chile.

"Mayor Rodríguez Carrasco was old friends with Calatayud; he had taken Alejo's daughter, Rosa, to be baptized, and he enjoyed the confidence of the entire family. An audacious and cunning man, with ambitions for titles and honors, he understood that he himself could come out of this critical situation in a tremendously advantageous position. First he came to an agreement with his most intimate supporters and friends; then he proceeded to contrive an evil plot.

"Calatayud, meanwhile, went about his life completely off guard. He only painfully witnessed the previous tranquility of his house upset by his wife's ceaseless complaints and reprimands. Her confessor, Don Francisco de Urquiza, a priest from the Church of the Matriz, tormented her soul by speaking ill of her husband's behavior.

"'Why,' Teresa would ask him, 'do you dare to carry in your hand the baton that does not belong to someone of your class? Don't you know that it is the will of God that we bow our heads before the preferred subjects of our Lord, the King?'

"And Alejo would answer with pride, with a profound belief in human equality that had been powerfully awoken in his soul:

"'Because I am just as much a man as they are; because I have the strength to protect my unfortunate brothers.'

"Other times his wife asked her husband about more dangerous affairs:

"'What are you doing with those papers? Who did you write to so mysteriously during the night, when you thought I was asleep?' she would ask him, and never received anything other than evasive answers from him.

"Things came to such a point that Teresa, afraid of losing her place in Heaven, abandoned her home to take sanctuary in the house of a notable lady, Doña Isabel Carera.

"One day, Rodríguez Carrasco appeared before his old friend with a smile on his lips, more cheerful and warm-hearted than ever, and invited him to celebrate some family holiday. Alejo accepted and went there by himself, unarmed, hoping to forget among friends the bitterness in his small house.

"But in the middle of the banquet—just when the guests seemed to exclusively be partaking in the spreading of friendship, while the wine passed from hand to hand, with words of affection and ardent toasts to prosperity and good fortune—a door leading to the adjacent drawing room opened suddenly. Many of the conspirators came in through the door in a mad rush; they overpowered the trusting Calatayud, and—"

"They hung him!" I shouted, believing I had correctly concluded his sentence for him. "They put his right arm on top of Mount San Sebastián where he had waved his black flag."

"They didn't hang him, not exactly," my teacher said. "Legend has it, and I believe it completely, that they choked him right there, or that they stabbed him to death, and that it was his corpse that they took to the jail house. The official reports insist that they took him alive, with his hands and feet securely tied, that he confessed in jail, and that he was then hung to death. In either case, it is true that he was already dead when they publicly hung him from the gallows, with the baton in his hand. Later, they distributed his limbs to the most crowded and visible places in town, along the roads and on the hilltops, and they sent his head to the Royal Audience of Charcas. But who told you about this?"

"Nobody," I answered, "I just heard a few mysterious words three years ago from my uncle the locksmith, and I have recently seen a piece of rope. . . ."

"That," the Father said calmly, "must be the piece that I found while hearing the confession of a dying man and which I later gave to your mother. That sad relic had been saved because of superstitions that attributed miraculous powers to it; but it was necessary for it to be respectfully kept by the descendants of Calatayud."

Imagine, if you can, how these words shook my entire being.

"My God!" I exclaimed. "Does that make me then. . . ."

"His great, great grandson by way of your mother," my teacher stated.

Until that moment he had been standing, and pacing at times, as he spoke. Now he stopped in front of me, curved his tall, thin body forward, rested his hands on the table, and looked at me with an affectionate smile.

"For this very reason you must hear the story out to its end," he continued, and went on with his interrupted account.

"The executioner Rodríguez Carrasco burned the capitulation and handed out dreadful punishments in the name of the King as vengeance for the offenses carried out against his Royal Majesty. He drowned any new attempts at insurrection in blood, and received the cheers, kind words, and declarations of gratitude from the Viceroy and the Audience in Charcas. He later received large rewards and honors, as decreed by the Crown. He had, among others, the satisfaction of declaring himself, in his deluded vanity, 'the Lord Captain of the Spanish Infantry of the Empire of the Gran Paititi'—a fantastic empire of riches that was said to exist hidden in the depths of our jungles. But the justice of posterity has made his very name, just as it has Judas', synonymous with 'traitor.'"

He paused here again, and then continued as he paced the room, as you will soon hear. Meanwhile, I remembered the words that *El Overo* had directed at me when he thought I had betrayed him to my mother—a shout from the mouth of a boy that represented the conscience still felt against the traitor, nearly eighty years.

"Agustina, Teresa, and the girl Rosa were locked up by Rodríguez Carrasco himself—just as if they had been imprisoned—in the Convent of St. Claire. That is why it was generally believed—and it still is—that Calatayud's family line was extinguished. But this was not the case; after her mother and grandmother died, Rosa, a young woman by then, managed to get out. She married a *criollo* peasant, a very poor, but honest and good man, in the vicinity of Pazo.

"Furthermore, the noble idea—the beginnings of which had been conceived by Calatayud—begins to shine in the souls of this the third generation since his death, who will erase the mark of infamy that has been left upon his memory. I have already told you, and I now repeat, that throughout these domains there are brave and enlightened men who are resolved to all manner of sacrifices in order to obtain the independence of our homeland. They are the ones who have fostered this spirit in the Colonies to form a government together, imitating the Peninsula, in order to repel the invasion of a foreign power. Last year, on the 25th of May, Chuquisaca took a step in that direction; on the 16th of July, inspired by Murillo, La Paz established the famous Junta Tuitiva. And it has not mattered at all that our dominators have suppressed these initial movements. One year after Chuquisaca's shout of freedom, Buenos Aires has let its own much more powerful one be heard; and from there, a redeeming crusade is on its way. Today, on the 14th of September, Cochabamba does what you see before you, and it does so with such determination and nobility that it seems certain to achieve victory.

"The only thing left to tell you now is the immediate cause of this «uprising». I will do so in a few brief words.

"You know that the governor, who has been removed from his post and is currently in hiding, sent Don Francisco del Rivero, Don Esteban Arze, and Don Melchor Guzmán Quitón to prison in Oruro. A few days ago, they managed to escape and came to the Valley of Cliza, where they enjoy a tremendous influence over the people. They induced the towns to rebel, came to an agreement with the patriots in our town, and this morning appeared in its outskirts. The daring advance of Guzmán Quitón with a few men on the quarters of the armed troops was enough for them to surrender. And not one single drop of blood, my son, has been shed! May God bless our people's ardent dreams!

"But enough for now. The meeting of the Cabildo must have finished. Those screams of jubilation, that joyful ringing of the bells, louder than this morning, tells us so quite clearly. Besides, your mother must be very anxious. . . . It's about time that this long lecture come to an end."

We thus left the monastery. But I had not taken more than one step outside, when I found myself snatched by María Francisca's arms. My mother was right behind her. She stopped to breathe freely for the first time that day, having found me after futile inquiries and anguished searches.

Leaving for later the reproaches and admonitions, she had me take the shortest path back to our house. I followed her silently, not worried about any trouble I might be in, lost in very different, deep meditations. Brother Justo's words, of which I have probably only been able to give a partial account, had opened my eyes to a previously unknown horizon. And if I was not yet able to take it all in, I began at least to spread my gaze in a wider circle than before. There were certain items, furthermore, that touched me intimately; I wanted to delve deeper into these; I promised myself that I would remove the mysterious veil of my origin. My wise teacher— whose name I wish to exhume from the oblivion in which it has been undeservedly buried—obviously believed, when he took me to his cell, that it is sometimes good to speak to children as if they were grown adults. That this is how they learn to think; that this is how they begin to seriously see life, where so many bitter trials and difficult battles await them.

How My Angel
Returned to Heaven

The following few days (until the end of October, at which point I could no longer pay attention to what was happening around me) were filled with jubilation, with all manner of activity, with busy preparations for the war into which Cochabamba had flung itself. I will only recount the main events here; or rather, whether they were the main ones or not, those that especially called my attention.

On the 16th or 17th of September—please forgive this lack of precision—the enthusiastic volunteers from the Valley of Sacaba arrived under the leadership of Don José Rojas. They were not as tall or as robust as the ones from Cliza, nor were they better equipped, but they were more alert, and rowdier.

On the 23rd of September there was a public ceremony in recognition of the Honorable Junta of Buenos Aires, which was followed by a solemn mass in the Church of the Matriz, "to give thanks to Don Francisco del Rivero, Intendant and Quartermaster General of the province." Before the groups from the Junta of War, the Cabildo, the Justice, and the Regiment headed to the church, Don Juan Bautista Oquendo pronounced the celebrated speech that has been recorded by historians (and which I will shortly recount in my own manner). He spoke from the gallery of the Cabildo to the entire town, which had gathered in the main plaza in complete silence.

On the 10th of October, the Junta of War arranged to send an armed dispatch to Oruro, led by Don Esteban Arze, in order to protect, as it claimed, "threatened public interests." But in reality, as my teacher assured me, it was to spread the spirit of Independence—an objective that would become clearer in future dispatches.

On the 16th of that same October, I heard they had named Don Francisco Javier de Orihuela as the representative to attend the Congress that was to meet in Buenos Aires. This seemed to transform my teacher and to fill his heart with happiness.

"When the representatives of the people of Upper Perú and the Río de la Plata meet in the Congress," he said to me, "the world will see that the Independence of America and the birth of our nation are unavoidable decrees that are willed by Divine Providence."

On the following day, the 17th, the false news—in the Church of the Recollect itself—that an enemy troop led by the old Commander in Chief Don Jerónimo Marrón de Lombera had appeared just outside the town caused such confusion, created such a tumultuous gathering of people in the main plaza, that I dare not try to describe it, even after I just attempted to give a brief idea of the uprising of the 14th of September. The call to arms that rang in all the church bells, which the governor was unable to stop, brought men and women, old and young, running to join forces, armed with whatever they could find: slings, sticks, hoes, plow-staffs, knives, frying pan handles, cobblestones pulled from the streets—any object that could stab, wound, or bruise the enemy from near or afar. The screams, curses, and howls must have literally caused the birds to fall from the sky. The news spread through the Valleys of Carza, Cliza, and Sacaba in a nearly miraculous short amount of time; today it could be explained, but only through the marvelous invention of the telegraph. An infinite number of volunteers arrived from a six-league radius, running desperately by foot and overriding their horses; they did not want to miss the occasion to prove their strength against the *chapetones* and to show their love for the emerging homeland. Suffice it to say that one could have carefully chosen, from those present, all the young, robust men, those fully fit for service, and formed an army of forty thousand soldiers who never would have demanded any payment for their services. Don Francisco del Rivero hurried to communicate this fact, as proof of the enthusiastic delirium with which Cochabamba challenged the secular oppression of the Spaniards, to the General who was leading his troops from Buenos Aires in our direction.

I received permission from my mother to go see some of these things in the company of Brother Justo. It surprised me very much not to find among the multitudes the individual who would have caused the biggest racket and the most confusion, the idler and vagabond per excellence—in short, my friend *El Overo*. I saw him only once, and from a distance. He looked very clean and was decently dressed, and he was standing next to a tall, fat man, who was blonder than him. A woman, speaking to another woman on her way out of church, referred to this man as the "*Gringo*,"[1] and they both crossed themselves as if they had seen the Devil.

Amusing scenes took place in our little house on the border of the Barrio de los Ricos—scenes of laughter and tranquil happiness, the memory of which moves me to the point of tears. I will relay just one to serve as an example of all of them, although this particular one did not end in the same manner as it begun.

The room described at the beginning of these memoirs also contains, in front of the dais, a small bedstead with tall columns and white curtains that were pulled back during the day and tied together with strips of blue silk ribbons. Do not ask me why we had such luxury in the middle of our poverty. You would give me the sorrow of believing that I have not been able to portray Rosita's soul, her affection and delicate attentions toward me—your humble servant who used to sleep in that bedstead like a prince in a soft, golden bed of feathers.

Rosita is sitting on her comfortable little stool. Since she is once again allowed to do a moderate amount of work, about two or three hours a day, she is embroidering in gold a red velvet baldric that a few of the notable ladies want to give to the new governor. Alejo, who has come by to say goodbye before leaving as a volunteer to Oruro with Don Esteban Arze's men, is leaning back against one of the panels of the door. Brother Justo, in his chair, with his hood over his eyes, seems more jovial than usual. I stand at attention in front of him like a recruit, ready to undertake my lesson. The dialogue between him and I begins:

"Have you learned Oquendo's beautiful words yet?"

"Yes, sir. And flawlessly, I believe."

"Can you repeat them like he spoke them from the heights of the gallery of the Cabildo?"

"Not quite; but . . . who knows!"

"Alejo, put this young man on the table for me."

The summoned man approaches silently with a smile that reveals all thirty-two of his teeth. He crouches back on his heels and offers me his open hand, barely an inch above the ground. I am not sure what I am supposed to do, but I place my right foot on his hand, straighten up like a cane, and feel myself being lifted almost to the ceiling, and immediately deposited on the table.

We all laugh; Alejo returns to his spot, and the conversation continues:

"Let's go, begin."

"'Brave citizens of Cochabamba; residents of the most fertile, beautiful, and delightful country in the world; most faithful subjects of . . . '"

"Ha, ha, ha, ha. . . ! We know this part; go on to the next."

"'Might they judge in the distant provinces that Cochabamba has caused additional harm upon the King's wounded chest. . . .'"

"Just like Don Juan Bautista! Let's get to the peroration. That's where the crux of the speech is, my son; the historians that speak of it will do well to transcribe it as the most beautiful example of the lofty feelings with which our country has cried its shout of Independence."

"'I see that you aspire to greater glories. Your strength will overcome the apparatus that the enemies of the State and your homeland still maintain in your region. The vigilance with which you amass your troops, the unity of feeling—in spite of the picture that Cañete[2] paints of Americans—with which you loath selfishness and strive to maintain with astonishing rivalry the rights of your homeland and of the State, is the most convincing argument that a single thought and a single sense of duty dictates your actions.

But what most elevates your homeland is the piety and devotion with which you have proceeded; from them springs forth the peace and tranquility that your homeland enjoys even in the presence of disorder and chaos. Nevertheless, even though this very honorable trait elicits my applause, I want to, thirdly, entrust upon you that from now on you must proceed in accordance with the same saintly law that you profess: that our European brothers, who you commonly call *chapetones*, far from having to endure any offense, be the first recipients of our affection. This is the time for the American character to shine. Do not ever bring harm upon your neighbor; do not avenge personal affronts. Demonstrate your temperament, the nobility of your souls, and the generosity of your hearts in everything: do not stain your hands with the blood of your brothers. Put aside your rancor: as you foster the most just of wars against your enemies, confer the sweetest peace upon your strong and brave homeland.'"

"Good. Wonderful!"

Then Alejo, who cannot contain himself, begins to yell:

"Long live Don Juan! And I'm not talking about Don Oquendo, but about you, young man! Long live Don Juan of—"

"Of nowhere, nor of anyone," my mother concludes with a loud and seemingly irate voice.

Alejo becomes as absolutely quiet and motionless as a statue. We all remain silent. I do not know what the others might be thinking, but I ask myself: what word was about to come out of the locksmith's mouth?

The following morning, on the day of the false alarm of the 17th of October, I awoke when I heard a cavernous voice in our room that sounded like a pig's raucous snorts. I sat up silently and very carefully opened my curtains just slightly. At first, all I could see was an enormous white mass, which I finally recognized as the Reverend Father Robustiano Arredondo. Sitting in one of the chairs, jammed between its armrests, he was talking with my mother, who was standing before him with the small *Imitation of Christ* closed in one hand. That strange, early morning visitor had arrived while she had been partaking of Brother Justo's prescription, probably not satisfied with only taking the nightly dosage.

I believe that there is not a single man more deserving of his last name anywhere on the entirety of our round earth than this Reverend Father Arredondo,[3] the Prelate of the Church of Our Lady of Mercy. His obesity in the town was proverbial. His entire body and each one of its composing parts aspired toward a spherical shape as much as possible: his swollen head, bald and shiny; his ruddy cheeks; his nose, red as a tomato; his shoulders; his hands; and, more than any other, his enormous abdomen. Morally, as he himself will reveal in the course of this story, where he will reappear several times in interesting occasions, he was also a well-rounded fool.

The first words I heard distinctly piqued my curiosity to such a degree that nothing in the world would have consoled me had I not been able to hear the conversation to its end. In order to prevent them from realizing that I was awake, I decided to lie back down on my bed, and to cover my head with the sheets; I even tried to restrain my breathing as much as possible without suffocating.

And what I heard is exactly the following:

"The noble lady wants to fulfill her husband's wishes, but with one condition, which she even told him in his last moments, and of which he approved."

"And what is that condition?"

"That your separation from the boy be definitive, that you do not set foot in her house, nor that he come to see you under any situation."

"Oh, the noble lady is so very generous!"

"You accept, then?"

"Can Your Reverence truly believe so?"

"You refuse, then. How ungrateful!"

"No, I do not think that either."

"I don't understand you. . . . But I have thought of something! In order to keep yourself from wanting to see him, why don't you cloister yourself in one of the convents for nuns. . . . Go to St. Claire, my daughter!"

"I do not believe that this will be necessary; no, Reverend Father. God shall arrange it elsewise!"

"Amen. So be it."

A very long pause.

"I need to think about it. If Your Reverence could return in eight days. . . ."

"Yes, I will return, my daughter. But try to send your response to me before then. I do not leave the confessional at noon, and I even tend to take my *siesta* right there, so as to be available to hear the sinners. Uff! Uff! It seems like this small chair wants to hold me here forever."

"God be with you, Your Reverence."

"And may He accompany you and light your way, my daughter. Uff! Uff!"

As soon as Father Arredondo had left, I jumped from my bed and ran as I was, in my undershirt, to kneel at my mother's feet. She, meanwhile, had collapsed into her little stool, pale as a corpse.

"No, mother," I told her, "I will never leave your side. . . . I despise that noble lady, whatever she may want from me!"

My mother gave me a fixed look with those eyes of hers that seemed even more beautiful because they were filled with tears. With a blood-curdling scream, she yelled out the word "son," which was so difficult for her to utter, and she held me tightly against her heart as she continued crying uncontrollably. She did not listen to my pleas, nor respond to my affectionate words, nor feel the kisses with which I persisted on trying to dry her profuse weeping. I believe hours on end transpired in this way. Finally, leaning on my shoulders with shaking hands, she stood up in order to go throw herself on the bed I had left, as if she had been broken by a long, physical torture on the rack.

That same fateful day the most alarming symptoms of her illness reappeared. At a moment in which I thought that my presence was not that necessary, for I was leaving the Aragonese Father, María Francisca, and two other women in care of our patient, I ran to the Church of St. Augustine to tell my dear teacher everything that had occurred. Listening to me, he began to shake with a nervous trembling. I saw him fall onto his bench and heard him murmur, in a muffled voice filled with infinite sorrow and unusual rage:

"They have murdered her!"

And effectively, there was nothing that could be done to save her. Despite the most solicitous care that once again surrounded her, she was dying, and quickly. And I believe—my God!—that she actually wanted to die before having to give Father Arredondo her answer. She received the viaticum and the extreme unction from Brother Justo on the day that Father Arredondo was to return. My teacher seemed to be in much greater pain than the dying woman whom he was aiding. When the Prelate of Our Lady of Mercy arrived, the victim was lying back on her pillows. He entered panting from fatigue after having walked, at a slow pace, the three blocks from his church to the dwelling where, one week before, he had unsuspectingly left that sentence of death. She did not see him, but she heard his loud breathing and the heavy noise of his steps.

"Your Reverence can take him," she said to him, "for I will not see him again on this earth, nor he me!"

Her eyes clouded over immediately; she looked at Brother Justo, standing at the head of the bed, and at me, kneeling at her feet. She wanted to convey her last farewell to me.

"I can no longer go with you; I am leaving. . . . I am being called!"

Having pronounced these words in the sweetest and most tender of voices, she raised her right arm slowly and pointed to the heavens with her index finger.

Who managed, by brute force, to tear me away from the arms of that stiff and frozen corpse that I would not stop embracing, as I asked to exchange my life for hers, or else be buried with her? What took place there? How did the time elapse until they nailed the black coffin shut and insisted on taking it away? What did I see, what did I hear—dumbfounded—during those moments in which I ran out of tears and was unable to hear my own painful screams?

I do not know when nor how, but I am aware that at some point I found myself at the door of our small house, between Brother Justo, blocking the entrance, and Father Arredondo, dragging me away by the hand. I remember that the former said to me:

"Follow him; it is what your mother wished."

I remember, also, that he made the following request of me:

"For your mother who is in Heaven and for the love of your teacher and friend who will still watch over you here on earth, do not give these people with whom you must live any cause to complain."

VI

The Márquez y Altamira Family

Although my guide, whom I followed in deep silence, carried his enormous body with difficulty, he did not stop until we arrived at a large arcade with thick adobe and stucco pillars. It supported an arch that had painted on it a monogram of the Virgin and below it what appeared to be the family coat of arms, something like a bull grazing in a field of wheat. The green door was reinforced by nails with large, copper screwtop heads; only the wicket was open. It was through the latter that we went in, once the Father had regained enough of his strength to cross the threshold of the tall, stone arch.

A spacious portico led to the patio, which was surrounded by the first set of rooms of the house. To the right there was a bench built of adobe bricks against the wall, which was the daily seat and nighttime bed of the *pongo*; above it, on the wall, could be seen a large oil painting of the Archangel St. Michael, his foot on the chest of the rebel and the tip of his spear in the rebel's mouth. Across from it, on the left-hand wall, there was a single door that opened into the head servant's, or the majordomo's, room.

The solitary, silent patio, with the small blades of grama grass growing in the seams between its uneven tiles, looked like a cemetery. To the right there were three doors, separated by three windows, all of which were hermetically sealed—and which I was never to see open—because they had belonged to the gentleman of the house, who had died a few days before. In front of the entrance, a large door gave light and passage to a drawing room that served as a dining room, and which continued on to a passageway leading to the second patio. On the left-hand side there were doors and windows like the ones on the right; these led to a reception room, an antechamber, and a small, private chapel for the lady of the house. The bedrooms, the servant's quarters, the pantry, the kitchen, and the other rooms could be reached—and were, as I later saw—from the inner patio.

Father Arredondo took me to the first door on the left, which led to the private chapel. This door was open; but inside a vestibule there was another, large door—with a white, plastered face painted on it of a grotesquely shaped angel advising one to keep silent—which was closed.

There the Father stopped once again; he coughed two or three times and finally knocked timidly on the door with the knuckles of his thick hand. We heard cautious steps; then the large vestibule door opened just slightly, only enough for a Negro woman's head—with thick, reddish, natty tufts of hair that were starting to go gray; a very flat forehead; small, squinting eyes; a flat nose; very prominent cheekbones; and a toothless mouth—to stick out. She spoke the following words, which we barely heard:

"The lady very bad; the sadness, the splitting headache. . . . Your Reverence come in without making noise."

We followed these directions, walking on our tiptoes. The large vestibule door closed behind us, and left us in the dark.

Once my eyes became accustomed to the dim light, which was provided by a single lamp shining from a *Berenguela*[1] stone hanging from the wall in front of us, I saw that we were in a room that was about eight varas long by six wide, whitewashed and burnished, and that it had a red and yellow socle, and a white curtain on the ceiling, with a star painted in its center, also in red and yellow. The entire wall underneath the vault light was occupied by a retable with stucco and wooden saints dressed in lamé and sparkles of gold, large silver candelabra with multiple arms, and crystal urns with veneered frames, also made of silver. To the left there was a large table, a prie-dieu chair, and two enormous honorary armchairs. To the right one could see another door leading out of the room, and next to it a dais covered with a soft spread and damask-lined cushions.

Resting there was a lady who was neither young nor old, much less obese than the Father, but more than simply fat, with a sickly complexion, gray eyes with a hard look to them, a straight nose, a large mouth almost without lips, a very prominent chin, and an air of extreme pride masked by feigned humility. She was wrapped in a rich estamin, silken shirt, and her head was covered with a black, mourning headdress. She had another mulatta servant kneeling in front of her—handing her a silver brazier in one hand and a cigarette in another—who was not as horrible-looking as the one who had let us in. Finally, a white lapdog, with the hair on the bottom part of his body shaved short, was sleeping on the same cushion where the lady was reclining.

The Father, who undoubtedly had waited like me to become accustomed to that semidarkness, was the first to speak.

"Noble lady, my dear Doña Teresa," he said, "here is the boy."

"Praised be God, Your Holy Reverence! God certainly knows how to try our weaknesses, doesn't He?" she answered in an unpleasant voice, and lit her cigarette.

A long silence followed. The two servants sat on either side of the dais, the Father settled in as best as possible in one of the enormous honorary armchairs, the lapdog growled and went back to sleep, and I remained standing in the middle of the room, turning my hat in my hands. Meanwhile, as the noble lady Doña Teresa exhaled pillars of smoke, the air became saturated with a strong smell of tobacco and anise.

"What torture, Your Holy Reverence!" she finally deigned herself to exclaim. "Only Our Lord has suffered for our sins more than I have!"

"He will know how to reward that suffering and anguish," the Father replied, "especially now that—"

"Yes, yes," she interrupted him. "I will be brave. . . ."

And finally, turning toward me, she added:

"What do you know how to do? What have they taught you?"

I felt more given to cry than to reply; but I remembered my teacher's order and answered:

"Madam, I know how to pray and read, and write, and count, and can serve at Mass in Latin."

"That's not bad," she answered. "The sinner . . . may God have forgiven her! At least she did not neglect the education of the poor boy."

When I heard her say "the sinner," a stream of tears sprung from my eyes, and my sobs began to choke me. Somehow I manage to hear the following words:

"He's very emotional," the Father said, "he needs nourishment and rest, as he has not done anything other than cry since yesterday."

"Take him, Feliciana," the lady of the house then ordered.

But I hurried to open the large vestibule door before her and exit, to go out and breathe, to see the sun, to run out—I know not where—and scream for my mother.

But the Negro woman took me by the arm, and more dragged than led me along the length of the patio. She continued to drag me through the passageway and on through the inner patio, until she finally stopped in front of a small, half-opened door and said:

"You can go in. The lady very sick. . . . I'm leaving!"

I went in. The room which I was to occupy was small; it had a tall, round, completely opened window through which one could see a roof full of yellowish moss and a piece of sky. I was surprised to find there, still unarranged, my small bedstead, the coffer, the table, and the chairs from our small house. I thought of them as old acquaintances suffering just like me; I thought that perhaps they had followed me to talk about Rosita. One of the chairs, which was placed facing the door, seemed to be tenderly offering its arms to me; I knelt down before it, leaned forward on the seat, and cried, completely losing track of time. Night had already fallen when I heard Feliciana's voice again.

"Dinner is served," she said.

I followed her mechanically to the dining room; we entered through one of the doors of the inner patio that faced my new room. It was a spacious hall with a burnished ceiling like the one in the private chapel. In the corners there were tall, large wood armoires that were painted red and had gold fillets. In the center there was a long, wide, sturdy table surrounded by chairs like mine, but with more intricate tooling; they were also painted red and gilded in gold, like the armoires. A single, metal oil lamp above the table lighted the completely empty room.

Feliciana left me standing next to the door, went to open another door that led to an antechamber, and repeated her laconic invitation to dinner. A moment later, I saw three other servants enter, one after the other, each bringing in a child. The first I recognized as the mulatta who I had already seen in the private chapel; the boy with her was my age or a little younger, pale, with listless eyes, covered from head to foot in a wool blanket. The other two mestiza servants, both very young still, each carried a smaller child in their arms. The latter were robust, fair, pinkish, and only partially dressed; they were laughing and playing with the braids of the women who carried them. The oldest was carefully placed in one of the chairs; the other two were made to sit on the table itself, on either side of the metal oil lamp. Meanwhile, Feliciana had opened one of the armoires that I mentioned with a small key attached to a large ring that hung from her waist; she removed three biscuits and the same number of bowls and cups, in which she served the children some kind of soup, and milk with sugar.

The mulatta made the child in her care eat with a spoon; the other two ate on their own, with their hands, finally throwing the leftovers on the table or the floor. Once dinner was over, they all left as they had entered.

I was about to do the same, in spite of the hunger I felt, when Feliciana tapped me on the shoulder to get my attention, and put a bowl with a spoon in my hands. I went to the table and ate avidly. Nature took over; it was able to ignore the suffering of the soul, which is what happens at that blessed age.

"Leave now," the Negro woman said to me as soon as I had finished my portion. "There's a stub of candle for you and the *pongo* will keep you company so you won't be afraid of the *duende*."[2]

That is what I saw of the primogenital family of Márquez y Altamira the first time I entered their house. I believe it is now necessary to finish introducing them to my readers and to say something about their customs, so that I may then continue with the humble story of my own life.

Doña Teresa Altamira, whom we left looking so plaintive, wearing her widow's headdress in her private chapel, had found herself as the sole heir presumptive of the estate of a wealthy primogeniture[3] when Don Fernando Márquez—a *criollo* like her, from one of the illustrious founding families of our town—had asked for her hand. She could not, nor did she want to, refuse the match; apparently, she did not have other options, nor would it have been possible for her to find a more handsome and elegant gallant who could have suited her any better. But there was an obstacle, which she expounded to him, shaking with fear. Her father, Don Pedro de Alcántara Altamira, who had founded the primogeniture in order to lend glory to his family name, demanded that whoever pretended to have the honor of being his son-in-law take the father-in-law's name and give it to his children instead of his own, as was the custom.

Don Fernando categorically refused to consummate the sacrifice, and I believe he would have directed his attention elsewhere, when it occurred to Doña Teresa to call to her assistance the most old-fashioned Baccalaureate of those times, Don Sulpicio Burgulla, who solved the entire affair in the simplest of manners and obtained the greatest triumph of his life.

"*Accentus*, my dear Don Pedro," he said to the obstinate father, "*est, quo signatur, an sit longa, vel brevis syllaba.*"[4]

"And what about it?" the father implored, not having understood a single word.

"By dropping the accent and changing just two letters, my noble and dear friend, one can change Márquez to Marquis."

"So that Don Fernando. . . ."

"Would be the Marquis of Altamira!"

"And my grandchildren. . . ."

"*Simillime*, Lord Don Pedro, *per omnia saecula saeculorum!*"[5]

The obstacle removed, the fiancés were joined in *facie ecclesiae*[6] with grand pomp and circumstance in the chapel of the wealthiest of their estates, with dances by their Indians organized in dance troops, and races and bull runs for their guests. And they received, above all else, Don Pedro de Alcántara Altamira's greatest blessing, as he was able to give his *nunc dimittis*,[7] as he saw that not only would his family name survive, but that he would have before him, with time, a title of nobility for his grandchildren: the Marquisate of Altamira.

The married couple lived in plenitude and was blessed with three legitimate children. But two weeks before my arrival, Don Fernando was summoned by God, by means of one of the fatal pneumonias that strike in September. And it had struck precisely right after he had been able to thank God for recovering from a wound suffered from a stone thrown during the uprising of the 14th. Doña Teresa wept over him bitterly, without forgiving the «rebels» for that wound that, according to her, had caused such irreparable and eternal misfortune. Furthermore, she said that because of all the love she had felt for him and in order to carry out the request that he had made to her right before he died, she was now consummating the sacrifice of taking into her house and placing next to her own children a vagabond boy who might very well be the Devil himself.

She had always lived withdrawn in her private chapel, but now she only left it at night to go to sleep. In addition to her confessors, she received many visits from her lady friends. Neither her lap dog nor her two favorite servants were ever absent from her side. When the administrators from her estates came for an audience, they would leave their spurs at the door and appear before her briefly in order to receive whimsical orders, which were almost always contradictory. If there was a serious affair, she would send for her confessor and his Honor[8] Burgulla in order to consult with them.

In the meantime, the children ran around on their own or were handed over to the care of the servants, over whom the Negro woman Feliciana exercised her tyrannical authority, beginning with her own husband, Don Clemente. The oldest boy, the primogeniture, had the same name as his grandfather, with the preordained additions. As I have already mentioned, he was weak and sickly; he did not even know how to read, and the only thing he thought about was entertaining his tediously vegetative existence by playing with his toys. The second, Agustín, was seven years old, healthy, alert, and lively, undertaking the most inconceivable of pranks, rummaging through everything from the barn to the drawing room, and even invading the private chapel at times. Carmen, the youngest of the three at five years of age, was an enchanting child, playful like Agustín, but obedient and very amiable.

Among the servants, the only ones I have not yet described are Don Clemente and Paula. The former was a *sambo*, which is to say a mestizo resulting from a cross between an Indian man and a Negro woman; he had the worst traits of both races: he was cunning, base, lazy, selfish, and cruel. Submissive to Feliciana's orders—who was the one of the two who wore the man's pants—he in turn tyrannized the others, especially the poor *pongo*, whom he always tormented without any reason whatsoever. As far as Paula, the cook, I have very little to say about her. I never saw her get involved in anything other than her stews; she did not even live in the same house.

The *pongo* was, as is known, some unfortunate, miserable, brutish Indian who came every week from the estates to fulfill his duties as a personal servant.

I did not know what the conditions were under which I found myself in that house. The following day I heard them refer to me as the «foundling waif»—in other words, the abandoned child. I was not given any servant duties, but I was also never told what to do. Left to my own devices, I became melancholy, taciturn; I would spend hours on end in my room, at times crying, at others lost in sad thoughts, some of which I could not even remember later. I would be called to eat after the other children had already left the table. I was warned that when night fell, as soon as I heard the ringing of the bells, I was to attend the saying of the rosary in the presence of the lady of the house while Don Clemente sang the melody. Finally, I was ordered not to set foot on the street. In only one person out of all those people, the young girl Carmen, did I inspire a deep sympathy, a feeling of tenderness and, surprisingly, of compassion. In order to amuse myself during the free time I had all day long, I decided to teach her the little that I knew. This stirred up her brothers' hatred toward me, each of whom, in their own way, wanted me to be «theirs»: one wanted me to be his biggest toy, the other his horse.

Luckily, before long, I made a discovery that made me very happy. Close to my room there was a passageway. To one side of it were the kitchen, the pantry, and the woodshed; to the other were the stables and henhouse, and it ended at a door with a large, simple handle. One day I saw Paula open and go through it and come back out with some printed papers in her hand, which she doubtless needed in order to make some pie in the oven. My curiosity was piqued; I could not keep myself from going to take a quick look at that unknown part of the house. Through the door I found a spacious corridor that faced a small, abandoned garden and led to a wide open room. Continuing my exploration, I saw that the room was full of parchment-bound books. From among these, four volumes that were better bound, in sheepskin, with decorations and gold lettering on the spine, drew my attention. I opened one of them. From the middle of a vignette engraved with figures of captured Indians and the spoils of war, I read the following: "*The General History of the Vast Continent and Islands of America, Commonly Called the West-Indies, From the First Discovery Thereof*, written by Antonio de Herrera, his Majesty's Chief Chronicler of the Indies, and his Chronicler of Castile."[9] Looking at once through some of the pages, I found engravings and read names that even I knew: Columbus, Cortés, Pizarro, and so on.

Those books represented a priceless treasure to me. I therefore decided to take them to my room right away; but in order to avoid Paula's daily destruction of the books, I stopped at the kitchen door and said to her, so that she would mend her ways, that the lady of the house must not know what she was doing.

"You're such a fool!" she answered. "Do you think that the lady of the house or the children would waste their time like you waste yours? Don't you know that my deceased master, Lord Don Fernando, may God keep him in His Heavenly bliss, never opened any of those books of his father's? And what would you want a primogeniture to do with them?"

Embarrassed, shamed by these explanations, I excused myself as well as I could and hurried back to my small room, while Paula kept laughing at my simplemindedness. The other servants who were gathered in the kitchen, as well as the child Agustín, all began to join in on the laughter. But I had at last something to console my abandonment; from then on I visited the room with the books frequently. With them, I slowly filled my long table, which for many years had only seen upon it the one solitary volume of Cervantes' novel.

VII

The Battle of Aroma According to Alejo

On the 16th of November, I had the great honor of being called by Clemente to the presence of the noble lady of the house, whom he said was in the reception room. I ran there quickly and saw her from the half-opened vestibule door of the antechamber; she was standing with Father Arredondo and his Honor Burgulla. The three of them were speaking animatedly, trying to lower their voices as if they feared that their conversation might be overheard, but then letting them grow loud again in the heat of their discussion. Since they did not notice my arrival, and since I did not want to interrupt them, I had more than enough time to examine that area of the house I had not seen before. I could also study his Honor Burgulla, whom I did not know, but whose name I had heard many times in the house, where his intelligence was always openly praised.

The large vestibule door was of the same size and shape as the one that opened into the private chapel. Instead of the angel demanding silence, however, it had painted on it an ostentatious animal that was supposedly a lion, because of its mane and claws, but in actuality was green in color and had an almost human face, like that of an old woman making a horrible grimace. I could see the majority of the reception room from where I was; it did not differ much from the other rooms, except for stucco moldings around the doors and windows that were painted in oils and depicted green velvet draperies, drawn and tied together by gold cords. The windows, due to the strange ideas of luxury at the time, were made up of large glass panels, all with closely woven copper gratings in front of them. Toward the front of the room, on each side of the door that led to the private chapel, there were large, round mirrors with silver frames, attached with chains that were also made of silver; these hung above tables with *Berenguela* tops and legs. White wooden benches lavished with gilding and furnished with cushions and damask covers ran along the length of the wall facing the entrance from the patio; several matching armchairs of honor were situated on either side of the large door to the above-mentioned vestibule, displaying on that side a gigantic and frightening halberdier. The floor was made of octagonal and smaller square tiles, seamlessly joined, with only a few narrow strips of thick carpeting from the Valley at the foot of the honorary benches. Finally, large, wooden shelves were solidly attached along almost all the walls, at a height which could be reached by a person standing on one of the benches; these held large vases, enormous wineglasses, strange goblets, and other silver and crystal objects.

His Honor Burgulla was the most laughable figure one can possibly imagine, although he himself assumed an air of importance and seriousness like no other learned man of his time. Shorter than average in height, almost completely bald, thin, with a reddish face, meticulously shaved, with a large, pointed nose, protruding and slippery eyes, and stiff ears that looked like the handles of some cup dug up from an Indian *huaca*[1]—that little man, dressed in a black jacket, white frock, blue trousers, and blue socks, made the greatest effort to keep straight as a board while he stood on the tip of his toes, clad in shoes with enormous buckles. Finally, his walking stick had a gold handle and long tufts of black silk, and he held it up in the air, halfway up the cane, with his thumb, forefinger, and middle finger only.

"I repeat: this kind of disgrace is inconceivable," Doña Teresa was saying. "Our Lord cannot allow it."

"I agree, and I have my reasons," added the Prelate of Our Lady of Mercy. "It should have ended on the afternoon of the 14th, and today is the 16th. Only two days have gone by and the man, who they say has submitted a sworn declaration before the unauthorized governor, cannot very well fly to our town like a bird. It is more than fifty leagues from here."

"*Distinguo,*" his Honor Burgulla answered in a falsetto voice, "the man should have taken a shortcut; he should have walked straight through the night. Because, as the prince of poets[2] says:

Monstrum horrendum ingens: cui, quod sunt corpore plumae . . .
Nocte volar coeli medio terraeque, per umbram
Stridens, nec dulci declinat lumina somno.[3]

Faced with such an argument, which one of them must have partially understood and the other not at all, the Father and Doña Teresa were left speechless.

"Well," the former of the two said timidly after a while, "your noble Honor might be right; but—"

"But what? *Quare dubitas?*"[4] his Honor Burgulla interrupted, raising his cane higher in the air.

"*Videre et credere, sicut Thomam,*"[5] the Father replied, very happily, almost triumphantly, because his Latin had not failed him.

"I cannot possibly know as much as Your Lordship and Excellency," Doña Teresa interjected; "but I insist that the best thing is to send the boy to the church, where they say that the «rebel» has gone, and get it out of him later, when he returns. . . ."

"*Accedo,*[6] that is to say, I am not opposed," the Licentiate replied. "*Feminae intellectus acutus. . . .*"[7]

But he was unable to conclude the erudite explanation of the tolerance to which he was inclined because Doña Teresa, who had turned toward the antechamber, undoubtedly to repeat her order to have me called, let out a scream: she had seen my head sticking completely through the opening of the large vestibule door.

"Juanito," she said right away, almost sweetly, trying to calm herself, "did you hear what we were saying?"

"Yes, madam," I answered in a normal tone. "His noble Honor was saying things in Latin that I didn't understand."

"What a good boy!" she said, reassured. Then, while the other two spoke to each other secretly, she continued to address me:

"You have not seen your teacher, Brother Justo of the Holy Blessed Sacrament, have you?"

"No, madam, because I was told not to step out into the street for any reason whatsoever."

"They have misunderstood. I only wanted you to stop roaming the streets aimlessly like the other idle boys; but I am not opposed to you going to see your teacher, with the condition that you come straight back before too long."

"Thank you, your Ladyship."

And without waiting any further, I ran out to the street, like a soul released from Purgatory.

When I arrived, I found the door to Brother Justo's cell was only half-closed, and I heard a very familiar voice inside. Then, putting my eye in the gap created by the hinge between the door and the wall, I saw my uncle Alejo sitting on the bench, and my teacher walking by in front of him, anxiously pacing back and forth. The locksmith, whom I had supposed very far away with the other volunteers, was almost completely black from exposure to the elements; he had grown thin, and his outfit was ruined and torn in several places; he held his hat in his hands, but wrapped around his head and tied on his forehead he still had a dirty bandanna stained with blood; and his feet, although he was only wearing a pair of wide sandals, seemed more comfortable, cracked and full of dust as they were, than they had been in the Russian shoes that always used to squeeze them in.

I was unable to hold myself back for more than a moment. I banged open the door, rushed inside, and hugged my friends, one after the other, without saying a word. The two in turn shouted out in happiness and hugged me back. Alejo then jumped to the middle of the room, crouched back on his heels, and offered me his open hand, undoubtedly to lift me up, balance me in the air, and continue rejoicing in that manner. But I did not have the strength to place my foot on his hand, nor did he hold it out for more than a brief instant; for I was soon forced to wipe off the tears in my eyes, and Alejo stood and faced away from me so as to do the same with the torn sleeves of his jacket. The sweet but at once sad recollection of my mother had risen simultaneously to our memories!

My teacher, who perhaps suffered the most when she was remembered, hurried to return to the conversation which I had interrupted.

"Come on, young man!" he said impatiently. "Sit back down and answer my questions. Juanito will enjoy hearing these things, like the good patriot he promises to be."

Alejo did as he was told, but only after giving me a look full of affection and compassion.

"What would you have had me do, Father?"

"Good God, the laziness! You should have continued on with the others, my good man of God! You should not have come back like a *guanaco* thirsty for the taste of chicha!"[8]

"But there are no traces of the *chapetones* left anywhere! And the others will also return, just like me."

"May the Heavens not allow such idleness! This would mean the miserable loss of the fruits of such a joyous victory. Oh well. . . . What can one do?! Tell me, at least, in some kind of orderly manner, what happened since you arrived in Oruro."

Alejo began to concentrate at once. He scratched the base of his head, behind his ear; he coughed, tried to talk, sat with his mouth open, and made an impatient frown. Finally, he began to recount for us, in his own manner, what was then the most notable event of the Independence Movement and the greatest triumph of the poorly equipped patriots in that region of South America.

"The people of Oruro had 'shouted' for the freedom of the homeland before we had even arrived. Their governor . . . I mean the governor of the *chapetones*, rather, Sánchez Chávez,[9] had fled with a lot of money from the royal offices; but, very happily, they captured him at Barca.

"And they gave us such a welcome! There was not a single person who did not come out to meet us, stretching out for more than a league from the town, and almost all of them on foot, because there are very few horses in the Puna. From far away they shouted to us: 'Long live the brave Cochabambinos!' And we paid them back in the same coin, and we continued with the happy shouts and whistles that we use in the fiesta of the bulls of St. Sebastian, the ones that are so loud that they can sometimes be heard as far away as Colcapirhua.

"When we entered the streets of Oruro, so many flowers rained down on us from the doors, windows, and balconies that I thought that behind the hills there must have been many more gardens than in Calacala. But then I saw that they were only pieces of paper and cut-up ribbons of every color—but perfumed, too, and with wonderful fragrances.

"We were there for two weeks. Don Esteban believed that we should set up the affairs of the government of the homeland there like we had done here. My compatriot Unzueta also told me to help him mount two useless cannons that had been abandoned in the Redoubt. But we were unable to do so, and I became so bored that I wanted to throw one of them into a pit; I already had it raised above my head when they begged me not to get angry in such an ugly and fearful way. 'Well . . . there you have it!' I answered, and went off to my quarters.

"On Sunday [it was the 12th of November, but Alejo, like the others of his class, knew nothing about dates and only remembered the days of the week], the leaders Don Esteban and Don Melchor had us get in our formation out in the plains of the Altiplano, near the Redoubt. And they told those of us on foot that we were to join with those from Oruro, men who were shorter than us, those youngsters. They're little fellows—but my oh my! They certainly know how to traverse the Altiplano! And how they yelled and whistled, and how brave they are in «war», too! You will soon see, Father, and you too, young man.

"After what I was just saying took place, they had us share our supplies of roasted corn, flour, *chuño*,[10] and *charqui*.[11] Then they distributed to those who had muskets, matchlocks, and rifles—and there were not very many, either, barely one hundred and fifty— gun powder, bullets, flints . . . whatever they needed, according to the condition of their firearms. The drums and the bugles struck up the march, and . . . Long live the homeland! We walked off across the Altiplano, on the road of La Paz, with the riflemen in front, followed by my group, wielding *macanas*; then came the cavalry, and finally several men with the two cannons that Unzueta insisted on bringing, although they had not been able to fix them.

"I think that you should know, Father, and you too, Juanito, that the world, beyond the slopes of Challa, is as flat as my hand, or like this table. In the middle of the long stretches of leagues upon leagues, there are only small hills like San Sebastián or Alalai, or a few groups of taller hills, like the ones that lead to San Pedro. I also believe that God did not put any trees or flowers anywhere other than in our valleys. The only ones I saw in that area is the *ichu*[12] and some grass or shrub that they call *tola*.[13]

"That day we only went as far as a town called Caracollo, still in the middle of the Altiplano. Those of us from Cochabamba and from the Valley, however, even as tired as we were, were unable to sleep. The cold, when it freezes like it did that night—and in the hot season, too—makes even the vicuñas scream out. They say that around San Juan the very rocks crack from the cold. But our compatriots from Oruro laughed at us; leaving us huddled in our hovels, they slept out in the open, on the ground, like little angels.

"The next day, on Monday, we continued marching, and it was only in the afternoon that we reached a few small hills. We camped out in the open because there was only one house, which belonged to the ranches of Pan Duro or Marquesado; in it, the leaders took their lodgings. Beyond, the Altiplano went on endlessly; it seemed carpeted with a greenish yellow, with denser and taller *tolas* than the ones we had begun to leave behind us. The only thing that stood out there, looking out in several directions, were the *huacas*, or the houses and raised burial grounds of the «heathens». Far away, toward the area where we were to continue marching the next day, the land was a little higher, like . . . look, Father: like right here, on my hand, where it rises up a little where my fingers meet my palm. And a lot further away, on top of that elevation, I could see two small, thin pilasters, almost touching each other, which I was told were the towers of Sicasica, still more than nine leagues from where we were. The road that led to it looked essentially like a white ribbon stretched out on the grass.

"Very early Tuesday morning, just when we were curled up praying to the souls in Purgatory to make the sun rise to warm us up, the drums, bells, fifes, cornets, and bugles began to play the reveille, but for a longer time and with more energy than ever. We formed into our columns to continue the march, but Don Esteban held us up, looking over the rank and file on horseback. And I heard him say to Don Miguel Cabrera, his secretary, that we would come face to face with the *chapetones* that day.

"At breakfast time [8 A.M.], we rested in the Old Redoubt, on the shore of the only stream that there is in the Altiplano. We started a fire with the shrubs of *tolas*, which burn even if they are green, and we made *lagua*[14] and had breakfast laughing happily, joking all the time. The Altiplano before us was deserted and quiet. A few llamas and vicuñas grazed between the *huacas*. Then, two vicuñas ran across the road, from this side to this other side [from left to right, according to his gesture]; this made us so happy that we all stood up at once, threw our hats and *monteras*[15] in the air, and yelled and whistled loud enough for us to have been heard as far away as Sicasica.

"'Well, well, men!' exclaimed Don Melchor, who had already mounted his famous bay. "This is proof that we shall have good fortune, although I never doubted it. Everything now depends on the spears and the *macanas*. Long live the homeland!'

"'Long live the homeland! Long live Quitón!' we answered.

"We kept on walking, walking across the endless Altiplano, until we could not see our own shadows at all [noontime], when we were told to halt, about half a league before the land begins to rise. We then saw a long file of bayonets shining in the sun above the *tolas*, approaching us very slowly from the direction of Sicasica. Then, when the head of that serpent with reflective scales reached the point where the land sloped downward, it began to gather its parts to one side and the other, until it appeared lengthwise before our eyes, so straight and close together that I could have sworn it was truly one single, long piece. All along its length it glimmered brightly; its head and tail stood out and shone even more, as it was made up of cavalry soldiers wearing polished helmets and steel breastplates that gleamed like silver.

"Don Esteban gave the call to the officers, and they all met in a circle to the side of the road to receive their orders. We looked at each other.... I think our faces were somewhat yellowish and that the spurs of the *huauques*[16] in the cavalry could actually be heard, as if small bells were ringing. But we tightened the belts on our trousers, placed our ponchos diagonally across our left shoulders, fixed our *leques*[17] and *monteras*, and prepared our *macanas*. We also told ourselves that there were not very many of them. We wanted to fool ourselves and encourage each other. The truth, *tata*,[18] is that there were more than twice as many of them as of all of us, and I have already said how their weapons gleamed in the distance.... Still, as long as I had my small staff, I did not envy any weapon or armor that they might have.

"When the meeting was over, Don Esteban himself came before us, on his tall and fast steed with the mark on its face, his sword already drawn and in his hand, and said to us:

"'Men! Long live the homeland!'

"'Long live the homeland! Death to the *chapetones*!' we answered.

"'Very well, my sons,' he replied, 'the *chapetones* are right over there. I shall be by your side, to see now what the *macanas* can do. Do not yell and follow my orders only! Form your columns! And prepare to march!'

"We disobeyed his request to be quiet unintentionally, without realizing it, for we yelled more than ever; but we followed his order and lined up in files along the length of the road. Meanwhile, Don Melchor had had the cavalry form two squadrons behind us, and the compatriot Unzueta insisted on having his cannons—or carronades, as he called them—dragged along trying to line up next to us, as had been determined he was to do, although he was never able to catch up with us.

"Organized in this manner, with Don Esteban in front, we marched quickly to meet the enemy. But they did not move; they stood 'as though nothing was happening,' with their weapons at ease. It seemed as if they had not seen us and that not even our yelling and whistling reached them. When we were within 600 varas from them, a few marksmen stepped out of their ranks and began a staggered drumfire. Our riflemen likewise stepped forward.

"'Battle positions!' Don Esteban ordered.

"We took our places, as best as we could, in two lines facing the *chapetones*.

"Then our cavalry advanced, each squadron on either side. I think that the thundering blast of the carronades went off at this time, too, although I don't know where.

"We continued running forward . . . yelling like you do when you are about to take the packsaddle from the bull. But bang! Bang! Two volleys were fired; a white cloud hid the enemy from us; many—I don't know how many—fell; the cavalry charged; and the firing continued in an incredible manner.

"I would like to know, *tata*, who was the first to yell at that point. I have heard so often all the *huauques* claiming 'it was me, it was me,' that I have even believed it might have actually been me."

"Be that as it may," my teacher said impatiently. "It doesn't matter at all."

"What do you mean that it doesn't matter at all?" Alejo replied. "It is for this reason that we were able to win the battle!"

"But, what did you yell? Come on, young man! Don't be roundabout."

"*Huincui*,[19] Reverend Father! I or one of us yelled *huincui* and we all fell among the *tolas*. So that if the *chapetones* saw us—which I doubt, because they were plenty busy with the cavalry—they must have thought that they had killed every one of us when they fired the first round of volleys.

"But we did not intend to just play dead. Without anyone telling us to—although we kept on yelling the entire time, unruly in this as we are and as those from Oruro had been—we crawled on all fours, like this, in between the *tolas*."

At this point the storyteller moved to the center of the room to have more space to continue. He wanted to accompany each of his words with the action or movement that best expressed it.

"The bullets whistled over our heads like mad, in heavy gunfire that sounded like the rocket loads on the holy day of the *Corpus Christi*. The smoke from the gunpowder was blowing our way, as the wind had shifted; it entered through our noses and into our brains; I believe it made us drunk. . . . We kept on going; every once in a while someone would raise his head, but psst! A bullet would fly by, and they would throw themselves down on the ground again, all the while continuing to move forward.

"When we reached the point where the land began to rise—which was not as easy as it had seemed from afar, and with mountain sickness, too!—we had to stand up in order to climb faster. Many—very many—fell there, never to tell this story. I thought that I saw our cavalry retreating to one side at that point; I later learned that they actually had to retreat in order to reform their ranks, because in their first charge they had met a formidable square formation that they were unable to penetrate in any manner whatsoever.

"There was no longer any *'huincui'* or anything else like that to do. At that point it was better to keep the enemy from reloading their firearms.

"'Take them, my sons! Take them! Raise your staffs and be brave!' Don Esteban yelled.

"I do not know, *tata*, if there has ever been a braver man in this world; but I do know that there is not another like him right now, nor will there ever be anyone like him. He was on horseback, without any armor, driving those slower than him on with his sword. The bullets seemed to fear and miss him in order to kill others, as the saying goes, because they seek out the cowards.

"'*Huactai, huauque!*'[20] we yelled to each other.

"And we climbed by jumping up the hill, without any order, like goats on a mountain.

"From this moment onward—please forgive me, Father—I can no longer give account of what anyone other than I and those nearest to me did."

"That's fine, my good man!" my teacher said, even more impatiently. He had stopped pacing to listen avidly and was undoubtedly annoyed by the merest digression.

"The smoke was so dense by then that we could not see any further than two steps away from us. I was also left essentially one-eyed: I was stunned by a very strong blow, and my warm blood, pouring from my head, made this eye [the left one] useless. I was jumping forward, yelling or maybe even roaring, with my staff in the air, when I found myself in front of a grenadier, tall as a tower.

"'Aha!' I yelled at him.

"My staff then fell on his leather cap, and. . . . May Our Lady the Virgin have mercy on him!

"Immediately everything turned red. . . . I wanted to kill, to kill without stopping, and I dealt blows to everything that came before me. I do not like to boast; but I believe that I broke and sent more than one rifle flying like a corn husk, and more than one head flying like a gourd. I don't know, I can't say how I defended myself. . . . One time I felt something ticklish under my arm, but only later did I realize that the bayonet of some *chapetón* had scraped my side.

"At the end, I found myself alone in the middle of the Altiplano. The cavalry was off in the distance, heading toward Sicasica, chasing down the *chapetones* who had fled.

"Don Esteban had to order us one by one to meet with the officers, because we did not hear the spoken orders, nor could we understand the call of the drums and the bugles.

"When we were finally united, with the prisoners in the middle—there must have been about two hundred of them—Don Esteban himself approached us on his distinguished horse, which was wet with sweat, lively, and wounded on the wide part of its neck, and said to all of us (although I thought that he was looking directly at me):

"'Brave Cochabambinos! The enemy shakes with fear before your *macanas*!'"

"Excellent! Long live the brave Don Esteban! His words are worthy of being remembered by history, my sons!" my teacher exclaimed enthusiastically.

But returning immediately to the thought that had worried him from before, he added severely:

"And yet you have returned here! And the others will come here as well. . . . And even Don Esteban!"

Alejo, excited by his own remembrances, did not respond to this comment and continued with his interrupted account instead.

"I cannot begin to explain our joy, the yelling and the clamor that we responded with. We then began immediately to pick up the weapons abandoned throughout the battlefield. An hour later, at the most, we were in Sicasica. It seemed as if we had grown wings on our feet. . . . What happiness it is to run like that, chasing after *chapetones*!

"But, unfortunately, there was nothing left to do. We found many dead along the road, and many others, in large groups, near the town. The *huauques* from our cavalry were waiting for us at the shore of the stream that flows by there. They had dismounted and were lying down on the ground and partaking in the food and the cups of liquor that the women from Sicasica were bringing them. They welcomed us with mocking whistles and yelled at us from every direction:

"'Hey! Where are the *chapetones*?'

"But it had not been them, either, who had finished off the last of the *chapetones*. The residents of the town and the Indians of that community had been brought together by the sound of the *pututus*,[21] and they had responded to the arrival of the fleeing *chapetones* by attacking them with sticks and stones. So the only enemies left alive were the ones that we had captured earlier on the «battlefield».

"I have been told that their leader . . . I don't remember his name . . . it was something like Peroles . . . managed to escape with a few of his officers, but I don't believe it."

"But you have come back like a guanaco![22] And they will all come back, thirsty for the taste of the chicha of San Andrés!" my teacher exclaimed again.

"I was resting peacefully when Don Esteban had someone send for me," Alejo continued, unperturbed by Father Justo's interruption. "He was in the nicest house in town, conducting a meeting with all his officers.

"'No, today, without losing any time . . . we should continue onward!' he was saying, very annoyed.

"'We cannot,' Don Melchor answered, 'let us wait for word from the patriots in La Paz.'

"'It's useless. Let's return to Oruro,' Unzueta shouted out.

"'Back to Cochabamba!' exclaimed a number of officers.

"At this point I was introduced to Don Esteban.

"'Alejo, your name is Alejo, is it not?' he asked me.

"'Yes, my general,' I answered him. 'Your Lordship met me when we spoke at the garden of Cangas, when I was the penitent on Holy Friday.'

"'That's true,' he replied, laughing, and shook my hand. It's no wonder that we all love him and are willing to die for him!

"'I wish to reward your courage and your strength, which have truly astonished me,' he continued. 'Ask me for something so I can give it to you in front of your compatriots.'

"'Sir . . . my general!' I answered. 'I would like to return to Cochabamba immediately!'

"'Good God! That's the only thing that these savages think about!' he exclaimed, and banged his fist down on the table."

"And he was right! That's how it is! You and all the *huauques* cannot live without seeing our green valleys, like animals," Brother Justo said angrily.

I thought Alejo would become furious then, as he usually did. But instead, surprisingly, I saw him sadly bend his head down.

"No, he was not right, nor are you, your Excellency, *tata*," he answered in a softened voice.

"And why not? Are you going to tell me now that you did not wish to return for the chicha of San Andrés?" my teacher insisted imprudently.

Alejo tried to speak; but he looked at me and once again bent his head down.

"Come on! Answer me!"

"If your Excellency really wants it this way!" Alejo finally yelled out with a sudden, frightful, and transformed expression on his face. "I had already heard the «bad news» in Oruro . . . I was not told that she—«the child»—had consented to having the boy live in «that house» . . . I wanted to . . . Good God! Even Don Esteban said I was doing the right thing, Reverend Father!"

"Stop! Forgive me, my good Alejo!" Brother Justo interrupted him, and grabbed one of his hands firmly in his own. I took Alejo's other hand and cried with him, because that strong and simple man needed to cry then. And cry he did, like a baby.

A moment later we heard all the bells ringing in their towers, and a mad rush of people shouting wildly and happily in the plaza. The priests ran through the cloisters of the church in order to join them as quickly as possible. One of them, who must have been a patriot, opened the door of the cell partially and yelled in:

"Victory! The *Porteños*[23] have won! And the good news from Aroma is also true, it's really true!"

My teacher did not wait any further. He went out as he was, without his robe. Alejo and I followed him out. But at the door of the cell the locksmith stopped me and said, with deep conviction:

"Young man, there are no traces of the *chapetones* left anywhere. Neither Don Francisco [Governor Rivero] nor the Father would believe me. But now they will see if there was any reason to stay out there in the Puna, in the desolate plateau of the Altiplano."

The crowd in the main plaza was enormous. On the corner, in front of the Cabildo, the Notary Don Francisco Angel Astete was standing on a table that had been brought out from a nearby store and was reading the proclamation in which the governor communicated to "the brave citizens of Cochabamba" the victory of the auxiliary troops from Buenos Aires at Suipacha, as well as the very joyous triumph of Aroma, which had not yet been officially confirmed.

It is impossible for me to attempt to describe the rejoicing of the people on that day and the next. Never, ever, not even when the final Proclamation of Independence was announced, after Ayacucho, has there been similar public demonstrations. More than anything, neither the new generation, nor any that is to follow it until the end of time, will ever hear a noisier clamoring of the ringing of the bells. And there are three equally decisive reasons for this: first, because they will never celebrate triumphs as memorable as those; second, because there were more churches active in the city back then than today; and third, because the great bell of San Francisco rang incessantly for forty-eight consecutive hours.

When it was already nearly nighttime, hoarse from yelling like everyone 'Long live the homeland!' I returned to Doña Teresa's house. I found Clemente at the door and grew frightened. His smile of content—once you knew his personality, as I already did—made me hesitate and tremble, thinking that something very bad awaited me. And sure enough, he grabbed me by the neck and dragged me before the noble lady of the house, who had once again retreated to her private chapel. With the strong smell of tobacco and anise, the air was less breathable than usual.

"Here is the vagabond, my lady, my noble *Marquesa*," he said. "Here is the one who yells the loudest among the rebels in the plaza."

"I was not wrong, my God!" the lady exclaimed. "He is the Evil One himself!"

She crossed herself twice, to free herself of the evil traps of the one whom she had named, albeit indirectly. Then she added:

"Take him away immediately, and carry out my orders."

I was to be—and was—locked in my room for two days, and fed only bread and water. Furthermore, after these two days, not only was I once again told not to step out into the street, but I was also not to "Take one step into the main patio, nor go one centimeter further than the hallway, except for going to say the rosary in the chapel, or to go to Mass very early on Sundays with Clemente."

VIII

My Confinement.
The News About Castelli

Although the "noble lady of the house" did not speak to me any more or less than before, and although the looks she gave me the rare times I saw her in the dining room, or when saying the rosary, were no worse than before, I knew, for two main reasons, that Doña Teresa's anger was not appeased for a very long time.

First of all, because Clemente's face lit up when he looked at me more than it did before. This told me that this monster was quite happy to be able to torture me and of having found a better "pain bearer" than the lowly *pongo*, whom he did not bother as much during this time. I will only recount the things he did regularly in his enjoyment of my punishment, leaving unwritten a thousand others he thought of and carried out in more unusual situations. In the mornings, as soon as I opened my door, he would quickly and excitedly look around for a piece of chalk or charcoal, even if he already had one in his hand, so as to draw a line on the ground at the place in the house beyond which I was not allowed to go. He would pretend to forget to call me at mealtimes until the food set aside for me, from which the children were served first, had grown completely cold. When I hid in my room to read, he would bring the boys Pedro de Alcántara and Agustín to the door so they could say to me something like:

"Don't you want to go to the main plaza, Juanito? The bells are ringing, Juanito! What do you think could have happened? We hear that Brother Justo is waiting for you out in the street. . . . Go on, Juanito. . . . The boys are calling you to come out and play *palama!*"

When he spoke either with someone from the household or from outside and was anywhere near me, he would never miss a chance to lament over the sufferings of the lady of the house and conclude by saying:

"What a terrible misfortune! Who would have thought that the noble *Marquesa* would end up having to raise ravens that peck her eyes out? How these little devils bite the hand that feeds them!"

On Sundays, he would get up with the second crowing of the rooster and take me to a Mass at dawn, which was led by an early-rising priest, so as to prevent me from running into anyone on the streets, even by chance, to whom I might speak. Every afternoon, when we met to say the rosary, or right afterward, upon leaving the small chapel, he would talk about the *duende*, saying it would probably come back out in the garden, or in the room with the books, or in my room, from where it kept away only because of the recent exorcism performed by the Reverend Father Arredondo. He would have Feliciana give me the shortest candle stubs possible. And he would often repeat that the *pongo* could no longer leave his guarding place by the door during those times of so much racket and so many disturbances, all caused by the «rebels».

And the second reason I knew that Doña Teresa must still have been very angry is because the joyous, incessant ringing of the bells, the victory hurrahs from the multitudes that reached me in my room every day, the noise from the groups on horseback that rode frequently through the streets, and the news that, in their own way, the servants talked about in the kitchen, because all of this left me no doubt that the revolution was gaining tremendous ground—if it had not already finished with the Spanish domination altogether, that is. The news from Chuquisaca, confirmed by a dispatch from Cochabamba led by Don Manuel Vía, arrived at almost the same time as the wonderful news of the triumph at Aroma. Also around that time, news reached us of the triumph achieved in Suipacha on the 7th of November by the Argentine troops, under the leadership of General Don Antonio González Balcárcel,[1] over the troops that had been amassed on the southern border of Upper Perú by Nieto[2] and Paula Sanz,[3] under the orders of Brigadier Don José de Córdova.[4] A few days later, it was known that the forces of Colonel Don Juan Ramírez[5] had completely evacuated from La Paz, and that they had come back across the Desaguadero River to join Goyeneche's troops because of Piérola's[6] defeat at Aroma. Armed dispatches, like the one that Don Bartolomé Guzmán led to La Paz, left our town frequently in order to correct the mistake made after the victory at Aroma. The enthusiasm and delirium of the people reached its climax, finally, when Governor Don Francisco del Rivero himself left with three thousand cavalrymen and two or three hundred infantrymen to join the auxiliary army. I must note, just in case it is necessary, that the house in which I lived—its residents and its visitors—were among the few exceptions to the overwhelming acceptance with which Cochabamba embraced the cause of the Independence Movement.

I would have given anything to go out to the streets or to the main plaza, to be among the multitudes, to relieve my heart by shouting what came freely from everyone else's—but which I could only let out, all alone, muffled between my pillow and the mattress of my bed! How I wanted to speak with my friends, with Brother Justo and Alejo, or even with *El Overo*, even if it were only through a keyhole in a door or through a wall! Why did the Father, who must have been able to gain entrance into any house, not come and see me? Why did my uncle not take advantage, at least once, of the rights he must have had, as my relative, to come and visit me?

The two things that consoled me remained the same: my reading, enlivened by the find of a tattered volume of the comedies of Calderón de la Barca[7] and a complete comedy by Moreto[8]; and the lessons I gave to Carmencita, or the innocent conversations we enjoyed together.

How did an angel like her come from Doña Teresa's insides? How did so much beauty come from so much ugliness? Such sweet, noble, and tender feelings from such arrogance and selfishness? I do not know. It is possible that she was an example that confirms the belief that girls are much more like their fathers than their mothers. Don Fernando, as I believe I have mentioned before, had been a handsome and elegant gentleman in his youth. I also believe that he must have been inherently good when he was born, and that the faults I shall later describe were a result of his foul and corrupt upbringing.

Carmencita had beautiful blond hair, destined with time to turn brown or completely black, as happens so often in our climate; an amusingly round, very white face, with rosy cheeks, dark blue eyes, and pupils that looked like sapphires; a somewhat aquiline nose; and a small mouth with perfectly shaped lips. She would have made an excellent model if one had wanted to paint a young Virgin Mary doing her lessons by St. Anne's side. But since her expression was also mischievous—although not malicious—she would have also been worthy of being represented as one of the Graces in a pagan painting. She was at times dressed in a skirt and shawl like a noble lady, and at others like a small version of a lower-class woman from Madrid; she could play either role exquisitely well. In the latter one, especially, with the mantilla across her back, her wide-flared skirt, her small red shoes, and, to complete the outfit, the appropriate garter and a small, golden tin dagger at her side, she looked so adorable that she could make even Doña Teresa laugh. I think that this woman did love her, and that she did not love anything else in the world, not even her other children; for although she demanded respect and unconditional compliance for Pedro, in light of the fact that he was the primogeniture, and although she allowed Agustín's pranks, I never saw her praise either one of them even once, nor did I ever hear her have them called to her presence.

Carmencita made me the confidant of her small secrets; she would show me the toys that she was given before showing them to anyone else, and she shared with me all the things that she liked the most. One day, in early March 1811, she came up to me with a charming, affected fastidiousness, making comical facial expressions, her hands behind her back. She then jumped up and down several times, alternately flashing before my eyes a bunch of ripe, golden grapes and hiding them again before I could determine what it was.

"What is it?" I asked myself. "Why can't I guess?"

"Who gave that to you?" I asked her.

"Go on! Who could it be? Luisito . . . that's who! Luisito!"

"And who's Luisito?"

"You're such a dummy! He's the *Gringo's* son."

"Where did you see him? Where does he live?"

"He always comes by our door; he lives there, over there, here. . . . I don't know where."

She was pointing all around my room with her little pink finger and hopping around as she spoke. Then she split the bunch of grapes, put the bigger half on the open book that I had been reading when she entered, and flew off like a bird.

But my second consolation did not last for very long. Clemente, my tormentor, must have told the noble lady of the house that the girl was learning to read with me, or that we spent time talking together; I was told not to receive her in my room again, nor to corrupt her with my company. From that point on, Carmencita was only able to send me a furtive kiss, or a smile from afar.

During that month of April 1811, in which, thanks to the triumphs at Suipacha and Aroma, the whole of Upper Perú felt free to pursue its own destiny, which had suddenly become linked to that of the Provinces of the Río de la Plata, I found myself in that house, without even knowing why. I grew so tired of my confinement that at times I would measure, by sight, the height of the walls of the patio, of the wood bin, and of the garden, considering a possible escape. I vehemently wished, at least, to speak with another rational person, or to hear another language other than the banter spoken by the servants in the kitchen. One afternoon, I saw the Prelate of Our Lady of Mercy and his learned Honor Burgulla enter the house, speaking spiritedly to each other. Unable to control myself, I made a heroic decision.

Pedro de Alcántara, who was always very susceptible to the cold, was sitting by the door of one of the rooms where the sunshine could reach him, playing with his toys. I approached him, pretending to be occupied with a piece of paper in my hand. From it, I first made a boat, then a rooster, and finally, when I had the boy's attention, that ingenious folding trick that I had seen my teacher do so many times.

"What're you going to do now?" he asked me.

"Nothing," I said. "But if you want, cut this here, with a pair of scissors, and see what comes out of it."

He immediately did this, and screamed out in amazement as he removed the cross, the crown, the nails, and the tunic—all the objects that appeared, and which I made sure to explain to him in careful detail.

"Show me how to do it, Juanito," he said to me in his most imploring and persuasive tone.

"Ah, it's not worth it," I answered him.

Meanwhile, I made a rabbit, or something like it, out of a handkerchief and tossed it beside him as if it were the actual live animal itself. This made him completely happy.

"Show me," he insisted, "don't be mean."

"It's too cold to stay out here," I replied, "and your mother, the lady Doña Teresa, doesn't want me to go into the antechamber."

"No, no, let's go. . . . This way. . . . Let's go, quickly!"

As he said this, he took me by the hand and dragged me into the room. I pretended to resist as we went in and made it so that he had to drag me into the antechamber. Luckily, the large vestibule door was closed, but in order to prevent any surprises, I made Pedro sit so that he was leaning back against the door, while I sat down with my left shoulder against the frame of the door. As I continued to entertain the boy in as many ways as I could think of, I was able to immediately begin to listen to the following conversation, which I shall recount without using any names, as the participants will make themselves known clearly enough through their own words.

"*Nihil novum sube sole,*[9] my dear Doña Teresa; irreverence has existed in the world for a very long time."

"And God consents, but not forever."

"Yes, yes, Father; that is understood."

"But how horrible! That irreverent, that Don. . . . What's his name?"

"Juan José Castelli."[10]

"That's it. . . . I don't understand how he could have been given the names of the favored disciple and of the putative father of our Lord."

"To go into the Church of La Paz during Holy Week! To receive gifts and organize dances!"

"And the inexhaustible blasphemies he continues to say all the time!"

"And in French, Father, in the abominable language of the Antichrist who dethroned our king!"

"He is terribly like a Frenchman."

"*Anibal in Capuae.*[11] Let him weaken himself with these pleasures, your Graces. . . . *Quos Deus vult perdere, primo dementat.*"[12]

"No, this cannot be. My God! What do these rebels say now? Are they Christians, or not? Were they ever honest subjects of Don Fernando VII?"

"The truth is that they themselves are unhappy."

"How right was the Most Distinguished Archbishop Moxó[13] in wanting to excommunicate them!"

"If one could only retrace one's steps! But, your noble Honor, what did you call their heresies before?"

"*Liberté*, which comes from *libertas*; *fraternité*, from *frater*, *fratris*; *egalité*, from—"

"I do not understand those words, but they must be very bad."

"Abominable, my lady, abominable."

At this point the large vestibule door, the one with the halberdier painted on it that leads out to the patio, can be heard to open.

"Who is it? How dare you enter, Clemente?"

"Forgive me, your Grace, my Lady *Marquesa*. It is the *Gringo's* son, who has come to pick up the Lord's altar platform that your Ladyship wishes to have gilded for the Exaltation of the Cross."

"That's fine then. Show him into the chapel."

Sound of two people's footsteps heading toward the indicated room. The conversation continues.

"And that devilish song that they say one of the insurgent officers began to sing, when he was drunk, I believe, at a soirée?"

"I don't remember it. It must be the one they sang when they beheaded the saintly King Louis XVI."

"But it seems to me that I have heard its name. *Capio, intendo*[14].
..."

"The *Marseillaise*, sir, the *Marseillaise!*[15] Written by the very Devil who built the Cathedral of Strasbourg."

This last was said by a mocking voice I knew only too well. My surprise was such that I screamed out; then, fearing my yell would make my tormentor come after me and denounce me, I bolted off toward the safety of my room.

On the Sunday of that week, I was going to Mass with Clemente when a man hiding behind the corner of the Church of St. John of God jumped out in front of the sambo, grabbed him with both hands by the belt, lifted him above his head as if he weighed no more than a feather, and said:

"Good morning, Don Clemente."

The wretch was so surprised and frightened that he could not even scream; he was barely able to move his arms and legs mechanically, as if he were swimming in the air. The man who had so unexpectedly, and in such a bizarre style, greeted us, finally set the sambo back down on his feet, all the while laughing at the latter's facial expressions and contortions. Clemente then gave him a pleading look, straightened his belt, tried to smile in his most paltry, complaisant manner, and exclaimed:

"Don Alejo!"

My uncle—for it was him indeed—grabbed the sambo by the ear, and said the following brief, imperative words to him:

"I want to speak with the boy, alone. Go on to Mass, and make sure that you are the last to come back out; then you can come get us at my workshop. And make sure that afterwards you don't tell anyone what has happened! You know me, don't you? Go on! Leave!"

And he ended his statement by giving the sambo a good kick in the rear, helping Clemente arrive even faster to the door of the Church atrium.

"Let's go now, young man," he added, and took me by the hand to his workshop, which was very close to where we were.

A forge occupied one of the corners of the room; in the middle, there was an anvil attached to a thick, pepper tree trunk; and leaning against it were hammers, tongs, and an enormous muckle hammer that could only be wielded by Alejo. The other end was taken up by a long table with many locksmith tools and instruments on it, but also with a group of wooden shafts and triangular iron heads and many tin bars, the presence of which was not so easily explained. A narrow door on that same side opened into another small room, in which Alejo—the locksmith and blacksmith—slept. It was there, on his bed, that he had me sit, while, for himself, he grabbed a small rough stool made from the trunk of a carob tree, with three thick stakes that served as its legs.

"I'm not allowed into the house where you're at," he said to me. "I don't know what's in that house! Luisito Cros told me that they're holding you prisoner there; tell me now, honestly, everything that the heartless woman does to you."

His appearance was frightening. I did not want to tell him how much I suffered, the abandonment in which I found myself, the confinement to which I had been condemned. I only had him understand that I wished for a little more room to move about; and, above all else, that they have something worthwhile, or some trade, taught to me.

"That's fine," he answered. "I will tell these things to the Father this very day. Luckily, I chose not to go with Don Francisco; I decided to work with the others from here and with the *Gringo*. You should know," he continued, calmer now and returning to the main preoccupation of the time, "that the homeland is winning everywhere; there are no traces of the *chapetones* left here; that is, of any with weapons or of any who still have the pride and the desire to fight. Here, take this; these papers will tell you what is happening better than I can. That's why you know how to read, Juanito."

He had just concluded when someone knocked softly on the door. He hugged me and ended the conversation with these words:

"The sambo must be more evil than Lucifer. Go on with him. . . . I don't want to look at him: he's always laughing with that face of his that looks like the mask of the large knocker at that hellish house."

At noon I saw my teacher's tall, hooded figure through the corridor as he crossed the patio swiftly and silently toward the small chapel. He entered there without announcing himself, as if it were his own cell. About an hour later, Clemente came to my room and said to me, in a submissive manner and with the deepest respect:

"Young Don Juan, the lady of the house, my mistress, wishes to see your Excellency in the chapel."

Upon arriving at the large vestibule door, I heard them inside, speaking heatedly. I stopped to see what I could make out. Besides, it seemed that the angel painted on the door was saying directly to me:

"Stop . . . and listen!"

And here is the part of the conversation I was able to make out:

"I have already told you that the horrifying upheavals of the times—that you yourself promote as a priest—makes it impossible for me to send him to study in Chuquisaca. Besides, what does he not have here? What is there for him to complain about? Is he not treated just as my own children are? What could a majordomo's daughter have done for him that I am not doing?"

"Teresa, for God's sake, be quiet! When I made this immense sacrifice to come to your house, I promised myself I would speak with you calmly, but you are trying my patience."

"You can abuse your sacred position if you wish. Praised be God, who has sent these new events to torture the heart of a sad widow!"

"Enough, Teresa!"

"Yes, enough! Don Fernando's wishes will be carried out as soon as these domains of his Majesty the King are once again pacified. Let the boy come here right now and tell you himself if I am lying. My God! If that's the case, I will grant you this, and much more, to atone for my sins!"

I thought she would repeat the order to have me called, so I backed up a few steps and came back again, this time making noise and running loudly into the door on purpose.

"Come in, Juanito," Doña Teresa said, almost affably, "come here. How come you have not gone to visit your teacher?"

I went first to kiss my teacher's extended hand; then I answered, somewhat daringly:

"Clemente has told me that your Ladyship does not want me to go out, nor—"

"Clemente is an animal!" she yelled, very upset. "That wicked sambo. . . . May God forgive me! He gets everything backwards; I'm going to kick him out on the street. What I do not want is for you to waste your time with your old friends playing *palama*; that you not got out and ruin the good lessons which you have learned; that—"

"Stop," my teacher interrupted. "From now on he will come to see me every Thursday, isn't that right?"

"Every day, if you wish it, Father," the lady of the house replied, changing the tone in which she addressed Brother Justo. He, in turn, immediately did the same to say farewell:

"Thank you, Doña Teresa. May God be with you, your Ladyship. . . . Until Thursday, my son."

I returned to my room as soon as he had left. I locked myself in and started reading the papers that Alejo had given me that morning. It was a copy of an announcement from the governor before leaving to join the army of Castelli and Balcárcel, and of the armistice they had reached with Goyeneche. Which is how I learned that the troops of the homeland and those of the Viceroy of Lima, led by the governor of Cuzco, were face to face on the shores of the Desaguadero River.

The Afternoon the Holy Rosary Was Interrupted. The Only Time Doña Teresa Was Friendly

My situation very much improved after my teacher's visit with the noble lady of the house. I was allowed to move freely throughout the entire house and even to go to the front door for a moment whenever a new event took place. Carmencita obtained permission to receive lessons from me at noon, in the dining room, with Feliciana present. An unkempt tailor came to take my measurements; he used a string, on which he tied a series of knots, and laughed at my clothes, which had become too small for me. I was given new shoes to replace my old ones, which were so worn that they barely stayed on my feet anymore. And Clemente was quite proper and very attentive with me in the various orders he had received in this regard.

On the first Thursday following the visit, when I was called in to lunch, I encountered Doña Teresa about to retire from the dining room with her children. Stopping at the door that led to the antechamber, she said to me:

"Make sure not to forget that today is Thursday and that you are to visit Brother Justo. He would be capable of believing—may God forgive his misjudgment!—that I had impeded it. That brute,

Clemente, has caused me a thousand inconveniences already."

The individual alluded to, who was just then placing my lunch on the corner of the table where I usually had it, bowed down to the floor as if those words had crushed him; but I saw that underneath the table he was smiling to himself maliciously.

During my walk to the main plaza, I began to think that I had been magically transported to a city other than Oropesa of the Valley of Cochabamba, one that was very similar, but livelier and more beautiful. And this illusion did not arise merely from being released my long confinement, either. The streets that had the best stone paving and were swept clean every day seemed wider; the houses that been recently fixed up, or at least painted, had a better architectural appearance. And when I reached the main plaza, my illusion only became more complete. The ground—which before was very uneven, with large potholes where water from the rains and piles of debris and trash always accumulated—had been perfectly leveled out. I thought I was laying eyes for the first time, in the center of the plaza, on the old public fountain, known as the fountain of Carlos III because this monarch had had it built explicitly "to reward the service of his brave and loyal Cochabambinos during the Indian rebellion." And finally, I did not see, in the entire plaza, a single one of those horrendous, ugly market stands; they had all been moved to another location, to a large stretch of land used for pasture behind the St. Albert schoolhouse.

All of this was due to an edict declared by the governor, to the efforts of the Cabildo, and to the enthusiasm of the citizens to dignifiedly welcome the promised, but never received, visit of the Delegate of the Honorable Junta of Buenos Aires.

Throughout the streets and in the plaza I saw many women gathered in small groups discussing, in their own manner, a proclamation made by the Provincial Junta, which was organized in the absence of Governor Rivero. The Junta had assured the populace regarding the false, alarming rumors that had been spread by the few who were opposed to the homeland's cause; it had also promised to announce any news it received from the army, whose situation at the shores of the Desaguadero River remained unchanged. But my attention was especially drawn by a large group of people involved in a heated conversation at the doors of the Cabildo; among others, it included two members of the Junta, Don Pedro Miguel de Quiroga and Don Mariano Antezana,[1] and at their side were the courageous Guzmán Quitón (who at that time was in the process of forming a new regiment of cavalry) and—surprisingly!—his learned Honor Don Sulpicio Burgulla!

I was only able to hear these last words spoken by Don Pedro Miguel:

"We have always told our people the truth. . . . Let those other evil individuals be silent now! We have already triumphed at Aroma. . . . And we shall triumph everywhere!"

His Honor Burgulla immediately took his place. He stretched himself up on the tips of his buckled shoes, raised his walking stick with its tufts high in the air, coughed to make himself seem more important, and shouted in his falsetto voice:

"*Excelsior! Audite, cives!*"[2]

The multitude, amazed by his genius, stared at him openmouthed and finally yelled back:

"Long live Don Sulpicio! Long live the homeland!"

I was very much surprised by his Honor's behavior. I later understood that I had seen, at that time, an exemplary model of the most harmful types for newly forming nations: those men known as men of science and experience who only worship success; those pedants who carry canes and deceive the innocent multitudes, making excuses for their own disloyalty with a faulty Latin quotation or a poorly uttered phrase in French, and who demand respect because of their white hair, while they themselves have bowed their heads all the way down to the ground to kiss the feet of the most despicable and vulgar tyrants!

My teacher was already waiting for me at the door of his cell. He led me by the hand, had me sit on the bench, and took a seat on his comfortable armchair.

"Tell me, before anything else, what your life is like," he said to me affectionately, and right away asked many questions of me, which I answered in the same manner as I had answered Alejo's.

Quite studiously, I related to him, in minute detail, my discovery of the books in the room of the *duende*. I knew this would make him happy, since studying was his sole joy in life; and I saw, effectively, his face light up with my words. As I was finishing my responses to his questions, I inwardly congratulated myself. I had just understood that the nature of my saintly mother, and all the advice she had given me throughout her sad and short-lived life had made me incapable of harvesting feelings of vengeance in my heart. Furthermore, I was finding an indefinable satisfaction in being able to hide my own suffering so as to not to add one single drop of anguish into the bitter cup of that just and good-natured man, whom I loved and revered by then like no one else in the world.

After this conversation about my daily life, however, I was not able to keep myself from asking him a question he himself seemed to expect and fear:

"Who am I? Can you tell me anything about my father?"

He thought for a moment, then answered:

"Your blessed mother wished you never to know this. Let us respect her will."

He went on after a long silence, undoubtedly to help shake me out of my sad reflections, to speak about the public events with which everyone was preoccupied. He told me that there were truly well-founded hopes for a great victory, perhaps a final one, for the armies of the homeland.

"I believe that Providence openly protects the cause of justice," he added enthusiastically. "I did not think, my son, that such a large revolution could lead so quickly to this happy outcome."

Finally, he spoke to me about my readings.

"You must have seen the horrors of the Conquest in the works of Don Fray Bartolomé de las Casas,[3] the Bishop of Chiapas," he said. "You should not believe, however, that the Spaniards were any worse than anyone else in the rest of the world at that time. It is no longer necessary to recall those dreadful crimes as a justification of our ardent desire for independence; the latter arises, rather, from other, more immediate reasons. Also, be careful not to let yourself be deceived by the books of Herrera and Garcilaso[4] when they talk about the solicitude of the Kings of Spain toward their subjects in these domains. The measures enacted by the Crown—from the

'Great' Isabel to poor Carlos IV—that they believed would result in their favor, have always turned out, instead, to be quite detrimental. The *encomiendas*,[5] the objective of which was to convert the Indians to Christianity, led to the complete enslavement of the Indians and to their brutalization, as they now believe in superstitions more vulgar than their old cult to the sun. From the Apportionments, with which they planned to place the goods from overseas that they needed within reach, came the most hateful abuses and monopolies, as well as the misery of those poor wretches who were cheated, stripped bare by the Royal District Officers, and finally massacred by the thousands when the Indians rebelled with Túpac Amaru.[6] From the Tribute, which they thought would alleviate their largest deeds and their personal servitude, was born their abjection, which, in all likelihood, is probably irremediable. From the *comunidades* maintained since the Conquest without the traditional customs that used to provide for everyone's livelihood, arose the greatest degradation of the so called Indian *forasteros*,[7] the laziness of the *comunarios*, and the overall impoverishment of the country.[8] Everything they tried became undoable; what is thought to be the best becomes the worst when it emanates from a distant power that can only see through foreign eyes and does not preside directly over the execution of its mandates."

"The Spaniards say that they have given us all the same things which they have; that if they have done us wrong, it is not on purpose, but from mistakes," I observed, timidly.

"They will never be able to convince us that the objectives of their laws regarding industry and commerce do not have the good of the metropolis, before all else, in mind," he answered. "With time, you will be able to see this better than even I have seen it."

"They have tried to enlighten us; their books reach even someone like me."

"They give us light through a screen; and even as such—opaque—they fear it, my son. If there were just one school in each location, it would be impossible for them to carry out their policies. I have told you how, in our country, using the uprising of Calatayud as a justification, it was forbidden for a time to teach mestizo and even *criollo* children to read and write. Just one single printing press run by an American in each Viceroyalty would all but kill their power. The books that you have luckily stumbled upon are all too rare in all of Upper Perú. In all of our city, I only know of three private libraries, each with at most 400 volumes: the one which, as you have told me, is currently being destroyed by the hands of a cook, the one belonging to the Boados and Quirogas, and the Escuderos'. And they each have cost tremendous work and difficulties, financial sacrifice, and personal dangers!"

"The revolution leads us into heresy, according to his learned Honor Don Sulpicio."

"Ah! The imprudence of Don Juan José Castelli!"

"But I heard him say in French that—"

"That which it would have been much better for him to say in Spanish—or in Quechua, if he knew it. Such is humanity's creed, like the evangel, from where philosophy has taken it, but which, however, it opposes."

"One of the officers wanted to sing the *Marseillaise*, which, according to my friend Luis, was written by the Devil in Strasbourg."

"That Luisito Cros is a scoundrel. His father, an Alsatian, must have taught him the truth, and he in turn must have wanted to have some fun on account of your ignorance. No, my son;" and here he stood up, proceeding in what seemed to me an inspired tone: "This cause is so great and just that one day even the Spaniards will respect those who have invoked it. You have already seen that Figueroa has died for our cause; soon you will hear mention of the brave Arenales."[9]

On subsequent Thursdays we continued discussing these same topics. I do not wish to recount these conversations in these memoirs any further. I would perhaps risk tiring the attention of my readers; this consideration keeps me from disclosing my dear teacher's speeches, which might seem trivial today, but were indeed admirable in those times of darkness.

Instead, I will move on to relate two events that are certain to amaze my curious readers, as they did me back then.

One afternoon, in which all the inhabitants of the house were united in the small chapel to say the holy rosary, we all began to wonder about something that Doña Teresa soon voiced: Clemente

—who was usually the most punctual, in order to sing the melody, as I have previously recounted—was not there.

"Where is that villain?" the lady of the house demanded, and crossed herself as she always did when she referred to the Devil, or to anything evil.

She was about to send us to look for him when the missing Clemente came in looking very agitated. "Captain. . . . Don Anselmo Zagardua!" he said to Doña Teresa mysteriously.

The lady of the house started.

"What does he want? My God! What could it be?" she exclaimed, quite vexed.

"He's in my room. He says that Don—"

"Yes, I know. . . . There's no reason to say his name, you idiot! What's wrong with him?"

"That he's sick. . . . That the swelling has reached up to his knees."

"Have him come in here at once, quickly!"

Immediately after Clemente left, Doña Teresa added:

"Feliciana, take the children away. . . . Have them eat dinner and put to sleep. Everyone, leave! What are you still doing there? Go to your rooms! And make sure not to open my door for any reason!"

As I crossed the patio, I saw Clemente returning with a strange-looking man, some sixty years old, tall and withered, dressed in a military uniform that was very much worn and threadbare. He walked with difficulty, leaning on a thick walking stick because he had a wooden leg, which was very crude, as they were in the country in those days.

On another afternoon—I do not recall if it was the 27th or 28th of June—I was called to dinner half an hour earlier than usual. Doña Teresa was smiling softly at the head of the table, surrounded by her children. She had me sit in my place to dine with them and told me I would not be made to wait from that day on. She lavished kisses on Carmencita. She patted Agustín's chubby cheek.

"Come here, my son," she went on to say to Pedro. After he had gone to her side, she went to button up his shirt, but was unable to. Addressing her servant, she said:

"Feliciana, my dear Feliciana, there is a button missing here.

Why have you let my heart's proud little boy get like this?"

She seemed another person, completely different from the usual Doña Teresa; she was an affable lady, a very affectionate mother, a mistress who ordered her servants without yelling angrily at them. Her kindness toward me went as far as all of the sudden giving me permission to go out wherever I wanted to.

Extremely happy, I went to see my teacher. Along the way I prepared in my mind a praise of my protectress to say to him, throwing in, if possible, a Latin quotation taken from the wise lips of his Honor Burgulla. The moment I opened the door to the cell, however, I was seized with the deepest feeling of distress at seeing the dejection, the unutterable pain depicted on the face of Brother Justo, and on his entire body, in fact. He was standing up, with his arms crossed on his chest, and his head bowed toward the ground, staring down as if there was a recently covered grave at his feet. I remembered seeing him in this very posture, through my tears, when my mother was being wrapped in the funereal shroud.

Neither the excitement with which I opened the door, nor the bright sunlight that came through it and covered nearly half his body, were enough to tear him away from his deep thinking. It was only an automatic response that made him cover his eyes against the glaring light with one hand, and stretch the other out in front of him as if he were protecting himself from some sudden threat that was about to strike. Then, regaining awareness as to what has happening around him, he looked at me sadly, and spoke to me as if I had confirmed for him the devastating news he had already previously received:

"I know; the disaster is complete. . . . It must have been the will of God!"

Finally, noticing my surprise and the astonishment with which I regarded him, he told me about the defeat that the armies of the homeland had suffered at Huaqui on the 21st of June of 1811.

Time has not erased from my mind the profound impression his words had on me. Today I believe that he was able to see at that point something he made clear to me as well: the dreadful consequences for the cause of our Independence that were to follow from that event.

The armistice that had suspended the hostilities could not lead to any favorable outcome. Any conciliation of the interests of Spain with America's interests by then was completely impossible. Goyeneche had dealt an irreparable, treacherous blow to the revolution under the pretext that Castelli, from the heights of the mysterious ruins of Tiahuanaco,[10] had spoken about freedom to the Indians and had reminded them of the *Tahuantinsuyu* of the Incas.[11]

"The Argentine campaign that had at most fifteen hundred men when it left Suipacha, arrived at the shores of the Desaguadero River transformed into a great and powerful army of twelve thousand men. Even Goyeneche's seconds in command—proud, haughty Spaniards—thought that it would be very difficult to confront this force, and this even though they held a position which was very well strategically chosen by their leader. This force surged across our territories from south to north, dragging along with it almost all the resources that our country had available from the revolution in Cochabamba and the happy victory at Aroma. Now that they are lost, I do not know how they can possibly be recovered. Our provinces—so distant from the rest of the world, separated by large mountain ranges and deserts—will not be able to replace a single, lousy rifle or even one musket gathered by the enemy as part of the spoils of war. From now on, the war in Upper Perú will be a desperate, heroic sacrifice. But it will, at the very least, achieve the Independence of the provinces of the Río de la Plata."

How I wish our national historians would repeat these words! They could then reply triumphantly to the ardent statements made by an Argentine writer[12]—ignorant of the thousand generous efforts from the provinces of Potosí, Chuquisaca, and La Paz—that only do justice to the province of Cochabamba.

On my way back to the house, crestfallen and deep in thought, I heard Alejo's voice call me from across the street. He was standing there with a large, heavy object, thicker than his own staff, and wrapped in a thick strip of cloth.

"I bet," he said to me, "that the Father has saddened you by going on about how hopeless it is. Don't believe it, young man. We are doing well, better than ever. Our compatriots had not entered into battle because they had been sent somewhere—I don't know where. But when they heard the cannon blasts, they returned, forcing the *chapetones* to retreat. Every single one of them—no, I'm wrong; all except the unlucky infantrymen, all of whom have been killed, including their leader and their officers—are heading for our valleys. We will then be ready to meet them face to face. The *chapetones* cannot imagine what awaits them!"

As he spoke these last words, he raised the strange object he held in his hand into the air.

"Father Justo," he continued, "believes that this, too, is bad. But you should know, Juanito, that I hold, right here in my hands, the means that could destroy the army of King Xerxes.[13] If you want, you can come to my workshop tomorrow . . . then you'll see! You'll see if the *Gringo*, the *Mellizo*,[14] the *Jorro*,[15] and I don't know more than Father Padilla, who invented gunpowder!"

Having said this, he quickly left, heading off toward the Cabildo. I continued my walk back, encountering groups of mestizos on the street corners already talking about the news with the same indifference or contempt as the locksmith had expressed.

As I entered through the portico, I saw Clemente speaking from the door of his room to Feliciana, who was inside.

"That's how they are, that's how those ingrates are," he said, raising his voice so I would hear him. "Does it surprise you, woman? They laugh when our mistress cries, but their faces are long and surly when she smiles."

And suddenly, turning around toward me, he yelled:

"Isn't that right, bastard child?"

I was unable to contain myself. Those insults, on top of all the times that he had humiliated and tortured me before, made me lose control. I struck his ugly monkey face hard with my hand, and then continued walking slowly toward my room.

"The nerve! You insolent «foundling waif»!" Feliciana yelled at me. But the wretched sambo remained quiet, probably rubbing his face, more frightened than angry.

That night I was not called to say the rosary nor to dinner. Luckily, I had a stub of a candle left; I went to light it in the kitchen. I tried to read but could not. Reflecting on what I had done, I congratulated myself just as I had on the other occasion, in which I believed I had vengeance within reach and had decided not to take it. I now knew that in the same way that I would never crush a defeated enemy, neither would I endure an excessive humiliating affront without confronting it right then and there with dignity.

Suddenly my door opened loudly, and a biscuit fell on the table in front of where I was sitting. I turned my head and thought I caught a flash of Carmencita's dress before the door closed. That beautiful girl, who had somehow escaped, had brought me what she could of her own dinner, then flown back so they would not notice her absence from the dining room. A very sweet tear fell from my eyes on the page of the book from which I was reading the comedy *The Brave and Just Man*, by Moreto.[16] I was hungry, but I never took a bite out of that gift that I had received from the only friend I had in that house. I put it carefully away in my coffer as if it were a sacred object.

The following day, one of the mestizas called me into the small chapel around the time when Doña Teresa tended to get up in the morning. I found the noble lady of the house holding the lapdog as she sat on her dais between two friends of hers who wore the habits of the third order of St. Francis. They must have undoubtedly been speaking charitably about me, because they crossed themselves when they first saw me, and both exclaimed, almost at once:

"Lord! He's so young still!"

"Poor child!"

"I have decided," the lady of the house said to me, "that you are to go this very day to Las Higueras."

"I will do whatever your Ladyship wishes and orders of me," I answered, not knowing what this was about.

"Pancho," she continued, "has come with his nephew, who has to stay behind in the city; you will go on his horse however you can manage. Tell me now what you will need."

"Nothing, your Ladyship."

"Good. Since «poor» Clemente has fallen ill and Feliciana must take care of him, Paula will look after whatever you need."

These words being spoken, she pointed to the door. But I was not able to leave as quickly as I would have wanted in order to avoid hearing the following additional charitable words spoken in Quechua by one of her friends, Doña Martina:

"Poor Teresa! What kind of snake have you taken into your house?"

Shortly thereafter, Paula came into my room. She placed a poncho and a cotton scarf, of the kind woven in Beni, on a chair and said to me:

"Don Pancho is waiting in the patio with the horse."

I picked up the poncho and the scarf, and followed her out. All the servants and the boys Pedro and Agustín were gathered around Clemente, laughing with him at the entrance to the corridor. None of them replied when I said farewell; much less did they come to shake my hand. The foundling waif was leaving; the lady of the house was sending him away with «Don» Pancho, because he had struck «Don» Clemente. . . . It was all very much fun to them. But no! A small blond head—more beautiful than usual in its disheveled morning look—leaning against the thick bars of her bedroom window, thought otherwise. As I was leaving that house, feeling completely insignificant, either for a few days or forever— I did not know which—I was comforted by the sight of my generous small friend, who blew me a kiss with her little pink fingers.

X

My Exile

The town of Oropesa in Cochabamba is the granary and storehouse of abundance for the bordering towns in the provinces of the Río de la Plata, which has led to its population being larger, because of the rabble that lives there, than other cities of greater character. . . . Nowhere else is this evil combination, which hates its own origins, more harmful than there.

MARQUÉS DE CASTEL-FUERTE[1]

Francisco Nina, the main tenant at Las Higueras—a small property belonging to Doña Teresa with six tenant farmers near the town of Sipe Sipe—was a forty-year-old mestizo man, very tall and broad, round-faced, beardless, and with a good-natured look to him, which indeed was not deceiving. He had a large hat made of sheep wool; a yellow scarf like mine; an alpaca poncho and spats that were beautifully woven in his own house; and shoes with rough soles and impressive iron spurs, well fastened just above the heels with long leather straps. He rode a white mare that was bloated as a *vinchuca*,[2] as he himself used to say, mounted on a saddle with front and rear saddlebows, a goat-fur saddle pad, and wooden stirrups that were too small for his feet.

I mounted a woolly nag as well as I could. It was part white, part black, very timid, and saddled just like the mare; and it always stuck its head under the latter's tail in order to walk, or else it would not walk at all.

We rode for three hours at a good pace, with Pancho in front and I behind, but we made over three hundred stops. And this was not because of me, either—for, although awkwardly, I managed to hold on to the front saddlebow and let the nag follow the mare as it pleased—but rather because of the incomprehensible signs and words my guide exchanged all along the widely populated way with the peasants who stood at their doors or behind the low adobe walls of their yards. At times, he would whistle and make a sign with his outstretched right index and middle fingers placed over of his outstretched left index finger; at others, after whistling, he would ask a question, but always with very few words, such as: "And?—You have 'em?—Ready?" In reply, the peasants in turn gestured in the affirmative, or also used very few words, such as: "Yes—Understood—Ready—We will soon—Of course." From all of this, the only thing I was able to infer is that it had something to do with horses, and with some festival or journey in which everyone very much wanted to attend or participate. Other than this, the beautiful countryside we crossed, although quite dry, constantly drew my attention with the pleasant, lively sights that it offered in every direction. It was filled with rich, green trees—such as the willows, pepper, orange, and lemon trees that bordered the road.* Large groups of women and children shucked corn or gathered wheat into sheaves, and laughed merrily. Every once in a while an extra loud burst of laughter could be heard. And more than once I distinctly heard someone shout "Long live the homeland!" Numerous flocks grazed in the stubble-field. Droves of donkeys carrying large packs crossed the road in every direction, and tiny kernels of corn that their wool reticulum could not hold fell from their mouths. The men with the donkeys were huge, svelte native sons of the valley. They walked behind the animals, with their thick whip, known as the *verdugo*, in their hands, and whistled and shouted to try to speed up the tired mules. Some had yellow aster

---

*At that time, the valley, especially in the area surrounding Quillacollo, was a beautiful forest of fruit trees. I am told that today my compatriots rudely cut down the trees in order to plant corn, and that along the sides of their wide roads they do not even plant the beautiful indigenous willows, or the poplars that have been recently imported from Carolina. And then they complain that the land dries up and that it doesn't rain!

flowers decorating their hats or *monteras*, and more than just a few carried a *charango*³ tied on and hanging behind them. With it, they would entertain themselves during their moments of rest, at the time of the *sama*,⁴ or when they ate.

Finally, around one in the afternoon, we arrived at Las Higueras. The place must have been named after the many beautiful tufted trees found there. The house was located in a large clearing in the middle of all the fig trees. It was simply one main room with two smaller rooms to either side of it. A long passageway connected the inside to the path leading to the entrance. The kitchen was a straw shed built against the right side of the house. The corrals with the oxen, donkeys, and chickens were spread out on the other side of it. The horses had their place out in the field, near the entrance to the house. When we arrived, there were two large, gleaming colts tied to a post; they raised their fine heads and their long, bushy tails, and neighed happily.

A woman of Pancho's same age, with fairer skin, robust like him, dressed in a Castilian *bayeta*⁵ skirt (everything that came from abroad was called "Castilian," even if it was not made in the Peninsula) and a *tocuyo* shirt, with bare legs and feet—like all women in their own homes in the country—was standing at the door, waiting. A young man of eighteen years of age—fair like the woman, already almost as tall and thick as Pancho, dressed in barracan trousers and a short-sleeved shirt, with wool socks and tanned leather shoes—rushed out of the main room to grab my guide's horse's bridle and help him dismount.

"Well done, Venturita," Pancho said as soon as his feet touched the ground. Then he gave the youth a good pull on the ears, which made him laugh with inexpressible satisfaction. The man then approached the woman and greeted her with a solid slap on the shoulder, a caress that she answered with as much finesse, giving him a strong fillip to the nose.

"Mariquita!" Pancho shouted out, happily. "Mariquita, where are you? I have something for you! Something really special. . . ."

"*Chunco, tatitoi*,⁶ I'm coming with the *merienda*," answered a girl's light voice from the kitchen.

Meanwhile, Ventura came up to me. Quite informally, he grabbed me by the waist, lifted me from the saddle, and set me down on the ground.

We went into the main room and sat on a bench that had no backrest and was placed against the wall behind a long, wide, crudely carved table. Two of the room's corners were taken up by adobe *poyos*[7]; these were Pancho's and his wife Petrona's beds. In one of the other corners there was a very tall table that held a large glass case, inside of which could be seen an image of the Virgin of Our Lady of Mercy, with eyes bigger than her mouth and cheeks redder than cherries, balancing a miniature of the child Jesus on the palm of her hand that was so small it looked like a toy with which she was playing. The other corner, in front of this last one, was the place designated to set down the saddles. Hanging from the ceiling tie-beams, which could be reached from the *poyos* or the bench, hung their Sunday clothes.

No sooner had we sat down, when a plump young woman entered, carrying a large tray with the *merienda* in her hands. She set it down on the table, then went to get a stack of enameled clay plates, four orange-wood spoons, and two knives from behind the glass case with the Virgin, and placed them next to it.

Few times have I seen such a beautiful model of a *chola*. Her wavy, chestnut hair; her large, brown eyes under long eyelashes that curled upward; her round, rosy cheeks; her mouth with lips that were a little too thick and bright white teeth; her neck, white as that of a woman of the purest and bluest blood: everything about her was somehow better, finer, and more delicate than in the majority of the women of the robust Cochabambian race—women who are more Spanish than Indian, who earned such poor esteem from the honorable Marqués de Castel-Fuerte, and whom European travelers, who have met them there in their valleys, who have received their friendly attention as hostesses, and of whom they keep fond memories, praise so highly. She was dressed like her mother; the wide sleeves of the shirt showed her round arms, with comical pockmarks on her elbows; and her tiny, bare feet deserved to walk on the richest of tapestries, but at best had to make do on

Sundays with the small, white and spangled sheepskin shoes that I could see hanging from a peg of carob-tree wood nailed into the wall, next to the hanging wardrobe.

The *merienda* she brought in, which was the main meal of the native children of those rich valleys, and next to which the famous Spanish stews pales in comparison, was an impressive display indeed. Arranged in artistic divisions, forming fanciful and imaginative shapes, it consisted of a pyramid of stuffed potatoes, at the center of which must have been the hot peppered chicken and rabbit; a circle of *habas*[8] and *charqui*; and rectangles containing different sauces, kidney, cheese, and eggs—all of which were seasoned with the unmistakable flavors of *locoto*[9] and the tremendous *ulupica*.[10]

When he saw his beautiful daughter, as well as the appetizing *merienda*, Pancho jumped up enthusiastically and yelled:

"Ah, Mariquita! Long live—"

But his wife pinched him and looked in my direction. Then, changing her tone, she said to me:

"Let us eat, my son, until we are satisfied and content, as is the will of God on all days except Lent Friday."

So we did, first with the spoons, and then with our hands. We talked about a thousand different things and laughed like mad, whether someone had said something funny, or not. How blessed I began to feel about my exile! In that house, among those good people, I felt in my heart the sweet warmth of a home—that indefinable charm that life holds in a family's inner sanctum.

Once we were finished with the *merienda*, Petrona climbed up on the bench. She took a small, bright red clay decanter and two wide-bodied, green-enameled glasses, known as *loritos*,[11] from a shelf and placed them ceremoniously on the table. Her husband's eyes glittered with joy.

"Do you want some?" he asked me.

I realized it must be chicha, the beverage commonly drank by much of the populace. I had a very bad opinion of the drink ever since, when I was very young, I had heard Don Francisco de Viedma call it "the poison" and attribute to it everything he believed to be wrong in the country.

"No, I'm too young still," I answered.

"Go on!" he replied. "What did they wean you with, then?" he added and burst out laughing, and his wife and children soon joined him.

He and Petrona were the only ones who drank; they had two or three *loritos* each. The children were not allowed to do so in their presence; they would drink later, as much as they pleased, but "they would never disrespect their parents."

Later, I was left to my own devices, without anyone telling me what to do, just like in the city. But out in the country, I was free to go wherever I pleased, to run around at will, certain that when I returned to the small house I would always be welcomed with a kind smile by my hosts. I was happy and enjoyed many days there, thanking Providence for having thrown me, without my knowing how, into that world—those beautiful fields that were the orchard and granary of Upper Perú.

During those times, the crops were threshed on the threshing-floors. I also saw there was no lack of horses, but they seldom used them, preferring the donkeys, instead.

"The horses are busy with other things," they would say.

I never passed the vicinity of an *era*[12] without hearing "Long live the homeland!" shouted out, repeated a thousand times by the country peasants in the middle of the joyous excitement of that fond occupation.

It was only in the small house where I lived that this topic was never raised. And if a visitor tried to say something about it, the head of the house would signal him to be quiet, or would abruptly change the topic.

One afternoon, I found Pancho and his wife speaking mysteriously in the hallway while she held a piece of paper in her hand.

"What should we do?" he asked. "I don't want the boy to know about these things. What would the lady *Marquesa* say?"

"We'll have him go with Ventura," she answered, pointing to the northern Cordillera.

"Yes, to the mountains . . . that's it!" Pancho replied.

But they saw me and stopped talking. Then they greeted me and told me that the *merienda* was awaiting us with two fat, juicy rabbits.

At night, as he was preparing my bed in his room next to his, Ventura said to me:

"They say that Don Enrique slept in this very spot. My father never stops talking about him. He must have been such a good man! So generous! And so courageous to walk everywhere! And such a good hunter! The *guemals*[13] in the mountains must be very happy that he has left them alone."

"I have never met him," I replied, "nor do I remember ever hearing anyone talk about him."

"He's no longer in this world," Ventura said. Then he rummaged under the bed, pulled out an old carbine covered with gold and silver plating, and went on: "Look at his rifle; he gave it to my father the last time they came back from hunting near the lakes."

Pancho walked in at this point, and spoke very naturally to his son, although they had the scene well rehearsed:

"That's what you do best, isn't it, you scoundrel, you. Every time you're told to go up to the Cordillera, the first thing you do is take out Don Enrique's rifle. Or maybe the boy wants to go with you, too?"

"Yes, I'd love to," I quickly answered, which pleased him so much that he could not hide his satisfaction.

It was barely the break of dawn when Ventura and I departed the next morning, he mounted on the mare and I, with the rifle, on the nag. We took the road I already knew for a good stretch, then turned onto another that led across the vast valley toward the Cordillera to the north. Before we had gotten very far, however, Ventura stopped his horse abruptly at a turn in the road and began laughing like a madman. He dismounted, took off his poncho and spurs, handed me the bridle, and said:

"That little devil is outside, waiting especially so she can see me coming. But watch. . . . Let me show you what I'm going to do. . . ."

Having said this, he started walking forward again, this time very quietly. I followed slowly behind him so as to observe his actions. A short distance ahead, to one side of the road, there was a house, more or less like ours. A young woman, whose figure and dress resembled Mariquita's, was standing on a *poyo* next to one of the columns of the passageway in front of the house; she was facing away from us, speaking with someone who must have been inside the main room. Ventura snuck up to her, grabbed her by the legs, and lifted her into the air; then he started shouting and running around in circles, carrying her on his shoulder. The young woman, for her part, after screaming out, soon began to laugh loudly. Meanwhile, two older people—a couple whose hair was completely white—came out of the house and also started laughing wholeheartedly.

The entire scene lasted until Ventura became too tired of running with his load on his shoulder. At that point, he lowered the young woman down gently on her own two feet. But the girl, who had by then turned red as a tomato, gave him a good pinch on the arm and made her getaway, jumping off into the house; the old couple never stopped laughing, growing more and more amused as the whole encounter proceeded.

The pinch seemed to fill Ventura with joy.

"Come on," he yelled to me. When I had reached him with the mare, and after he had mounted again, he spoke to the inhabitants of the house from his horse: "I'm going up to the mountains. . . . I'll see you tomorrow!"

About half a kilometer later, he turned toward me, his face glowing with happiness. "What do you think?" he exclaimed. "That's Clarita, my cousin. . . . My fiancée!"

"She's very beautiful, almost as beautiful as your sister," I answered.

"Oh, much more! She and her brother—the one who went to the city the other time—live with our grandparents, who you saw at the door. They're already saying that when we get married in San Andrés, every single person from the entire area will come dance in the lean-to that will be set up in front of the house."

I do not know what else he was going to say, for suddenly he stopped talking and became visibly agitated.

I looked around in every direction, but did not see anything that could have caused this reaction in him. The only unusual thing I noticed was a few violin notes that seemed to be coming from a decrepit, old house up ahead, to one side of the road that continued across the valley.

The house was tall and had a tiled roof, as opposed to the majority of the others I had seen in the area, which were of one level and had straw or simple adobe roughcast roofs. The rickety balcony only had part of its railing left, and it was held on with leather straps; one side of the roof appeared to be partially caved in; and the adobe stairs—or as much as I could see of them above the adobe wall surrounding a patio overgrown with grass—had a number of steps that had been ruined by the rains. Finally, in the door leading into the patio, I saw Captain Don Anselmo. He was not wearing his old military uniform this time, but rather the jacket and trousers worn by well-to-do country people. He was peacefully enjoying the sun and smoking a large, clay pipe.

The harmonious instrument, the notes of which began to reach my ears more distinctly, must have been played by the masterful hands of an inspired artist. I shall never forget that tune which, to this day, I still frequently repeat for Merceditas, and which she says would make even a stone shed tears. It is at once humble and angry, peaceful and violent, tender and threatening, but always expresses the same cry of a heart from which all hope has been extinguished.

"The old house . . . the madman . . . I'm such an idiot!" Ventura murmured.

And immediately he led us in a wide roundabout detour through a corn stubble-field. In vain did I ask him the cause of his anxiety and disturbance; in vain did I attempt to have him tell me something about the inhabitants of that house. He continued ahead in complete silence, spurring on the *Vinchuca* and not saying anything else to me for the duration of the trip through the populated areas. He was plenty busy, besides, in gesturing, like his father, to the peasants we encountered along the way or who came out of their houses when they heard Ventura whistling.

When we reached the rocky terrain that is found at the base of the Cordillera along with the wheat stubble-field and the groups of dwarf pepper trees, he suggested I watch the ground carefully around me as we continued along the way. In this manner, perhaps, he aimed to avoid any new questions he feared I might pester him with.

"There are many partridges," he said, "but it's very difficult to see them because they hide under the rocks."

And, in effect, we did not find any that we were able to shoot, although two suddenly flew off from right under the feet of my frightened nag, who came very close to throwing me off and cracking my skull on the rocks.

Later, we turned down a dry riverbed and proceeded into the ravine until its walls were no longer climbable. At that point, my guide stopped; he dismounted, then lifted me off my mount. Immediately he asked me for the carbine. He walked a short distance ahead, very quietly, until he reached a turn in the riverbed. From there, he aimed carefully to his left, and fired a shot, loud as a cannon blast, which was heard more than six times because of the echo.

Ventura disappeared behind the turn in the ravine and hopped back moments later holding a beautiful mountain *viscacha*[14] in his hand.

"Now we have to cut off its tail, so it won't ruin the meat, and then put the animal in the saddlebags," he said, very happy. "We'll take it to Mari-quita; she'll know how to prepare it, and to cut half of it for «the others»."

We had to climb the slope to the left along a steep, winding path. We went up in this very tiring way, both of us on foot leading our horses by the bridles, for an hour. We then found ourselves on the first level of the Cordillera, where the *ichu* begins to grow and potatoes are cultivated. Ventura stretched out the fur saddle pads near a small stream of water that dripped down into the sands of the ravine below and took our cold meal out from the saddle bags: it consisted of a chicken stuffed with peppers, *chuño* with cheese, and a corn *tamal*. I sat facing the valley, looking out at the wide, vast, and splendid panorama now visible before my eyes, and exclaimed:

"Oh! How beautiful!"

I shall try to describe it. Perhaps I will be able to provide my readers with at least some idea of what it was like, although words can never come close to describing even a fraction of its beauty.

The sun was shining in a sky that had a crisp clarity that can only be observed from those heights, and only during the dry period of winter. Not even the slightest bit of haze was present in the serene, transparent air. My eager eyes could gaze out freely in a semicircle of a diameter over fifteen leagues in length.

The inner Cordillera, known as the Royal Cordillera of the Andes, stretched out to my right at a uniform height. It rose and fell at intervals near Tunari and reached its tallest height at the peak of that mountain, whose snowcap can be seen from great distances like a white pearl set against blue enamel. Beyond, the Royal Cordillera dropped immediately down into the Chocaya ravines. Then it rose again, continued toward the Northwest, dropping to the East in a straight line to a branch that leveled off at the same height as the one I was on. Then it continued until it was lost in the distance, but not before rising abruptly into a groups of peaks that were taller and had more snow than Tunari. It is from all that snow that that area gets its name of *Yurackasa*,[15] or in other words, the White Valleys.

The ridges of these two great branches, stretching out at times into chains of hills, thus form the four valleys: Caraza, Cochabamba, Sacaba, and Cliza. Between the first and second of these, in a depression among the hills, sparkled the great Lake Huañacota. Also, on the ridge beyond Cliza, at the very edge of the horizon, could be seen the reflection of the Vacas Lakes.

The floor of the valleys, the prairies found within the lowest foothills of the ridges surrounding them, must have offered during summer's rainy season—with the many orchards, the forests of willow trees, and all the different kinds of fields that would be in full growth at that time—a sight filled with all shades of green, from dark and somber to the lightest yellowish green. In winter, when I admired them, they contained large stretches of the dark green of the perennial trees; between these, I could distinguish the red tiles and bell towers of the small towns. The rest, covered with underbrush, offered the most varied shades of brown and yellow, from the most opaque to the whites of the *eras*. From where I was, I could see the southern part of the Caraza Valley; the more picturesque half of the Valley of Cliza, from the town of Orihuela on; almost all of the Valley of Sacaba, except for one of its most beautiful little areas, near the White Valley; and all—absolutely all—of the Valley of Cochabamba, down to its smallest detail. I could have drawn its entire configuration on a piece of paper, the course of its torrents and rivers, and the most perfect map of the towns of Pazo, Sipe Sipe, Quillacollo, Tiquipaya, and Colcapirhua.

The queen of those valleys, the city of Oropesa of Cochabamba, stretched out at the end of the Valley of the same name, at the base of the chain of ridges that separate it from the Valley of Sacaba. Its southernmost neighborhood was partially hidden by the gentle hills of Alalai and San Sebastián; the westernmost one reached the gullies around the Rocha River; and the northern and eastern ones disappeared among the orchards and gardens. Above the tall columns of the so-called Castilian willows, above the tops of the more beautiful native willows, and above the fruit trees, rose the city's white towers and the red-tiled roofs of its many houses. Finally, outside the city, on the other side of the riverbed of the Rocha—whose abundant waters were extensively drained for irrigation—stretching out almost as far as the base of the Cordillera, and actually reaching it through of the Taquiña ravine, were the rich and abundant orchards of Calacala. And above its forests of eternal green foliage rose the tops of two or three enormous ceibo trees that must have been hundreds, if not thousands, of years old.

"Oh! How beautiful!" I repeated, admiring the details after first having taken in the whole.

And even today, after having seen in the course of my adventurous life many renowned places throughout the Americas, only able now to admire those valleys in my imagination, knowing their beauty surpasses even the best reproduction that I may be capable of drawing in my mind, I say these words without fearing that those who hear them might suppose them to be the products of exaggeration because of my love for the land in which I was born—which I will not see again, but where I would like my bones to be laid to rest, under the rich foliage of one of its willow trees. I remember that Governor Viedma used to call my country "the Valencia of Perú," adding that it was as lovely as the most beautiful areas of his beloved Spain. Also, I have before me D'Orbigny's book,[16] which my comrade-in-arms Don José Ballivián has recently sent me. This wise French traveler says that, "Those prairies, sown with buildings, those rich and abundant fields, awake in him the memory of his own homeland!" Why, then, would an actual native son of those sweet valleys not be allowed to proclaim that they are, in fact, "the most fertile, beautiful, and delightful country in the world"?

These last words of Oquendo's came naturally to my mind on that occasion.

"Brave citizens of Cochabamba—" I began to say.

But Ventura interrupted me. He wanted to say himself the speech that I have previously recounted.

"What? You know it?" I asked him, surprised.

"How could I not? Who doesn't know it? I thought, rather, that you didn't like such things?"

"But, they're the only things I dream about, Ventura! If only I could be as big as you so I could fight for our homeland!"

"Ha, ha, ha, ha, ha!"

"Why are you laughing?"

"Because my father sent you up here thinking that you might have his lands taken away by Doña Teresa. But read this; I'll tell you the rest afterwards."

Having said this, he handed me the paper that Petrona must have held in her hands when I surprised her the day before speaking mysteriously with her husband. It was a proclamation from Governor Rivero to the province under his command after his return from the defeat at Huaqui. I shall copy only a few fragments of it here:

"Children of the brave province of Cochabamba, compatriots, and brothers! As you know, the auxiliary army, which our troops had joined, had situated itself on the shores of the Desaguadero River with the objective of stopping the progress of the opposing army, then located on the other side of the river. We suffered a defeat there this last June 21. . . .

"With this fact in mind, I have determined that every single man in Cochabamba between the ages of sixteen and sixty is to take up arms. . . .

"If there are among you any who, because of illness or other justifiable reasons, are unable to take part in the joy of our sublime purpose, I am certain that you will fulfill your duty instead by extending your weapons and any other services which you are able to contribute to this great endeavor. Tomorrow we shall all begin to gather, in the towns grouped by neighborhoods and in the fields by estates, and then head towards the Arque and Tapacarí ravines, where the orders and maneuvers will be assigned. Each of you must bring enough supplies to last you until you reach these first locations. . . .

"Make haste, my brothers, knowing that your vigilance will assure our victory; choose captains to lead you whose voices you trust; and repeat the vows you have made with God, who looks over our armies. . . .

"And finally, my brothers, work for the good of our common interests, without giving me cause to exercise the authority that you have placed upon me; for, if necessary, I will use the full force of the laws against any among you who are indolent. . . ."

As the child I was at the time, I was deeply moved by the direct, loving, and insinuating patriotic language in the beginning, as well as by the severe and threatening language used toward the end. Today, old as I am, comparing the times in which I now live with those back then—with their noble sacrifices, demanded and given so naturally and simply—it is impossible for me to rewrite those words onto these pages without feeling even much more touched by them. And . . . darn it! I do believe I am crying, for a burning tear has just fallen on my trembling hand!

When I was done reading, Ventura spoke to me, saying the following:

"The army has already left in order to move into the ravines. But today and tomorrow my father still has to gather anyone who is left that can fight and has horses. He has sent us here, under the pretext that time is running out to fallow, so that you would not tell Doña Teresa that he is a rebel leader and also to prevent me from following him to «the war.»"

"Let's go back, Ventura!" I exclaimed.

"Don't get too anxious," he replied. "Today I'll do what he ordered me to do. Tonight we'll sleep in the house of one of the Indians, very close to here. Tomorrow we'll descend like greyhounds; I'll get Clarita to pinch me again; we'll arrive for lunch; and you can tell my father that you are annoyed with all this, or, to make it more clear, that you are a good patriot."

After having said this, he stood up. We mounted our horses and continued climbing up the slope, now at a gentle gradient. About a hundred paces later, Ventura whistled loudly. As if by magic, a black dog appeared; it had rigid, sharp-pointed ears and was somewhat woolly—it was, in a word, the intelligent American *alco*.

"It's *Ovejero*[17]; he watches over more than a hundred sheep by himself," his proud master said to me.

Following *Ovejero* on a narrow path that wound through an area thick with *ichu*, we reached the rancho that Ventura had told me about. It was located at base of the second level of the Cordillera, considerably lower than the first.

That night, lying down on as soft a bed as Ventura was able to set up for me, I dreamt that I had turned into a giant, ten times bigger than Pancho and a hundred times stronger than Alejo; and that, using a cedar tree from Tiquipaya as if it were a *macana*, I was crushing hundreds of grenadiers who wore tall, downy fur busbies. My victims were screaming out very sad laments; the air around me was filled with the violin melody I had heard that morning. Then, suddenly, without knowing how, I found myself as a gentleman mounted on my nag. It was carrying me away from the battlefield, running behind the *Vinchuca*, heading toward the old house. There, at the door, Doña Teresa was waiting for me with the lapdog in her arms, laughing in a frightful manner.

I also remember—but how could I forget?—that when I woke up, scared by Doña Teresa's laughter, I heard Ventura singing at the door of the hut, by the light of the moon, a *harahui*[18] similar to the Ollanta[19] one:

Urpi huahuaita chincachicuni . . .

But what am I doing? Can my young readers even understand that language, which is as foreign to them as Syrian or Chaldean?

It will be better for me to write down a poor imitation of it here in Spanish instead. This will at least give you a partial idea of those sweet popular songs, which are already forgotten today as the new lyrical muse of our national literature—quite sickly and affected, unfortunately—is only just being born.

I have lost my dove
   In the bower.
Perhaps you will find her—oh swallow, how anxiously
   You skirt by!

Listen here to her description—I'll sing it as well as
   Possible in my sorrow;
For no one can put words to
   Such beauty.

Beautiful Star of Happiness*—
   That is her name.
Her eyes the two lights
   Of morning.

Never have you seen another on this earth
   As white as her;
For she is even whiter than the pure
   Mountain snow.

Seeing her face, the proud flower
   Of the *achancara*,**
Bowed low upon her stem, humbled
   In comparison.

Her tender cooing softens the hardest
   Hearts of stone;
And a sweet aroma that gives life
   Is her breath.

When you see her, tell her that her poor Ollanta,
   Who is always with her,
Does not envy the Inca's golden litters, nor
   All his emeralds.

---

*Cusi Coyllur, daughter of the Inca Pachacutec.[20]
**White and red, it was used for the plumage as part of the decoration of the headdress, for the crest.

And tell her, tell her, that if she does not return,
  If she is not grateful,
She will die alone, by her own fire, which is
  Already dying![21]

XI

The Army of Cochabamba.
The Fields of Amiraya

The next day, everything took place just as Ventura had said it would, except for the part about Clarita's pinch, for as we approached the grandparents' house down a different path from the day before—so as to avoid the old house this time—his fiancée saw him just in time and ran to hide behind her grandmother, who was sitting at the door.

"Fiend! Scoundrel! Villain!" she yelled at him, alternatingly sticking her head out from behind the old woman's shoulder and ducking back down again.

His response to these kind words was to throw the *viscacha* at her without altering his countenance, forgetting that Mariquita was first supposed to take part of it for us, as he had said when he had cut off its tail and put the animal in the saddlebags.

I should also note that only the grandmother was there to enjoy this new pleasantry with a somewhat forced laugh. Her husband, Venancio Fuentes, had left very early for Sipe Sipe, saying that it was very much understood, following the governor's proclamation, that he was "more of a man than any of them." And no one was able to convince him that he was already ninety years old, and that, furthermore, since he would be a gentleman on a donkey, he would not be able to charge at the enemy with a lance in his hand.

When we arrived at our small house—I say "our" because, as a poor orphan, I had begun to think of it as the home of my own family—we found the entire clearing in front filled with horses, most of them hacks used as workhorses, or nags as woolly as mine. Throughout, one could see crude lances stuck into the ground or leaning against the adobe walls and trees. The riders of the horses completely filled up the passageway, the main room, and the kitchen of the house. Commander «Don» Francisco Nina, with a larger and brighter lance than all the others—which still had attached to its end the plume with the red and yellow colors of Spain—was standing near the door, on a stone *poyo* that usually served as a step for women to mount horses on their own. With the seriousness of the most consummate of brigadiers, he was ordering his soldiers to record their names on a piece of paper, with the sacristan from Sipe Sipe, «Don Bartolito», serving as his secretary and chief of staff.

When he saw Ventura and I, his normally friendly, good-natured face all of a sudden contracted and was transformed in a frightful manner, much like Alejo's—and I noticed at that point the resemblance between the two men's faces. I delivered a long speech in the appropriate manner, but his anger only grew with each one of my words, until he finally struck the stones of the *poyo* with the end of his lance and exclaimed:

"I could pierce both of you with a single thrust of my lance! This is unbearable! Grandfather has already twisted his ankle when the donkey knocked him over—he's inside, screaming in bed. . . . And now this other wretch comes back to follow me to «the war»!"

Ventura kneeled down at his feet and said to him:

"Take me, *tata*, or I will go and join the *Porteños*."

These simple words had a greater effect on him than all my previous rhetoric.

"May God bless us all!" he replied, and solemnly assented, dropping his head to his chest.

At about noon that day—it was the 13th of August of 1811—a large cloud of dust was seen in the direction of the Putina ravine. The army of our province was returning to the Valley of Cochabamba, leaving behind the useless positions it had occupied in the Arque and Tapacarí ravines.

"Mount your horses, men! Mount your horses!" Pancho yelled.

Everything was noise and confusion until finally, about a quarter of an hour later, the squadron had formed almost orderly out in the clearing. Pancho and his son mounted the beautiful horses I mentioned earlier, which they had undoubtedly kept ready and in excellent condition for this very occasion. After begging the father a thousand times and even shedding tears, I was allowed to follow them on the nag, led by an old Indian, *tata Tuli*, who rode bareback on the *Vinchuca*, with only a bridle, because the saddle was needed for the son. I and my new guide were to remove ourselves to a safe distance from them if there was any danger, far enough so that the bullets could not reach me.

As the last to head out on the road, I saw Mariquita standing at the door of the house. So as to honor the family in the presence of the patriots, she had put on her Sunday clothes, her sheepskin shoes, silver earrings, and a large silver pin—all of which were the "something really special" that her father had brought back for her from the city. She held her hands together on her chest, praying silently while two thick tears ran down her cheeks from her beautiful eyes, which were raised to the sky. Her mother must have had to stay inside to take care of the grandfather, who, although he could not put any weight on his foot, still insisted that he be given a lance and helped to mount his donkey in any manner whatsoever.

I remember hearing him yell, and more than once:

"I'm more of a man than any of them! Long live the homeland! Don't they know that «Nicolás Flores» was my father-in-law?"

It must have been around one in the afternoon when the entire army of Cochabamba was finally gathered in the prairie of Sipe Sipe, near the Amiraya River, which is the continuation of the Rocha River, but augmented by the Sulti, Anocaraire, and Viloma Rivers, and by all the torrents of the valley, before it makes its way into the Putina ravine. It was already known that Goyeneche, with his army of eight thousand men, exalted after his victory at Huaqui, had climbed up from the surroundings of Tapacarí to the heights of the Tres Cruces and descended straight through the spur of the Royal Cordillera, which levels off in the Valley of Cochabamba near the aforementioned prairie. This was the same route later taken by General Pezuela,[1] as we shall see later, and it will surely be the same route that any other general in a similar situation will take if he wishes to avoid the deep gorge of the Putina ravine, which, with its steep, rocky slopes, is as easy to guard as the unassailable Thermopylae.

I very much enjoy the writings of the Spanish historian Don Mariano Torrente about the Spanish American Revolution. He is a fanatic who always includes many charming details, and I also like the grandeur that he attributes to the patriots. He says: "The rebels' army of twelve thousand men, most of which was mounted cavalry, with its front next to the Amiraya River and its rear in the tall mountains behind it [he is referring to the low sierra that runs across the valley and separates Sipe Sipe from Quillacollo], with heavy sections detailed in the town of Sipe Sipe, would have driven back any other army which had not learned by then to match its efforts and courage to the size of the obstacle before them."[2] Meanwhile our national writers, on the other hand, assure us that the number of rebel soldiers was half as many and also stress the inadequacies of the patriots' weapons. Finally, a Chilean historian has even expressed his bizarre idea that there was no battle at all and that Goyeneche entered Cochabamba without any resistance.

From their opinions (the Spanish and the Bolivian ones only, that is, because the Chilean one is utterly foolish), I can now, as an eyewitness of all these events, solemnly clarify for my young readers that, as strange as it may sound—just like in Moliére's *Sganarelle*[3]—both are correct.

There were, in effect, more than ten thousand men gathered there to defend the nascent homeland. But the number that, for all effects and purposes, could be counted as regular troops did not reach six thousand. And included among these were some six hundred men that Brigadier Don Eustaquio Díaz Vélez[4] had brought from Chuquisaca, these being the only sections of the auxiliary army left after the defeat at Huaqui.

The infantry accounted for less than a quarter of the total number, and not all of it was armed with firearms, either. There was a long battalion with slings made of wound leather straps and the well-known *macanas*. The best armed had appalling rifles, and these were the kind with flintlock, of course. It was not unusual to see muskets and wide-mouthed blunderbusses that stood out among the files, disrupting their uniformity. And one column of about two hundred men, among whom I recognized Alejo, was quite proud of itself because of some very curious weapons of theirs, which had been recently conceived and built in the country with childlike naiveté and heroic determination. These deserve their own description and a corresponding explanation of how they were operated.

They called them cannons, but in reality they were more like harquebuses. Very white and shiny, as if they were made of silver, but actually made of tin, they were one and a quarter varas long, and thick-barreled so as to make them more stable; because of this very reason, however, they were of scant caliber, some two ounces or so. They had trunnions like regular cannons toward the middle; the vent was made of bronze; and at the back there was a very crudely built wooden butt. One person, exerting much effort, would lift the weapon up to his shoulder, where he had a small, but thick, sheepskin cushion on which to rest it; another would place a large, pitchfork-like tool in front to support the trunnions on the forked ends; and a third, who would light the fuse, was also in charge of carrying the ramrod and a jug of water to cool off the outside of the weapon after each shot. Other cannons were later invented, but it is not yet time for me to talk about them.

Half of the cavalry consisted of good troops, disciplined and trained in the previous campaign; they carried real lances and many sabers. One squadron had helmets and breastplates; two others had only breastplates. The other half of the cavalry resembled, in varying degrees, the first cavalry troop I saw back during the uprising of the 14th of September. This included the brand new squadron that the Commander Don Francisco Nina had just formed, the tail end of which was brought up by *tata* Tuli and I.

Finally, there were a few artillery men with one mortar and Unzueta's two infamous carronades. The latter were the topic of a specific remembrance by the historian Torrente because of their problematic, and hence disastrous service, at Aroma.

After recounting all these details, which are in fact the most important ones, I do not think I have the strength left to describe the outfits and the wide variety of uniforms worn by these soldiers. Suffice it to say that the most veteran among them came from a long campaign and a horrendous defeat, with their basic uniforms in shreds, and that the newest recruits had responded to their sacred obligation dressed, at best, in their Sunday clothes, without asking nor expecting to be given anything—their saddlebags were filled with the cold foods prepared by their wives or daughters, who had stayed behind, crying under the straw roofs of their ranchos. And yes, I will add that just as they were, as my imagination is able to paint them in my mind—and I regret that I am no Goya[5] to reproduce them in an eternal painting—they seem to me a thousand times more beautiful and respectable than today's soldiers, who dress in elegant, French-styled materials, who wear white gloves and false beards,* who break up congresses with the brute force of their weapons, who pitilessly murder the defenseless populace, who hand over Bolívar's blood-stained medal to a backstabbing idiot, who laugh at the laws, mock the constitution, betray the country and sell themselves. . . . No, I cannot go on! . . . Mercedes! I'm choking! . . .

As you can see, I have had to interrupt my story and scream out for my Merceditas. The anger was suffocating me. But I am calm again, and shall now continue.

That motley and ill-clad army had one sole emblem—of which my sweet, lifelong companion has just reminded me—shining brightly with her gold and silver, her pearls, and her other precious stones. It was the image of the patron Virgin of the city, worshipped at the Church of the Matriz ever since the founding of the city. Every year, the most illustrious ladies tended to give very luxurious lamé dresses and the most valuable jewels as offerings to her. She was now called "*la Patriota*," because hers was the most majestic religious ceremony performed after the first "shout" for independence was heard. This is also why she had been brought to the battlefield.

She was on her platform, on the shoulders of four colossal *val-*

---

*I have already stated at the beginning the year in which I began to write these memoirs.

lunos,[6] in the middle of the column of the harquebusiers that I described above. When I went to look at her, with my hat in my hands, I saw a group of women from the hamlets surrounding Suticollo, Amiraya, and Caramarca arriving before her. They flooded her with wildflowers that they had collected in their skirts, and said to her, in Quechua:

"Merciful mother, guiding light for those in distress, protect us and all the patriots with your beautiful cloak!"

I can only say a few words about the main leaders commanding the army, for I did not know very many of them by name.

Governor Rivero looked like he was over forty years old, very respectable, majestic even. A pure *criollo*, white and blond, he had light eyes, an aquiline nose, and a thick mustache that drooped down over his Spanish-style mutton chops. He wore a gallooned tricorn and a red silk poncho draped over his shoulders, revealing below it his blue, embroidered jacket and the baldric that I well knew, for it had been made by my mother's hands. He also wore tall riding boots with silver spurs, and his horse, which he rode very skillfully, was one of those beautiful dapple-gray horses from the Andalusian race that Goyeneche later destroyed and that has only recently, with much difficulty, been brought back.

I saw Don Eustaquio Díaz Vélez for the first time when he passed quickly in front of me, and I later learned his name and post from Ventura, when the troops cheered him on. He seemed shorter and portlier than the governor. He had very intense, bright eyes, his face was darkened from the sun and the elements, and his beard was thick and full. His military uniform was worn out and discolored, and he commanded—like only an Argentine can command—a gorgeous, sorrel-colored colt with a waving mane worthy of a lion.

And from a distance I was able to distinguish Don Esteban Arze, the delegate representing the troops from Cliza, in front of his gigantic *vallunos*, as well as Guzmán Quitón, who was leading the new regiment that he had formed in the country, as I stated earlier, in the absence of the governor.

As soon as the troops were in their columns, Rivero and Díaz Vélez proceeded to examine the rank and file and then address them. From where I was, I could only hear the "hurrahs" with which they were greeted. I believe I only heard the name of Fernando VII invoked once, and that the response to it was much less raucous than the cheering at the mention of the Junta of Buenos Aires, of our province, and, above all, of the magical name of our homeland, which, although not yet widely known, was already the main yearning desire of all my plain and simple compatriots.

Just when the most enthusiastic "hurrahs" were heard throughout the field, a group of men on horseback appeared on top of the hill coming from the direction of Sipe Sipe. The man in front waved a white and red flag, which had probably just recently been put together. A moment later, a column of smoke was seen, on the same hillside, from a fire that one of them had lit.

This must have been the party assigned to be the lookout, for immediately the generals shouted out their urgent orders, and everything became a coming and going of mounted officers riding across the entire field. The infantry, with the exception of the column of harquebusiers, marched ahead to the town of Sipe Sipe; as I later observed, they then took their positions in the surrounding hills and behind the walls of the cultivated lands and the lands used for pasture. The harquebusiers, for their part, occupied the banks of the river, hiding along the walls of the ravine. The bulk of the army, in other words, the cavalry, took its place to the left of river and formed into its squadrons in the fields of Amiraya. Finally, the image that served as the army's emblem was taken to the rear and placed in a prominent location, at the base of the low sierra which, as I have said, runs across that part of the valley, between Sipe Sipe and Quillacollo.

The lookout party, meanwhile, was quickly descending the slope on foot, each rider leading his horse by the bridle. An endless line of bayonets had begun to sparkle on the long crest behind them—these were the first troops of the vanguard of the enemy army.

My companion, *tata* Tuli, as much for his own personal safety as to obey the orders of his master «Don» Pancho—who now repeated it with a hand signal—took me at that point where he wished to go. I had no choice but to follow him, for even if I had not wanted to, my nag, as I have said many times, was a mere extension of the mare's tail.

He took me very far away, as far as Caramarca, where we took our position at a knoll in the low sierra. It was a clear day; small white clouds, like puffs of cotton, drifted across the sky. A strong, but pure wind, which was normal for that season, was blowing from the Viloma ravine; it effectively swept away the dust raised by the troops in the fields so that we were able to see, from where we were, the great battle which, by then, was obviously imminent.

The vanguard of the enemy army descended into the field in many parallel lines, trotting down the hill in a tight formation, just as one would expect from well-disciplined, veteran troops. It was composed of the Royal Battalions of Lima and Paruro, a light column of chasseurs, and six pieces of mountain artillery. These last had already been mounted on the crest of the hill, and they must have caused an incredible amount of work for the men who had pulled them up that very steep slope. Their leader, the Brigadier Don Juan Ramírez, whom I believe I saw more than once throughout day, always on horseback, in front of his men, was to reach great fame during the war for his diligence and his coarseness and his stupidity. One could say of him that he was at once a lion, an eagle, and a rhinoceros.

It must have been after three in the afternoon when the cannons of the vanguard opened fire on the positions of our infantry. The famous carronades from Aroma fired back immediately and with good aim, according to later accounts by the Spaniards. Then, at that point, the slope became filled with the bulk of Goyeneche's army.

It is said that Goyeneche ordered Tristán[7] to speed up the pace of the rear and hurried the advance of the core divisions in order to be at the head of his own grenadiers from Cuzco and personally direct the vigorous attack. Half an hour later the infantry of the army of the patriots was dispersed by the attack. After a disorganized retreat, they were able to reorganize themselves at the hills of Suticollo, but only briefly, before being definitively beat back to the banks of the river, where the column of harquebusiers was still in position.

Then, there was a moment of rest. Goyeneche wanted to gather all his troops and arrange them in the best manner to send them again into the field of Amiraya.

"Let's get away, my son. . . . Let's go to that hidden corner near Vilomilla!" *tata* Tuli said to me, terrified.

And without waiting for an answer, he spurred on the *Vinchuca* and headed away from the knoll. He crossed the river and would have continued on to where he had said, forcing me to go along, had I not begged and threatened him a thousand times for us to stop at Payacollo and take another prominent position there, on the hill that rises there out of the prairie like a natural cone.

The sun was now nearly touching the crest of the Cordillera, and the wind was more severe, blowing clouds of dust and smoke toward the opening of the Putina ravine. We could still see the main action of the battle.

The enemy's army was moving into the banks of the river with its vanguard deployed in small sections, while its cavalry advanced along one of its flanks, and their cannons fired from their perfect position abandoned by the patriots on the ravine. I do not think that the bullets of our harquebusiers would have slowed down their attack even for an instant. Their range was too short, the projectile could not be forced without ruining the weapon's bore, and, finally, it became unusable after at most six or seven shots.

The numerous cavalry of the patriots took on the main charge of the first enemy columns on the left side of the river; they were driven back and lost their formations, and the defeat seemed to be consummated. A very small party along the rear fled toward the rugged low sierra. I remember very well seeing a shiny object that must have been the image of the Virgin. She was saved—except for the fingers of her right hand, which had been shot off—by Jacinto Gómez, who was the first to reach the city with her and the terrible news.

The Brigadiers Rivero and Díaz Vélez, the inexhaustible Don Esteban Arze, and the strange Guzmán still managed to reorganize a few squadrons. They tried to flank the enemy's army along both sides, so as to then attack it from behind. This last effort, which seemed at first to promise good results, ran aground, however, before the tactics and discipline of the opposing side, which presented compact and formidable cadres of sharp bayonets along the left wing, while, at the same time, the Spanish cavalry victoriously drove back the attack along the right wing.

As night began to fall, all that was left was the pursuit and pitiless massacring of the patriots. The majority of these fled to their right, climbing up the riverbed toward where I was. This was, in essence, the safest path of retreat, since it was very difficult and dangerous for the troops on horseback to climb the low sierra that I have mentioned often in this chapter.

Tata Tuli once again dragged me along with him, and I could hear rifle shots in the direction of our small house. My entire body trembled nervously; I wanted to go there at all cost; and, with an extraordinary effort, I managed to take control of the halter with which the mare was muzzled.

"Let's get away! Let's get away, for God's sake!" the Indian was screaming desperately.

A stray bullet—either from those who fled or from their pursuers—whizzed over our heads. This made *tata* Tuli decide to jump off the horse. He crept down into a deep trench and ran off like a madman, while the frightened *Vinchuca* pulled away from me and ran through the field, followed as always by my nag.

Night was growing darker; my mount was out of control, and I did not know where I would end up—that is, if I was not first thrown and torn to pieces on the rocky ground, for it was very difficult by then for me to stay on my saddle. I had let go of the reins to grasp the front saddlebow with both hands. The nag had gone wild, jumping trenches, ridges, and walls in order to catch up to his inseparable companion, the mare. Finally, I saw before me a thick column of smoke, followed by the actual flames of the fire, reaching higher and higher toward the sky. And, illuminated by the evil glow of the fire, between the rocks, I thought I saw our small house, the grove of fig trees, and some strange-looking shapes in the clearing out in front of the house.

A moment later my horse stopped so suddenly and gave such a violent jump that it threw me over its head. Then, instead of breaking my skull, as I was sure would happen, I landed on a soft, furry body which did not move nor give any sign of life.

I stood up. At first I saw that the shed used as a kitchen was burning. Then, by the light of the flames, I recognized the body on which I had landed as Ventura's beautiful horse, which he and Mariquita called *Consuelo*[8]—I had seen Mariquita pet and feed ears of corn or clumps of salt with her gentle hands to that horse so many times! Its head had been smashed by a bullet, and there was a pool of blood in front of its snout.

Not far from there, I found human corpses: a grenadier with his leather cap down by his beard, lying on his back with a broken-off lance sticking into his chest; and near him, the bodies of Pancho and of his son, lying so close together that I knew they had either been killed as they hugged, or that they had dragged themselves so as to die in each other's arms.

I ran screaming toward the house, but at the door I tripped over another body, which I thought would have been Petrona's. I went to the kitchen to get a torch, came back, and—my God! I don't know, I cannot believe I have to write these things! I thought I saw on the ground—or rather I did actually see, for, horrendous as it was, it was undoubtedly real—the body of Mariquita. She was stretched out on her back, her arms crossed on her chest, her body half-naked as the embers from the burning roof fell on it! At that point, the roof collapsed, and a volcano of black smoke and burning sparks rose into the sky.

And that is how I saw, as a child, one of the most dreadful scenes of the war! Oh! War must not be waged again in the world except by desperate peoples with a purpose as grand and just as that which America invoked in 1810! Its consequences are always the cruelest for the most innocent and the most helpless, like that poor girl who I saw alive for the last time praying silently at the door of that small, humble house, in which none of its previous owners would live again!

How can I now—if that is what you expect—express what I suffered, my horror, my fright? . . . I believe I fled, that I circled round the clearing, falling and getting up many times. A deep silence surrounded me. The calm moon had risen and spread its silver rays over these scenes, and I do not know if it was from the glow of the fire or from this gentle light, but they now seemed even more terrible and painful.

I heard a few soft whistles from among the fig trees. A voice that I recognized at once cautiously called out, one by one, the names of all the inhabitants of the house—who of course could no longer answer him. A moment later Alejo was at my side, and I held on to him strongly, sobbing.

"What is this?" he asked me. "Where are they?"

"Dead!" I answered.

"My God!" he replied. Then he set down on the ground another inanimate body, that of a boy of about my age, whom he had been carrying draped over his shoulder. "Before hearing what you have to say," Alejo continued, "he," pointing to the child, "is to blame for me not being killed in the battle. He insisted in carrying the ramrod and the fuse, he was wounded very early, he grabbed on to my feet, crying, calling out for his grandmother, and I had to flee with him to save him. Poor Dionisio!"

Then he ran off to identify the corpses. He entered the house and looked among the debris from the kitchen, burning his hands in the process. He took a long time to return to where I stood, silent, trembling, with Dionisio's body at my feet. He came back crying. He was sobbing more than me, and I was a child. . . . What am I saying?! He was crying and sobbing, I should say, like those strong, simple men, those primitive natures who are all heart and soul when they love those who know how to be loved!

"There is nothing for us to do here," he said to me after a while, when he could speak again between his sobs. "We can no longer help, nor receive help from anyone. I want to assure you, though, that I will come back to bury them, even if it gets me killed in the process. . . . Which would be better yet: I wouldn't have to go on living! And this one," he said, referring to Dionisio's body, "we'll leave next to his poor grandfather, who is also dead, on the dais."

I followed Alejo blindly. But before we got very far, he stopped and asked me:

"Why didn't they run away?"

"I believe," I answered, "that the women stayed behind to care for the grandfather, who couldn't walk. . . ."

"And the others," he finished for me, "returned to defend them and were killed in their own home!"

Of what we did afterward I have only vague recollections. I believe that at one point, when we came near a torrent, which must have been the Viloma River, I threw myself face down and drank avidly from the warm, brackish water that runs over the red sands, like blood. I remember that we arrived—I do not know if I was on my own feet or in my guide's arms—to a hut, and that some dogs were barking furiously at its door. And I also remember that several people forced me to lie down on a bed of sheepskins; that these burned like the embers I saw falling on Mariquita's body and which were also falling on mine; that I tried to flee, but was either held back or weighed down by a very heavy weight, such as the horse that lay dead in the clearing of Las Higueras.

XII

An Astonishing but True and Well-Known Event

When I awoke, I was lying on the ground, on top of the sheep-skins, with a coarse, wool blanket wrapped around me, and a very low and completely smoke-darkened roof above me. I turned on my side with some effort and saw on Indian squatting on his haunches, leaning back against the rough stones of the wall, wearing a dented *montera* and a black poncho that covered his entire body, down to his feet.

"Where's Alejo?" I asked him in Quechua, or rather in that awful dialect used by the brutish descendants of the sons of the sun.

"He left three days ago," he answered.

"But I came here with him last night!"

"That was the night of «the war»."

"And how many days has it been since then?"

"Today is Sunday; «the war» on Tuesday. One, two, three, four . . . five days!"

"But . . . what has happened to me?"

"When «Don» Alejo brought you in his arms, like a little baby, you didn't want to lie down. You were very angry and fought us. The next day the *Callaguaya* came; he gave you some water with boiled herbs that smelled very strong; he put a mustard plaster of *centella** on you, and I think he has cured you. This morning he drew some lines on a stone with a piece of charcoal; he blew into a handful of coca leaves; he studied how the leaves fell; and he told me that when you woke up today you would be healthy and ask me for food."

The *Callaguaya* must have been one of those Indian doctors and fortunetellers, from the Province of Larecaja of La Paz, who still travel even today throughout much of South America practicing their strange profession, carrying herbs and drugs that only they know about.** I understood that I had had some kind of cerebral fever. I felt very weak, and my whole body hurt, but especially my neck, arms, and legs, where the terrible *centella* had taken its repulsive effects. Still, I sat up and began to get into my clothes, which I found at my side.

"Don Alejo," the Indian was saying in the meantime, "left me a royal peso for the *Callaguaya*, another so that I could fix him a *merienda* and buy him some *mistela*,[2] and a *tostón*[3] for myself. He left very distressed, to 'bury them.' He wanted the priest to go with him, wearing his choir cloak and carrying the high cross, out to Las Higueras, to take them back to the graveyard."

"My God! I haven't been dreaming!" I exclaimed.

"The others," my interlocutor went on impassively, "were buried, without anyone saying prayers over them, in very long, deep ditches dug out by the Indians from the communities of Olmos-Rancho and Payacollo. There were a lot of them. . . . I don't know how many, but alive they would have filled an entire plaza during a fiesta."***

He stopped talking for a moment to put the *aculli*, in other words a bunch of coca leaves, followed by the corresponding little

---

*An herb with fleecy, star-shaped leaves.

**Editor's Note: Mr. Claudio Pinilla, an adjunct to the legation that went to represent Bolivia in 1883 for the Centenary of the Liberator Bolívar, recounts that he encountered one of them on his way back from Venezuela, on a steamboat heading down the Pacific.[1]

***There were close to one thousand of them. Torrente comes up short when he says: "The main spoils of that celebrated victory were: 8 cannons, one mortar, one flag, 70 prisoners, and 600 dead which were found the next day strewn out on the battlefield." I will add that the cannons were the tin ones that we already know about, and that no one can truly be made to believe that there were 70 patriots left alive in the hands of the victors.[4]

piece of *llucta*, or the ashes mixed with potatoes, in his mouth. Then he went on talking as he chewed:

"Don Alejo asked me to take you to the Church of St. Augustine on my donkey."

"And where did he go?" I asked him.

"To mourn with the Grandmother Doña *Chepa* and with Clarita," he answered. And he added, "Poor Dionisio had not died; they're giving him all their care, but they say that he will still die soon," always completely impassive.

"Do you know who Dionisio is?"

"Clarita's brother, who went to the city to make lances with Alejo."

"This, too!" I said to myself and started crying, while the Indian kept chewing his *aculli* with that indifference brought about in his oppressed race by unremitting suffering and with which they face all miseries of life.

Two days later—for it was necessary for me to wait this long until I was recovered—the Indian *Hismicho*, my host, led me to the banks of the Rocha on his donkey. From there I walked very slowly the rest of the way to the Church of St. Augustine. The streets were full of drunk soldiers who were shouting threats against the incorrigible Cochabambian rebels. Yelling, and *huainos*[5] and *sacaqueñas*[6] were heard from the *chicherías*[7] playing to the beat of the *quenas*[8] and *charangos*.

The victors from Amiraya had pursued the fleeing patriots for a league and a half, as far as Vinto. There, they were ordered to regroup by their general, who chose not to move into the feared city at night, when he knew that he could enter it a few hours later, by daylight, and not face any resistance at all. Thus, he took another road, to the left, climbing half a league up the banks of the Anocaraire River, and camped in the Anocaraire hamlet, a wooded area that is one of the most pleasant of the vast valley.

The next morning, he received a delegation from the Cabildo in Quillacollo asking him to guarantee the protection of the defeated city, which he granted. A short while later, Governor Rivero and one of the members of the Junta of War, Don Pedro Miguel Quiroga, appeared before him to make the same request. A few days before, Rivero had written him quite a noteworthy letter appealing to him, as an American, to stop the imprudent resolve to continue ahead with such a disastrous war, the unavoidable conclusion of which would be the triumph of the new ideas. "After everything has been said and done," the letter said, "your Lordship will not have achieved anything other than to have your name be execrated, and you shall miss the opportunity to erase the horrible impressions left by the event that took place in La Paz in the previous year of 1809. . . ."[9] Imagine the satisfaction that Goyeneche must have then felt with Rivero defeated and begging before him!

That day he moved into the city, victorious. But before doing so, he stopped his royal troops at the outskirts, at Chimba de Vergara, and proudly placed his flag on that prominent, overlooking position.

In a written statement to the Provincial Junta, or rather to the only member of that body who had given in, he said: "Tomorrow, between ten and eleven, I shall realize my entrance into the city, wherein I will proceed directly to the Church of Our Lady of Mercy, where the Sacrifice of the Mass will be celebrated with a simple *Te Deum*[10] before the entire clergy. . . ." And he concluded with these very strange words: "«It being my exclusive right to choose my lodgings», I will confirm from there to the entire community the peaceful nature of my intentions."*

The victor from Chacaltaya, Huaqui, and Amiraya was not all there! He thought the public buildings were mined and that the insurgents could blow him up into smithereens!

My beloved teacher welcomed me with open arms and held me tightly while I cried for a very long time against his chest. Then he had me sit down and began to speak first, as if he feared what I might have to say:

"Alejo sent someone from Vinto, where he is staying with the poor Grandmother, who has told me everything. I have been impatiently waiting for you, worried about your health, my son. I had predicted our side's unfortunate outcome. What could our simple and naive peasants, so proud of their tin cannons, do against an

---

*I wish to clarify, once and for all, that I have before me, on my table, the documents from which I cite, which help to refresh my own memories.

army with such immensely superior resources, weapons, and discipline? But what happened with Francisco Nina and his family. . . . My God! It's horrible! I can barely stand to recall it, and I quivered at the very thought of hearing it from you again."

After a sad moment of silence, he suddenly said to me:

"Have you ever seen anyone more ingenuous or of nobler intentions than that humble family?"

"No, sir," I answered; "I had begun to believe I was among my own blood, as if I were related to them."

"And you were not altogether wrong," he replied. "The Grandmother's father was Flores, who was related to Calatayud and whose death he tried to avenge with a new rebellion, but this only got him a dreadful execution. She and her entire family consider themselves your mother's relatives. They did not come to see her because of their sensitiveness, common to peasants. They believed that this would not have pleased 'the child,' or that she would have been embarrassed of them. But they loved her from afar; they served her without her knowing it. . . . Do you remember the black cow that Alejo used to bring by the house every morning so triumphantly? The Grandmother . . . poor old woman! She must be weeping so much now! The Grandmother, I was saying, sent Dionisio to the city when Alejo told her the prescription I had ordered!"

Then, as if to escape his sad thoughts in any way possible, he loudly opened the door and rushed outside, saying:

"Let's go, quickly! Let's go!"

I followed him, silently. But I was unable to hide my surprise, my chagrin, and my vexation when we turned town the street that led to Doña Teresa's house.

"It is absolutely imperative," he told me; "the lady has offered and even sworn to send you to Chuquisaca in less than ten days. You need to study, Juanito, now more than ever. One day it will be necessary for you to serve your unfortunate country, and to be fully conscious of your duties as a man and a citizen. For your homeland has not died; it cannot be buried in the trenches of Amiraya. Your homeland will rise again a thousand times from the very blood of those who have sacrificed themselves on her behalf."

As the door that led to the small chapel was locked, my teacher, without announcing himself, opened the vestibule door with the halberd on it. When we entered the drawing room, we saw Father Arredondo sitting comfortably on the widest armchair at one of the *Berenguela* tables; within his reach there was a small tray with pastries and a large glass of a well-aged Spanish wine known as "*el Católico*,"[11] but which was actually more Moorish than Boabdil, and did not have one drop of baptismal water in it. A very happy, rejuvenated Doña Teresa, in half-mourning, wearing enormous diamond earrings and a necklace with pearls the size of pigeon eggs, was sitting on the cushioned bench on the other side of the room. My teacher greeted them by nodding his head and began to say:

"Pardon me, your Excellencies. The need to bring—"

But Doña Teresa, who had already seen me, interrupted him, exclaiming:

"What joy! There is the poor boy! My remorse would have been eternal if anything had happened to him. For I sent him with Pancho—our Lord is listening to us; may he punish me if I am not speaking the truth—without knowing what that family was. . . . May God forgive them!"

My teacher made a gesture of impatience, but he controlled himself and went to sit at the opposite end of the bench. I followed, and remained standing by his side.

The lady of the house continued speaking:

"As I have said to your Grace, and also to the Most Reverend Father, the Prelate of Our Lady of Mercy. . . ."

The individual alluded to acknowledged by gesturing. He tried to speak; but his mouth was full of pastries, so he opted to drink half a glass of wine instead.

"Now we can calmly, without fears—blessed be our Apostle St. James!—worry about the education of this luckless little orphan. You will go to Chuquisaca, to the University of San Javier, young man. . . . See how fortunate you are! And you will be going with my own son, Don Pedro de Alcántara 'Marquis' of Altamira, and . . . this truly is beyond your wildest dreams! You will go as part of the entourage of his Lordship the Illustrious General Don José Manuel de Goyeneche y Barreda!"

"Oh! His Lordship's kindness is endless!" added Father

Arredondo. "Such Christian feeling! Such wisdom! Such excellent judgment in all his words and actions! It was inspiring to see his humility and compunction at the solemn *Te Deum* that we sang for him at our church. And afterward, in the humble collation at the banquet that we gave for him in our refectory, he amused us so with his affability, with his charming speeches, and with his cordial acknowledgments. Above all is the generosity and liberality he has shown to these rebellious people, to whom, far from punishing, he throws handfuls of money from his balcony!"

At this very particular moment, we heard hurried steps out in the patio. The large door slammed open, hitting against one of the armchairs to the side of it. The servants then entered, terrified, in the following manner and order: Feliciana, carrying a silver tray on which there was a grenadier with a golden rifle made of almond paste; Clemente, with a crystal platter covered by a very finely laced cloth; the mulatta, barely balancing in her two hands an enormous crystal glass containing some precious refreshing drink that I did not recognize; the mestizas, carrying wicket filigree baskets on their heads filled with exquisite preserved fruits; and the *pongo*, all cleaned up, wearing a new *tocuyo* shirt, and loaded down with a heavy tray of ice creams molded into the shapes of eagles and lions. All these things were set down on the tables in the middle of a grave silence. At first, Doña Teresa looked on bewildered. Then she became distressed, irate, and finally mad with pain and anger. She proceeded to hold the following conversation with Feliciana, who was confused, trembling, and out of breath:

"What is this? For God's sakes, what has happened?"

"Oh, my mistress! I don't think I can speak!"

"Go on, speak, girl!"

"I don't know where to begin with all this."

"Begin wherever you can."

"Well, here I go. . . . But, no. . . . I can't!"

"You're killing me, you wretch!"

"Well, when we reached the door of the antechamber, the gentleman aide-de-camp told us to give these things over to the majordomo, in the dining room. But I told him that we were to deliver your Ladyship's present in person."

"Yes, that's right."

"We went into the drawing room. The good gentleman general, more beautiful than the sun, was surrounded by many people, but still he deigned to come to see us."

"I don't doubt it. And then?"

"I gave him your Ladyship's present."

"Did you tell him everything that I told you to, or did you leave anything out, or decide to add some stupid thing of your own?"

"No, madam, my mistress. I only said to him what your Ladyship has had me memorize since yesterday: 'That it is to the one who has defeated the rebels, to my *chunco*,[12] that the grenadier has been brought so as to greet the invincible general—'"

"Fine . . . go on!"

"His Excellency grabbed the piece of paper that the almond paste grenadier carried in his rifle and lifted the laced cloth covering the royal dish a little, but. . . . I don't know. . . ."

"What? Go on, finish!"

"He smiled in a frightening manner. Then he read the paper, and he crumpled it up and threw it to the ground."

"Blessed Virgin! This is unbearable!"

"'Tell your mistress,' he yelled, 'that my generosity and clemency with this country of incorrigible mestizos does not give her the right to mock me with these idiotic and—'"

"This is unbearable! What does his Excellency mean by saying that thing about the mestizos? Doesn't he know that I am a Zagardua y Altamira, and that I do not have a single drop of Indian blood in me? I am a pure Spaniard, a descendent of Adam himself! What a thought! It's as shameless as if I were to call him 'the *cholo mocontullo*[13] from Arequipa'!"

"At that point the good learned Honor Don Sulpicio came in and said something I didn't hear to the aide-de-camp. 'What does that stuffed doll want?' his Excellency asked. 'He is asking if the verses that the grenadier carried have already been read,' the aide-de-camp answered. 'Yes, the Devil take it!' his Excellency replied. 'They're horrible, evil words. Have that ridiculous monkey taken to the barracks of the grenadiers in Cuzco, where he'll learn how to make them more harmonious!'"

"My blessed, strong, eternal Lord, what sins of ours are we

being punished for? And what will become now of the poor god-mother of my child, and of my poor Little Seraph?"

"Then his learned Honor, very afraid, yelled out: 'But the Most Reverend Father Arredondo has said to me that my verses would very much please your Excellency!' 'The Father,' his Excellency yelled back even louder, 'is a jackass. . . . No, no, I'm wrong. He's a well-fattened pig!'"

"What? That's what his Excellency said about me?" the individual alluded to blurted out, jumping out of his seat as if he were shot from a spring in spite of his immense bulk.

"Yes, sir, that's what he said," Feliciana confirmed, and went on with her story: "An officer dragged his good Honor out by his lapels, and another pushed him from behind, while he said things I didn't understand in Latin. I thought that we should leave at that point, but first I picked up the paper and have brought it back with me."

"Give it to me!" the Father snorted, and grabbed it from her hand at once.

Doña Teresa, for her part, ran over to examine the tray with the royal dish. The following exclamations were then, in turn, heard from her lips and from Father Arredondo's:

"My god! This says: 'Long live the homeland!' But I myself wrote 'Long live Spain!' on it with fragrant cloves!"

"And this is the most abominable of heresies! It's a copy of what the infidels call *'los droites del home'*!"*

General shock and astonishment on the part of all of them. Doña Teresa could not control herself. She exploded and jumped like a wild beast on the luckless servant. She tried to scratch her and pushed her back very hard, so that she nearly toppled over.

"Leave, you dreadful Negro! And take these animals with you! I don't want to see anyone! Absolve me of my sins, Father! I'm dying! It's hopeless. . . . I'm dying!"

---

*Editor's Note: The Father must have pronounced these words as they are written, in a grotesquely adulterated French, in the manner of the most renowned men of letters of the time. It should be added that we have heard this episode recounted with a few variations. It is possible that the very worthy Colonel La Rosa has embellished it slightly, carried away by his vivid imagination.

Then she turned quickly toward my teacher. Her appearance was horrible, livid; she looked like a Gorgon.

"How you must be enjoying this!" she said to him. "Go on, laugh, you rebel rouser!"

My teacher opted to pull his hood over his head at this point, and to depart without saying a word. I more than hurried off toward my room. At the entrance to the hallway, I saw the poor servants, all gathered round Clemente, and I heard him say to them, with deep conviction:

"Her Ladyship, our mistress, doesn't want to believe in the *duende*. But it's the *duende*, the very same *duende* as the last time, girls! No one could have gone into the cool of the garden passageway where we placed the sweets. The lady of the house herself closed the door and locked it twice. . . . I saw her put the keys away in her pocket. . . . I saw it with these very eyes that you see before you!"

At night, in spite of the events of the day, they did not fail to call me into the dining room. The children were still there. Carmencita came to sit on my lap. She put her little arms around my neck, and I kissed her beautiful head of hair. Pedro de Alcántara looked at me like an idiot; he did not say a word, nor did he make any gesture when I greeted him respectfully. Agustín came up to me, took a chair at my side, and wanted me to tell him what a battle was like. I offered gladly to tell him everything that he wanted to know, but not until the following day—the strong impressions I had suffered and my recent illness had left me somewhat stunned.

After eating my dinner, as I headed back to my room, I saw that the servants had once again gathered round Clemente, this time in a corner of the dining room. And I heard him once again say, with the same conviction and seriousness:

"It's the *duende*, girls."

To distract my mind, I opened Moreto's comedy to the place where I had left it, which was marked by a tear of mine, as is stated in Chapter IX of these memoirs. It was scene XIII of act III, between King Don Pedro the Cruel and a Dead man. These last two words made me tremble, but I went on reading:

Dead man: Wait.
King: Who is calling me?
Dead man: 'Tis I.
King: Who is this? Shadow or ghost, what do you want?
Dead man: To tell you that as of now
You shall be turned to stone. . . .

At this point two very cold hands covered my eyes. My hair stood on end; I was so frightened that I could not even scream. A somewhat restrained laugh behind me calmed me down a little; the hands lifted off; I turned around. . . . But my curious readers, who surely believe in *duendes* much less than I did back then, must have certainly guessed who it was by now. It was my friend *El Overo*, in flesh and blood—the *Gringo's* son, the "scoundrel" Luisito Cros, as my teacher called him.

"I gave you a good fright, didn't I!" he said, laughing.
"And with good cause," I answered, very upset.
"I'm sorry, Juanito . . . but that's how I am!"
"I know you too well, and I don't ever want to see you!"
"But I'm dying to see you."
"What do you want? How did you get in?"
"I'll answer these questions and many others that I can guess you have in a moment, but then you'll have to answer the ones I ask you. First of all, you should know that over a year ago I used to come to this house, like I do now, to amuse myself. I won't tell you all the things I did to frighten the sambo and the Negro woman; it was more evil than the things real *duendes* do. But my father came back from Santa Cruz, where he had gone to make bronze sugar presses, or to bring back some boxes filled with dried herbs, stuffed mounted birds, and bottled snakes for the *gringo* of all *gringos*, Don Teodor Hahenke[14]; and he set me straight with beatings. . . . Such beatings, Juanito! Unbelievable! I turned into a saint, even more of one than you are . . . I swear. And only one thing has brought me out of my praiseworthy path toward reform. Yesterday I heard a lot of noise in the garden—since, you should know, I live right over there, under that roof that you can see through the round window

that lets in light during the day and the cool wind from the Tunari at night—and I watched, and saw, and came in at night with a lantern of my father's, and . . . and so on, and so on, because the rest I'm sure you can figure out for yourself."

"But how did you do the thing with 'the rights of man'?"

"My father spends much time with those things. I stole one of his papers, knowing that he'll have my scalp for it. His Honor's verses are right here. They're very beautiful, I don't understand them, since they're in Latin. Listen! '*Invictus Caesar.* . . .'[15] But you can read them better than me, since you know how to assist at Mass."

"Tell me, instead, how you got in?"

"Through the round window, my friend. Could anything be easier than that? Then I hid under the bed, not to scare you, but because I was afraid you would come in with another person. And now, will you answer my questions?"

"I will do it so as to be rid of you."

"That won't happen! Let's take it one thing at a time. Do you forgive me?"

"Well. . . . I forgive you!"

"Will you want to talk to me sometimes?"

"Frankly, I think that I will eventually like having your company."

"Long live—Oh, hell! I almost yelled and had us both beheaded."

"Yes, it's better to be discreet."

"I'm going to be a. . . . What does his Honor call it? Ah, a Ulysses.[16] And what have they been saying around here about my prank?"

I recounted to him parts of the scene I had witnessed. But I was not—I could not be—in the mood to laugh like him, and I soon wanted to put an end to our conversation. So he hugged me affectionately, gave me a kiss even, I believe, and left like a cat, climbing back up and out the window through which he had entered.

XIII

Arze and Rivero

As ordered by your Excellency in your written communication of the 22nd of January, the dispatches of Don Rivero—the Colonel and Brigadier as per the titles bestowed upon him by the Junta of Buenos Aires—have been gathered under the Prefect Don Mariano Antezana. . . . His current condition is of concern to me. . . .

WRITTEN COMMUNICATION FROM ARZE TO PUEYRREDÓN[1]

The General Don José Manuel de Goyeneche, a native of Arequipa, who was destined to be the Spanish Grandee and the Overseer of Huaqui—although his fame would have been better served if he had been simply a good American patriot—did not speak without cause when he bragged of the generosity with which he would treat that country of incorrigible mestizos, of "that evil mix, which is worse there than anywhere else," as the Marqués de Castel-Fuerte said in his writings about the uprising of Calatayud.

After his victory in the bitterly fought battle of Amiraya and the slaughtering of the defeated patriots that followed it, when the committee of peaceful residents from the city and, a short while later, Don Francisco del Rivero himself appeared before him asking him to guarantee the protection of the city, he declared that he would be "as merciful as Caesar after Pharsalia." Perhaps that is what his learned Honor Burgulla's beautiful Latin verses were meant to express, only better. The general wanted to try a policy that would be the opposite of the one of the terrifying atrocities that he and all the Spaniards had at first attempted, when they tried to drown the revolution in blood. And, although it was actually better, it was not fated to give him any more satisfactory results. Even if the entire Colonial system had been burnt to the ground, there would have been no way to put out Murillo's fire. The revolution was one of those great historical events, disastrous according to some, but destined to succeed according to all of us who believed in Divine Providence, as was the custom—and perhaps the only good one—during the times of which I speak.

Blind to this truth—which unfortunately did not illuminate his mind—and under the illusion that the country had been pacified, he continued on to Chuquisaca, leaving Don Antonio Allende behind him as the governor—a praiseworthy and peaceful resident, well respected by everyone—and a garrison of a hundred men under the Commander Santiestevan. He also wished to take with him—which he did—a squadron from Cochabamba, to prove to the Viceroyalties of Perú and Buenos Aires, where his name was already well known, that he now counted on the loyalty and support of the "most rebellious of all the provinces."*

His personal entourage, however, included two people less than it should have: the primogeniture Don Pedro de Alcántara «Marquis» of Altamira, and Don Juan of . . . "of nowhere, nor of anyone." Thanks to the *duende*, General Goyeneche would never think of him, nor much less feel any great loss. I do not know what my traveling companion thought, if it was possible for him to have any thoughts at all, about the renowned University of San Javier. For my part, I confess I did not regret it at all, namely because of how utterly repugnant I felt it would be to travel in that manner. And neither have I ever regretted, in the rest of my life, the tragedy of not having my mind enlightened by that source of light, nor of failing to drink from the waters of the Inisterio³ found there, which they used to say were as wonderful as the ones from the

---

*Editor's Note: The Spaniards kept the name of Cochabamba for one of their army units up until the very Battle of Ayacucho, even though there was not a single soldier from Cochabamba in it.²

Peninsula. What would I have been able to learn there? Did I not have something closer to me in the books, even torn and mutilated as they were, of the famous room of the *duende*? How could I have learned there everything that I have learned about the world from the misery and misfortune that is taught in the school of the infinite, unexpected turns provided by Divine Providence?

Even Latin, the most emphasized and best taught subject at the university, yes, sir, even my phrases of Latin did I learn from my dear teacher during my Thursday visits, using the book by Nebrija.[4] This helped to distract both of us from our suffering.

"The study of this dead language," my teacher used to say to me, "is only necessary for clergymen, and that is certainly not what you are going to be. But it can also offer any intelligent man—as it will offer to you, since you are not an idiot—the wonderful satisfaction of reading the esteemed classics of Virgil and Cicero,[5] which lose much of their beauty when they are translated into another language."

Furthermore, I also eventually found that I could live much better, if not actually fine, in the house of Doña Teresa. In addition to the affection of my charming pupil Carmencita, I thought I could count, and finally did, on the friendship of the restless and whimsical Agustín. In keeping with my promise, I told him what I had seen of the battle. On another day, I convinced him to listen to a scene that I read to him from Moreto's comedy. Then, the day after that, he actually came to me, asking to have it read to him in its entirety, and not being fully satisfied until I had read some scenes twice, as he insisted I do. He swore he would memorize scene XI from act II, between the king and the wealthy man of Alcalá, and this turned out to be quite simple for him, for he was intelligent and had a good memory. After this he often sought out my company, and no longer tried to have me carry out humiliating tasks as part of his pranks. I, in turn, was kind with him so as not to harm his estimation of me. I would make for him, for example, tricorn hats out of paper, wooden swords, and epaulettes from yellow strips of cloth. With these items, acting out the role of King Don Pedro the Cruel, it was a pleasure to watch him recite his part from his favorite scene, especially the stretch of lines that begin with:

> So . . . art thou the one from town
> Who will not extend a chair to the
> King himself in your house?
> Is the wealthy man of Alcalá
> More than the King of Castille?

And not even on these occasions would he strike me with the famous blows to the head with which this scene concludes.

Finally, the servants now treated me with more respect, but this was not due to an explicit order from the lady of the house. All the physical exertion I experienced during my sweet exile, combined with the dreadful drama I had witnessed, as well as my illness, had seemingly sped up my physical growth a little and helped to give my countenance a look of seriousness. This made them see me as a different person than the poor «foundling waif» who had first come crying into their house.

The only thing I never managed was to make myself liked, or even tolerated, by Doña Teresa, who always looked at me with evil eyes and avoided speaking to me as much as possible. In vain did I heroically offer my services to read the corresponding saint's life for that day. And two or three times I also timidly proposed that I could do some tasks in one of her estates, or take on any kind of work—all in vain. She, for her part, not only wanted to keep the promise she had made to my teacher, but seemed desperately to want to be freed of my presence. But, although a muleteer had already been hired, the political events did not take long to unravel, once again making my trip to Chuquisaca impossible.

After the battle of Amiraya, Don Esteban Arze, the most inexhaustible caudillo of the nascent homeland, had taken refuge in the deep ravines that separate the Valley of Cliza from the Río Grande, on the southern border of the province, in his private estate in Caine. The moment Goyeneche had left—the very moment Don Arze himself saw the last helmets of Ramírez's departing soldiers from an inaccessible height at a turn of the deep banks of the aforementioned river—he moved once again to continue working for liberty, the endeavor to which he had devoted his entire life. He went first to Paredón, the town closest to his estate, and, with the magical shout of "Long live the homeland," brought the entire town en masse, armed with slings and *macanas*, to rebel. He soon found himself, through similar actions, in control of the rest of the vast Valley of Cliza. Finally, it did not take him long to appear at the outskirts of the city, as he had done previously for the uprising of the 14th of September 1810 with Rivero, arriving there on the 29th of October of 1811.

Governor Allende, in spite of having trenches dug on the street corners in a one-block radius surrounding the main plaza, did not, in the end, offer any resistance. This was due as much to his conciliatory character, as to the fact that he must have been, deep inside, as a good Cochabambian, sympathetic to the goals of the revolution. Thus, with the exchange of only two parleyers—I believe that Brother Justo served as Arze's—Don Allende surrendered, turning over his arms with only one condition: that Santiestevan, and any of the soldiers who might want to follow him, be allowed to leave freely to rejoin Goyeneche's army. This was carried out so nobly by the populace that not even one single word of insult was directed to the departing officer, nor was his march, nor that of the soldiers who chose to follow him to Chuquisaca, hindered in any manner whatsoever.

A new open meeting of the citizenry in the Cabildo was called. It named the honorable «citizen» Don Mariano Antezana as the «Prefect» and constituted a new Junta of War over which this same Prefect would preside. I remember I only heard occasional, isolated shouts of "Long live Fernando VII!" The shout for the homeland, however, came out of everyone's mouths spontaneously. The revolution was now present in its most direct and resolute terms. Even the exotic title of the new authority, and the word «citizen» that adorned his name, stated it quite clearly.

The euphoria, the noise, the zeal, the tireless preparation for war, all returned, as in the days after the first uprising that were filled with so much hope. Don Esteban Arze undertook a new dispatch to Oruro, but did not have the firearms necessary to fight the enemy that had dug themselves into trenches around the main plaza. He was turned back and rushed to the Province of Chayanta instead, where he managed to defeat two companies of good, strong troops, sent there under the leadership of the Commander Astete. The name of the highly active and brave caudillo resounded everywhere alongside the shout for the homeland's independence. But such was not the case with that of his old compatriot, of the people's previous idol, Governor Rivero, who was now accused of disloyalty.

One day toward the end of February 1812, in which my teacher was very happy to see me pass the "what's what"—in other words the *quis vel quid*—of Latin grammar, a gentleman dressed in a very ornate military uniform suddenly came into the cell.

"Esteban!" my teacher exclaimed, immediately rushing to welcome him. "What are you doing in the cell of a poor friar? I would never have expected such a high honor."

"Yes, Enrique," the other man answered very fondly, "I know your soul, and I have chosen this place, and I beg your assistance, to carry out a very sad duty."

They shook hands. Then the Father offered the unforeseen visitor his comfortable armchair, and took a seat on the bench in the place I had just abandoned in favor of a corner of the room where I could stay out of the way. I looked on at those two extraordinary men very much like a fool, with my small mouth wide open.

When Torrente, my favorite historian, is astonished at the ingratitude of the Americans before the generous and loving metropolis, and when he furiously aims his indignation at "Guerrero, Arze, Bolívar, Lamar,"[6] and the other principal American «insurgents», I am happy to see the inexhaustible caudillo from my country in such good company. He had "the kind of faith that moves mountains"; he did not lose courage, nor grow disheartened for even an instant during any mishap; "he had learned to win even in defeat," like the glorious Liberator. . . . God only knows what heights he might have reached if a sad and dark death had not rudely interrupted his endeavors!

Don Esteban Arze was a pure *criollo* like Rivero; he was tall, anxious, and also endowed with admirable physical strength. On horseback, with a soldier's lance in his hand, he could have fared very well against one of the Centaurs of the Argentine pampas,[7] who earned so much fame under Güemes.[8] He had a quick temper and was prone to letting himself get carried away by his anger; he had received a very limited education, but worked within his own admirable school in which, with his natural talent, he had advanced as much or more than Páez,[9] for example.

The other man before me, the poor friar who had taught me to read, and who had always been an impenetrable mystery for me, was now transformed in my mind into the sparkling, generous gentleman «Don Enrique» about whom Ventura had spoken to me. He was now the hunter who had traveled everywhere with his ornate carbine, from the peaks of the Cordillera to the vast, pleasant valleys, leaving behind him indelible memories of his kindness in the hearts of the simple peasants, whose misfortunes he still remembered and mourned over like a true friend.

"I have been ordered by Don Martín de Pueyrredón, who is currently reorganizing the auxiliary army," the victor from Aroma said, "to take back without delay the titles of governor and brigadier that the Junta of Buenos Aires had previously bestowed upon my old comrade-in-arms Don Francisco del Rivero. I know what is in Don Francisco's heart; I believe he is weak, but not a criminal, and I want him to be able to defend himself. Therefore, as much to carry out my charge in the least painful manner, as to explain to him how much better it would be for him to accept the decree himself, I have asked him to come here, where he will be arriving before very long."

And, sure enough, as soon as he had said these words, Rivero came in, well hidden with his hood pulled over his head. He closed the door quietly behind him, approached the other two men, and removed his cloak, revealing his worn and pale face, which showed every sign of carrying a heavy burden, of deep dejection, of the fatal illness of the sadness that would accompany him all the way to the grave.

He was welcomed with the greatest display of kindness and even respect by his old comrade-in-arms and by the Father, who had been his fellow student and friend since childhood, and was offered the seat of honor, which he refused. Instead, he remained standing, leaning against the table, and looked distractedly in my direction. My teacher then motioned for me to leave, but Rivero quickly interrupted, saying:

"Let him be. . . . I might hide from my enemies, but why should

I hide from that poor boy? I wish every plain soul who has not yet been blinded by hatred would come listen to me!"

Arze, deeply moved, delicately explained his orders to him. The Father, for his part, added a few words of support.

"So be it!" Don Francisco answered, bowing his head in resignation. "The truth is that after the battle of Amiraya, during that time of anguish and terror, a thousand arms reached out imploring me to save the country from the Spanish vengeance—the same arms that today would tear me apart pitilessly for having listened to their wailing back then. But what else have I done, in actuality? They say I accepted a dispatch to be a brigadier for Goyeneche. . . . But did anyone take into account the treachery and shrewdness of the «Three-Faced Man»? Would anyone believe me now if I were to say that I accepted the dispatch without intending to make use of it, promising to myself never to draw my sword against my own country? No! But let history judge me—a day will come when it will be seen that Rivero would not have been capable of betraying the land in which he was born, that he was not another Goyeneche. . . . How much better it has been for Quiroga, the Quiroga who is cursed as I am, but who, when he was furiously pursued by the same snake that has betrayed us both, has fled to the impenetrable mountains of Chapare, among the wild beasts that might put an end to his suffering with more compassion than the men who are killing me with this slow torture of endless calumny!"

How wise it turned out to be for the defeated brigadier from Amiraya to allow a poor boy to hear him speak those words! It is thanks to this fact that our national historians will, I believe, now correct the very severe judgments they have dealt out in regards to his conduct.* Rivero's sin was quite similar to that of the glorious

---

*Well after I had written this section of my memoirs, my friend Don José Ventura Claros y Cabrera, the current patriarch of my beautiful country, sent me a brief book, entitled *Notes for a History of Cochabamba*, by Eufronio Viscarra, treating this matter in a much better fashion. My friend also told me that the author was a modest, studious young man, who was fond of rummaging through old papers. I hope he continues his very praiseworthy projects! May he also not lack the enthusiasm that public opinion should lend to those who work toward creating something in our incipient literature, but who almost always end up discouraged![10]

Miranda in Venezuela when he surrendered to Monteverde think-ing that his cause was lost.[11] If Rivero had had the same strong will as Arze, Antezana, and the other members of the Provincial Junta, and if he had absorbed all the consequences of the defeat, Cochabamba might have suffered, from that point on, the same kinds of tragedies that were to take place in 1812. And yet, if the governor had done so, his glory would have grown to be much greater in the eyes of his fellow countrymen, as Arze's did after his fall, and, to a larger degree, as Bolívar's did after Miranda's. And this is not because of the blind injustice of man, but because, deep in their hearts, despite all their bewailing when misery strikes, na-tions want their heroes to consummate not only their own sacrifi-ce, but, if necessary, that of the people themselves in order to per-severe in the greatest causes of humanity!

In that same year of 1811, throughout Upper Perú, in the places left behind by the victor Goyeneche, the popular masses preferred their own destruction to the old, subservient condition. The *ail-los*,[12] the hamlets, and the towns from the province of La Paz rose up when they were called out by the bold caudillos, those men whose names are forgotten by today's generation, and thousands of Indians and mestizos rushed to participate in the siege of the sa-cred *Chuquiaguru*[13] against the garrison troops left there by the victor from Huaqui.* In vain did the hordes come from Cuzco with Choqueguanca[14] and Pumacagua[15]; in vain did Huisi[16] return with his hired assassins; in vain did fires devour the ranches and the crops; in vain were thousands of prisoners, women, and children beheaded with a savageness that horrifies everyone, and—how bad it must have been, my God!—is even repugnant to the fanatical Torrente! The "shout" for Independence resounded in the smoke from the fires. It arose, I should say, rather, from the very wounds

---

*The city of La Paz is so revered by the Indians that when they enter or leave it, as a way of greeting or saying farewell to it, they kneel down and make the sign of the cross facing its heights. If they laid siege to it before, and again at this time, it is because they were driven to it by their desperation in their condition of slavery and by their ardent desire for freedom. This liberty, however, has only been given to them quite parsimoniously by those who, in this as in all else, have made a mockery of the great Independence Movement, without un-derstanding the expressed dreams of Bolívar and of the victor of Ayacucho.

opened by the weapons, and became louder and grander with the more blood that was spilled from them!

What occurred in that meeting spoke very honorably of the personal sentiments of those who started the American revolution in my country. But perhaps it no longer interests my readers as much as the events that I very briefly mentioned above.

XIV

The Weapons and Resources of the Homeland

My friend Luis did not come back to my room through the window, nor did I see him anywhere else, until some forty days after Goyeneche had left the city, when I ran into him out in the street quite unexpectedly. He looked very sad and pale and was walking with difficulty. A friendly smile lit up his face when he raised his eyes and saw me right before I nearly knocked him over.

"How are you? What have you been doing with yourself?" I asked him.

He looked at me as if he wanted to cry and answered:

"Oh, my friend! I haven't been able to do anything. . . . I haven't been able to move even!"

"Have you been ill?"

"I wish I had! I wish I had gotten the most horrendous typhus fever, even if the Aragonese Father had had to bleed me three times a day and then apply mustard plasters from head to foot on me permanently!"

"Well, then! Tell me, what happened?"

"I told you before that I knew my father would wring my neck. But this beating. . . . Oh, my! This thrashing was the worst one ever, Juanito!"

Then, all of the sudden changing his tone as he was wont to do, he started laughing, and also became more excited as he went on:

"But the matter was quite serious, my dear friend! Because of the audacity that someone had had of rubbing his nose in all that 'rights of man' stuff, the '*Invictus Caesar*' got angrier and more worked up than he had even for the battle of Amiraya. He learned that the beautiful verses written by his learned Honor had been substituted for these others and demanded to be told about everyone who knew French in the city. They reported to him that several people did, but none as well as the *Gringo*. Without further ado, he had the *Gringo* brought before him by four grenadiers from Cuzco, Indians who are even bigger brutes than our *tatas* from Arque and Tapacarí. He treated him worse than if he were a Negro and ordered that he be executed without a confession, facing the firing squad wall like the heretic that he must surely be."

With these last few words, his tone once again became melancholy, and I believe his eyes even became wet with tears. But it did not take him long to laugh again and to go on, saying:

"Luckily, Father Arredondo, who was present at the time, was shocked by what he had heard and tried to jump up. But the arms of the chair where he was sitting broke, and he fell sideways. . . . Are you following me, Juanito? Father Arredondo fell, and the whole floor of the room shook as if there had been an earthquake! This helped undo some of the Caesar's anger. Meanwhile, his Honor continued to implore him, with many, many words in Latin, and finally my father was allowed to return to his home with his life intact. He was red as a pepper when he came in. He searched through his papers, grabbed a whip, and—"

"Poor Luis!" I exclaimed, solemnly. He nodded in agreement and continued, even more excited than before, as if he were speaking about someone other than himself:

"Have you ever seen a rosebush pruned down all the way to its very last leaf, so that later it will grow back full of fresh, beautiful, fragrant roses? Do you know how they thrash wool to make the soft stuffing for cushions and pillows? Well, my friend, all of that pales in comparison to what my father did to me! Forty days! Forty days I have had to keep to my bed from the pain, Juanito!"

"How I wish I could have comforted you with a visit!" I said to him compassionately.

"I would have loved to see you," he replied. "But I have had plenty to occupy my time. I memorized his Honor's verses, and, besides, I made an incredible discovery. Don't laugh, my friend! Or I'll get angry.... Even my father says it's good, and you're going to see it right now, in a moment. We're going this very instant."

It is probably unnecessary for me to add that as he said these last words, he had grabbed my arm and was already dragging me in the direction he wanted to take me, throwing in a thousand things as we went along.

"While we walk, and since it's impossible for me to leave my tongue idle once I have found someone who will listen to me, I shall tell you how I made the discovery. On the other side of the large patio where my father and I live in two rented rooms, lives the lay sister Doña Martina, a very close friend of Doña Teresa's. She has never been able to look at us without crossing herself, as if we were both devils: my father because he is a *gringo*, and I because one day I tied a cracker to the tail of her chihuahua and let it back into her room while she was deep in prayer. When she found out about my misfortune, she came to my door, pretending to be offering her compassion. But instead she said a thousand things about my evil creator, including that he has a tail, and ended with the moral that, sooner or later, Heaven punishes those infidels who disturb the just in the middle of their prayers. I begged her, I implored her for everything that is sacred to let me suffer in peace that which I certainly deserved. But she didn't let up. She continued her sermon for over an hour, until my father finally came back home, at which point his mere presence frightened her away, since, as I have already said, he is like the Devil himself to her.

"I swore to myself that I would do some mean trick to get her back, and I came up with quite a good one, if I may say so myself. Among the many odds and ends that I always have in my pockets, I had half a cartridge of gun powder and a little copper bell that I had taken from the end of one of the ornamental feathers of a dancing Indian during the last celebration of the *Corpus Christi*. I took the cartridge apart, transferred the gun powder into the bell, and put in a fuse of the appropriate length. Finally, I tied a piece of rope that was about half a vara long to it so as to make it easier to throw the petard that I had just invented. Armed in this manner, I waited until it grew dark. Then, when my father placed a candle near my bed to lovingly care for my wounds with the same hands that had caused them, I asked him to leave me the light so I could study my verses. He laughed and gladly agreed. Then he had to go out for some reason, so I sat up right away, moaning, of course, as I did so. I lit the fuse, spun my bell in the air, and tossed it with such good aim that it exploded loud as a bomb inside the lay sister's room. Oh, Juanito, you should have heard the shrieks she and her chihuahua let out! Frightened to death, she ran into my room looking for help, crossing herself, saying the Devil had caused a thundering explosion in her room. I crossed myself in the same way that she does, and then I told her, very seriously, that without a doubt this must be how God punishes those who do not honestly pity the misfortunes of their fellow men."

"Go on! You're incorrigible!" I exclaimed, but could not help laughing.

"Wait, you have to hear how it all ended," he replied triumphantly. "For this, my friend, is the most glorious thing of my whole life! When my father found out what happened—in other words, how the Devil had caused a thundering explosion in Doña Martina's room—it didn't take him long to guess who was behind such an extraordinary event. He came to see me, looking very serious and with his arms crossed, and, without saying a word, he gestured with his head, indicating that I should explain everything to him. Completely frightened to death, I told him the whole story, in minute detail, and he listened without making any interruptions or asking any questions. Then he thought for a moment, and said: 'Ah, *mon Dieu!* This can be put to use!' And this because he was unsatisfied with the copper and bronze vents that he had made for the tin cannons—he has been searching more than ever for something that would avenge the insults he received to 'his personage,' as he says, and, he adds, the grenades made by 'the system of the *garçon*' will be the end of Goyeneche's army."

"Well, that's incredible!" I exclaimed at this point, unable to put up with his lies. "Do you know something, though, my friend? I don't believe a single word that you're saying now, and I'm even beginning to think that perhaps you were ill with typhus fever or whatever else, and that your father never gave you any such beating!"

"But why?"

"Because I already heard a while ago about the grenades invented by someone in Tarata, better than the ones you describe. Because you're an incorrigible scoundrel, a jester, a—"

"Whatever you want to call me. . . . But stop lecturing me and judge with your own eyes. We're here already."

Distracted by Luis' story, furious for having fallen for his trickery, I had not been paying attention to where we were going. When I realized we were at the door of Alejo's workshop, I stopped in amazement. The sounds of a volcano and the activity of a wild beehive reigned within; it was so unusual that everyone who passed by in the street stopped to look in, as open-mouthed as I was. The bellows were blowing without rest, and the red coals in the forge and in a furnace built next to it sparked brightly; the hammer struck the glowing orange steel on the anvil incessantly; the file spattered as it bit into the steel and the bronze; and young men in short-sleeved shirts, completely blackened with soot, were coming and going, carrying various steel, tin, copper, bronze, and wooden objects through a door that had been recently installed on the wall opposite the entrance. Dionisio, looking very pale, working the bellows; Alejo, swinging the large hammer; the *Gringo*, working the file restlessly on the table; and the *Mellizo*, who I saw then for the first time, walking around everywhere without doing anything: all were shouting out orders and were answered just as loudly by the young men. All of this was occurring in the middle of a bluish smoke or gas from the coals, in the glow of the forge and the furnace, and in temperatures as hot as Hell's antechamber, according to Luis.

"Ho there, boys! Long live the homeland!" Alejo shouted when he saw us. "Come on in, my sons! And off to work you go, just like everyone else!"

"And none of your pranks, either!" the *Gringo* added, taking his large Santa Cruz cigar out of his mouth for a moment so he could say this.

We walked quickly through the shop, bumping into the young men more than once, and out into a large yard full of sounds and activities similar to the ones inside, and just as loud. The carpenters' saws, chisels, and mallets created their dissonant noises among the constant shouting of orders and answers, much like the ones inside the shop. From a pipe that was sticking out of the wall and that came from the furnace inside, molten bronze dripped over small, round molds. From another pipe that came from the forge, tin spouted and then flowed along a groove, and was dispensed into other, bigger cylindrical molds. A few men were removing the molds with the aid of large tongs, shovels, and pikes, and replacing them immediately with empty ones. Others were taking the hollow bronze balls, or the tin cannonballs, out of the molds. The carpenters were building rifle butts and gun-carriages, and, with nails that were still hot, since they were also made inside, they were attaching them to the pieces of steel coming from the shop. The *Mellizo* was also roaming around outside, going everywhere without doing anything, getting more agitated and yelling louder than anyone else.

My friend explained each and every one of the activities to me in minute detail. It would be impossible to repeat even a small fraction of what he said to me. But I have not forgotten the solemn words with which he concluded, taking on the air, stance, and voice of his learned Honor:

"*Per istam*,[1] Goyeneche!"

And I believed every word he said.

"My teacher is wrong," I said to myself; "this country has but one sole thought, there must be over forty thousand soldiers, and the weapons. . . . Well, here they are, right before my eyes!"

Such enthusiasm for the homeland! Such simple determination in undertaking the most heroic sacrifices! Such innocence! Such unshakable confidence in the *macana*, in the tin cannon, and in the grenade made with the system of the *garçon*! Today, as I recall what I saw then, what I as a child believed among all those men-children, it seems to me that we were much greater then, in our ignorance and naiveté, because of our faith, because of the sacred fire which we all fully and joyfully and wholeheartedly embraced!

While today. . . . My God! What do we think about today? What are we doing for our homeland today?

The frightful and constant noise that my ears had grown accustomed to was suddenly interrupted by a solid silence. This had the effect, because of the contrast, of waking me from the ecstatic admiration in which I found myself before a large tin cannon, recently mounted on its gun-carriages, with one-piece wheels that were made out of carob-tree wood—like the ones used in those small carts for carrying heavy rocks with the help of a team of mules. The time for taking a break had arrived, and the sweat-covered workers all put on their jackets or ponchos, and were given a very meager salary, the absolute minimum needed for their sustenance. It was handed out at once by a commissary from the provincial government.

I went back into the shop with Luis. The only ones left there were his father, the *Mellizo*, and Alejo. The first of these, as I have mentioned before, was a tall, large man, very blond, with bright red coloring. He must have been over fifty years old, he wore the same outfits as the *criollos*, quite simply, he did not speak Spanish very well, and he liked to laugh and throw in a few words in Quechua, in a sincere attempt to be closer to the mestizos. Why had he come to our country? Was he a humble adventurer looking for work, who had emigrated in search of a fortune in a distant corner of the New World? Or was he a Jacobin[2] who had been thrown into the prison of Cayenne,[3] and had somehow escaped from there, fleeing to the valleys below the great peak of Tunari? I am not able to answer any part of these questions. Luis himself did not know. Many years later, he told me that his father had come over with Haenke, but he did not know under what circumstances. Also, that he had married a good, young mestiza, who had died when she gave birth to my poor friend. I believe even his surname, Cros, must not have been the actual family name, but some distortion of it that was nevertheless later used by all his descendants in our country.

The *Mellizo's* Christian name, which I believe I finally learned after quite a bit of work, was Sebastián Cotrina, but it was useless to use this name when speaking about him with anyone at all, even with his closest friends, nor to get his attention, for that matter. As happens so often even to this day among the common people, the nickname had replaced the person's real name. Speaking about Sebastián Cotrina would only get everyone around you to look questioningly at each other as if you were speaking about a total stranger. If you were to say *Chapaco* (another nickname for Sebastián), you might sometimes get the individual alluded to to realize that you were addressing him. But if you just said *"Mellizo,"* plain and simple, there was not a single person in his class that would not answer, "I know him!" And if he was present, he himself would jump up in response to the name.

I don't know that I would count the Cotrina who was a compatriot of Calatayud among his ancestors. The *Mellizo* was more cupreous than white, and he was close to thirty years of age. I can still see him in my mind when I recall him today: short and chubby, with bright, deep-set, little eyes; round-faced, with a flat nose; completely bald; restless, a troublemaker, and quite rowdy; and always the loudest of anyone around him. His head was covered with a blue handkerchief, tied at the nape of his neck; he wore a large leather apron; he would grab the first tool before him when he entered the shop and then not set it down his whole time there; and he moved around and shrieked more than anyone, but without ever accomplishing anything productive. When Luis and I came back into the shop, he was going on about his fatigue and the tremendous amount of work that he had done with his hands, or that which had been done by others', but always under his indispensable supervision and direction. And, saying that he would take advantage of the break to carry out a thousand other patriotic duties, which only he could carry out, incidentally, he ran out of the shop just as he was, with the tool in his hand and the apron still around him, and headed straight for the nearest *chichería*.

The *Gringo* was drawing deeply on his Santa Cruz cigar in silence, although no one would have had more of a right than him to boast about their work. He was organizing, in a corner, the bronze balls to which he had given the finishing touches, putting the corresponding short strip of esparto rope they required on each one of them for their use. Then he arranged his tools carefully on the table, and, finally, went over to wash his hands in a wooden washtub.

My uncle, the strong, good, and simple Alejo, his head covered, wearing an apron like the *Mellizo*, was completely soaked in sweat after having worked so eagerly. He was stacking a few small silver coins—his salary—on the anvil with his blackened, callused hands, and more than a few gleaming drops fell on them from his face as he did so.

"What do you think about all this, young man?" he asked me.

"Oh! It's beautiful, amazing!" I answered, truly carried away with happiness after what I had seen.

"Now, they will learn, revolution," the *Gringo* said, letting the cigar fall out of his mouth, and proceeded to calmly put on a kind of greatcoat, which he had left in the back room or in the bedroom.

"Yes, young man," Alejo replied, "this is a revolution!"

"There is a lot of *saltpêtre* in the valley; the gentleman Haenke has taught how to make very good gunpowder; the hills are full of lead, there is no lack of tin, and one can also find a bit of copper; and we have «many worlds» of people," added the *Gringo* from inside.

My uncle was enthralled, listening to him with that smile of his, in which he displayed his infinite satisfaction and all thirty-two of his teeth.

"That's it, boys!" he exclaimed. "Long live the homeland!"

"Hurrah! Hurrah!" Luis and I answered.

"Now, another thing. Do you have a paper in your pocket?"

"Yes. Coincidentally, I just got a copy of the proclamation from the Junta of War."

"Very good. You're going to make a clean roll for me, a very clean and neat roll for me with those *reales* from over there. But let's hear the proclamation from the Junta first."

I unfolded the paper, pretended to put on a pair of eyeglasses, coughed, straightened myself up like the Notary Don Angel Francisco Astete, and prepared to begin reading, ready also to imitate the Notary's somewhat nasal voice.

"Wait!" Luis yelled, and ran to arm himself with a lance and stand up behind me, representing the public forces.

"Let's have it," Alejo said.

"Go on, you little devil," the *Gringo* added, for his part.

And I read, in the manner I just indicated, that famous proclamation, from which I shall copy only a few of the main sections here:

"Don Mariano Antezana, President of this city's Provincial Junta, along with the other members of the Junta, in the name of his Majesty the King Don Fernando VII, may God keep him forever in good health, etcetera.

"It being necessary in the current circumstances to resort to all available resources. . . . And it being one of them that the entire community contribute to the saintly and worthy aims of the defense of the homeland and the arming and keeping of its troops. . . .

"Therefore, I decree and command that every person in this city and in the entire province, regardless of sex or age, agree to give what each finds appropriate, for the maintenance of the troops. However, so that the expenditure not be unreasonable the contribution is set at the sum of «eight *reales*». . . ."

"Long live the homeland!" the public forces yelled behind me.

The *Gringo* shrugged his shoulders and walked out into the street. Alejo was thinking, scratching his head behind his ear, as he always did when he could not figure out what he should do.

"Well," he said after a while, "my eight *reales* are right there. Set them aside and roll the rest up for me."

I did as I was told, as well and neatly as possible, and put the roll into his pocket for him, since he did not want to touch it to avoid getting the paper dirty with his hands. Then he looked at me angrily and said:

"I bet you won't be able to guess! Go on, you fool! It's for the Grandmother!"

And right away he lowered his head, adding, with much emotion and, I believe, crying:

"She's here with Clarita. They came to have Dionisio cured. She's gone blind! . . . They're living in my small house in the Barrio de los Ricos. . . . Where you used to live with 'the child.'"

XV

An Inventory.
My Visit to See the Grandmother

Those last words of Alejo's, with which I ended the previous chapter, made me stop and think in a manner that it had never occurred to me to do before. For, although I had always lived in poverty and known that I had to make do without a thousand different things that others had, I was always provided for by the work of my mother's hands. And, afterward too, as the orphan that I was, I never had to think about my daily bread, nor of the way in which—regardless of how bitter it may have been—it reached my lips.

"The Devil! Money is obviously very important," I said to myself, "and it must be much more so when one is suffering greatly and when it is not possible to even think about how to go about getting it, nor to earn it by working. The Grandmother, who must somehow be related to me—and who, if she is not, I wish she were—the poor, blind Grandmother is apparently able only to stay alive thanks to Alejo's and Dionisio's work. . . . Is it not my duty to protect and serve her as they do? But what could I give her, the loafer that I am? And what are all my big, old books or my foolish presumptuousness at having passed the 'what's what' of Latin in my Nebrija good for now? Can I possibly go see her as I am, empty handed and with my eyes full of tears, only to make her shed the last of the tears that might be left in her eyes?"

I reached my room as I thought about these things, very sad and crestfallen. I locked myself in and looked in a desk drawer for the key that opened the coffer that contained my entire inheritance, of which I had not as of yet taken inventory.

The only clothes, either white or of some color, that were inside were mine, and these were very worn and threadbare. My mother's clothes must have been distributed, according to her wishes, to the poor women who had always attended to and assisted her. The only item left was her newest pair of shoes, very small, made of varnished leather, with red heels. I contemplated them for a long time before finally kissing and putting them back in their place. Then, carefully wrapped and to one side, I found the painting of the Virgin. I put it up on the wall, above the headboard of my bed. I noticed at that point that it looked like a portrait of my mother, and that on a fold of its blue mantle, almost as imperceptible as shadows, were the letters "C. A.," signed with a rubric. A black package, which I touched distractedly with my hand, sent a sudden shiver through my body. I left it alone; it was the piece of rope, the relic believed to be part of the rope used for hanging Calatayud. Finally, I found a small, wooden chest, with its key in its lock, I put it on the table, opened it, and took out of it the following items, in this order: a partially embroidered piece of cloth with a round blood stain on it, a small cardboard box, and the money box, the broken pieces of which had been stuck back together with glue and sawdust.

The small cardboard box contained my mother's brooch, earrings, and her small, ivory ring. I noticed for the first time that this last item was very delicate and had been skillfully engraved with a burin. On the outside, around a small space with a little gold top, the Quechua words *Cusi Coyllur* were engraved, and the little top, in turn, had a rose engraved on it, which, when opened, revealed at the bottom of a tiny hollow the same two mysterious letters as on the fold of the Virgin's cloak.

The money box was very light, but when I shook it in my hands, I heard a slight metallic sound, the unmistakable sound of coins hitting against its sides. I immediately grabbed a nail, removed one of the pieces of the lid that had been glued back on, and screamed out in happiness with as much satisfaction as if I had discovered the treasures of *Tangatanga*.[1] There were a few small gold coins, some five or six, very new and bright. I took one, put it in my pocket, rearranged everything as it was before, and ran off toward the small house that I knew so well.

I turned the corner, and when I was about half a block away, I saw poor Clara sitting on a tall stool, leaning back against one leaf of the door. She was dressed all in black and looked very pale, and right then and there, she seemed to me more beautiful than Mariquita and almost as beautiful as my mother. She was working with her hands, unraveling the edges of a very fine piece of linen on her lap without looking down, while one of her feet was resting on the stool's thick cross-bar, and the other, white and pinkish, was playing distractedly with her shoe, barely hanging by her toes. Her beautiful eyes were looking up at the sky, above that large, ugly house across the street. And she was singing to herself, like my mother used to do, the following *harahui*—which I recognized as I came closer—from the chorus of the maidens of Ollanta:[2]

Iscay munanakuc urpi . . .

I shall transcribe it here in Spanish so that you can understand it. However, since it is untranslatable, it will inevitably be very poorly translated:

Two doves were cooing
Back and forth in the hollow
Of a dried-out tree trunk, wanting
There to nest and live together.

One of them one day
Is caught in a traitorous trap
In agony he writhes. . . .
Dies far from his beloved.

And the other does despair
On the old tree trunk, and in moans,

Asks the swaying breeze: do tell me,
Where is my companion?

Will I be able to proudly gaze
At myself in his eye once again?
Will peaceful sleep ever find me
Without his sweet cooing and his lulling?

And because the wind only murmurs,
does not respond to her lament,
She leaves at last—not knowing where,
And leaves behind the empty nest.

Flying from branch to branch
And from one boulder to another,
Always bent on somehow finding him,
Always grieved does she call him.

When she can no longer her yearning wings
In the blowing wind stretch,
She keeps moving on her feet,
Not ever stopping for a rest.

And running ceaselessly,
Dragging herself along the ground,
She dies at last, inconsolable,
From her fatigue and from her sorrow.

This was the young woman's sad response, without her knowing it, to the last *harahui* that her fiancé had sung to her by moonlight, at the top of the mountain, the night before his death.

Either from that inexplicable magnetic feeling that always lets one know, or because she heard my loud, agitated breathing from the sprint at which I had come, Clara sensed that someone had stopped at her side. She turned to me, startled, and became very flushed. Then she asked me quite rudely in proper Spanish:

"What are you looking at? Is there something in my face that lazy boys might find amusing? Why don't you go off to play the *palama*? Who is helping your mother while you are out causing trouble?"

"I wish to embrace you," I answered. "I wish to weep with you, if you will let me. I'm Rosa's son. . . . You've seen me twice, when I was with. . . . Don't you remember?"

"Let him in, my daughter. . . . Bring him here," a woman's strong voice yelled from inside before Clara had gotten the chance to say anything.

The Grandmother—for she had been the one who had spoken with that loud voice that seemed to have come from a much younger body—was standing next to a dais, which was placed in the same location as the one that had belonged to my mother, and from which she had obviously just risen to receive me. Her completely white and very thin hair, like combed cotton, was gathered in two braids that barely reached her shoulders; she was brown-skinned; her face, spotted with those dark stains common to old age, did not have deep wrinkles other than between her eyes and on the ends of her mouth; her lifeless, grayish-green eyes remained absolutely fixed, like those of a corpse; and her wide forehead, long, straight nose, and square chin indicated a steady and resolute character. She was quite tall, and not at all shrunk over by her nearly one hundred years of age. She wore a black mantilla draped over her back and attached in front by a large silver pin, the end of which was partially shaped like a spoon; a very simple, white doublet; and a coffee-colored, Castilian *bayeta* skirt, pleated and adorned with black merino fringes. She had thick wool socks and shoes with uppers, eyelets, and shoelaces. In her left hand she held a staff, like a shepherd's crook, and her right hand was extended out at chest level, waiting for mine.

"Come," she said to me after I had grabbed her hand and pressed it against my heart; "come and sit by my side. I cannot see you with my eyes . . . but I want to touch your face, your hair. You must be very pretty, like 'the child,'" she continued after I had done as I was told. "Your face is soft and delicate; your hair is nice, fine and curly; your long eyelashes tell me that your eyes must be like those of a *chasca*[3]. . . . What color are your eyes, my son?"

And she asked me a thousand other questions about myself, my life, and my mother's. However, since I tried to answer her in a manner that was as little sad as possible, fighting hard to contain my emotions, she said to me:

"Liar. . . . Do you think that the Grandmother can't see everything around her with the eyes that her many years have given her and which are much better than yours? You're trying to fool me. You said to yourself: 'Poor Grandmother! She has cried so much, I don't want to upset her any more.' But I have just felt in these old, crooked fingers of mine a small tear trembling at the end of your eyelashes, and I know that it is not possible for you to be happy. . . . Who could be in this world, with the *guampos*⁴ here? Look, I was a small girl, as young as you, when I saw one of your grandfather's arms displayed on a pole on the crest of Mount San Sebastián. A year later they had the body of my father, Nicolás Flores, drawn and quartered right in front of my eyes, and they forced my mother to come out of her house, holding me by the hand, so that it would go to the King, as they used to say. A lot of time has passed. . . . I married, had many children, and have raised my children's children. But do you think I have forgotten any of those things? No, no! No one used to remember anything about those times, and then, at times, they would see me very sad and thoughtful, and they would ask: 'What's wrong, Grandmother?' And I would answer: 'There are no men left!'"

"Oh! Don't talk about all that, mother!" Clara shouted, or sobbed rather, at that point. She had come in and taken a seat in front of us in the adobe *poyo* on which she must have slept. I saw that they had done the same for her brother with another *poyo* on the other side of the room.

"And why not?" the Grandmother replied. "Do you think, girl, that there's nothing left of me, that I'm nothing more than a dry, termite-eaten tree trunk like the one you were singing about in that *harahui*?"

"No, it's not that, mother," the unhappy Clara replied; "it's just that I can't. . . . I can't. . . ."

"Be quiet! I cannot believe this is a daughter that actually came out of my womb. . . . You're a sad, little dove. . . . *Palomita!*"⁵

I do not know what else she would have said had Alejo and Dionisio not entered at that point. The former carried some object in his arms, wrapped up in his poncho, and was laughing to himself in that familiar manner of his, while the latter carried a wicker basket on his shoulder, which seemed very heavy to him, and was also smiling with a roguish look on his face.

"Did you bring it?" Clara asked Alejo.

"No, I wasn't able to," he answered, but when Clara approached him to see what he was hiding, he jumped back and added: "It's a little baby. . . . You'll wake him."

"And you?" the young woman asked, turning toward Dionisio, but he proceeded to raise the basket high above his head with both hands, keeping her from seeing its contents, and said:

"They're oranges . . . not ripe at all and very sour still. I brought them from the Antezana garden."

"Enough!" the Grandmother yelled authoritatively. "I will examine all the items with my hands, right now."

Immediately Alejo and Dionisio set their loads down submissively on the dais. Then the former unveiled the very same tin cannon that I had earlier admired in the workshop, and the latter produced four or five of the bronze grenades from his wicker basket.

I watched then as the old blind woman studied those implements of death with her trembling hands, paying the same careful attention, and demonstrating the same—there is no other word for it—affection that I had seen in her before when she was touching my face and hair. Her lips, at first very tightly drawn together, began to relax and unfurl, until she finally broke into a wild laughter that actually scared me. Then she quickly bent over the cannon, and putting her mouth right to the vent of the piece, as if she were about to speak to a person, to ask them to execute her vengeance for her, she yelled with her sharp, vibrant voice, even louder than she had before:

"Speak up, my son! Tell the *guampos* to get out of our land and to leave us alone to live our lives! They will listen to you better than they will to us. . . . And hopefully God above who protects us all will listen to you, too!"

Then she grabbed one of the grenades, stretched out the thin length of esparto rope that was wound around it, swung it in circles in the air like a sling, laughed as she had before, and said to Alejo:

"How many can it kill?"

"More than fifty, grandma!" the locksmith answered, rubbing his hands together, and he himself must have believed it.

"Good," the old woman replied, "if the *guampos* come back again, I'll go out with you and Dionisio to welcome them myself, and greet them with these beautiful fruits of our land."

"But can't I go with you?" I asked her, stung at the thought that she might have already forgotten me.

"Yes, my son," she answered with a smile, "we will all go, all of us. . . . Even the poor *Palomita!*"

"Oh, no! No. . . . For God's sake!" exclaimed Clara, terrified.

If my young readers think that this scene is not believable, or that I have exaggerated in writing it, please indulge this poor veteran from the glorious era of the Independence Movement. Why, really, should I be surprised if you doubt what I say? Has anyone actually told the story of all the events that took place as they truly occurred? Can our national writers possibly understand them when, with the sole objective of further incriminating Goyeneche, they lessen the value of the most characteristic and frequent episodes of the time? I cannot, thus, and I should not wonder in any manner whatsoever at the fact that my country's young generation does not understand the degree to which the Spanish domination was abhorred, and the delirium brought about by the love for the homeland that had just only around that time been born, with so many promises that were as of yet unrealized. It is necessary for all of this to be especially known from now on, for I still have a thousand things, more incredible yet than those I have recounted so far, to tell: about the women of Cochabamba, about the children—who at the same age today play with toys—but who back then did not have any other source of amusement but the weapons which they themselves invented, and no other game to play besides soldiers and war.*

---

*Finally, after so many years, a beautiful book has reached my hands, although not written by someone from our country. I am speaking about the *History of Belgrano*, written by General Don Bartolomé Mitre. I hope it serves as an incentive for today's young generation

It was already very late—almost the dreaded hour at which I had to appear before Doña Teresa in the small chapel—when I was finally allowed by my new family to leave that small house in which I had spent the happiest years of my childhood. Touching those implements of death—those weapons that she believed would be so formidable in the defense of the homeland and in executing the vengeance for the horrors that her loved ones had suffered—had aroused an excitement in the Grandmother that took a long time to subside. Afterward, the only thing she thought about was trying to please me in every way possible, even as Clara and her brother competed with her to do the same. It was not until I was out in the street that I remembered the main objective of my visit. I went back to the door of the house and called in for *Palomita*. I asked her to give me her hand, as if I wanted to say another farewell to her, and then I deposited my small coin in it and ran off like a deer, not turning my head to look back at the young woman until I had turned the corner. She stayed behind, shouting and calling my name, without a doubt to try to return the coin to me.

of Bolivians to present to the world in much broader terms the glorious ways through which our homeland obtained a place as one of the republics of South America! Until such a day arrives, I declare that the illustrious Argentine writer has understood quite well the heroism of Cochabamba in its struggle against the scheming and cruel Goyeneche.[6]

XVI

The Entrance of the Governor of the Gran Paititi

Earlier in these memoirs, I mentioned the children, and now I shall describe some of what they used to do in those times.

One afternoon, Agustín came into my room, a gentleman riding a stick, with military trappings that I had invented, wearing a paper tricorn and epaulettes, armed with a bent quince-tree branch that served him as an enormous scimitar. He pretended to bring his spirited battle steed under control with much difficulty; then he stood at attention before me, as if he were acknowledging someone of higher rank, and said:

"My Commander, his illustrious Lordship, the Delegate from the Most Honorable Junta of Buenos Aires, has ordered me to accompany your Excellency to his camp."

"And who is this new Lordship who has replaced the post held here by Don Juan José Castelli?" I asked him with as much seriousness as I could muster.

"Don Luis Cros y Cuchufleta, Knight of the Order of St. John the Baptist, Field Marshal of the armies of the homeland, Quartermaster General of the Gran Paititi,[1] General in Chief of the Auxiliary Army, etceteras, etceteras," he answered, parodying the many titles that Goyeneche generally used in all government proclamations and announcements.

"And where is he?"

"In his camp, at Las Cuadras. Tonight, when the moon comes out, he is to make his triumphant entrance in this, the brave city of Oropesa of the Valley of Cochabamba."

"And how did you learn of all this?"

"Because yesterday, when your Excellency went to take your lesson in the church, he came by our door with the artillery. . . . Oh! The cannons were so beautiful! He left the order with me himself, to carry it out properly as a good soldier. I'm a captain! And I've been made no more and no less than his aide-de-camp!"

I realized that my friend was putting together another one of his pranks, so I categorically refused to follow Captain Don Agustín where he wanted to take me. He implored me in vain, and finally became quite annoyed with me.

"Fine, then . . . the Devil's tale!" he said to me at last, imitating the Brigadier Ramírez, who was known for using this expression. "I'm going alone, and if I have to run my horse into the ground to get there on time, I will, too. And:

'Since we are alone, know, Tello,
That it was to free you that I was moved to set out!'"[2]

Half an hour later a frightening confusion broke out in the house. Doña Teresa was shouting angrily in the patio, and the servants were coming and going, searching everywhere in great alarm.

"They have stolen my son!" the lady of the house was screaming.

"Little Agustín has disappeared!" the servants were wailing.

But then the lady remembered me. She had me called to her presence and told me to go and retrieve the boy, and not to come back to the house without him.

Luckily, I knew more or less in what direction he had gone. However, it took less than five blocks before the loud whistling and tremendous shouting of a large band of boys indicated to me the precise point of the camp of the brand new Governor of the Gran Paititi. It was situated in a small square—which is perhaps still there today—located about a hundred paces in front of the Viedma manor. From the moment I turned the corner onto the street that led to the small square, behind the Church of St. Claire, I could see, even from that distance, that the army was already in formation. Eight cavalrymen came away from it at a good trot on their magnificent long-reed horses, and these soldiers, as they passed by my side, yelled out that they were going to alert the Cabildo and the priests in the Church of the Matriz so that the bells could be sounded at once and the whole city could come out.

There must have been over four hundred boys gathered in that small square. The majority of them were more or less about my same age, or that of their leader; many were not even seven years old; the number of grown-ups or bigger boys was very small. The smallest had been assigned to the infantry, and they were armed with reed rifles, willow-tree staffs, or any other stick or cane. This was the case for all but about forty of them, or perhaps a few more, who carried especially noteworthy firearms, for they had loaded gunpowder into the upper end of their reeds and carved up a vent to make a place for the fuse near the knot of the reed. Then came those of medium height, who were the artillerymen. They held in their hands small tin cannons, with wheels and gun-carriages that were also made of tin, which they had either cast themselves or had gotten from a store, as most stores in the city around that time were filled with these kinds of toy. A larger piece, the pride and joy of the regiment, was placed in the middle, with a beautiful dog attached to it. The dog was one of those known as the *choco*,[3] and it already seemed well trained and accustomed to gunfire. Finally, the larger boys, mounted on sticks, made up the cavalry, and they were armed with long canes that served as lances, which were adorned with green leaves or handkerchiefs as streamers. The uniforms worn by this army were even more incredible than those of the province's real, adult army. *Mamelucos*, simple trousers and common shirts, the clothes of the son of a man with a title, and the rags of a bricklayer's son—all were mixed together in those motley groups. And there were also a few very small boys wearing only a long shirt, opened in front as if it were a gown worn as a *negligée*.

The different corps also had their corresponding musical band, each appropriate to its branch of the army. The smaller boys in the infantry had four or five drums, a *pavillon chinois* consisting of a number of small bells, sheets of tin that were being used as cymbals, and many *herques*—whistles made from thin pieces of cane, that is—that produced an infernal sound, the most horrendous noise heard by any eardrum since that endured by the patriarch Job. The cavalry and artillery regiments, for their part, had a real—although cracked—bugle, reed pipes, and countless other wind instruments that could also be heard in their bands, and which were almost as good as the *herques* which I just mentioned.

The main drum of the infantry band deserves its own special mention. It was played by a grown man who was over forty years old, a giant among all those children. He was laughing and, I do believe, enjoying himself more than anyone else there. His shaggy hair, which was not covered by a hat, made his head look enormous, monstrous in fact, and his yellowish face, already quite wrinkled, showed two very small, bright eyes nearly hidden in their thick and fleshy eyelids, as well as a pug nose, and a mouth that opened as far out as his large ears, which flapped forward like a dog's. He was dressed like the most well-to-do mestizos. It was, in a word, Paulito, Paulito the deaf-mute. He was the most loyal, noble, and intelligent creature among Governor Antezana's servants, and an individual whom—as my young readers shall see in due time—those who have written the history of my country were very wrong to leave out.

When I arrived, the officers were gathered around their leader. I remember seeing many among them whose names would later become famous in the fifteen years of the Wars of Independence, either for their heroic fighting or their martyred deaths. I do not know how many, like myself, are still alive today, and could give testimony to all these events.*

The noble general of those bright troops, the Marshal Don Luis

---

*Justo Guzmán has not written me in a long time. However, I do have right here in front of me the last letter he sent me, in which he says: "I still remember, my dear Juan, the famous entrance of the Governor of the Gran Paititi. Everything from those times has stuck to me in an unbelievable manner. Would you believe that after fifty years I still had inside of me the bullet that I was wounded with in the hills of Pirhuas? It hit me in the groin, but it was just recently taken out when they removed a tumor that had been bothering me in my ankle!"

Cros, was wearing a grand military uniform made out of rags of clashing colors and strings of dazzling tinsel. His hat was a masterpiece of golden cardboard, spangles, and chicken feathers. He had riding boots that came up nearly to his crotch, and he explained, in a very loud voice, how the *Gringo* used them for his trips to Santa Cruz. He was actually mounted, too, and in quite a regal manner, on a white, filthy donkey, which was saddled with Argentine riding gear, silver-plated bit and harness, and with a lot of additional tinsel and glitter everywhere. In spite of the arduous labor with which he held it up, his extraordinarily enormous, rusty saber would occasionally slip out of his hand. His imposing air and his every word and gesture reminded one of the victor from Huaqui and Amiraya. I have never in my life seen another general as elegant and handsome as him, and this includes, my dear readers, the ruffians who, dressed like French marshals, have made off with everything from the Republic that they could get their hands on! And finally, he had an assistant pillioned on the croup of his mount—this was Captain Agustín, the one I was looking for and had found at last, beside himself with joy.

"Ho, there he is! Here comes the deserter!" the assistant screamed out as soon as he laid his eyes on me.

"Seize him!" the general yelled. "He is court-martialed right here and now; he shall be shot four times in the back!"

The entire infantry band jumped on me at that point. Between the dreadful shouting and the loud whistling and horrible noise from the *herques* and the reed pipes, it is a miracle I did not end up as deaf as Paulito. And with all the hands that pulled and dragged me from one place to another, grabbing anywhere they were able to, I do not understand how I managed to escape with any item of untorn clothing left on my body. The meekness with which I tried to turn myself in was of no use whatsoever, and it probably would have been even more fatal for me to fight back, as my anger was on the verge of inciting me to do. But luckily, at this point, the magnanimous general rode up on his donkey and extended his protective hand in my direction.

"That's enough," he said, "release him, for God's sake! He'll be quite safe by my side. . . . I need another assistant. . . . These eight that I have are insufficient for all the orders that I have to dispatch. . . . Let's go!" he added in his commanding voice. "Form your columns! In silence! To teach you a lesson, I now order everyone to serve in the company."

"Hurrah! Long live the general! Long live the Governor of the Gran Paititi!" the imps yelled, and quickly returned to their files.

I was free and could breathe again. I wanted to be angry and leave, but I could not; I laughed, and finally took my post by our general's side.

"Don't be a fool. . . . This is fun!" Agustín said to me from his post on the donkey's croup, as happy as could be.

Order having been reestablished with much difficulty, the general and his principal assistant spurred on their battle steed as well as they could to position themselves in the best location, on top of a pile of rubble from a fallen adobe wall. From there, the absolutely unique caudillo, who was as eloquent an orator as he was a courageous soldier, addressed his troops in a manner that I would never dare to even attempt to emulate with my humble prose. However, I do remember word for word how he concluded, and I shall transcribe it here as a model, as a helpful instruction for all present and future captains who wish to make a triumphant entrance in as dignified a manner as possible:

"My soldiers! Do you see my jacket, my boots, my hat? The moon has come out with the sole purpose of admiring them, but I fear she may soon hide, blushing at the sight! Stop right where you are, my poor little moon! March, soldiers, march! Long live the Governor of the Gran Paititi!"

"Hurrah! Hurrah! Hurrah!"

The troops began to march. The rear, however, was soon detained in some sort of dreadful commotion. They had gathered around something that we could not see and were whistling and throwing fistfuls of dirt at whatever was in the middle of their circle.

"What's going on?" the general demanded angrily, and sent me to reestablish order, giving me full authority to do so by any means necessary.

No one answered my questions, nor much less allowed me to get through to the middle so that I could ascertain with my own eyes what was going on. So I began to swing a tucuma cane—the unmatched sword of one of my fellow assistants—to the right and left, dealing out blows until I was at last able to penetrate the mass. A man, a bearded giant, was rolling about on the ground, desperately trying to stop some ten or twelve boys from tearing off his trousers. I became quite infuriated, yelled, and kept on dealing out blows with my sword. But one single word disarmed all of my anger.

"It's the *Maleso!*[4] It's the *Pallaco!*"

"Well, well!" I answered, laughing. "Carry on, then."

They managed to tear off the man's trousers, and tie them around his neck as if it were a necktie. Then they took him off looking like that to the head of the column and forced him to walk there, publicly humiliated.

Plagued by drunkenness and his addiction to the vice of the *coca* leaf, the *Maleso* was the most debased of men. He was also a beggar, a thief, and perhaps much worse than that, for I heard as much evil spoken about him as can possibly be attributed to a human creature. . . . When the victor from Amiraya had thrown money from his balconies with the generosity that we have heard so highly exalted by Father Arredondo, that wretch was the first to run, joyfully screaming to pick up the coins that fell on the stone pavement. He was soon followed by others of his kind, and since then they have been given the disgraceful name that they rightfully deserved: the *Pallacos.*[5]

The children of Cochabamba—I have already stated that our band included, without distinction, the sons of the most distinguished families as well as those of the poorest—were thus carrying out, right then and there, a kind of popular justice with that miserable wretch who had dared to approach them in their games. And they were right to do so! Even today, as the old—very old—man that I am, I would applaud them! It is a shame, and a big one at that, that my brave people did not later tear the trousers off the vile political extortioners—the *capituleros* and the other vermin who are such a disgrace to a democracy.*

---

*Editor's Note: *Capituleros*: "Name given to those who led the scheming and plotting of

From then on, the parade continued without any other interruptions. The general, with his assistant on the donkey's croup, went first; his nine other assistants, including myself, went next; we were followed by Paulito and the *Maleso*, and the infantry band and battalion; then came the cavalry units; and finally the artillery. As soon as we started marching down the streets, the officers began to light the petards that they had brought with them in their pockets and throw them up in the air. Then, at the first corner, and afterward on all the subsequent ones, we stopped so that the artillery could fire a round of volleys. And at no instant did we stop the yelling and the whistling, carrying on in a manner that was certain to alarm the entire city. The frightened residents at first rushed to close their doors. But then they peaked out through a window or a small shutter, and when they saw what it was, they came out in a mad rush to cheer us on and join the fun.

"It's the boys," they would say, "there goes Luisito. Let them have their fun! Let them learn to be soldiers! Long live the homeland!"

And their applause became louder, too, when they saw the miserable *Maleso* beside our main drum.

"Ho there!" they would say. "They have the *Maleso*, and he doesn't have any trousers on. . . . That's it, boys! Excellent! Only these rascals would think of these things. Ha, ha, ha, ha, ha!"

Our band grew with every step we took. No boy in town wanted to be left behind, and not one single curious resident either, man or woman, regardless of class, could resist the desire to follow us to see where all of this would end up. Never had such a racket been made, nor a better laugh been had, in the city of Oropesa than with our parade.

By the time the general reached the corner of the Barrio Fuerte, his troops and the multitudes of curious onlookers behind them stretched back more than three blocks. Here he doubled back to his left and gave us, the assistants, orders to have the army fall into battle formation on that entire side of the plaza, facing the Cabil-

elections, some more skillfully than others. There are men whose only employment is that of being *capituleros*, and this is more than enough for them to live comfortably. . . . Each *capitulero* is worth proportionately as much as the number of men who follow him to the election booths." Juan Espinoza, *Diccionario Republicano*.[6]

do. Despite the most infernal din and clamor, this was somehow finally achieved.

"Fire!" he yelled then, with that sharp and vibrant voice of his that even Neptune would have coveted to aid him in mastering the roaring of the tempests and the thrashing of the tumultuous waves.

And an endless drumfire shot off from all the reed rifles, cannons, and petards as loud as that from Amiraya, I thought.

"Long live the homeland!" we boys shouted repeatedly.

"Long live the homeland!" the curious onlookers answered back.

Somehow, too, four of the officers whom I had first seen when I arrived at the square had managed to get into the Church of the Matriz and climb up the tower to reach the bells, and these were now tolling almost as loudly as when the news from Aroma had reached the city.

Meanwhile, the Provincial Junta and the Cabildo had met to deliberate about the proper measures to carry out and had decided to send an order to the soldiers in the barracks to have them move in on the army in the city. But the same thing occurred with them as had occurred with the rest of the residents. Once they realized what was really happening, they cheered the boys and their idea and laughed readily now that there was no cause for alarm.

They concurred, at last, that it was amusing, but a bit much. Therefore, since there was no other way to bring them under control, they sent for the governor, and for council members Arriaga, Vidal, and Cabrera,[7] as well as for our general's father, to come out on horseback to help silence the mob of imps.

As soon as we saw them by the light of the moon, which luckily had not been too embarrassed by Luis's bright uniform, we yelled with even more enthusiasm:

"Long live the homeland! Long live Don Mariano Antezana!"

"That's very good, my sons," answered this venerable gentleman, whom I consider the first citizen of Cochabamba. "Long may she live! Yes, may she live forever, our beloved homeland! But these things should not be done at night, depriving the neighbors of their sleep and perhaps even scaring a few poor, sick people to death."

"Yes, yes! Long live the governor!" we answered in turn, and obediently began to disperse.

"Oh, Juanito!" our general said to me in a tearful tone when he saw his father approaching him. "This time I've really done it. After this one I'll need bed-rest for at least two months!"

But contrary to what he feared, or what he pretended to fear—the scoundrel that he was—the *Gringo* ran up to him quite joyfully. He grabbed him in his arms to help him dismount from the donkey, and gave him such a big kiss that it sounded like a shot had been fired from one of our little cannons.

"Bravo! Oh, *mon Dieu!* This is my son!" he exclaimed proudly.

How different was Doña Teresa's welcome for Captain Don Agustín! She got so worked up when she saw her son that she reached out and scratched him and began to drag him straight off, holding him by his hair. She was about to do the same with me when the noble boy pounced back at her, and Carmencita, shaking and white as paper, grabbed her pleadingly by the neck, sobbing. I do not know, I do not wish to recall what I felt at that moment and what action I had already decided to take if that beast had scratched my skin with her nails.

The following day, precisely at twelve o'clock, the community was called out to the sound of the tolling bells. The Notary Don Angel Francisco Astete, followed by the best battalion of militiamen, made public the following announcement of the government, which deserves to be known by this and all subsequent generations:

"The Gubernatorial Junta of this province, as formed with the approval of the Honorable Junta from the capital of Buenos Aires, in the name of the King Don Fernando VII, may God keep him. . . .

"It having come before the attention of this government that the boys of the town make much raucous noise at night with drums and cracks and reports from little cannons, which inconveniences, shocks, and disturbs the community, especially the ill. . . . Thus, we declare and order that all judges and subaltern magistrates prohibit such boys from playing at games of war at nighttime. The parents of these are also hereby notified to control them.

However, it is understood that this order does not extend to disallowing them from entertaining themselves, in a moderate fashion, during the day. . . .

"Signed in Cochabamba on this date, the 24th of March of 1812.

"Doctor *Francisco Vidal*. — *Manuel Vélez*. — Doctor *José Manuel Salinas*.[8]

"*Note:* This is to be published in the customary locations and with all due solemnity. Date *ut supra*.[9]

Astete."

XVII

My Appearance Before Father Arredondo's Dreadful Tribunal, in Which I Am Declared to Be a Philosophizing Heretic

Blessed months of March and April! In such glorious beauty do you dress the gorgeous land where I was born! If only the other months of the year were like you—if at least September and October were not so niggardly with their rain, and if they could only be encouraged by the fine example of February's generosity to prevent the hot, thirsty sun from drinking up all the waters of the Rocha River and of the lakes—I would have every reason in the world to believe, even if they brought the Inca Garcilaso de la Vega before me and had him swear in my presence that the first apple trees in this area were brought from the Peninsula, that it was in Calacala that Eve had eaten from the forbidden fruit. For Genesis does not state that the fruit was specifically an apple. It could have been a cherimoya, a pacay pod, or any other of the delicious fruits from our beautiful native trees.

Oh, I say it again: you are blessed! For how beautiful you were to me in that dreadful year of 1812, in spite of Goyeneche, in spite of Doña Teresa!

And the fact was, my curious readers, that no one in Cocha-bamba paid any heed to all the fierce barking and the furious foam-ing at the mouth of the pacifier of Upper Perú, who was later to re-turn like a wounded wild boar. Nor did the noble lady pay any attention to her «foundling waif.» She never asked whether he went out to the streets, whether he ate at home or not, or whether he was still wasting his time with the books from the room of the *duende*. Thus, I gave up my best intentions and resolutions, and abandoned myself to the *rocheo*, which is somewhat akin to "play-ing hooky," or however else it might be called in other places, as long as it is understood that I dedicated myself to truancy, and to stealing the tempting, ripe fruit from the orchards and gardens on the shores of the Rocha River. And it is from this activity by the river that this very common term of *rocheo* is derived in my coun-try. I should add, however, that back in my days it was very normal for boys to participate in truancy and in this kind of stealing, to the extent that if a farmer or a landowner tried to stop or sic his dogs on the poor *carachupas*—or *pilluelos* in Spanish, or *gamins* in good Frenchified Spanish[1]—they would be the ones who were seen as strange criminals, or as horrible monsters.

Luis and I—do I even need to say it?—were inseparable com-panions. Dionisio would frequently follow us, but he was more se-rious than we were, for he liked to work and did not want to quit the bellows at the blacksmith's shop for very long at a time. If we were trying to climb over an adobe wall with plenty of cracks to use as foot holds, I would be the first to charge on up; if the adobe wall was too tall and smooth, Dionisio would offer me his shoulders so I could climb up; if this did not suffice, Luis would up climb on mine; meanwhile, some dog would inevitably be barking on the other side. Dionisio always tried to be the first one to go in, to be the one to meet the possible danger of being bitten by the dog, or to be shot with a sling by the owner, who would have been alerted by the dog's barking.

"This is an outrage," the "Governor of the Gran Paititi," would say in such situations; "it is unacceptable; look at this little hyp-ocrite, always acting so small and humble, but then insisting on taking the biggest risks. He's as quiet as a stone saint figurine, but he's braver than we are, and he has already taken a wound to the chest. No, a thousand times no, for God's sake! I will not permit him ever again to go without me to come face to face with the Governor of Cuzco, the Knight of the Order of St. James, etcetera, etcetera."

And he would immediately turn to Dionisio, demanding explanations from him, putting him on the spot in a terrible manner.

"Tell me, you died, didn't you? Well, then! I want you to tell me right now what you saw in the other world. What do they say over there about the *chapetones*? Speak up! Answer me, you little Devil!"

And poor Dionisio, who loved his friend better than he loved himself, would laugh to himself, like Alejo, and get out of the fix by timidly proposing some new caper.

I do not want my readers to think, however, that the only goals of our outings were to satisfy our capricious stomachs. We also had the tastes of sybarites and poets. We were intoxicated by the fragrances that filled the warm, moist air; we were enchanted to no end by contemplating the flowers and listening to the warbling birds; we spent lovely hours enjoying and admiring the beauties of mother earth—with whom, by then, we had fallen deeply in love.

One day we stripped a long hedge of fresh, fragrant flowers from the Rosal estate. Then we made a very soft bed with these under a group of beautiful acacias, and we dove on it, screaming out in our happiness. We threw handfuls of leaves at each other, and buried ourselves in them. Then Luis said the following words to us, which I have never forgotten:

"How beautiful it would be to fall asleep like this, here, forever!"

On another day we walked a league so as to admire the great, hollowed ceibo tree out in the Linde. We measured the thickness of the trunk with a long rope and saw that it was nine varas around; we went into the hollow, which is big enough for twelve people to fit in it; we cleaned it out and made a rug out of wildflowers inside it. We widened an opening on the side of the tree above us, through which a ray of sunlight shone in, into a perfect oval. But then I made a discovery that dispelled my happiness at once.

"What did you find?" my friends asked me.

"Nothing," I answered, but could not pull my eyes away from

the two mysterious letters, "C. A.," which were carved deeply into the wood next to the window that we had just been opening up.

I remember that on another day we took a beautiful acacia that was about three varas tall from the shores of the Rocha River and transported it to the plaza on Mount San Sebastián, promising each other to water it every day.

"This will be very beautiful one day," Luis said, "when this little tree grows and can cast its shade like those in Calacala, I will come here with my uniform—my real brigadier's uniform, that is, for I will be a general for sure—and I will take a seat between two of its branches and enjoy the running bulls that we will celebrate the homeland with."

Tired, covered in sweat, we would go bathe at Carrillo. We would take our clothes off, run, and jump into the deep pool; we floated up to the surface, light as corks; we swam "butterfly" style, fooling more than one gullible individual, who would jump in without knowing how to swim, and sink like lead, until we would pull them out, half-drowned; we would get out a hundred times to stretch out on the fine sand; we would crawl around like caymans; we would jump back in the water a hundred more times. . . . Oh! It was so beautiful! If I could take one bath like that now in my river, with my friends from childhood, I believe that it would make my blood race vigorously through my veins again, just as if I were to drink all the water from the fountain of youth! But . . . will I ever be able to see my country again? And where—my God!—are my friends?

In the afternoons, when we did not have some military parade, review, or a meeting of our academy to attend, I would go visit the Grandmother and Clarita. We talked about so many things, all of them so wonderful, that I would gladly give up all the knowledge I have today in exchange for hearing even a few of those words that used to come from the lips of the old blind woman. I believe that she saw everything more clearly than everyone else with the eyes of experience and with the light—if I may be allowed to say so—of her large heart. I want to recall here—even if it may seem like a triviality to you, like a doting obstinacy of my senility—the stories that she used to tell me of the lay sister Quintañona and of Don Ego, which were meant to serve as examples for me. Reprimanding me in my pranks and for my attempts to make Dionisio as much of a truant as I was, she tended to conclude her speeches with these words:

"Well, you will have plenty of time to do those things when you are older and have more sense, my son. The important thing is never to be a hypocrite, or selfish, or a coward. Listen: Quintañona used to put a mustard seed in her coffer every time she said her prayers, and she said so, so many prayers for over a hundred years. But at the time of her death, when she thought that her coffer would be completely full, the only thing she found in it was one small, wrinkled-up little seed that she had put in there after giving some poor child a crumb of bread. This was the only one that her guardian angel had saved for her. And poor Don Ego, who loved himself so much and who never wanted to extend a hand to anyone, nor to fight the Moors, was turned into a tree trunk in the middle of a deserted countryside. There, he felt his heart claw its way out of his body with sharp nails, and when he looked down, he saw that the only thing that he had had in his chest all his life was a black, pustular toad."

Clara—the poor *Palomita*—listened to these things in silence. She would go off to the kitchen for a moment, where I could hear her bustling about and singing her *yaravís* to herself, and she would come back with some simple, delightful dish prepared especially for me: a plate of potatoes, baked or broiled in hot embers, with peppers or with *soltero*,[2] or some *humita*[3] in a corn husk. In short, she would prepare something like this and bring it to me in that humble, generous, and good manner that the people of my hospitable country regale upon their visitors, or even upon an unknown traveler who might come to the door of their huts with the sole intention of getting out of the sun for a little shade.

Oh, blessed be the months of March and April of 1812!

But how quickly they passed by! How horrendous the fury of the «Three-Faced Man» when he turned toward my people again! How awful it was for me to appear before the dreadful tribunal of the Reverend Father Robustiano Arredondo, to be declared a philosophizing heretic, and to have to suffer the punishment suited to my misconduct!

It was vanity, my desire to excel over my enemy Clemente, to strip him of his laurels, that brought me to this last, painful extreme.

One evening, when she was not discomforted by her flatulence nor by her terrible migraines, the noble lady Doña Teresa was in the small chapel chatting delightfully in Quechua behind closed doors with Doña Martina and the worthy godmother of her child, Doña Gregoria Cuzcurrita, his learned Honor's wife. They had their corresponding bowls of chocolate, and her "Little Seraph" was stuffing himself with candies and pastries. The other children had wanted, for their part, to stay a while longer at the table after dinner, and were listening to the sambo Clemente telling a story of *duendes* and apparitions, just when, as my luck would have it, I arrived at the dining room.

"Come here, vagrant, vagabond from the streets," Carmencita said to me; "I'm angry with you. . . . Don't speak to me, and don't look at me, either."

"Have a seat, sir commander," Captain Don Agustín added, "this is even better than the comedy *The Brave and Just Man.*"

"Go on," I answered disdainfully, "you don't know anything about stories if you haven't heard the one about Quintañona."

"Quintañona?" Carmencita asked.

"Yes," I answered with an important air. "But I feel I have a slight head cold; I will have to tell it some other time."

But once the children's curiosity had been excited, it was impossible to keep them waiting for an hour, or even a minute, for that matter—a fact I knew quite well. And although I wanted to tell my story more than they wanted to hear it, I made them beg, and went as far as demanding a kiss from Carmencita, before I began.

They interrupted me a thousand times, shouting out in admiration, and just as many times did I pretend to have a sore throat and be extremely fatigued, so that they would continue begging me to go on, until I eventually finished the story to a resounding round of applause, from the servants as well as the children. But I knew I had also incited, more than ever, the anger of the dethroned storyteller toward me. When I retired to my room, I even believed that with time I would challenge the fame of the well-known Father Jaén, whose book was passed from hand to hand back then.

The next day, when the sambo called me to the reception room on behalf of the lady of the house, I trembled with as much fear as if he had said that the Marshal Goyeneche was waiting for me and if I were the *Gringo*, suspected of having written the paper with "the rights of man" on it.

The lady was sitting on a bench with her golden denarius in her hand, looking up at the ceiling as if the red and yellow star painted in the middle of it were completely absorbing her attention. I calmed down a bit. But then, at the door that led to the chapel, occupying its whole width with his white cassock, I saw Father Arredondo armed with a scourge, holding a crucifix up in the air, looking severe, imposing, and unabatable, just like Torquemeda[4] must have looked to Fernando and Isabel[5] when he appeared before them demanding the establishment of the Inquisition. I broke out in a cold sweat, and felt my legs about to give.

"Come here, you infidel!" the Father snorted. "Get down, on your knees!" he continued when I was two steps away from him. "Listen and answer like a Christian—if you are one, that is," he added when I had knelt at his feet. "Why did you say that Quintañona's prayers were in vain? Don't you know that *'oportet semper orare'*?[6] That *'Majestatem tuam laudant Angeli, adorant dominationes'*?[7] That *'prima via veritatis est humilitas; secunda, humilitas; tertia, humilitas'*?"[8]

Each one of these questions was followed by a blow from the scourge, and then by my painful scream.

"Sir. . . . Reverend Father. . . . I didn't . . . do . . ." I started to say, but a deluge of whips from the scourge fell on my body as if I were uttering some atrocious confession of unbelievable irreverence. And I was forced to endure the blows, writhing and screaming, despite the fact that I already considered myself more than just a child by then, for the respect that the religious cassock inspired in me at that time did not allow me to even consider the idea of defending myself against the dreadful scourge, nor of running away from where I was, at the feet of the enraged Prelate of Our Lady of Mercy.

"There it is, just as I have been saying all along, Reverend Father!" Doña Teresa was crying in the meantime. "He's the Evil One himself!"

The Father did not stop beating me. Growing more and more furious, he stomped on me with his legs, big as an elephant's, until he saw me lying unconscious on the ground, and until he was actually so tired that it became necessary for someone to bring him a large glass of the *Católico*.

I came to in the arms of the mulatta, who had sat down on the floor to put my head on her lap. She was splashing my face with water, unable to hold back her tears. The lady continued screaming that I was the Devil. The Father was wiping off his sweat with a handkerchief, and he now held a parchment-bound folio under his arm.

"He is to be locked in his room until he memorizes the *Flos Sanctorum*[9] in the minutest of details, or until he dies of old age," he said. "Have all the books that he spends his time with and that feed his arrogance removed. It would not surprise me if, among them, there were some that the Quirogas managed to bring somehow from the City of Kings.[10] . . . One of the ones from what they call the Encyclopedia of Diderot or Astarot[11]—it's all the same. I will examine them when I have the time. But if I don't come back soon, have them burned in a large pile, your Excellency, my noble lady Doña Teresa."

"Above all," she shrieked, "I don't want him infecting my children. It only takes one rotten apple—"

"Oh! Absolutely," the Father replied; "the disgraceful infidel should have to wear a millstone around his neck and be made to jump into the depths of the sea. Has your Excellency had Brother Justo informed of what has happened?"

"I thought about that, Reverend Father, but it was not possible. . . . He is not here. . . . I was told that he went to see the «other one». Oh, my God! How many crosses will I have to bear in my long, torturous life!"

"Poor Ladyship!"

"I believe, in any case, that Brother Justo would have laughed at that irreverent story anyway and that he would have tried to assure us that there was nothing wrong with it, as he does with everything that harms and insults our lord, the king, and our holy religion."

"Yes, yes. . . . How slow of me! I had forgotten that. . . . I believe, if your Excellency, my noble Ladyship, will permit me, that the despicable wretch and ungrateful disciple of the Great Fathers of our Church is firewood that is quite ready to be thrown into the bonfire of the Inquisition."

"May God's will be served, Reverend Father!"

"Come!" the Prelate said right away, pulling me up. "Take this precious treasure in your irreverent hands and go to your room, you miserable, lost lamb. I wish there had been some gentler way to get you out of the brambles!"

I took the folio in my irreverent hands and left, crying, not knowing what horrible sin I had committed, nor why I was a heretic, or the Devil. Today, as I read and re-read the most orthodox book that we had at that time, *The Mystical Realizations* of the Reverend Father Brother Antonio Arbiol[12]—and which, incidentally, I have saved as the last vestige of the library of the room of the *duende*—I do not believe that there was anything reprehensible about the story of Quintañona. On the contrary, I see that the good Father Arbiol states conclusively: "Regarding the number of prayers and catechisms, it is necessary to warn those who attempt to gain spiritual advantage from them not to say too many of them in succession, because praying too much in that manner can wither one's mind and fatigue one's soul. Christ Himself admonished us not to speak too much when we say prayers out loud, which is why he taught us the very brief and holy prayer of 'Our Father.'"

My punishment was that much more difficult to bear with the thought that my dear teacher would not know of it, as, according to Doña Teresa, he was not in the city. Who could that "other one" be who had made him leave me behind? Would he be back soon? Could I have lost him, too? I asked myself these questions, spilling many tears on the *Flos Sanctorum*. I opened the book automatically, but then I read with indescribable emotion the following words that were handwritten on the first page of the manuscript: "Blessed be those who shed tears, for they shall be comforted." It was the sweetest promise offered by Jesus! And it was printed in my mother's handwriting! There was no way for me to mistake those round, minute letters with which she used to correct my writing exercises! That book had been in her hands. . . . When, though? What immense suffering would have made her take refuge in the memory of that divine promise—that, for her, would only be kept in Heaven?

I do not remember how many days my new confinement lasted. I was forbidden to have any of the books that I had been saving from Paula's devastation, nor even my innocent *Don Quixote*, which must have suffered, along with the others, an *auto-da-fé* crueler than the one executed by the priest and the barber, and assisted by the niece and the landlady, against the Ingenious Gentleman.

In the judgment of the Father and of Doña Teresa, every book that was not a catechism or one of the lives of the saints was necessarily heretical. Herrera, Garcilaso, Las Casas, Moreto, Calderón, Cervantes—all undoubtedly spoke very poorly of Quintañona, and by ridiculing this respectable person, insulted in turn all devout souls. And these, of course, could only be people who said the rosary, the hymn of the Holy Trinity, and the rosary of the seven decades all day and all night. It was impossible for the Prelate and the lady to realize that the Grandmother was the only responsible person in what they called my lamentable misguidedness. Nor did Doña Teresa know of my visits to the old blind woman. Besides, I believe that if she had, she would have been that much more angry with me. There was nothing left for me but to read and re-read the *Flos Sanctorum*, but my mind was completely preoccupied with very different things. For some reason, I heard the melody of the violin from the old house at all hours; all the letters I looked at seemed to transform themselves into those two, very mysterious ones from the painting of the Virgin, from the ring, and from the trunk of the giant ceibo tree; I dreamt of battles; I rode quickly on my nag across the rocky plain of Sipe Sipe; I saw tin cannons and bronze grenades everywhere. The idea of running away, and of becoming a soldier, was slowly starting to take control of me.

Carmencita and Agustín would come furtively to my room and speak to me through the crack of the door, each one trying to comfort me in his own way.

"I care so much for you. Learn the book quickly. . . . Don't be an oaf," the first one said.

"We're going to make you colonel. . . . They're saying that Arze has destroyed Goyeneche," the second one added.

It did not take long for Luis, for his part, to sneak into my room through the window.

"Long live the homeland! Death to the *tablas!*"* he exclaimed as soon as his feet touched the ground. "What's happened? Why can't you come outside? Have they locked you up? Do you want me to help you escape?" he proceeded to ask, firing question after question at me, as he always did, without stopping to hear my response.

Covering his mouth with my hand, I finally told him everything that had happened.

"The Devil! This can't be!" he yelled then, which made me have to cover his mouth again so that the servants would not hear him. "No, sir!" he went on very angrily, refusing to alter his tone. "It's one thing if my father skins me alive—even though he didn't actually do it, and I did lie to you, like a scoundrel, like a true, live scoundrel, as you were very right to call me. But who is Father Arredondo to whip you, my friend? . . . That walking wine barrel! And why did you put up with it, my soft-souled friend? No, sir! No, no, and no! We're not little anymore. . . . There's a whole world out there. . . . They're saying that Goyeneche is coming, and I think that Don Esteban won't know what to do without us."

"Have it your way," I answered, "we'll be soldiers. . . . We'll go give our advice to Don Esteban. But be quiet—we have to wait for the right time to make our escape."

He kept coming to see me every night. He told me, in his own way, everything that he saw and heard as he pried restlessly through the whole city—in the Cabildo, in the Junta, in the Offices of the Prefect—for he could get in anywhere, slivering into every place like an eel.

"Don Esteban," he told me, "has an army so large that when it

---

* This is the term they had begun to use by then for Goyeneche's soldiers because of the long, stiff coats that they wore, which truly did look as rigid as *table* tops. In the Valley (that is to say in the Valley of Cliza, which, because it is the largest and widest of all the valleys, is referred to even today, by antonomasia, simply as the "Valley") they were also known by the name of Saracens, because of a statement that Arze made in one of his proclamations: "We Americans must fight without rest against the Spaniards, just as they once fought against their conquerors, the Saracens."

takes its battle formations it reaches from Tarata to Angostura—
no less than four leagues! Don Mateo Zenteno's people have
stretched out along the entire Cordillera, from Tapacarí to
Quirquiave. A general, Pueyrredón, is coming from "below" with a
hundred thousand cavalrymen. . . . The horses are like churches
and their riders like towers. . . . Their lances put together must be
countless varas taller than the cross of the Church of the Matriz!"

One night he arrived happier than ever.

"There are six hundred cannons and two thousand grenades,"
he told me. "But that's nothing. . . . Look!"

And he placed before me a glass ball, larger than an orange, and
he added, growing more and more excited as he went on:

"This is it! This is the real thing! 'My' grenades can only kill fifty
chapetones."

"And this thing . . . ?"

"Go on! You're such a fool! This is glass. . . . It's made in
Paredón. . . . I think, actually, that I was thinking of it and that they
stole my idea. . . . This thing explodes into a thousand smithereens.
. . . And each small splinter, like the end of my finger nail, look, like
this. . . . Each one rips into a *chapetón*, and penetrates as far as his
bones, and . . . *brum*! That's all there is for Goyeneche's army!"

Oh! I cannot, I must not ever forget those childish thoughts! I
am very old now, and I still have a thousand much more serious
events to recount to you—the great sacrifices, the eternal glories of
our America. But I have stopped to recall fondly these small, insignificant details of my dark life, which took place during the
months of March and April of the very memorable year of 1812.

XVIII

A Pull From Behind.
Quirquiave and the Quehuiñal.

In the meantime, Goyeneche, blind with rage and thirsty for vengeance, was about to turn back against the untamable Oropesa.

When he had continued his triumphant march "to Buenos Aires" after the battle of Amiraya, he believed that the hordes of Pumacagua and Choqueguanca, combined with the regular forces from his army assigned to that area under the command of Lombera, would easily extinguish the fire that seemed to be starting again behind his back in the province of La Paz. And he certainly did not figure that Cochabamba would rise up again, as completely helpless as he had left it.

He continued on his way to the city then known as Charcas confident about his rear, receiving as he went the surrender of the defenseless towns, the cheers of the few supporters of the Colonial regime, and the incense burnt for him at the church altars by the weak souls who, after having joyfully welcomed the nascent homeland, believed that it had now been drowned in the blood of the martyrs of the 16th of July and in the very plentiful amounts spilled at Huaqui and Amiraya.

The patriots who still had hope and spirit fled before he arrived and gathered again once they had crossed the border with Argentina. From the entire auxiliary army—whose leaders Castelli and Balcárcel had fallen into disgrace and had been called by the Junta of Buenos Aires to account for their actions—there were only two small groups of brave soldiers left: the first, led by Pueyrredón, traveled through unfrequented roads with the fortunes from the Mint of Potosí, with which Belgrano's glorious army would later be formed; and the second, which had survived the defeat of Amiraya, followed the lively and courageous Díaz Vélez, and much later they would make up the nucleus of the vanguard of Belgrano's army.

The evil American, the unworthy compatriot from Melgar, could consider himself, at that time, the master of Upper Perú, and promise himself that the dreams that stirred his treacherous, vulgar soul would very soon be realized. He would be the Grand Pacifier of the Viceroyalty of Buenos Aires! He would arrive triumphantly from the mountains of Cuzco to the mouth of the Río de la Plata! Victory would accompany his carriage for over six hundred leagues, through the mountain ranges, plains, valleys, and pampas of South America! Arbiter then of so many provinces, he would choose the master who best suited him from among Fernando VII, Joseph Bonaparte,[1] and Carlota[2]—whichever one he chose to lavish him with honors, to double his copious fortunes, to name him the Grandee of Spain or of Portugal, and to give him the right to appear donning his hat before the majestic presence of the monarch! The outcry of his brothers—of the anxious *criollos*, of the contemptible mestizos, and of the brutish Indians among whom he was born—did not matter to him at all. He did not think that following behind him, counting his victims, rummaging through the rubble and the ashes that he was leaving behind, most grave and indignant, was History, the only one who allots men their eternal rewards or their eternal punishments, and that she would call him, throughout the centuries to come, voiced from a thousand different mouths—including from that of the poor child who was then locked up under bread and water by the obese Father Arredondo—a vicious and vile snake that fed on the heart of the great American homeland!

But the "shout" of my noble and valiant Oropesa did not take long to dispel all his dreams and show him the dreadful reality. Murillo's fire was indeed inextinguishable! The cold ashes would burn forever, as hot as a wildfire, the very moment the victor's foot ceased to be on them! Goyeneche would never reach as far as the Argentine pampas, where, thanks to Cochabamba's sacrifices, the invincible "Centaurs" were to be formed!

It is said that when he learned of the new uprising, he was overcome for the first time by the violent and painful convulsions that would later serve as his excuse for abandoning the impossible enterprise that he had undertaken, and eventually to retire to the Peninsula to vegetate, feeling quite smug with his title of Count of Huaqui—which I, my readers, would never exchange for mine, that of Commander and Aide-de-Camp of the Grand Marshal of Ayacucho, which I am honored to have here in my small vineyard, hidden deep in the Valley of Caracato, next to my sweet and loving companion Merceditas.

His fury rose to delirious levels when the unfortunate Santiestevan—who, as I have previously recounted, had surrendered on the 29th of October of 1811—appeared before him. Goyeneche exploded, shouting all manners of vulgarities at him, and he jumped on him, swinging his fists, so that his followers had to forcefully hold him back. He wanted to have him executed by firing squad at once and did not consent to holding a court-martial for him until they convinced him that this would be a better way to make the judgment more solemn and have it serve as an example to others. But when the court-martial absolved the offender, Goyeneche became enraged, and he decided on his own that if Santiestevan's life was to be spared, he would have his honor destroyed instead. Thus, Goyeneche declared in a general order that: "Santiestevan was unfit for duty, and that he was not to be assigned to any position requiring of his personal responsibility."

The truth was that the poor Don Miguel Santiestevan was a good soldier and that he had been rightfully absolved by his military judges. It would have been impossible to expect the future hero of Mount San Sebastián, with only one hundred soldiers, to resist an entire people whom Goyeneche himself found it necessary to resort to all of his forces to subjugate. And if Santiestevan had resisted on the 29th of October, it would have been even less prudent than Cardogue's course of action, which led to his being torn to pieces with all of his men by the multitudes who were led by my ancestor, the silversmith Alejo Calatayud, in the year of 1730.

It was not possible for Goyeneche, nor would it have been possible for anyone else in his position, to leave behind him an adversary like the Cochabambian people. For disarmed as they were, which made them very weak against a well-organized and hardened army, they had instead an untiring and even a feverish spirit and ability to bring in an instant the whole of Upper Perú into upheaval and to spread their traditional hatred against the Spanish domination, and the courage that they had already proven more than once, and their resources of resistance—such as, for example, their famous tin harquebuses and their no less famous bronze and glass grenades. The victor of Amiraya could already feel them stirring, beginning to surround him everywhere. Without making the efforts necessary to organize a strong government or regular army troops, the impatient patriots who exercised influences over any group or territory were content to form large or small bands of guerrillas armed with lances, slings, and *macanas*; they asked the new Prefect and the Junta for whatever resources they could send them, and sometimes they would make do without; and each one rushed on his own to spread the uprising, to sever the lines of communication between Goyeneche and the Viceroyalty of Perú and to antagonize the enemy of the homeland in every conceivable way. I have already recounted how Arze did not pause for even an instant before bursting into Oruro, and then immediately rushed against Chayanta, where he had more success and obtained the triumph at Caripuyo. Don Mateo Zenteno followed his example, stirring the uprising in the area of Ayopaya and leading groups at times as far as the outskirts of La Paz, and at other times retreating across the heights of Tapacarí to antagonize Lombera's troops,[3] which were then crossing the Altiplano. While Don Carlos Toboada, with his inexhaustible Mizqueños, would threaten Chuquisaca as quickly as he would retreat to the Valle-Grande. Other guerrillas who did not become as well known, but who were no less active and enterprising, carried out incursions as far as the outskirts of Potosí on one side, and as far as Santa Cruz de la Sierra on the other, achieving successes over small groups of enemy troops. The most noteworthy triumph gained by one of these was by Don José Félix Borda's second in command, whom his superior did not even mention in the report sent to the Provincial Junta. It occurred in Samaipata, on the 26th of March, against the reinforcements for which Goyeneche had sent. The fighting lasted sixteen hours, was extremely bloody, and left the leader of the enemy troops, Joaquín Ignacio Alburquerque, a Portuguese Brazilian, dead on the battlefield.

Goyeneche wanted to retrace his steps immediately. I do not believe that he wavered between continuing his march to the provinces of the Río de la Plata and taking this course, as some writers of history have proposed without any proof. If he remained in Charcas and Potosí for five months, it was only because the rainy season did not allow him to come back on the road that cuts through the valleys, as he would have had to cross the unfordable Río Grande. Nor was it possible for him to take the road through the Altiplano, as it is even colder and more rigorous there during this season than in winter. This road, besides, is also cut, like the other one, by the torrential floods from the Arque and Tapacarí ravines.

His forced stay in the south of Upper Perú gave him time to execute contemptible acts of vengeance as he pleased. The hypocrite ordered the presidential house that had been previously inhabited by "the infidel Castelli" to be purified with solemn religious rites before he proceeded to move into it. The same man who confessed like a good penitent and took the Holy Communion every eight days, kissing the tiles of the church, and who boasted of his generosity and liberality—this same man had respectable ladies accused of having called him a sambo or a *cholo* gagged and publicly displayed, while he had others, even with small children, exiled, driven away on their feet. He confiscated goods, ordered bloody executions daily, and watched from his balconies as half a dozen men were hung to death at the mere hint of being suspected of conspiring against him.

He did not miss the opportunity, either, of utilizing the time to take possession of as many fortunes as could be found in what had been an affluent province. And not just for the service of the King, either, but also for his own personal hoard, as is well known and has already been brought to light by other historians.

He was aided in this last act by his accomplice in Carlotist schemes,[4] the Archbishop Don Benito María Moxó y Francoli.[5] This Prelate, a fanatic for the cause he embraced, be it in favor of the legitimate king or of the Infanta, dealt out excommunications to patriots who were just as good Catholics as he was; he said that the war of the people against the kings was horribly impious; he preached the doctrine of dejection of "these Caligulas and Neros"; and he willingly handed over to his accomplice the treasures of the wealthy church, which were under his charge.

The plundering was confirmed before the dignitaries of the Cabildo—

But: "*Les chanoines vermeils, et brillants de santé,*"[6] one of them said at last, daring to protest; "*d'abord pole et muet, de colére inmobile.*"[7] The Basque canon Areta, a hero who eclipses all of those recounted in the heroicomical poem *Lutrin* by Boileau,[8] then spoke—the illustrious and brave Areta spoke, that is. Thus, putting his arms round one of the gigantic candelabrum that still remained, he said the following memorable words, which could only have been uttered at that time by a Spaniard from the Peninsula and which reveal the contempt that everyone felt deep down toward the *criollo* general:

"That *zambillo*[9] Goyeneche is mocking us!"

At which point all the other canons stood up, following his example. They felt overwhelmed by holy indignation and swore to die as martyrs if need be to protect, as was their duty, their blessed candelabra.

The desired season arrived. The month of April was drawing to a close—the time when, according to the farmers of my land, "it rains a thousand rains, but it doesn't fill a single barrel"—and the flooded rivers and torrents could no longer protect the heroic Oropesa. Goyeneche took one last glance at the road toward Buenos Aires and let out a long and loud sigh. His vanguard, under the command of the brave Picoaga, had cleared out the Argentine border for him; Díaz Vélez was running to hide on the other side, with Belgrano; this most eminent American was making extraordinary, but quite useless efforts to reorganize the auxiliary army, for he barely had two or three hundred men with him. Without the evil Oropesa, the Grand Pacifier could have reached the Río de la Plata without firing a single shot, while the Brazilian troops drew the attention of the Junta of Buenos Aires down the other side!

He made his decisions then, full of rage. He planned to surround the ceaselessly rebellious province in a circle of fire and steel and pull it tighter and tighter until the queen city of the fertile and lovely valleys was crushed. He ordered Huisi, who was then destroying the Laguna, to take the road through the Valle Grande. Lombera received the charge to come down from the Altiplano on the route across Tapacarí or Chayanta, whichever one was preferable; he even asked for reinforcements from as far as the distant Santa Cruz de la Sierra; and he himself, with the core of his best troops, took the road through the Valley of Mizque, placing the atrocious, unforgettable Imas[10] in charge of his vanguard.

"Soldiers!" this villain would say, removing the mask with which he had tried to convince everyone of his magnanimity, but that never truly covered the stigma of his horrendous crimes of 1809. "You are the owners of the rebels' lives and of their properties. The only thing that I forbid," the hypocrite who desecrated the churches would add, "I forbid you only, under penalty of death, to invade the holy houses of the Lord!"

Was Goyeneche really a Christian? Did that villain ever think about God? I believe not. I can concede to him, at best, the superstitious religion of the Calabrian brigands, who light tall candles by the image of a saint before or after committing a robbery or a murder. As I have stated, Goyeneche confessed very often, but he could not possibly have revealed the entire leprosy of his soul to the priest. He must have set out, more likely, to quite shrewdly fool the Father in order to continue to count on the support of the powerful Church. Much more of a believer was Belgrano, the great caudillo of the homeland who tried to dispel the prejudices of a section of the common people, which had been fomented by Moxó in consequence of the indiscretions and imprudences committed by Castelli.

The patriots of Cochabamba realized the need to gather their forces and prepare for a vigorous defense. But the caudillos, who until that moment of imminent danger had been accustomed to leading their own *republiquetas*[11] or groups of *montoneros*,[12] each following his own initiative, created a breeding ground ripe with disputes and personal grudges. In a book like this one, which follows a specific plan that is quite different from the dry and certainly more useful investigations of a critical historical study, I only mention these lowly events here in passing.

The best organized forces were those that followed the untamable Arze. He aspired to discipline them and unbendingly punished those who used the cause of the homeland as an excuse to carry out criminal excesses. I have before me several of his proclamations and general orders that have not yet been published in any book in print so far. Many villains paid the ultimate penalty, imposed on them by Arze himself, because of the little respect that they held for the people whom they called *tablas* and *sarracenos*, or for their goods and properties.

Arze had more or less four thousand men in the area of Cliza, with Tarata serving as his general headquarters. The infantry was, by then, already much larger than the cavalry. In addition to the thousands of horses that had been destroyed in the war, Goyeneche had seen to it that not a single one was left alive after the battle of Amiraya. The only ones saved were the ones that were led away by their owners to the most inaccessible peaks of the Cordillera. It is the weapons and equipment of these troops that will leave for all posterity the clearest idea of the enthusiasm and determination with which these men battled for the sublime ideal that filled their souls, without consideration of the immense obstacles before them, or of the weakness of their material resources. The number of rifles they had managed to gather, and after incredible efforts at that, did not reach five hundred, and not all of these were in regular operating order. I saw many that only had a functioning barrel and were attached to very crude butts, without anything other than a loose fuse tied to the vent, therefore requiring someone other than the man aiming the weapon to light it. Of the tin harquebuses, which I talked about earlier in some length, there must have been around six hundred in total, but Don Esteban only received half of these, while the other half were distributed among Zenteno's troops. There must have been over a hundred cannons—also made of tin, of course—mounted on gun-carriages that were so crude and primitive, that, as I have already stated, they resembled small carts used for carrying heavy rocks. And there were not even two thousand of the famous bronze and glass grenades. Thus, the majority of the defenders of the homeland were only armed with slings, *macanas*, and lances; and these, although they had proven so successful in the victory at Aroma, did not stand a chance against forces of the likes of Goyeneche's. But those men were driven by the most joyful of illusions, and would have gone after the *tablas* naked, armed with only stones and sticks if they had to. They likewise cared very little about the personal privations that they had to put up with. The clothes that they were wearing when they left their homes were now falling off their bodies in shreds, and when they received their handful of toasted maize and a bit of *charqui*, they yelled: "Long live the homeland!" They followed their bold caudillos through rugged hills and cold, barren plateaus. I also have, right before me on the table where I am writing, an order from Don Esteban to his majordomo in Caine to hand out a certain ration of corn to each of the soldiers who were to accompany him to Chayanta.

The number of troops with which Zenteno was to defend whichever road Lombera chose to take did not reach three thousand men, and their discipline and weapons were considerably inferior to those I have just briefly described. Try to imagine, my dear readers, what they must have been like! Tell me, more importantly, if today's men can be compared with the ones from back then! Tell me. . . . But, no, for God's sake, don't tell me anything! For the blood rushes to my head and the pen falls from my hand!

The two caudillos who I have been speaking about met their corresponding adversaries at the same time. Zenteno courageously stopped Lombera for a few hours at the heights of Quirquiave, but he was defeated, for there was no possibility other than for him to be defeated. And he fled to the mountains of Hayopaya, in that area of the territory of Upper Perú where the Andes themselves form very deep ravines, quite different from the ones that barely open between the barren spurs of the gigantic Cordilleras—to *Hayopaya*,[13] in a word, which holds quite a glorious name in its own right, and does not need to be called the Asturias of Perú, as American historians insist on doing.

Arze headed out to face Goyeneche. . . . But this caudillo, for a thousand reasons, deserves our attention more than any other from those times. Therefore, we will follow the details of his moves a little more slowly.

The eastern border of the vast Valley of Cliza is composed of a wide and tall ridge of the Yurackasa Cordillera, which separates it from the Valleys of Mizque and Pocona, and forms a tableland that is not as cold, and is consequently more fertile and cultivated, than the great Puna, which geographers today call the Bolivian Plains. Goyeneche had to climb precisely to this area by one of two roads, either through Curi or through Pocona, both of which were equally steep and rugged. Then he had to cross the whole length of the tableland, opening him up for possible attacks, first by the infantry along the slopes, then by the cavalry in the high plateau. Arze understood this perfectly. Therefore, he decided to take his troops to the town of Vacas, which is located in the center of the tableland, on the shores of the large lakes after which the town and the tableland are named, and from which he could keep a lookout over both of the roads I have mentioned.

But time—that element that is more precious in war than in all other human things—did not suffice for the caudillo of the homeland to carry out his well-conceived strategic plan.

On the morning of the 24th of May, he learned in Sacabamba—which is on the heights of Tarata, the position he had first occupied—of the entrance of Goyeneche into the old city of Mizque on the night of the 21st, and of the clever retreat of the caudillo Toboada, who, sliding back to the left of the enemy, had tried to break up its rear and force it across to the other side of the Río Grande. Certain, then, that Goyeneche would come through the Vacas meseta, he set out to occupy that town, as I have said, pushing the pace of the march and not allowing his men to rest for even an instant, until, well after night had fallen, he accepted having to make camp in Paredones, not far from the town of Vacas.

One of his men has recounted to me how Arze did not want the horses to be unsaddled that night; that he ordered the march to recommence the moment the first bugles had blown; and that, in his hurry, he rushed ahead on his horse down the road many times. He has also assured me that it must have been four in the morning when Arze learned—from an Indian from the area who had gone to Pocona the day before and returned through hidden paths—the news that the enemy was probably going to pick up camp from the town of Chapín de la Reina* before sunrise. At that point, letting out a loud, angry scream, he ordered that the agreed-upon signal to take up the march be sounded at once.

He wanted to take the top of the slope before the enemy could reach it. From such an advantageous position, he could have brought down enormous harm on Goyeneche, forcing him to retreat from all the punishment, or perhaps even defeating him definitively. The disadvantage of the patriots' weapons would have been compensated by those offered there by nature's hand. The robust *vallunos* would have buried their dominators under the rocks of the slope, like the mountaineers of Switzerland, who fought in this same manner for their liberty without weapons. But time did not suffice, as I have said, and the caudillo of the homeland found himself in the position of having to fight in the worst of circumstances. By the time the patriots could distinguish the slope in the first rays of sunlight on that ominous day of the 24th of May, the vanguard of the enemy, led by Imas, had already crowned its peak.

Tricked cruelly by fate, the brave Arze decided at that point to wait for the enemy where he was, which was called Quehuiñal, and which was as far as he had been able to get despite the efforts he had made to move quickly. He placed his large tin cannons on a small mount to his left; he formed the front lines with the few

*It was called by this name because the Tributes paid by the Indians from the region with bitter tears tended to be sent to Spain in gold, "for the footwear of the venerable feet of our Lady, her Majesty the Queen."[14]

riflemen and harquebusiers he had; and he ordered the cavalry, in an advantageous formation, to make up the rear, placing himself at its head. He understood that on that terrain the only thing he could count on were his lances. In the meantime, Imas was spreading out his band of guerrillas, and the core of Goyeneche's troops was quickly mounting the last steps of the slope of Pocona.

From the very first shots exchanged by the combatants, the patriots understood the tremendous disadvantage of their weapons. The projectiles fired by the tin cannons and harquebuses barely harmed the enemy, while the other side's bullets were already starting to spread death among their files. The same occurred, but to an even larger degree, with the grenades. Very soon, too, the explosions of the real bronze cannons of the enemy artillery resounded, and they found themselves exposed, without any defense, to the case shot from the blasts. What else can I tell you? The only real serious threat that the patriots could, and did, offer was the charge of their brave squadrons, led by their caudillo. But Goyeneche's soldiers had been trained, above all, to resist cavalry in cadres, and this is what their enemies relied on primarily. They would fall into these formations, assembling together at the opportune moment, without even having to wait to hear the orders from their leaders. Thus, Arze's squadrons, small to begin with, crashed uselessly against those walls of men bristling with bayonets that are seldom broken even by the strongest and best organized cavalry units.

An hour after Imas's band of guerrillas had fired their first shots, Goyeneche found himself once again the joyful victor, for the third time, of "those incorrigible rebels from Cochabamba." The field was littered with more than a few bodies. They say that only thirty of the casualties were from the victorious army. I do not believe it, but I shall not quarrel about it. What I can assure you is that there were many patriot deaths—but no one bothered to take the time to count them.

"What were we going to count them for?" one of the Spanish leaders said. "What good was that rabble of mestizos anyway? All they did was force us to come back to kill them off when we could have been well on our way to Buenos Aires!"

Don Esteban Arze fled with a few of his soldiers from the cavalry, taking the road through Curi to their right. But he did not do so to save his own life, as the victor claimed—having the audacity to call him a "frightened, cowardly rebel"—but rather to meet up with Taboada immediately. Together, a few days later, they tried the bold undertaking of attacking Chuquisaca, with the idea that from there they could then attack their enemy again from the least expected of places. But pursued by the bad luck that all the great caudillos of the Independence Movement shared in the first few years of the war and which was only to be overcome by their extremely admirable heroic perseverance, Arze was once again defeated, this time by the garrison troops from the main plaza of Chuquisaca, at the point of the Molles, barely one league away from the old city of Charcas. He could see, from the battlefield, the white towers and elegant buildings of the city where he longed to raise his flag, and he was forced to retreat to the Valle-Grande, continuing to fight for his homeland his whole life, suffering many bitter disillusionments along the way. Eighteen patriots who were taken alive at the hands of the victors at the Molles were executed by firing squad that same day. Taboada went further south with a few of his followers; he was captured at Tinguipaya and hung to death, along with three of his men, in Potosí. His head, dried out with salt, was sent to Chuquisaca, and displayed at the Molles for a long time. And the last of the patriots from those brave and untiring troops, who undertook grave dangers to cross the border with the hope of joining the auxiliary army, were finally captured in Suipacha. Of this group, those who were not hung to death were sentenced to suffer slowly in the dreadful prison of Casas Matas, about which I shall have plenty to relate to you at the appropriate time and place.

XIX

Woe to the Rebels!
Woe to the Chapetones!

On the morning of the 25th of May, Luis snuck into my room through the window with the soft light of dawn, and although he brought with him the horrible news of the defeat at Quehuiñal, he was still unable to resist pulling off one of his jests: he woke me up by brushing my nostrils with the ends of a feather lightly powdered with snuff.

"Listen, my friend," he said very seriously, ignoring my curses and my sneezing, "you should know that I'm not up to fooling around today. They have handed us patriots a thrashing worse than the one Father Arredondo dealt you. I have informed myself of everything there is to know. Just imagine. . . . I don't know when, nor where, nor how the thing happened. . . . What was poor Don Esteban supposed to do without us? In any case, last night I saw a large number of gentlemen and ladies go into the Prefect's house, the men whispering and the women moaning. 'Aha!' I said to myself. 'Why am I not included in these events?' So I followed behind them and went as far as the vestibule door of the antechamber. Inside, an important gentleman from the Cabildo was speaking very angrily, saying that it was necessary to save Cochabamba from Goyeneche's rage. The others were applauding him, while the ladies were imploring the Prefect, begging him in the name of all the saints, to soften his stance. 'Let me be. Your Excellencies may do as you please, but there is nothing else left for me to do,' the Prefect answered. 'As far as I am concerned,' he added, more angrily than all of them, 'I am not going to see that man from Arequipa for anything in the world. I will not make the same mistake that Don Francisco committed, nor will I write him a single letter, nor do I consent to anyone going under my name, even if your Excellencies explode at me and call me a heartless monster, and even if Goyeneche himself comes and hangs me and has me drawn and quartered!' 'Hurrah! Long live Don Mariano Antezana!' I yelled, sticking my head in the door and then running off into the street at once. A little later, they all came out, the men very angry and the ladies in a sea of tears. 'This man has no soul,' they said about poor Don Mariano, who is actually so pious; 'he wants to have things his way, to see his countrymen beheaded, and to be left without anyone standing in the whole city.' 'That raving man must not have a wife, nor children, nor even a dog to bark at him,' the ladies added about the praiseworthy gentleman who has so much love, even for his deaf-mute Paulito. Then they headed off toward the Cabildo. Such efforts! Such running around! They have decided to send representatives. . . . They had the learned Don Sulpicio called in from wherever he was, out in the country. He said the most astonishing things to them in Latin, which no one understood, of course. I think that he doesn't want to go with the representatives. But, in the end, we'll let them be, my friend! You and I, we know what to do, don't we?!"

Each one of his words was a blow to my heart. But it was not because I understood the full magnitude of the misfortune, nor because I had already learned to love the homeland to such an enormous extent, but rather because I felt that I myself was lost, without any hope. "What's to become of me? Where am I going to go? What good am I in this world, now that I can't be a soldier anymore?" I asked myself sadly, with a forgivable selfishness for someone of my age and in my highly unusual circumstances.

"Be quiet, for God's sake!" I exclaimed at last. "I know you too well. You're a liar. . . . But for some reason—I don't know why—this is the first time that I believe you to be telling the truth in your whole life."

"I, lie?!" he replied indignantly. "Don't you know that I am nothing if not a fountain of truth? Do you want to see it with your own eyes, you heartless creature? Fine! . . . Come, come out to the streets with me, and you'll see! Oh, such long faces, my friend, on some of those handsome gentlemen, who were ready to eat the *chapetones* alive when they taught us to yell 'Long live the homeland!' Oh, such looks on the noble ladies, fleeing on donkeys to their estates before sunrise, as if they were Calacanians on their way to Quillacollo with vegetables! You haven't seen any of it, my poor friend! Do you want to go, or not? Yes or no? Come on! Oh, but you can stay here with your book about the saints if you want. . . . Here comes Father Arredondo with his scourges to give you your lessons! I'm leaving. . . . I'm going to see the *Mellizo*, and the *Jorro*. There's good people for you! There are no men left, like the Grandmother says!"

"Where did you see her?"

"Everywhere. Where doesn't the Grandmother Doña Chepa go? Ever since it was known that the «Three-Faced Man» is coming back, she could be seen in the main plaza and in the streets, with *Palomita* leading her from place to place. She didn't want a single man to stay behind in the city. One day she ran into the sacristan of the nuns of St. Teresa in the small plaza, and said to him: 'Doña "Sissy," you've put my trousers on by mistake and left me with your skirts. Return them to me immediately so I can go right now to present myself to Don Esteban.' The poor sanctimonious man was so embarrassed that he headed out that very moment on the road to Tarata."

I remembered the promise I had made to accompany the Grandmother, so I jumped out of bed to follow my friend at once.

"Let's go! I want to go take *Palomita's* place right away," I told him, and began quickly to get dressed.

At that point we heard the hurried steps of someone who was coming toward my room. The key turned in its lock and Luis fled like a cat, so that the Negro woman Feliciana did not see him when she opened the door and said the following brief words to me: "You can go out. . . . The captivity is over!"

I sat on my bed. The news of my freedom sent a thousand ideas spinning through my head. "I must not, I cannot run away now," I said to myself. "I have to leave this house in some way other than through its window. I will go see my teacher, if he has already come back. . . . I will tell him that I am leaving. . . . That the only family I want is the Grandmother's. I will give Carmencita one last kiss, and. . . . And why should I not also tell Doña Teresa about my resolution to be a soldier? Let her get angry! Let her call me 'the Evil One himself'! It would be worst for her to be able later to say that I had fled like a thief. . . ."

The beautiful sunlight was already coming in through the half-opened door, and I could hear more activity and commotion than usual throughout the house. Doña Teresa's shrill voice reached my ears distinctively several times, even though she was not an early riser—she normally got up around eight and went straight to the small chapel, where she would have her chocolate and start her constant complaints about her flatulence and her terrible migraines.

"Feliciana! Everything must be as clean as a reliquary, girl," she was shouting out in the patio. "It's been so long since these rooms have been opened, they must be full of cobwebs by now."

"Oh, how wonderful!" Clemente came to say in a loud voice near my room so I would hear him. "His Excellency, the gentleman Cañete[1] himself is coming to live in this house, in the «very same» rooms of my master, his Lordship the «Marquis» Don Fernando!"

"Cañete? Could it be Doctor Pedro Vicente Cañete, the man who is supposed to be half a fox and half a snake, Goyeneche's secretary and advisor, of whom I have heard my teacher talk about at times?" I asked myself. "No, sir! I am leaving this house no matter what!" I added resolutely. But in vain did I head to the door a hundred times, for the same one hundred times I retreated, frightened by the image of Doña Teresa's face. And in vain did I look to the window another one hundred times, for just as many did I feel disgust at the thought of leaving the house in that manner.

It was getting toward ten in the morning when the noise, the commotion, the shouting was slowly coming to an end. I believed I had finally set my mind definitively to what I was to do, but once again I heard steps, this time of several people approaching my room. When the door was opened as wide as it could go, I saw the most imposing group that I could have possibly have had before me in that place.

Doña Teresa was luxuriously dressed in a pleated petticoat made of very fine velvet, a white satin doublet with gold embroidery, and a blue, velvety silk mantilla, known as a *vellutina* from Naples; she was adorned with her large earrings, her necklace with the enormous pearls, and countless rings on the fingers of both hands; and she wore a chignon hairdo, with her braided hair wound around a tortoiseshell comb, rising above her head into a coronation inlaid with gold and plenty of pearls—it looked just about as large as the back of a modern cane chair. She was leaning on one of the arms of his learned Honor, who was holding, on the other, a new walking stick, with bigger and shinier tufts than ever. And everything behind them was covered by the Prelate of our Lady of Mercy in his white cassock, over whose shoulder Feliciana's face would at times appear, when she got up on her toes to give me looks of hatred with her crooked eyes.

I walked backward until I hit the wall facing the door, the one with the window on it, and greeted them, bending down as low as the floor. None of them seemed to take any notice of my presence, but rather entered solemnly into my room, looking up at the crossbeams of the ceiling. Feliciana pulled chairs up to the table, where they sat, with the lady of the house in the middle. Then the Negro woman looked in the drawer for the key to the coffer and proceeded to open it and take out of it my inheritance, item by item.

"Let's be finished with it, oh Blessed Virgin! He is finally leaving tomorrow, just as soon as his Excellency frees us from the rebels!" Doña Teresa shrilled.

The father took out a yellowed piece of paper from the sleeve of his cassock, slowly unrolled it, and signaled to the servant with his hand to begin.

"Some clothes of his. . . . Very old and unusable," Feliciana said.

"And how could they be in any other condition? Can anything

last on that wicked and vagabond boy?" Doña Teresa asked, bothered by the Negro woman's comment. "All right," she went on impatiently, "if anything is still usable it can be put in the trunk for the muleteer to pick up. Go on! I don't want my migraine to come back today."

"A new pair of women's shoes. They must belong to 'the child'...."

"That's impossible! They're too small. That wretched sinner had feet that were much larger than mine.... Leave them in the coffer! Go on. I can already feel my flatulence coming back!"

"A small, black package, with a piece of rope...."

"Yes, I know. The Reverend Father Brother Justo told me that it was a family keepsake," the Prelate interjected.

"Some witchery, I suppose.... Such lowly people!" the lady spoke again.

"A small wooden box...."

"Yes, yes. Let's see what it contains," the Father said, and he began to read from the paper. "A partially embroidered piece of cloth with hemstitching and lace and....'"

"Here it is, Most Reverend Father."

"'A small cardboard box.'"

"With earrings, a brooch, and a ring."

"Correct. 'A money box.'"

"Broken; a piece of its lid has been removed."

"It had been fixed. It should have...."

"Four small gold coins."

"There were five! I counted them myself. I put them in there with my own hand and had the lid glued back while I watched."

As he said this, the Prelate was looking at me with the eyes of a basilisk.

"What's so surprising about that? Don't we know that he's a scoundrel? Won't you ever believe me when I say that he is the Devil himself?" the lady yelled.

"*Ingeneratur hominibus mores a stirpe, generis,*"[2] his learned Honor—who until then had sat with the walking stick between his knees, seemingly absorbed in contemplation of a cobweb in the cross-beams—said solemnly at this point.

"That's right! His wise Honor has said it very well," Doña Teresa replied even louder than before, although she did not understand a single word of his Honor's poor Latin. However, ever since Don Sulpicio had succeeded in getting her unbending father Don Pedro de Alcántara to come to reason through the utterance of just one of these phrases, as I have previously recounted, Doña Teresa had nothing but the utmost admiration for each and all of the Latin words spoken by him.

This scene was painfully cruel to me. Each of Doña Teresa's words revealed the hatred she had toward me; the reference to my poor mother was a blow to my heart, as if I had been bitten by a snake; the contempt that she held for Calatayud's rope made the blood rush to my head. . . . I understood that the lady was trying to rid herself of my presence in the house as soon as possible. Her first worry, after preparing the rooms for the "Illustrious and most learned Cañete," was to arrange the trip of the "foundling waif" to Chuquisaca. I promised myself never to have to owe her anything in my life, to escape in any way possible, anywhere, even as far as Buenos Aires, where I could still become a soldier for the homeland.

As I thought about all this, Feliciana closed the coffer and left, taking my old and raggedy clothes to prepare "my bags." The other three most respectable personages had already forgotten about me, and were talking about more interesting things. They resumed the conversation they had had to interrupt in order to honor my humble room with their visit.

"*Excelsior*,[3] as your Excellency, my good, learned friend, says. Oh! There is no one in this entire area who knows how to run things better!" Father Arredondo said, admiring the man whom he truly believed was wiser than any of the Seven Sages from Ancient Greece.

"*Odi profanum vulgus, et arceo*,"[4] his Honor answered. "When the people went back out to the country to yell: 'Long live the homeland,' I said to myself: 'Sulpicio, *nullam, vare, sacra vite. . . .*"[5]

"Didn't I say so! Your Excellency is a well of knowledge, oh good Honor! You fled from the torture and—"

"And I came back when I had to come back. They called me.
... They wanted me to beg for compassion on their behalf!"

"I dare say! Let them pay for what they have done!" Doña Teresa exclaimed, quite angered.

"And what did your Excellency respond?" the Father asked, ready to hear an answer worthy of that oracle.

"*Justum, et tenacem prositi virum....*"[6]

"Oh! Admirable!" the Father and the lady exclaimed simultaneously.

"*Haud flectes illum, ne si sanguine quidem fleveris!*"[7]

"Ohh!"

"That's for the 'homeland'!"

"Woe to the rebels! We won't be the ones who'll cry tears of blood when we're honored once again with the visit of Don José Manuel Goyeneche y Barreda."

"*Nunc est bibendum, nunc pede libero!*"[8]

"Mercy!" the servants suddenly yelled out in the patio at this point. A moment later they rushed into my room, trembling with fear, bringing the livid children—who looked ill with fright—in their arms.

A threatening uproar could be heard, and tremendous blows resounded against the front door.

"It's the rebels...! They want to come in...! They're saying that they're going to behead everyone who's a friend of the *chapetones*," the terrified Negro woman stammered.

"Oh, my mistress, my lady *Marquesa*! Run away, for God's sake, your Excellencies!" Clemente managed to say, completely frightened to death. "They're enraged.... They look like a bunch of criminals.... I was barely able to close the large, front door...."

I shall not describe the terror that overcame the three personages who, just a moment earlier, were speaking with so much charity toward the rebels. Doña Teresa stood up, shaking as if she had tertian fever. She snatched Carmen from the mulatta's arms, and held her tightly in her own. His Honor somehow disappeared, and neither I nor anyone else could have said where he had gone to, or how. The Father remained glued to his chair, but it did not take him long to calm down, undoubtedly remembering, and quite rightly so, that the cassock made his nearly spherical body quite immune to any attacks.

"The *Mellizo*, the *Jorro*, the blacksmith—I mean Don Alejo— are all out there," Clemente continued.

"The blacksmith! My God, those raving lunatics are going to behead my children and I!" Doña Teresa exclaimed, very distressed, as if that word, "blacksmith," represented for her the very image of Death wielding his scythe. "Oh!" she then shouted joyfully, as if she had found a new source of hope in her heart again. "Go up there, Juanito. Look at how pale my poor Carmen is! Run to the door, my son. . . . Tell Alejo to take those men away with him. . . . Beg him in the name of your mother . . . of Rosita!"

"*Excelsior! Feminae intellectus acutus*,"[9] his Honor's falsetto voice added from underneath my bed.

The learned man had hidden there, leaving his hat behind in the process, but not forgetting to take his walking stick with him. Neither was he cured with the fright from his mania of inserting his phrases of poor Latin into every conversation around him.

I looked at my noble and loving little friend. She was truly pale as a corpse, holding onto her mother's neck very tightly, so I went out, determined to do whatever was necessary, to beg like a child or be killed like a man, in order to defend her. But I was only halfway down the patio when I noticed that the tremendous blows that had been heard coming from the front door before had completely ceased and that the shouting of the large mob was slowly dissipating as it headed away from the house.

In the portico, I found the unfortunate *pongo* sitting on his *poyo*, in the position of one of those mummies that are dug up from the *huacas* of his ancestors. He was so frightened that his teeth were chattering, but he had not abandoned his post, undoubtedly because the fear he had of bringing upon himself the ire of the "Grand Mistress," whom he was accustomed to revering like a frightening and wrathful deity, was even greater than the fear caused by the uproar from the mob.

I opened the wicket very cautiously and stuck my head out. The street was deserted, and the doors and windows of all the other houses were closed. The large mob was still shouting, in the distance, on another cross street. They had ripped stones from the stone pavement to throw against the door, and had seriously damaged its thick cedar planks. One of these had been completely split in two and was almost loose from the cross braces, in spite of the enormous nails that held it in place. I thought I could distinguish the mark from a tremendous blow by Alejo's large iron bar at that spot.

I wanted to investigate the situation further, so that I could then return to calm down Doña Teresa's family. I ran to the corner and saw, a block down, along the cross street, a completely unruly mob of men, women, and children, all common people, crowded around a man on horseback and yelling loudly at him. The latter, in turn, was also yelling and waving his arms wildly in the air, alternatingly gesturing and raising them up toward the sky. I approached at a hurried pace. The gentleman, whom I recognized immediately, was the Prefect Don Mariano Antezana. He was both imploring and threatening the crowd to stop its undertaking of breaking into the houses of the members of the community who were considered to be attached to the government of the *chapetones*. He had with him six or seven Franciscan monks who were helping him in his efforts, preaching liberality and clemency, peace and harmony, thus fulfilling their priestly duties in the most praiseworthy of manners.

Then I saw the deaf-mute Paulito, armed with a three and a half-inch caliber musket, uttering inarticulate guttural shouts, and holding onto the tail of the horse to avoid being separated from his master even for an instant. Finally, I saw Alejo, the *Mellizo*, the *Jorro*, and several others whose names I do not recall. They were leading the mob, inciting it and spreading to them the savage rage that possessed them. The first of these was brandishing his large iron bar in the air. The *Mellizo* had a tin harquebus in one hand and a lance in the other; he was dragging along an enormous saber; two daggers shone on his belt; and he was so drunk that he could barely stay on his feet. The *Jorro*, whom I present to my readers here for the first time, was, as his nickname implies, a wild mulatto who always had the worst of reputations in my country. He was armed to the teeth and as drunk as the *Mellizo*.

I was not surprised, but I was certainly saddened—it grieves me even now when I say it—to find there my rash friend Luis, armed with his saber as the Governor of the Gran Paititi, and leading the dregs of his army from Las Cuadras. His high-pitched voice stood out above the howling of the women and the yells of the hoarse drunkards, as if it were the soprano of that infernal chorus. But I must also say that he did not understand, in his rashness, that that could have quite easily led to pillaging and butchering, and I beg you to wait a few moments before you make your final judgments about his conduct on that day.

"My children, my fellow countrymen. . . . Damned rabble! I beg you. . . . This can't be! For God's sake! For the Blessed Virgin! I'm going to have this whole vile mob hung to death," the good Don Mariano exclaimed, nearly smothered by the mob.

"Are we not Christians? Savages! Excommunicants! Dear brothers," the priests yelled, raising the crosses that they had armed themselves with above their heads.

"We won't surrender. . . . Death to the *chapetones!*" Alejo answered, brandishing his large iron bar.

"Aha! So they're going to make us surrender?" the *Mellizo* clamored, unable to handle the bountiful arsenal he carried on his body—nor himself, for that matter—when he did not have a wall on which to lean.

"Let's get on with the beheading! Let's go, men!" the evil *Jorro* howled like a jackal.

"Death to the *chapetones!* Death to the *tablas!*" *El Overo* was shrieking, although I am sure that his eyes would have shed oceans of tears if he had seen even a single drop of blood spilled in that manner.

"Long live Don Mariano Antezana! Let us go, sir! Death! Death to the *chapetones!*" the mob was yelling.

The Prefect and the priests had already managed to draw them away from the doors of Doña Teresa's house, explaining to them that they would only find a widow and small, harmless children there, regardless of how much of a *Chapetonist* she was. But their task now was more difficult, because the house that the mob was trying to break into was one in which an officer of Goyeneche's army lived, an Andalusian who had been wounded in Amiraya, a Treasurer of the Royal Audience of Charcas, and someone whom we shall get to know quite well later on, Don Miguel López Andreu. He had been exiled by Nieto because of his unfavorable opinions regarding Goyeneche's Carlist schemes and his participation in the events of the 25th of May of 1809, but he was poorly thought of by the patriots because he was a Spaniard and because he would not embrace the cause of the Independence Movement definitively. This separated him from the faction that Arenales had embraced, as much because of his convictions as from the persecution that he suffered from Nieto.

I do not believe that my readers expect me to recount to them all the details of that unruly scene, which was so characteristic in those times. Who can explain how a group like that moves and is incited, or how it calms down and regains control; what makes it howl and wail, or grow quiet; how it becomes enraged to the point of delirium, or is appeased and humbled—in short, who can explain what drives that monster, made up of so many bodies, known as a mob? At times one sign, one word is enough to hurl it into the most criminal of excesses. At others, one smile, one joke, one sarcastic comment can stop it, leading them to disarm and disperse. . . . And this is what happened in this particular case, in the least expected of ways.

The house that the mob was trying to break into had several stores, which had been very well sealed, on either side of its large front door. Just when the mob was at its most frenzied, and the Prefect and the priests were losing any hope of keeping it under control, the small postern above the door of one of these stores suddenly opened. The beautiful, small head of a little girl, an eight- or nine-year-old, appeared there. Her face was white and pinkish, she had large, lively eyes, and her hair was curled into ringlets—it looked like the head of one of the angels of a painting by Murillo, in which the angels are depicted up in the clouds with rosy colored wings.

"Oh, Jesus! How ugly they are! And it looks like you've all been drinking!" she exclaimed, with a marked accent that was somewhere between Andalusian and Limean.

"There, there you have the *chapetones*! A girl! A little angel!" The Prefect yelled to the mob, which immediately stopped shouting. "Let 'em be, sir!" the girl answered. "Don't bother yourself. . . . Let 'em come in! There isn't anyone in here but me. The shopkeeper Don Ramón left on his donkey for his farm. . . . Then Papá Alegría left at dawn. . . . And then they went and took Don Miguel Andreu who was shaking with the ugly fever from his bed."

After saying these words, she made a face at the *Mellizo*, who was still pointing his lance at her. She stuck out her little tongue, winked at him, and disappeared, laughing and closing the small postern a moment later.

Everyone—all the people who before were uttering those cries of death—responded to the charming girl with a loud burst of laughter. The *Mellizo*, furthermore, lost his balance and fell to the ground, increasing the laughter in which the rage of the mob was quickly diffusing. The women said that the gentleman Prefect was right, that what they had seen was not a girl, but a little angel. And the priests added that God had sent the angel to prevent a crime from occurring. Alejo stood there with his mouth wide open, scratching the back of his head, as he did in his most difficult moments. Finally I heard him say the words with which he always declared himself defeated:

"Well . . . there you have it!"

The *Jorro* was still howling and trying to force open the door to the store, while the *Mellizo* stumbled back to help him. But the blacksmith decided then, resolutely, to defend the house. He grabbed both of his companions by their lapels in one hand, raised his large iron bar in the other, and stopped all of their efforts with one good stare.

Those two villains—I cannot think of another name for them—were also prophetic types of another kind that is very harmful for democracies. If his learned Honor, whom I left hiding underneath my bed, announced the courtly group of the Excellencies of the rising empire, these two preceded the boisterous and reckless phalanx of the common people, which encourages riots, which pushes its brothers toward death and crime, but trembles and is speechless, runs away and scatters when it itself is faced with danger.

While Alejo dragged his humiliated companions away, I seized my friend, "the Governor of the Gran Paititi," by the ear.

"You are the most evil of *duendes*," I told him.

And immediately I explained to him how and why his conduct had been so ugly. He looked at me surprised. Then he blushed, slapped himself hard on the cheek, and ran off, refusing to tell me where he was going.

I went back to Doña Teresa's house, very happy with the news I was bringing back, which would surely ease their fears, but I found the front door hermetically locked. In vain did I call with the knocker and shout with all the strength my lungs could muster. No one answered. The house seemed completely abandoned. I later learned that the moment I had left, the lady had taken refuge with her children and her servants in one of the neighboring houses.

I headed to the Grandmother's small house. Half a block before it, I heard the old woman's voice angrily reprimanding someone, and from the door, I saw a very curious scene that I have not forgotten in my whole life. The Grandmother was standing in the middle of the room, leaning on her staff with her left hand, and swinging a thick whip made from several belts wound together in the other down at the poor Dionisio, who was kneeling down at her feet. Behind her, with his back against the wall, turning his hat in his hands, with his large iron bar between his crossed legs, I saw Alejo, confused and ashamed. Clara was sitting on the dais, crying silently. And Luis was cowering behind her, occasionally peeking over her shoulder and then hiding again, as if his guilt made him fear that the old woman's blind eyes would look in his direction and see him. I have not told you yet that Luis had become a daily visitor of the family during my confinement and that he was already good friends with Clarita and a passionate follower of the Grandmother's ideas and beliefs. The old woman, in turn, treated him with affection, and endeavored to correct his ways, like mine, in our pranks and mischief.

"Look at how much fun we've been having!" the blind old woman yelled indignantly. "Throwing stones at the doors, scaring the ladies and the poor little children! Wanting to steal! The *chapetones* are not in the city! They're coming across the Valley!

Since there are no men left. . . . The ones that said they were going to eat them alive have run away. That's for the *chapetones*, you scoundrel! I don't want to hear a word from Alejo . . . that drunkard, that animal!"

As she said this, she kept swinging the whip and striking terrible blows on the boy's head and back, or on the bricks of the floor when the poor Dionisio, who did not dare run away, did try to avoid the blows, writhing on the ground like a snake.

"Stop, dear Grandmother," I exclaimed, walking into the room, "it's not Dionisio's fault. . . . It's someone else, some very evil *duende* who must have forced him to yell: 'Death to the *chapetones*!'"

"Yes, madam Doña Chepa," Luis added, jumping from the dais and kneeling down beside his friend; "I'm that *duende* . . . that scoundrel; whip me, not him."

The old woman stopped with the whip raised in the air. Then she smiled and searched with her shaking hand for the urchin who had just spoken.

"It's all right," she said sweetly, "you must have done it without thinking. . . . You won't do it again, will you, my children? Alejo, that brute," she added, getting worked up again, "he's the one who's going to pay for this whole ordeal and for Clara's tears!"

The blacksmith, encouraged by Luis' example, thought it was his turn to beg the Grandmother for forgiveness, so he approached, muttering some unintelligible words. But the old woman refused him quite harshly and told him to leave and not to return until he had gone to the Prefect and become a militiaman and a true patriot.

"And I will go as well," she added, "I said as much before, and now I will go, and we'll see then if those cowards follow me or not. Oh! There are no men left today, there are no men left!"

She would not yield until Alejo had left, rushing off toward the Cabildo.

I led the Grandmother, as she wished, to take her seat on the dais, next to Clarita, and she had me sit on the other side of her. Then she called my two friends to come before her. She had them stand in front of her and spoke the following words to them:

"When I was a little girl . . . up to around here, about halfway up my staff, they hung a man in the plaza. Everyone said: 'That was the right thing to do; he was a thief.' A few years later, they hung my father and had his body drawn and quartered, but everyone cried. A man dressed in black came to our house, with some dirty papers in his hand, followed by ten militiamen, and ordered my mother to leave the house with me, because it now belonged to the king. We roamed through the countryside. . . . We had no where left to go but to my mother's family. 'Was he a thief?' I asked her. She turned bright red with anger and shame, and slapped me across the face. Then she sat down on the ground, took me in her arms, cried a lot, and said to me: 'If he had stolen, I would have been glad that he was killed. No, my daughter. The *guampos* hung him to death because he did not want them to be our masters. He said that only those who are born on this land and who know how to love their brothers should be district officers, justices, and magistrates.' If you are a patriot, you cannot be a thief. If today's *guampos* hang those who are going around breaking down the doors of the *criollos*, I will be the first to be happy about it. The patriots must go fight with the soldiers. . . . I'll show them how! There are no men left!"

That day, the uproar did not go beyond the stoning of a few houses that belonged to *chapetones*, or to families thought to be *Chapetonists*. Kept under control by the Prefect and the good Franciscan brothers, the city remained peaceful. Patriotic *criollo* families were seen fleeing by foot or on the backs of donkeys to their estates, especially in the direction of the Valley of Sacaba. Complete anarchy reigned in the Cabildo. Many notable members of the community spoke only about appeasing the victor's wrath. They dispatched two groups of commissioners to this end. A few zealous patriots said that it was necessary to resist Goyeneche until the end. They believed that they could still count on the troops that could be formed with the survivors from Quirquiave and Quehuiñal, and they rested their last hopes on the harquebuses and tin cannons and the grenades and lances that were still left in the storehouses of the provincial government. This faction included Lozano, Ferrufino, Ascui, Zapata, Padilla, Luján, and Gandarillas,[10] among others. The Prefect Antezana declared that, to his way of thinking, the situation was indeed desperate. He decided that he would resign his post in the Cabildo, but that he would never implore the victor to take pity on him. This man, the first citizen of Cochabamba, as I have referred to him earlier, was certainly not someone who could take up arms, nor could he lead the multitudes into war, like the lively and bold Don Esteban Arze. But he had the conscience of his civil duty and the courage to face the most impending of deaths straight on, without ever bowing his head to anyone other than God.

Luis and I spent the entire day of the 25th, as well as the next, with the Grandmother. His father was plenty busy with the grenades and cannons to have any time to worry about his son, while I could not, nor did I much wish to, return to Doña Teresa's house. The old blind woman sent us several times to find out what was happening in the Cabildo and what news was being brought by the very few survivors who were arriving to present themselves before the authorities. She listened to the reasons given by those who intended to surrender with the greatest contempt, she applauded the opinions of the zealots, and she got angry with the Prefect.

"He is a very good gentleman, quite respectable," she said, "but he is not a man! There are no men left, my sons!"

On the morning of the 26th, it was learned that Goyeneche had entered the town of Orihuela and had had the "Rebel leader Teodoro Corrales"[11] immediately executed by firing squad. The word was that he did not pardon any patriot who was unlucky enough to fall into the hands of his *tablas*. This news increased the fear of some and the rage of others. An enormous popular mob came together, and, like the day before, it was led by the *Mellizo* and the *Jorro*. Alejo was already honorably occupied with the *Gringo* in making preparations for the resistance. The rioters tried to break into the Church of St. Francis, where they claimed that the *chapetones* had hidden. They threw stones at the doors, and were about to break down the one that opened into the church atrium, when a member of the congregation appeared in one of the windows of the tower, placed the consecrated Host in the sacred monstrance, and raised it in his hands. At the same time, the large bell that been cracked by the repeated ringing after the victory at Aroma rang its rasping gong three times, like at the hour of Mass, when the Holy Sacrament is raised. This caused the entire delirious mob, intoxicated with liquor and thoughts of vengeance, to drop down to their knees, cross themselves, and leave immediately.

XX

The Women's Uprising

On the 27th of May, after finishing the frugal lunch that Clarita had prepared, we were gathered around the table, the Grandmother sitting in the only chair and the rest of us standing, when some ten or twelve women appeared at the door, panting and gasping for air. I recognized my poor María Francisca among them, looking more tattered than ever.

"They're coming. . . . They're at the Angostura already. They're saying that they're killing everyone along the way. . . . That they're burning houses. . . . What's going to become of us, oh Holy Blessed Merciful Virgin?" they said in Quechua, all speaking at once, uttering these and other phrases like them.

The Grandmother stood up and hit the table very hard with her staff.

"There are no men left!" she yelled. "They ran away when they heard that the *guampos* were coming, those wretches! Come on . . . let's go, my daughter!" she proceeded to say, reaching out with her hand for Clara. The latter, shaking and very pale, approached to offer her shoulder. "Let's go, everyone!" the Grandmother concluded, pointing to the street with her staff.

We all went out. María Francisca was told to lock up the house and then follow us. Our fearless generaless would not allow anyone, not even the poor, half-witted woman, to stay behind and fail to participate in the glory that it would be to force them to have to conquer the patriots.

"Long live the homeland!" we shouted when we were out in the street.

"Death to the *chapetones*! Now, now is the time to yell: 'Death to the *chapetones*,' my children!" the old woman exclaimed in a resounding voice that rose above all the others.

We turned down the Calle de los Ricos, which leads straight to the main plaza, yelling these phrases constantly as we went. The doors of the houses along the way were hurriedly closed as we passed by, and we could hear them being bolted and secured from inside. Along some stretches, and especially on the corners, there were small groups made up mostly of women and boys; they joined our band, or could not help getting dragged along with it. When we reached the corner of the Church of the Matriz, the Grandmother asked:

"Why aren't they ringing the bells?"

And a moment later, as if her wish had been magically answered, the bells suddenly began to toll in the other tower.

Groups like ours could be seen on other streets. The largest of these was coming down the Street of St. John of God, which runs through the neighborhood inhabited by the common people. It was led by the *Mellizo* and the *Jorro*, both armed to the teeth, and both showing signs of having been drunk without a moment's rest since the morning of the 25th.

"Now we'll see what those ruffians can do," the Grandmother said disgustedly as the two bands inevitably mixed together at the intersection of the two streets.

There were already about a hundred people or so in front of the Cabildo. Our group joined them, and soon afterward nearly the entire plaza was filled.

Peasants arrived from the outskirts of the city, armed with slings and cudgels. The butchers, known as *mañazos*, arrived with long knives attached to the end of their poles; their wives followed them, armed in the same manner.

The entrance to the Cabildo was guarded by two sentinels, and the rest of the guard was lined up in formation in the portico of the

Cabildo. A few beautiful horses could be seen with luxurious velvet saddles embroidered with gold and silver and plated belts in the patio inside. The yelling did not die down for an instant, and the bells were uttering that terrifying and gloomy wailing with which they announce the imminence of danger at the same time that they call for help.

The ruffians who had been leading the rowdy mob for the last three days wanted to force their way past the guards of the Cabildo. But as soon as they saw the first rifle pointed at them, they immediately became frightened and retreated to hide among the women.

"We want the Governor!" someone yelled from the crowd, and right away everyone repeated: "We want the Governor! We want the Prefect! We want Don Mariano Antezana!"

He appeared in the upper galleries a moment later, followed by a few *criollo* gentlemen from the resistance faction. He was not wearing a hat, and he carried a piece of paper in his hand. He was average in height and a little stout; his completely beardless face—with light eyes that had a pleasant look to them, a wide forehead with a retreating hairline of chestnut-brown hair streaked with much venerable gray—inspired respect, but it could never instill fear in the multitudes that had called him and who greeted him with a general applause.

"What are you doing, my children? Are we back to our incorrigible and noisy old tricks?" he asked calmly.

"We won't surrender. . . . We won't be sold out. . . . Turn the weapons over to us! Death to the *tablas*!" many voices replied.

"That would be madness, my children," the Prefect answered. "They say that José Manuel Goyeneche is coming in peace. I shall turn over the government to the Cabildo, but I declare that I am a patriot and that I shall not beg for mercy. Yes, my fellow countrymen, I shall stay until the end. Long live the homeland!"

The multitude answered his shout enthusiastically.

"Well, then," the Prefect went on, "that's what we all wanted. . . . And a lot of blood has been shed for the homeland, but God's will would not have it so."

"No! No! That's what cowards say! We won't surrender! The

weapons! We'll see what happens with the *chapetones*!" answered those from the *Mellizo's* band.

"We don't want the *chapetones*! That's all we need! What do they want in our land? Why should they come if we don't want them to?" the women yelled.

"There are no men left! Come, your Excellency, our Governor! I am here to lead them face to face with those vile *guampones*!"[1] the Grandmother yelled, with Clara in front of her, completely frightened to death, and us behind her, more enthusiastic than ever.

"What am I to do, my daughters? Has there ever been a more insane scene than the one caused by these mad, devilish women? 'We don't want the *chapetones*! Why should they come if we don't want them to?' Fine! Sure, they'll leave, scared the minute they hear the shrieks of these raving women and the boys!"

"No, sir!" one of the gentlemen who was on the gallery with the Prefect exclaimed at this point. "The people are right. . . . To arms! Long live the homeland!"

The uproar of the delirious crowd that followed this was such that nothing else after it could be made out distinctively.

The Prefect—I could see him quite well, and I have never forgotten it—turned calmly to the man who had spoken in that manner and said a few words to him. Then they all withdrew from the gallery, and a moment later they came out to the plaza on horseback. One of them rode toward the old Jesuit church, where the survivors from Arze's and Zenteno's troops were quartered who had been arriving to the city. Shortly afterward, a scant battalion that was very poorly armed, and even more poorly dressed, came out to take their formation in the street. The crowd, shouting the whole time, broke into the Cabildo and took ten or twelve cannons and more than fifty harquebuses that were inside. Everyone argued over who had the right to have a weapon. The women did not want to turn over to the men those that they had managed to get, and they furiously defended their possession of them. I saw old people who could barely drag themselves along, as well as children of both sexes, proudly and triumphantly hold up in the air the grenades they had obtained.

Around that time four *criollo* gentlemen arrived in the plaza, mounted on horses that were covered in sweat and foam. The first of these men held a rolled-up piece of paper in his hand. They must have been the last group of commissioners dispatched by those in favor of compromise, returning now with one of those threatening or elusive responses from Goyeneche, the kind that revealed the evil cunning of his soul: "The disloyal Province of Cochabamba has drunk its fill from the cup of clemency," or, "His Majesty's good subjects shall be protected by the arms of the king."

The crowd saw and ran at them; it surrounded and mocked them, yelled and whistled at them; it threw handfuls of dirt at them, so much so that they were engulfed in a cloud of dust—and all of this happened so quickly that it takes longer to recount it than it did to occur. Confused, covered in dirt, they also did not take long to get away in whatever manner and direction each of them could, without trying to speak or much else to calm down the angry multitudes, tearing at the sides of their tired mounts with their spurs.

It was impossible to place any kind of order in that chaotic and raucous popular mass, which only wanted to rush out and face Goyeneche's army. The good Prefect simply took the lead; a few gentlemen came next; then followed the militiamen and the few soldiers; then the *Gringo* and Alejo, the women, and those in the *Mellizo's* band, dragging the cannons along. As they passed by the door of the Church of the Matriz, the women yelled out, asking for the image of the Virgin of Our Lady of Mercy, *la Patriota*—which had already been wounded in the battle of Amiraya. But the priest of the parish, Don Salvador Jordán, dressed in surplice and holding the aspergillum in his hand, came out to the doorstep, and he was followed by the sacristan, who was carrying the basin of holy water for him. The former said:

"No one will come into the house of the Lord in this manner. ... Get back!"

"But why, Father?" the Grandmother asked. "We come for our Mother. ... You cannot abandon us like this," she yelled at once, and a thousand voices repeated her words.

The parish priest, completely enraged, sprinkled the women with the aspergillum and repeated:

"Get back! Infidels! Anathema!" and other words that were not very productive, for they were drowned out by the clamor of the multitudes as soon as they left his lips. The first waves of people advanced toward him and retreated less and less before the aspergillum each time.

"Yes, Father!" a voice yelled at his side, making me tremble with joy. "They're right! Let them take the Virgin. . . . And the sooner, the better!"

"Long live Brother Justo!" the women exclaimed.

The parish priest looked at my dear teacher with astonishment.

"What else can we do?" he continued, "let them take Our Lady of Mercy! Let them show Her the sight of human blood! Let the Mother of Christ the Redeemer, the Queen of the angels, go and hear the blasphemies and the shrieks of fury and desperation! Since She and all these stray women are the same, it does not matter if bullets tear her apart and rip her head off! They have already taken two of her fingers at Amiraya!"

At these unexpected words, the women lowered their heads humbly. My teacher knew the secret to bringing the popular mobs to reason. He had pretended to be on their side to get their attention and then used the language of irony to serve his purposes.

"Come now!" he went on. "Why don't you take her? Our Lady very much likes bullets. . . . Who doesn't know that it has been impossible to replace her two missing fingers? The *Cuzqueño*[2]—I think he's over there with the *Mellizo*—he can say precisely what he has seen with his own eyes. Three times he tried to attach the fingers that he made for her, and the same three times they fell right off! It was impossible to keep them glued on! Let the *Cuzqueño* come forward! Let that fool come and tell us if this isn't true!"

The women were shaking.

"Come on! Who wants to come in and take the Virgin with them?"

His question was answered only by sobs and moans.

"Good, my daughters," the Father then said, exchanging his ironic tone for one that was deeply tender and melancholy. "The Virgin will come out here, as far as the door, and give Her blessing to those who are going off to die for the homeland."

I then saw, my dear readers, I then saw the most moving scene that I recall ever beholding in my long life as a soldier of the Independence Movement. The image was placed at the door of the church on its platform, held there by four of the women. Then the parish priest and the Augustinian Father knelt down on either side of it, and the crowd fell to the ground on their knees. And the sweet singing of the *Salve Regina* was tenderly taken up after the silence that had followed all the screams of rage, of death, and of vengeance.

"Be gone!" my teacher exclaimed, standing up. "It is utter madness. . . . God bless you, my daughters!"

And he covered his face with his hands, and his chest shook in strong convulsions.

"Forward!" the Grandmother yelled, and pushed Clara—the poor *Palomita*, who could barely keep herself standing—ahead.

Behind them, continuing on with my friends, I passed the door of the bell tower that opens onto the plaza. I was already shouting again like everyone, and I was excited about the idea of being present for the battle and about throwing one of the grenades myself. But I felt someone with fingers that seemed like bone grab and pull me back by the ear. Then I was dragged inside the tower by an insurmountable force, and the door closed immediately behind me, leaving me in the dark.

I let out a scream of fury. I became enraged and swung my tight fists against he who dared deprive the homeland of one of its defenders, and. . . . And I found myself cold and mute in front of my teacher's sparkling eyes, shining uneasily in their sockets.

"It is utter madness. . . . Oh! I understand it, though. I would go and die with them, my son, if a very large duty did not ordain that I now live my life for 'another,' who is yet more unfortunate than I," he said to me. "But you, poor child," he continued in a persuasive and paternal tone, "why would you present yourself—weak, defenseless, unarmed—before those whom you shall be much better able to battle later in defense of the homeland? No! I will not allow it. . . . I order you to stay by my side . . . in the name of your mother!"

I grabbed his thin hand tightly in mine and was going to beg him to allow me to go back by the side of the Grandmother. But he leaned forward and murmured the following words into my ear, which would have been enough for me to follow him obediently to the end of the world:

"Do it for your father! For you will be able to see him, to mercifully close his eyes for him at the hour of his death!"

Then he immediately climbed up the stairway of the tower. I followed him to the landing where the first level of windows of the belfry open up and stopped to catch my breath. The Father began pacing back and forth anxiously, speaking to himself in the already deserted and silent belfry.

"It is utter madness. . . . Oh! If we only had the weapons that were lost in Huaqui! If there was some way to communicate with the rest of the world! . . . But closed in like this, in the bottom of our valleys, with the sling, and the staff, and the tin cannon, and the glass grenade as our only weapons—what's left for us now? Death, only death!"

Then, all of a sudden, he stopped pacing.

"Come," he said, and jumped into the dome of the church through one of the windows that led to it. I followed, less nimbly than him despite my young age and my many outings of physical exercise.

There were already a few people in that prominent location that overlooks the red roof tiles of the houses of the city and further out to the entire countryside. Among these, I saw the parish priest dressed in the surplice and the sacristan who, in his confusion, had followed him with the holy water basin still in his hands. A gentleman wrapped up in a long Spanish cape, with his hat pulled down to his eyebrows, drew the Father's attention. It did not take him long to recognize him and start up the following conversation with him:

"What? Your Excellency around these parts, Don Andreu?"

"Indeed, it is I, in person, Reverend Father. The day before yesterday I was brought in my bed to be sheltered in one of the houses of this neighborhood. My tertian fever is not as severe today. Since I am able to walk, and since the danger for me has increased,

I came to take refuge in the church. Then I followed the good priest of the parish up here out of curiosity."

"Well, Don José Manuel de Goyeneche is on his way. . . . Now we're the ones who will be looking for sanctuary. And who knows . . . we might not find it anywhere, not even in the center of the earth."

"Like I just said, the danger for me is indeed growing."

"I do not understand. Is your Excellency mocking me, Don Miguel?"

"Not at all, Reverend Father. A Peninsular Spaniard, a very loyal subject of his Majesty the King Don Fernando VII, may God protect him, can be in greater danger today than the rebel Don Mariano Antezana. The 'Three-Faced Man' . . . that's what the patriots call him, isn't it?"

"Yes, Don Andreu, that is what we call him, because of the three charges that he received: from the Junta of Seville, from Pepe Botellas,[3] and from the Infanta Doña Carlota."

"That man will never forgive me because I was one of those who tore off his mask and revealed those three faces of his, which all together make up the face of one true, deceptive schemer."

"And of one abominable American."

A gust of wind from the south brought us a confusing clamoring, a mix of all the sounds that the human voice is capable of producing. It reminded me of the comparison that Alejo had made between the shouting and whistling of the patriots at Aroma and those of the crowds at the fiesta with the bulls for the Patron St. Sebastian. The two men became silent so as to observe, from there, the unbelievable battle that was about to take place between an unarmed people and one of the best organized armies, with all the resources available to it at the time, of the Spanish domination.

Light, white clouds that looked like floating pieces of gauze that were symmetrically folded at intervals decreased the glare from the sun, making it appear to be a white dot in the middle of an iridescent circle—a common phenomenon in those skies at that time of the year. If I believed that nature took part in men's bloody battles, I would say that this was her way of flying the flag of the republic, which would eventually be raised in the sky, after many years, thanks to this and a thousand other sacrifices that seemed so senseless at the time. . . .

At the foot of Ticti, a peak that rises from the hills of Alalai, a large cloud of dust, inside of which evanescent flashes could be distinguished, announced the arrival of Goyeneche's army. The multitudes leaving the city were flooding onto the small hill of Mount San Sebastián. The city, meanwhile, appeared to be completely abandoned.

Supplementing my own memories with all the detailed reports that I gathered afterward from many people who witnessed the events up close and who participated in them, I shall now recount to you everything that followed, and about which our national writers, due to their sole objective of incriminating Goyeneche, have not said a thing.

The Grand Pacifier of Upper Perú, the Count of Huaqui—whose real historical names had just been uttered from the mouths of the treasurer Andreu and of my teacher on behalf of the moral awareness of Spaniards and Americans alike at that time—was approaching at the front of his troops. He came quite satisfied, with his secretary Don Pedro Vicente Cañete and his vast military staff, thinking that at any time now he would see before him the repentant people of the already submissive city of Oropesa. He figured that the clergy would come first, bringing the baldachin that would provide shade for his laureled head; that they would be followed by the members of the Cabildo, the justices, and the other institutions; that a delegation of ladies with welcoming hands and teary eyes would follow; and that the multitudes would come crowding behind, crying out: "Mercy! Compassion!" And he promised himself to be deaf to these cries for clemency. That he would be severe, relentless. It was necessary for the rebellious city to atone for its repeated treacheries against the loving monarch! What would his brave soldiers—to whom he had promised the ownership of the lives and the properties of the rebels—say otherwise! But all of a sudden he heard a strange clamoring, a kind of mocking hooting and bellowing, that at once brought to him the ceaselessly rebellious and untamable people of Cochabamba. He looked up the road, but did not see anyone. So he raised his head and looked to the left, toward Mount San Sebastián, and what he saw there woke him up from his daydreams. With fury and desperation, he exclaimed:

"There is nothing else to it but to kill every single one of those damned Cochabambian rabble!"

He then ordered his troops—more than five thousand men from the three branches of the army—to take their battle formations, with their right against the Ticti, and their left at the banks of the Rocha River, and to charge forward so that the wings spread out in a semicircle and then met on the other side of Mount San Sebastián, thus surrounding it in a circle of fire and steel that would start to close in and pitilessly destroy the patriots. The terrain was completely clear for this maneuver to be executed. It was a plain of clayish ground, naturally flattened out, that barely contained a few, scattered, rickety carob trees. The public cemetery, which is now at the very base of the hill, was built many years later, during the government of the Grand Marshal of Ayacucho. At the time, the small hamlet of Jaihuaico consisted of only one estate house with a very small chapel.

Meanwhile, the patriots had set up their tin cannons at the crown of the hill, with men, women, and children indistinctively preparing to operate them under the instructions of the *Gringo* and Alejo, and driven on incessantly by the resounding voice of the Grandmother. Those who had rifles, harquebuses, slings, or grenades took their places in a disorganized fashion to defend the sides of the hill. A completely unarmed multitude of women and children was behind them, around Antezana and the other gentlemen with him, growing more and more anxious. The yelling of the senseless challenges, the mocking whistling, the loud bellowing did not stop for an instant. These sounds even reached as far as where I was, filling me with a nervous quivering and rending tears of rage and shame from me. More than once I was about to run off and go jumping down the stairs, to fly to where I thought my post should be. But just one glance from the Father would keep me still, and I would go back to looking through my tears to the distant hill where a hopeless people was about to die. The first shots from the cannons and the harquebuses were fired from there. The enemy troops continued to charge around the hill and did not begin firing until they were within striking range. The clamoring of the multitudes grew at that point, an immense howl of fury and pain that must have come from the mouths of everyone there upon seeing the first blood spilled. I also saw, starting at that moment, a number of frightened people running down the side of the hill that had the mildest slope, where it descends down to the plaza of San Sebastián. I noticed that there were more men running away than women, and I later learned that that example of cowardice had been instigated by the *Mellizo*, the *Jorro*, and the most raucous ones from their band.

It took Goyeneche's troops less than an hour to completely surround the hill. There were about two hundred patriots still there at that point, of both sexes and of all ages: mothers hugging their children desperately against their chests, youths who were going to pay dearly for their lives, old people who were not even strong enough to throw a well-aimed stone at their enemies. The Prefect Antezana and the gentlemen in his party managed to save themselves thanks to the quickness of their horses, but not without most of them suffering some kind of wound and without leaving two dead behind them in the field of battle.

Longer than the battle—I say "battle" because I do not wish to contradict the accounts of the Count of Huaqui—was the time it took to complete the killing, the pitiless slaughtering of those who were trapped without a way out of that circle of death that became more insurmountable the more it closed in on them. Goyeneche's soldiers gave no quarter, not even to the women who dragged themselves at their feet. . . . It was time for killing. There would be plenty of time later to satisfy other brutal passions in the city, as their general had handed its future over to them. . . .

I shall recount to you now what became of a few humble people whose names do not appear in the annals of history, but who have appeared so often in this, the story of my dark life.

Clara, the poor *Palomita*, had fainted and fallen in front of the Grandmother with the first shots and was saved while she was unconscious by the women who fled with the *Mellizo* and his noble companion. Dionisio took her place, and his skull was smashed.

My friend Luis immediately and unhesitatingly replaced him. His voice resounded with that of the old woman, until a bullet penetrated his lungs. His father, the *Gringo*, made incredible valiant efforts, operating the tin cannons with Alejo. When he saw that there was no hope of coming out of there alive, and when he saw, above all, that Goyeneche's inexorable soldiers were forcing the patriots to kneel before them, he exclaimed in French:

"Non, sacré Dieu! Non, par la culotte de mon père!"[4]

And turning the mouth of the cannon that he had just loaded with the case shot against his own chest, he lit the fuse and landed far off, torn to pieces.*

Alejo, even happier than him, felt the blood rise to his head. He remembered Aroma and attacked the first grenadier who appeared before him, took his rifle, and managed to escape with his life, although he was wounded, and although he did not know himself how he did so, thanks no doubt to his Herculean strength and the quickness of his legs.

On the crown of the hill, the victors found a pile of corpses, dismantled and partially melted tin cannons, and, sitting on one of their crude gun-carriages, with two lifeless children at her feet, an old blind woman with hair as white as snow.

"On your knees! We'll see now how witches pray," one of them said, pointing his rifle at her.

The old woman aimed her blind eyes in his direction, gathered the blood that was spilling from her chest in the palm of her hand, and threw it on the soldier's face before receiving the *coup de grâce* that awaited her!

Despite all this, the historians from my country barely mention in passing the "Battle of the Tin Cannons"! They have not seen what the newspapers of Buenos Aires said about it, which was repeated in those of all the Americas and which had more than one echo on the other side of the Atlantic!

---

*This event has been incorrectly recalled by my friend Don José Ventura Claros y Cabrera, who has confused his notes for his telling of the life of the youth Viscarra with it.

I thought I had finished with this chapter, but Merceditas, who does not leave me alone even for an instant, and wants to have a part even in the writing of my memoirs, and comes to read what I write over my shoulder,* suddenly said to me:

"I would put four sentences here from a book that I know of, which had great fame in the glory days of your country."

"And what is that?" I asked her, smiling a bit mockingly, because I have the fault of believing that I know more than her, even though she has proven me wrong innumerable times.

She took the small volume entitled *The Education of Mothers*, by Aimé Martin,[5] from my shelf. Then she opened it to a page that she had marked with a ribbon with the design of the three colors of the flag, and held it out before my eyes.

"You're right, and you're always right, damned woman!" I exclaimed at once, and copied the following down from the book:

"The United States of America is a new world born from and for new ideas. . . . Such will also be the case with South America, after it triumphs in its battle for its independence. And it will triumph, because it is impossible for a nation in which the women fight for the cause of Independence and die beside their brothers and husbands to do anything but triumph. A nation in which an officer stands before his army every night and asks: 'Are the women from Cochabamba there?' and another officer responds: 'Praise be God, they all died for the homeland in the field of glory,' will inevitably triumph."

"You're right!" I said again. "I remember that the first night that I heard the drums call the rolls in Belgrano's *Porteño* army, I heard those very same words with an emotion that I cannot describe, which cannot be described in any other way than with tears. That

---

*Editor's Note: At the bottom of the page on which the worthy Colonel La Rosa has written this, there is a an envelope that has been sealed onto it. On it, the honorable wife of our veteran has written the following words: "Do not believe the doddering old fool. Actually, it is he who follows me around like a shadow, like a pest. . . . He won't leave me alone! He wants me to be at his side all the time as he writes his rambling, foolish stories! But what he recounts right after this, however, is very much the truth. — M. A. de la R." We do not know if the author had noticed these comments before sending us his manuscripts, and we beg his forgiveness if we have committed an indiscretion by including them here.

great native son of America, about whom I shall have much to say in my own way, offering my country's eternal gratitude to him, had wanted to instill his soldiers with courage by honoring the women of Cochabamba in the same manner in which the French army honored the memory of their first grenadier, La Tour D'Auvergne.[6]

Many years later, it makes me proud to see these events treated so well by the illustrious Argentine writer Bartolomé Mitre, who says the following:

"Giving in to the influence of the authorities, the Cochabambians sent a new dispatch to Goyeneche. . . . But this was not the will of the people: determined to perish before surrendering, a group of about one thousand gathered in the main plaza. There, asked by the authorities if they were ready to defend themselves down to the very last, a few voices answered yes. Then the women of the populace present at the plaza began to yell that if there were no men left in Cochabamba to die for the homeland and to defend the Junta of Buenos Aires, then they would go out to face the enemy on their own. The men's courage being inspired by this heroic determination, they all swore that they would rather die than surrender. Thus, men and women alike took up arms and prepared their resistance by taking the hill of Mount San Sebastián, which is right outside the city, where they gathered all of their forces and the last of their tin cannons. The Cochabambian women, infused with a manly spirit, occupied the battle positions next to their husbands, next to their sons, and next to their brothers. They inspired the men with their words and their actions. And when the time came for it, they also fought and knew how to die for what they believed in.

"In spite of this heroic persistence, in spite of so much sublime sacrifice, Cochabamba succumbed. . . ."

These things should be remembered in as many ways as possible: in books, in bronze, in marble, and in granite. Why do my fellow countrymen not erect a simple monument at the top of their pleasant and historic hill? A stone column, truncated to indicate the grief, with a harquebus and a tin cannon—made exactly of tin, just as they were back then—and with this inscription at its base: "May 27th, 1812." This would be so useful in teaching the new generations the sacred love for the homeland that—God forbid!—already seems so deadened today.

XXI

The Great Heroic Feat of the Count of Huaqui

The slaughtering of the patriots on Mount San Sebastián had barely ended when the city began to suffer the most horrendous, the most savage, and the most merciless acts of war imaginable. The victors were "the masters of the lives and of the properties of the rebels," as the Grand Pacifier, the Count of Huaqui, had told them more than once. Without any order whatsoever, without leaders or officers to control them—or at times given license by these same who led them by example—the soldiers committed crimes and killed men, women, and children without distinction in the streets. They pursued the fugitives, calling for their heads, encouraging each other with their boisterous yelling, as if they were hunting wolves. They knocked down doors of stores and houses, pillaging freely, becoming more and more excited the more liquor that they drank. They abandoned themselves to their hearts' delight to the most brutal excesses of which man is capable—transformed, in these situations, into a more loathsome monster than the wildest of beasts.

Thousands of unfortunate ones, condemned to death and shame, turned instinctively to seek refuge in the churches and monasteries. But unfortunately the majority of these sacred sanctuaries had shut and locked their doors. Only three or four, located in the center of the city, opened them at last before the wailing of the desperate multitudes, who thought, at that point, that they had been abandoned by everyone, including God.

My teacher was the first to remind the parish priest of the Church of the Matriz the duty imposed on them by humanity as well as by their sacred ministry.

"Our place is at the door of the church, my good priest," he said to him; "from there we shall extend a helping hand to our brothers, or else we shall stand and be killed by the pitiless victors. Follow me, your Grace. . . . This is more important than preventing the poor women from taking the image of Our Lady to the battlefield to protect them."

He leapt down the stairs, and the parish priest followed him, although not very willingly, as did all the others, all in a deep silence.

As we went out the door of the tower that opens into the plaza, so as to immediately take the door of the church that opens there, we saw three gentlemen stop in front of the Cabildo. One of them was Antezana. Not wearing a hat, he sought to enter the building while the other two were trying to prevent him from going in. I remember quite well that one of them was waving his hand, which was stained with blood, up in the air, and was heatedly talking to the Prefect. I believe it must have been the patriot Córdova, who managed after some time to convince Antezana to seek refuge outside the city instead of succumbing to what would have been a certain death by staying at the post that he had declared he would not abandon.

In the meantime, Goyeneche, followed by Cañete, his military staff, and a small escort of dragoons, was continuing ahead of his troops so as to avoid disturbing even indirectly the pillaging and plundering that his soldiers were enjoying. He was calmly on his way to take the lodgings that were now his in the house of government, located a block from the main plaza, on the same street as the Church of St. John of God, facing one of the exits of the Church of the Matriz. In those times, the house of government had the most beautiful engraved wooden balconies of the city, as well as a great stone arcade on the wide pillars of which one could see, in high relief, two musketeers serving as sentinels with their weapons over their shoulders. I believe it is necessary to record these details here, in passing, for I have been told that the new owner of the house has had those monuments destroyed, although they very much deserved being preserved, and that he has replaced them with modern stucco constructions, more elegant, in accordance with today's taste, but which I do not share.

Two blocks before arriving at these lodgings, the Count of Huaqui heard a great rush of people coming down a side street to his left. He stopped the spirited horse on which he was mounted and drew his sword. Looking in that direction, he saw a large group of fugitives from the hill, men and women, come running down the street and then stop suddenly at the corner. They had probably sought to seek refuge in the Church and Hospital of San Salvador, but now found themselves in danger of falling before the sabers of the unexpected cavalcade.

"At them, men! And I don't want anyone in that rabble to remain standing!" he yelled like a Cid before a Moorish army.[1]

And spurring on his horse, he charged the fugitives. His men followed with their sabers in the air.

The poor fugitives could not turn around and run back the way they had come because a large number of soldiers had been chasing and firing at them. Some of them continued forward, toward Las Cuadras, and must have kept running until they reached the brambly grounds of San Pedro. The majority turned to their left, heading away from the cavalcade, with the hope of reaching the desired sacred sanctuary at the Church of the Matriz.

It would have been necessary to be able to run faster than a rabbit, however, to escape from the fearsome Count and his men on foot. The victor from Huaqui, from Amiraya, and from San Sebastián had the satisfaction of killing almost all of those unfortunate people with his own hand. He wounded them with the blade as well as the point of his saber as they ran, terrified, or dragged themselves on their knees at the feet of his horse. He swiped and slashed indiscriminately, cutting and sending hands that had come up to try to stop the blows from his *Tizona*[2] flying through the air. His steed stomped on the quivering bodies with its iron-plated hoofs, and his escort of men easily completed the rest of the killing as necessary. The screams of these victims were so loud that they rose above all the other wailing that could be heard from every part of the city where the victors had already entered.

The Count, maddened with fury, continued to pursue them, and only one woman, whose fright had given her feet wings, and three or four of the strongest and quickest of the men, managed to reach the doors of the atrium of the Church of the Matriz and rush into the church to fall on the grounds, completely out of breath. The woman was very young, white, and blond; she had a saber wound on her head and had lost her mantilla and one of her shoes while running; her screams, her contorted face, her eyes that seemed as if they were about to pop out of their sockets, and the trembling that shook her entire body would have inspired pity even in a panther. You might be able to better imagine her condition when I tell you that the unfortunate woman had seen her father and her fiancé killed on the hill, and that, pursued in that manner by the Count of Huaqui, she eventually lost her reason. Many years later, in 1825, when I returned to my country as part of the entourage of the Grand Marshal of Ayacucho, I saw her again. She was constantly fleeing, hiding behind doors or wherever she could, and she said that she was being pursued by a fiendish beast who rode on a horse of fire that burned her back with its breath. One of the men who managed to save himself along with her was sooted black with gunpowder and completely covered in blood. Although it was not easy, I recognized him to be Alejo. His body was full of wounds and bruises, although luckily none were fatal.

Goyeneche had wounded the woman when she was just about to escape him and enter the atrium, but he lost a moment at that point because he had to turn his horse away from the door. To compensate for this, he kicked with his spurs deeper and even more enraged into the sides of the noble animal. This put him at the door of the church in just one leap. Thinking that he would catch his victim there, he swung his sword and struck a tremendous blow on the upper part of the wicket, which was open at the time, and I believe that over half a century of successive layers of paint have not managed to cover the mark that can still be seen there today. Oh! How I would like his name to be engraved right below it as an eternal reminder of his infamy!

The woman's screams, the wailing from the group, and the

sound of the horse's iron-plated hoofs on the stone pavement of the church reverberated in the sacred dome and drew the attention of everyone who was gathered in the Church of the Matriz to that area of the building. The clergymen—there were already five or six of them, in addition to the parish priest and my teacher, at the main door that faces the plaza—marched forward, full of wrath, to meet the defiler, whom no one had as of yet recognized.

"Desecrator! Infidel!" they exclaimed, while a shout of panic and fright came from the mouths of all the people amassed inside the church.

Goyeneche stopped his tremulous horse, which was covered in sweat and foam, and he raised his hand automatically to his hat, but he did not take it off his head. As he stared at the priests who were coming to face him, and at the multitude that was crowding on the other side, near the altar, and at the tabernacle where the Holy Sacrament was uncovered and surrounded by many lighted candles, he looked stunned, as if he were awaking from a dream.

His appearance impressed me so deeply that I feel that I can still see him right here in front of me now. He was taller than the average man, with thin and straight chestnut-colored hair and a wide, protruding forehead that could be seen because his hat was tilted backwards; his eyes were large, of a clear, grayish-green color; he had a bulky, straight nose, thin lips, and a large, protruding chin. He was wearing a military uniform that was full of dust, and tall riding boots covered in blood and mud. He was mounted quite unskillfully on a luxuriant square saddle, in the Limean style. The horse he rode was one of the most beautiful of the Andalusian breed of horses raised in the Rimac Valley that I have ever seen: a ruddy bay, bright as burnished copper, with a long mane, and a thick, jet black tail.

The parish priest, who was out in front of everyone, was the first to recognize him. He took two steps back and looked again. He was as stunned as the man on horseback, as if he refused to believe what he was seeing with his own two eyes. For the parish priest, who thought of himself as a realist, it was impossible for that man, who was on that horse inside the church grounds, to be Don José Manuel Goyeneche, the grand Christian, the defender of the

Church, the man who confessed and received the Holy Communion every week! And the same happened with the other priests, with the exception of Brother Justo, who proceeded to make his way past the others and to the front. My teacher looked paler than I had ever seen him. He was trembling with wrath, his lips quivered convulsively, and sparks flew out of his eyes, which were more jittery in their sockets than ever. A sepulchral silence now reigned in the church. The only thing that could be heard was the occasional sound made by the front legs of the spirited horse when it stamped them on the stones, while it chewed its bit. Is neck was arched back, it was breathing vigorously through its fuming nostrils.

"Scoundrels! Wretched rabble!" murmured the hero of San Sebastián, and finally sheathed his sword to turn to leave that place and rejoin his escorts, who had not dared to pass beyond the door of the atrium of the church, as Goyeneche had.

But at that point, unfortunately, Goyeneche spotted López Andreu, who had gone toward the front along with the priests. He became livid with rage, his eyes shone like those of a starving tiger that has just found its previously lost prey, and a horrible curse came out of his mouth that froze the blood of everyone who heard it, as none of them would have ever imagined that it was possible to hear anything like it in that sacred place, and even I dare not copy it here on these candid pages on which I am loyally putting down my memories.

"At last!" he then shouted, raising his sword and kicking his spurs.

"Villain! Despicable, unworthy, unfaithful American!" my teacher answered him with a resounding voice and stepped forward between them at once, grabbing hold of the horse's reins with his strong hands.

The horse retreated a few steps, even though its rider continued to tear into its flanks with his spurs.

Goyeneche then sought to swing his sword down on the priest's head, but the horse rose on its rear legs, forcing him to loose his balance, let go of the sword, which remained hanging from his sword-belt, and grab the horse's mane with both hands.

The Father, meanwhile, once he had taken hold of the reins, did not let go of them. We saw him hanging from them. Dumbfounded, we watched the unfolding of the struggle, which ended shortly thereafter in a disastrous way for the priest, as the horse finally knocked him down and trampled on him maddeningly on the ground before carrying away its rider, who, completely unable to control or direct it by then, barely held on to its neck.

A general scream of horror and distress resounded in the church. I rushed to help my teacher, running over whatever was in my way. I sat down on the ground, raised his venerable head, and rested it on my knees. Alejo was bellowing beside me like a wild beast. The priests gathered round and leaned forward anxiously. The people crowded in from everywhere, uttering screams of pain.

Brother Justo looked as if he were peacefully asleep. Appearing suddenly as if by magic, a woman brought a jug of water and sprinkled some on his face two or three times. Her own was flooded with tears. The Father then opened his eyes and looked at us. A serene smile appeared on his lips, and he said:

"It's nothing, my children."

But right away his face became contorted from the pain that he felt from having spoken these words.

"The infidel . . . Oh! My God!" he said, and lost consciousness again. A stream of bloody foam spilled from his mouth.

The parish priest kneeled down by my side and sprinkled his face again with water from the jug that he had taken from the woman's hands. He took his pulse, wiped his mouth with a handkerchief, and, very moved, exclaimed:

"He's dying! He was truly a just man, a man of the Lord. . . . We must save him. Let's take him elsewhere, where it will be possible for him to receive the aid he needs in his condition."

"I'll take him in my arms, Father," poor Alejo sobbed.

Then he lifted him immediately from the ground, with the tenderness and care that a mother would take to place her sleeping baby in its cradle. Unable to leave his side for even an instant, I helped, for my part, by holding his head up in my hands.

"Let's go! Everyone out of the way!" the blacksmith said, heading toward the door that led to the main plaza.

"Where are you going, you poor fool?" the parish priest asked him.

"To the monastery, *tata*," Alejo calmly replied.

It was undoubtedly the best thing to do, but it was impossible to get there without running the risk of perhaps dying along the way. Goyeneche's soldiers were already roaming throughout the entire city by then. Rifles shots and screams could be heard all across the very plaza that we would have to cross.

"Nothing matters," Alejo answered as different people made these observations to him; "there is no *chapetón*, nor any Indian from Cuzco, who is a more evil fiend than Goyeneche. Everyone will respect the Father, and me, because I'm carrying him in my arms. Let's go, young man!" he continued. "If they do kill us, then we will have all died 'together' on this day."

No one dared come with us. As we were leaving the church, I saw the poor Don Miguel López Andreu to one side of the door, sitting on a bench, overcome by an attack of his tertian fever. Many compassionate people surrounded him and lent him whatever assistance they could in that place.

"Are there no more thunderbolts in the sky for that infidel who has desecrated your house, oh, eternal God?" the Treasurer of the Audience of Charcas exclaimed through his chattering teeth and the convulsions from the fever.

Groups of soldiers, some of them led by contemptible Spanish officers, were running in every direction to pillage the houses of the wealthiest *criollos*. On the Street of Santo Domingo, I saw one of Goyeneche's aides, the fierce Zubiaga, defending for himself the house of one of the members of the Provincial Junta, that of the patriot Arriaga. This same thing is what other prestigious leaders did with the utmost insolence, managing to impose respect from the wild troops only for themselves and only to this end. It did not occur to any of them to protect the life or property of any rebel or of any peaceful inhabitant of the rebellious Oropesa.

Alejo kept marching forward at a quick pace, and I followed with difficulty, but still holding my teacher's head in my hands. When we reached the middle of the plaza, near the public fountain of Carlos III, I heard blood-curling screams from a woman on the corner of the Barrio Fuerte. A young woman—who had barely a few shreds of her black basquine left, no mantilla, torn doublet and shirt, bare shoulders, and her hair loose—was fighting there with two unarmed soldiers who must have abandoned their rifles to partake more freely in the pillaging. Her desperate situation gave the timid girl incredible strength to fight off her adversaries. She was able to push one and the other away with her bare arms. She tore into their fierce, repugnant, and bestial faces with her nails, and, afraid that she would scratch their eyes out, the villains were forced to cover themselves with their hands.

That lioness was Clara, the poor *Palomita*! Try to imagine my astonishment and my suffering when I recognized her. How beautiful she looked like that, my God!

"Let's go! We're almost there," Alejo said without slowing down, continuing on toward the door of the monastery, which was half opened. I could see the patriotic Father standing at its threshold, holding a holy crucifix in his hand.

I let my companion continue ahead with his precious cargo, while I ran like a madman to defend the young woman.

She had managed to get away from the two villains, but it was inevitable that they would soon catch her again.

I then saw one of those sublime acts of heroism that a woman is capable of in such extreme situations to protect her honor. The young woman picked up the wad from a rifle that she must have spotted burning on the ground in front of her, she took a grenade from her bosom, lit the fuse, and turned back to face her pursuers. Then, just when the soldiers were about to grab her in their arms, a horrendous explosion separated the three bodies. They landed far from each other, on their backs, and a whitish cloud of smoke was left in the place where they had met.

I rushed toward Clara's mangled body and found the patriotic Father already there before me.

"May God welcome her into his heart! How awful!" the good priest exclaimed.

I fainted. The Father, as I later learned, took me in his arms to my teacher's cell. He then went back with two other priests to retrieve Clara's body and take it to a bier in the church, where it could be buried in the sacred grounds.

When I came to, I found myself lying down on the bench. Alejo, kneeling on the floor beside me, was trying to wake me up by making me smell whiffs of vinegar from a bottle. I sat up and saw the Guardian, Brother Eustacio Escalera—a venerable octogenarian who had rebuilt the church and sought, in vain, to reestablish the order of the monastery—sitting at the head of my teacher's bed with his head bent down, either to hear the wounded Father's confession or some wish of his.

"That's fine," he said to him out loud, "you can rest in peace now, my son."

That day Alejo and I stayed in the monastery, attending to my teacher with the other priests. The locksmith also wanted to dig the grave of the poor Clara with his own hands. He would not hear from anyone about the need for him to take care of his own wounds.

"This is nothing," he would say, "I'm used to being shot to death, ever since Aroma"—an expression that has become proverbial among the common people of my country, and one that no one knows by whom it was said for the first time and under what circumstances, which is why I want to make sure to record it here for you.

Meanwhile, the city, as I have said before, continued to suffer the most horrendous acts of war imaginable. And I repeat it yet again, because I cannot find other words with which to describe it. . . .

But no! Here is Don Mariano Torrente, who will speak for me on this occasion, and whom you are more likely to believe than me! This Spanish historian, who is so calm when it comes to the great crimes committed by monsters like Calleja, Bobes, Morales,[3] and others—the memories of which still make one's hair stand on end—cannot help regretting Goyeneche's behavior after his victory at "The tall mountain of San Sebastián," and this even despite the fact that the Count of Huaqui is one of the heroes on whom he dotes the most. Carried away by his blind Peninsular fanaticism, he tries to make excuses for him in the following manner:

"The position of a virtuous leader who finds himself forced to authorize or overlook such a violent course of action on his own soil (for Goyeneche was American) is certainly a painful one. And it is even more so when it is seen executed by peoples from the same family (Indians from Cuzco under the command of Spanish officers). But what can a loving father do when his repeated warnings, advice, generosity, tolerance, and pardons for the misguided criminals produce no other effect than to incite the same offenders to commit other, even greater crimes? What was this dignified leader to do with a populace that had so many times mocked the personage of the victor. . . ?"

Don Mariano does not care to remember that Goyeneche had already shown his true colors in 1809; that it was from Potosí that he had promised the pillaging of Cochabamba; that the rebels from my homeland, for their part, never abused any of their victories; that, in fighting for their liberty, they were doing the right thing by rebelling a thousand times, without giving in to the flattering offers, nor to the threats of that treacherous American; that. . . . Ah! I must seem very old indeed when I waste so much ink on matters that the whole world has already judged!

As night fell, the neighborhoods around the center of the city became somewhat tranquil. Goyeneche had found himself forced to control his own soldiers because they had started to set fire to the city in the neighborhood where his lodgings were situated. The slaughtering, the pillaging, and all the other unnamable crimes continued in the outskirts of the city, and did so for three more days.

The Father Escalera wrote something on a piece of paper on behalf of my teacher, gave me the carefully sealed manuscript, and said to me:

"You must go deliver this to Doña Teresa right away. One of the brothers will accompany you to her house."

I wanted to say goodbye to my teacher, but the Guardian did not allow me to do so.

"Let's leave him completely in peace for now. He must not speak nor move. . . . Go on, my son. You can return another day," he said, accompanying me to the door himself, where the patriotic Father was waiting for me.

XXII

The Wolf, the Fox, and the Parrot

Even though Don Pedro Vicente Cañete had been forewarned by an early letter from his learned Honor Don Sulpicio, a great friend and admirer of his, and had gone straight to honor her house with his presence, Doña Teresa had not been able to avoid a part of the same fate that indistinctively befell on all the wealthy *criollos* of the city. A large group of drunk soldiers still broke into the house. They killed the unfortunate *pongo* first, and then began their pillaging in the small chapel and the reception room. They did not respond at all when they heard Cañete's sweet, pleading warnings, nor did his angry threats manage to stop them. Luckily, the fierce Imas arrived just in time. He had gone there to arrange with Goyeneche's noble advisor how to carry out certain orders of their leader's, "in the very urgent service of the King," which we shall hear more about in a moment. A single shout from him was enough to chase away the wild group of soldiers, who decided then to carry as much as they could in their packs and pockets as they fled.

I found the doors fallen off their hinges. The *pongo* was hollowed out, naked in a pool of blood on his dais, at the feet of the painting of the Archangel St. Michael. The whole patio was littered with broken furniture, destroyed urns, and stucco saints that had been cruelly mutilated and stripped of their valuable lamé clothing and of their gold and silver. The lady had returned that morning with her children and servants, very confidently, and had happily welcomed the illustrious doctor into her abode. But then she had had to hide in the inner rooms, where she suffered the most fatal of afflictions, until Imas arrived to save them.

Her room reeked with the smell of tobacco and anise—a sure sign that she was absolutely furious, as my good readers already know. When I entered, she jumped like a wild panther at me, as if I were the one responsible for everything that had happened.

"What do you still want here, you intolerable vagabond?" she asked me, posed as if about to scratch my eyes out.

I handed her the Guardian's letter without saying anything. She opened it quickly and read it by the light of a tall candle that was lit at the feet of a St. Anthony, one of the saints that had been saved and was still in one piece, although it was just as naked as all the others.

I am not certain, but it appeared that she was actually moved for an instant, for I thought I saw a tear about to fall from her eyes. But her fierce selfishness immediately overtook any other emotion.

"Oh, for God's sake!" she exclaimed. "Yes, that's fine . . . but it's impossible now. . . . Tomorrow . . . we'll see him," she said, pointing me toward the door.

I cannot tell you precisely what was in that letter. I think, though, that it must have been the final farewell from a dying brother and that it implored the lady to protect "another more unfortunate than him."

I walked toward my room automatically. I wanted to lock myself in there, to be all alone and cry. . . . I believe there is no need for me to describe my state of mind to you after everything that had been impressed upon it on that ominous day of the May 27th, 1812!

As I went out to the patio, I saw that the rooms that the Doctor Cañete was to occupy were brightly illuminated.

"Do it any way whatsoever. Capture them and hang them or send them to the gallows! What else does your Excellency need?" was said, or rather howled, by a man, or rather by a wolf in the shape of a man.

"It will be done. Anything can be accomplished with the right touch, my dear brigadier. The only thing soldiers want to do is go out and use their bayonets. . . . Be calm, my dear friend. 'Slow down, for I am in a hurry,' I dare say, as did his Majesty the King Don Carlos III,[1] may God keep him in His glory," answered another person, with a sweet and cajoling voice that made him sound like a lay sister.

"There won't be even a trace of the rebels left. *Delicta majorum inmeritus lues, Romane!*"[2] yelled our old acquaintance, his Honor, in his falsetto voice.

I went up to one of the windows. Between the metal lattice and the glass, I was able to see those who were speaking inside. I stayed where I was and continued listening to their clandestine meeting.

The two personages whom I saw then for the first time were sitting in comfortable armchairs, facing each other. A glowing candelabrum with five burning lights and a silver-plated writing desk rested on the large, round table that separated them. His Honor was standing up, with his hat under his arm, holding his beloved walking stick with its tufts halfway down the cane as always, and keeping a respectful distance.

The man who howled when he spoke was over forty years in age, of medium height, cold, and stiff. He had thin, gray hair, a low forehead, jumpy eyes that seemed to be swimming in blood, a bulldog's nose, a large mouth, and a protruding chin with small bristles that the blade had not been able to shave clean in his many days of traveling and campaigning. He wore a worn-out military uniform and kept his greasy and dented hat on his head, tilted back. He was smoking paper cigarettes constantly, lighting a new one as soon as he had thrown the butt of the previous one on the table or on the carpet. From time to time he would brush off some dust from his flat-heeled boots with a whip that he held by a silver handle.

The man with the sweet voice who sounded like a lay sister was younger in age, taller, thin, quick, and bright. He seemed especially ready to perform the most graceful of courtly contortions, or to sliver through the ground like a snake. His long, black, curly hair; his pale coloring; his small, lively, penetrating eyes; his flat nose; and his thick lips—all indicated that he was probably a mestizo of three bloods: Spanish, cupreous, and African. His outfit was similar to his Honor's, but finer and better kept, like that of a dandy of the time. At that instant he was writing quickly on large, yellowish sheets of official paper.

I later learned that the man who howled was the famous Colonel Don Juan Imas, the most fanatical for their cause of all the *chapetones*. The most relentless of them all, his thirst for blood and gold was insatiable. He would have well deserved to end up like one of the famous conquistadors from the sixteenth century, the one who was forced to drink the molten metal that he so desired. Insofar as the other man was concerned, the one with the voice that sounded like a lay sister's, I realized at once that he must be, and in fact he was, the Paraguayan Don Pedro Vicente Cañete, the advisor to Goyeneche. He already enjoyed much fame back then among the Spaniards and their supporters as a very learned magistrate and an admirable politician. This was due in part to his "Advice Regarding the Situation of the Spanish Colonies,"[3] dedicated to the viceroy in 1810, and published by the patriots in the *Gaceta de Buenos Aires*.[4] This very praiseworthy document exposed with piercing insight the dangers that then threatened the colonial regime, and it cynically advised that it was necessary to corrupt the influential Americans with gifts, honors, and distinctions until the Spanish domination was once again solidified, at which time it would be possible to severely punish that which, for the time being, had to be tolerated and overlooked. No one knew as well as he how to capture someone's heart through flattery; every single one of his words was meant to cajole; a perpetual smile adorned his pale face; his manners were enchanting; "he was quite a lady," as his admirers said in praise of his charm and kindness. He also knew, better than anyone else, how to dazzle the uneducated and common men of his time by letting some deep maxim fall from his lips, or by opportunely—or inopportunely—bringing in some historical quotation, making him appear very erudite. We have already heard him, from the very first, refer to his comrade, the military man, as "his dear brigadier," whereas the latter was only a colonel. We also heard him turn to a saying of Carlos III's when he was being pressed to act. I believe that he constantly used *The Prince* and the *Discourses on Titus Liuvius*, by the Florentine politician, as his sources of inspiration. This Paraguayan Machiavelli, finally and most unfortunately for the future of the republic, was to leave a large, active clan behind him, like some of the other types that I have mentioned in my memoirs. There is not a single tyrant who has not had a Cañete at his service. I have heard the expression "he is quite a lady, and a fountain of knowledge, too" said so many times, just like in those days, in reference to some of these cajoling and deceiving "Men of State"!

"This is where we must begin, my dear, spirited Don Juan," Cañete said, placing his quill on the corresponding place on the writing desk.

"Let's go, then!" Imas answered impatiently.

"His Lordship will send the following letter to have it circulate among the magistrates and the members of the Cabildo, among the priests and the Guardians of the convents and the monasteries: 'The peace of the loyal and brave City of Oropesa of the Valley of Cochabamba having been reestablished by the arms of our Majesty the King, may God protect him, it is at all costs essential that sacred homage be celebrated with the splendor and glory worthy of an excellently apostolate Roman Catholic people. And seeing as how tomorrow is the day reserved for the celebration of the solemn holy day of the *Corpus Christi.* . . .'"

"The Devil take it! I don't understand a single word of what your Excellency is reading there, my good doctor," the colonel interrupted him, striking the table with his whip. "His Lordship told me that we were to form a Junta to purify this rebellious city, to judge and summarily hang every vile rebel. But your Excellency comes out with this religious holiday and *Corpus Christi* procession!"

"Don't worry, my dear brigadier," Cañete replied with his most pleasant smile. "Soldiers are explosive. . . . The thunderbolts of war, as—"

"I don't care who said it. The important thing is. . . ."

"Yes, my brave friend. The important thing is to punish the ungrateful, rebellious subjects of our Majesty the King, may God keep him, in an exemplary manner. That's where we're going, Don Juan!"

"Hm! . . . I don't understand."

"Your Excellency will now understand it."

As he said this, Cañete took out another piece of paper, smiled again, and read:

"In the name of the King, general exoneration. . . ."

Imas stood up and howled a spirited Spanish interjection that cannot be found in any dictionary, nor can it be copied down on paper.

"I can't stand this any longer, my good doctor," he said, suffocating in his anger. "I. . . . I. . . . But enough! I am not a toy to play with!"

Cañete seemed very contented.

"*Divis orte bonis, optime Romulae . . .*"[5] his Honor Don Sulpicio started to say. And he would have recited the entire ode by Horace, if a look from Imas had not shut him up and made him stay as still as a statue.

"By the way, what does this eccentric character want?" the colonel asked Cañete.

"Oh! I had forgotten. . . . He's my learned friend, his Honor— no, the good doctor, rather—about whom I have spoken so many times with his Lordship," Cañete answered, with his most enchanting smile. "Please forgive me, your Excellency, my Don Sulpicio," he continued, addressing his Honor and accompanying him to the door, "please forgive me, your Excellency, for having detained you so long. It was such a pleasure to see you, to embrace you in my arms. . . . So be it! Your Excellency is not *lingua amicus, verbo tenus*! Until tomorrow, when we will be able to see each other all day long."

His Honor was undoing himself in reverences and bows, but he barely dared to breathe, and he was looking frightenedly out of the corner of his eye at the enraged colonel as he walked backwards all the way to the patio. Once there, he finally breathed. Then he quickly put his hat on and sprinted all the way to his house. Cañete closed the door behind him and returned laughing to his armchair.

"That puppet will now go around everywhere repeating what he has heard," he said. "Come now. Listen to the conclusion of our exoneration, my exalted and beloved brigadier."

Imas made an angry motion.

"'Strike, but listen,' I dare say, as Themistocles[6] said, my spirited Don Juan!" the Paraguayan exclaimed. "Listen, your Excellency."

And he continued reading:

"In the name of the King, exoneration, etc. . . . With the condition of apprehending or denouncing the leaders and instigators of the rebellion, warning, furthermore, that if the guilty parties do not present themselves to the established authorities or to their respective parishes at once, or at most within three days, they shall be militarily found to be guilty of contumacy. And. . . ."

"Good Lord! Your Excellency knows more than anyone. Go on! Let's hear it. . . . On it with it, my good doctor!" Imas exclaimed, beside himself with happiness.

At that point, unfortunately, I heard footsteps coming from the portico and saw a group of officers appear. They were undoubtedly coming to receive orders from the personages inside. I was therefore forced to abandon my observation post and head to my room once and for all.

"My God! What terrible clutches has my poor country fallen into!" I thought, despite my young age.

I threw myself on my bed, fully dressed. I wanted to cry, but was unable to. I cannot tell you the pain, the fatal anguish that I suffered throughout the night. I thought about my friends, the ones who had been killed. . . . About the dangers threatening those who were still alive. . . . And making my torture even worse, I started hearing a sad wailing near my room, from the garden. They had deposited the body of the *pongo* in the passageway, and his poor wife, who had somehow arrived from the country that night, was keeping vigil over him, joined by Paula. They alternated in addressing their moans to the dead man, in that kind of monotonous cry used by Indian women on such occasions.

"You were my father and my mother," the wife wailed in Quechua; "you were my sole support and comfort. . . . What audacity drove you to leave me behind? Can't you hear my laments?"

"Why did you have the nerve to abandon your poor companion?" the charitable Paula said in turn. "Can you not hear her when she calls you now? Will you now sleep, just like that, in the heart of the frightful *Pacha mama*?"[7]

Nature eventually overcame the suffering of my soul. Already close to dawn, I fell heavily asleep. . . . You must remember, my dear readers, that I—who am now an old man simply and truthfully recounting to you the horrendous events of 1812—was then barely a boy of twelve years of age!

XXIII

*The Edifying Piousness with
Which the Count of Huaqui
Celebrated the Holy Day of the*
Corpus Christi *after His Victory
at "The Tall Mountain of
San Sebastián"*

It must have been about eight in the morning when I woke up the next day, fully dressed on my bed. My pillow was soaked with the tears that I had shed throughout the night. The bright winter sunlight—the sunlight from the season that in my country of perpetual spring we call winter, that is—was shining in my small room, coming in through the door that I had forgotten to close the night before. I heard the servants bustling about in the patio as usual. It seemed to me that they talked to each other joyfully, that they were laughing, that they were excitedly preparing to attend a large fiesta. The bells from the Church of the Matriz were ringing loudly for the Solemn Mass; small cannons and petards were going off; a group of dancers was passing by in the street, playing drums and reed pipes. . . . "Could it be that I have had some kind of horrible nightmare that seemed to go on forever?" I asked myself. "It's not possible that Goyeneche has come to my city! My longing to be a soldier has made me dream an impossible battle between the women and children of Cochabamba and a powerful army. . . . I'll go find Luis, and we'll go visit the Grandmother in her small house together. They'll make so much fun of me when I tell them what I have dreamt and imagined!"

"Clemente! The Doctor, his Excellency the wise Cañete needs warm water to shave," Feliciana shrieked in the passageway.

"I'm on my way! How wonderful it is to serve the most illustrious Doctor Cañete!" the sambo replied from the kitchen.

These words brought me back to the horrible truth of reality.

"Oh, my God! This is the celebration of the *Corpus Christi*,[1] ordered by Don José Manuel de Goyeneche, whom I saw yesterday on horseback in the Church of the Matriz, trying to kill women and old people!" I exclaimed, running out to go to the monastery were my teacher lay in pain.

"Ho there, young Don Juan, good morning to you!" Clemente yelled at me as he stepped out to the patio with the cauldron in his hands. "Today is the day of the celebration and performances. . . . Why doesn't your Excellency try on the new suit that her lady the *Marquesa* ordered for you?"

I looked at him with disgust and continued on my way. There were several Indians with long, black wool ponchos in the main patio. After having attended to the burial of their companion, they were now cleaning the house under the command of an old majordomo whom they had come with from one of Doña Teresa's estates nearby. The lady had not yet come out of her room; she was still there with her children. Feliciana stopped me at the front door of the house and took me to her presence.

I saw her, fully dressed, sitting in her wide, varnished wood bedstead, with the red damask curtains drawn back. She had a yellow silk handkerchief tied around her head, and she was smoking her indispensable paper cigarettes, in which she put two-thirds tobacco, one-third anise, and a pinch of musk. She looked straight at me and said:

"If you are going to the monastery, tell Brother Justo that I am ill and in much pain. . . . Oh, these migraines! I must bear so many crosses for my sins, dear Lord! Tell him, also, that I will send the Aragonese Father himself out to the country tomorrow, and perhaps even the 'physician' that the good Cañete has offered. . . . Oh! I can't stand this . . . I can't even talk, Juanito! Finally, I will later send my confessor, the Reverend Father, the Prelate of our Lady of Mercy. Go on, my son. . . . Oh! One more thing: have them give you some lunch in the kitchen, because the dining room is at the service of Don Pedro Vicente and his friends."

"Everything will be done as your Excellency has ordered it, your Ladyship," the Negro woman said right away, and took me to the kitchen.

I avidly ate what they gave me. I had not had a bite to eat in over twenty-four hours.

The streets were deserted and completely silent. I could see everywhere evidence of the pillaging and the killing from the day before. Meanwhile, the joyful ringing of the bells did not cease for a moment. On the corners of the main plaza they were hurrying to put up wooden posts, to raise as altars. I saw two or three dance troops at the doors of the Church of the Matriz. They were being given something to drink by their respective "Elders"—in other words, by the lay brothers or sisters who had organized them so as to solemnize the procession.

I must tell you at this point, but only in passing and very quickly—for it is not the most opportune moment to go into it—that the celebration of this holy day was the most noteworthy annual event in the otherwise apathetic life of Colonial times. It would be impossible for you to imagine today the enthusiasm that it stirred up; the sacrifices made by the poorest and humblest classes for the celebration and performances; the large altars that were raised higher than the roofs of the two-storied houses and that were covered by precious cloths, mirrors, items from silver services, urns, saints, and candalabra; the infinite diversity of dancers that participated in it; and the immense number of pitchers of *chicha* and bottles of *mistela* that were consumed in the week before the fiesta, which was celebrated on the octave. What you see these days is nothing. Between town-councils on the one hand and the establishment of new schools on the other, these customs from the "good times of our Majesty the King" have been almost completely extinguished. Some old people, from my generation, claim that piousness is dying out. But I think that it is actually fanaticism and ignorance that are no longer able to live as they did under the sun of 1810. If the wise Baron de Humboldt[2]—who was alarmed by these things to the point of believing that the Indians were more plunged in the practice of idolatry when he saw them than they had been before the Conquest—could rise from his grave today and once again visit the "sights of the Cordilleras," he would say with much astonishment: "This is the same magnificent nature that I have described, but I no longer see the savages that I once saw, but rather men who seem quite civilized." And if he were to ask, "Who was able to carry out such a miracle?" I would answer, "The swords of Arze, Belgrano, San Martín, and Bolívar. Murillo's blood and that of thousands of other martyrs, among which can be counted that of the poor women and of the noisy children of my dear Oropesa!"

Despite the power of the customs of the time, it was impossible for the Count of Huaqui to have the holy day celebrated with the same excitement and splendor as I have just briefly described. My readers will be surprised, rather, after the horrors that the city had suffered the day before, and when large groups of wild soldiers still continued committing them on the outskirts of the city, that he would try it at all. But the Count was also counting on a feeling that touches the weaknesses of people and leads them to take the most unbelievable actions—terror, my young friends. The terror that deifies the Caligulas and the Neros; the terror that dries the tears of those who are suffering and makes them smile pleasantly at the executioners; the terror that drags the multitudes along the feet of the tyrants; the terror that even gives men courage to fight and defend themselves from ones that scare them more than death itself; the terror, finally, that transforms simple people into inexorable persecutors of their own brothers, whom they never believed before to have caused them any harm, and whom without it—the terror—would continue loving and comforting in their sufferings. And if the tall, large altars, the infinite different dance troops, the innumerable devout multitudes were not present that year, there was no lack of people who hurriedly erected the altars, albeit at lower heights than usual, who participated in three or four costumed groups, as well as in the procession, all in order to gain a favorable glance from the hero of San Sebastián. There was also no lack of people who tried to assure that their heads stayed on their own shoulders by turning in their friends or by applauding the bloody executions that were carried out that same day in the middle of the ringing bells, of the religious songs, of the music, of the dances, and of the drunkenness of the Catholic populace—essentially in the same way that their conquerors had been transformed, in their case by fanaticism and greed!

The famous exoneration in the name of the King was announced that morning. I saw it posted on all the street corners, displayed on large pieces of papers—manuscripts, of course, for there was not a single printing press anywhere in Upper Perú at that time. As soon as the first inhabitants learned about the posted exoneration, they left the churches or monasteries where they had taken sanctuary and hurried to examine their pillaged houses. They consoled themselves with the thought that they had come out of it with their own skins intact, at least. But they were immediately told that they were to appear in the presence of his Lordship, so they went to pay him homage.

"That's fine," the triumphant general would answer; "I have come to clean the tears of the loyal subjects of our Majesty the King, those who have been grossly tormented by the rebels, by the ungrateful, evil enemies of the altar and of the Crown, who have forgotten that their hateful lives depended on my clemency. Today, all good people are under the protection of his Majesty's arms. But the evil ones must be punished. . . . The commission that is currently in charge of judging them needs to know their names and be able to capture those who are trying to get away. Woe to those who lend them sanctuary in their escape! He who does not denounce the criminal becomes his accomplice, and shall be equally punished."

At these words, even those who seemed the least timid would tremble with fear before him. Many were struck dumb and collapsed, their legs failing them. His Lordship would then smile, give them a friendly pat on the shoulder, and add:

"But your Excellency has nothing to fear, my dear friend. I know that you have never been contaminated by. . . . Come now! It is essential that all the good subjects of the King Don Fernando VII, may God keep him, assist me in my efforts. Does the commission already know what your Excellency has to tell them, for your part? What do Imas, Berriozábal, and Cañete say? Oh! The duty of punishing people is so painful!"

You can imagine, then, the infamies that this villain thus created in this manner!

A few notable patriots had already fallen into the hands of the victors the day before. Many were imprisoned on the day of the *Corpus Christi*, as it was later called. They were in the chapel, awaiting their death by firing squad or at the gallows, as soon as the procession ended. There were thirty of them, more or less, even though our historians only recall the most important ones: Gandarillas, Ferrufino, Zapata, Azcui, and Padilla.

I found the venerable Guardian at the door of the monastery speaking with a soldier who was dressed in a very proper uniform. This was no other than Zubiaga, the same one who had taken possession of the house and of all the goods that were most susceptible to being easily apprehended, of the member of the Provincial Junta Don Juan Antonio Arriaga.

"Forgive me your Excellency, honorable commander. . . . I beg you for God's sake and for that of all the saints in the Heavenly court," the good Father Escalera was saying, stretching his shaking hands out to the villain. "The brotherhood must aid the dying man right now. . . . Listen, your Excellency: they are already starting to sing the solemn *Miserere*³ in his room. . . . As soon as we are done, your Excellency will be able to go in."

"Well, fine . . . but I will do it, too! I've had enough of being run around!" replied the very noble Aide and Quartermaster General of the army of the most Christian Count of Huaqui.

The Guardian turned to return hurriedly to be by my teacher's side, but he saw me and stopped for an instant to stretch his hand out for me to kiss it.

"Follow me, my son," he then said, very kindly.

The commander sat down, in a bad mood, on a wooden bench that was there at the time, and turned his attention to lighting a cigarette. His presence at that location could be explained by the order he had been given to take possession of all the books and papers that might be found in Brother Justo's cell, as the latter was considered to be: "A heretic and a rebellious priest, who was an unworthy disciple of the teachings of the Fathers of the Church, and who was to be sent before the Inquisition in Lima, if, unfortunately, he were not to die." I learned this a few years later from Captain Alegría, who heard Goyeneche's verbal order word for word. In all likelihood, one of the "King's good subjects"—whose devotion to the Monarch the Count was so apt at awaking—had given the most reliable of reports about "the insolent priest" who had taken a hold of the Count's horse's reins in the church to prevent him from punishing the "evil Spaniard Don Miguel López Andreu" with his own hands.

The singing of the *Miserere* resounded in the silent and deserted cloister as the Father Escalera and I walked quickly toward my teacher's cell. "*Ecce enim in inquitatibus conceptus sum,*"[4] sang the brotherhood of at most five or six priests who had lined up four steps away from the bed of the dying man. The Guardian immediately took his place and joined in at that point in the song. His voice was less broken than one would have expected for someone his age. "*Ecce enim veritatem dilexisti....*"[5] I got down on my knees in a corner of the room, from where I could see the dying man.

Nothing more solemn than that scene. The *Miserere*, which is always moving when it is heard inside the dome of a church or in any other situation, is tremendous, irresistible when it is sung at the side of a man who is on his deathbed.... It would be impossible to replace that psalm that is used by the Church with anything that could be conceived by even the most inspired of musical geniuses. The man who lay there in his deathbed, furthermore, was a martyr, a just man who had suffered all the agonies possible in this Vale of Tears, and who fought the battle of life nobly and courageously. His head was resting on his pillows with his eyes closed, but his lips were moving, following his brothers' singing with a barely perceptible murmuring. His pale face reflected the peaceful conscience inside! . . . Forgive me, dear readers, you who have arrived to this world in a time so different than mine, but I saw a halo of light encircling his large head! When the brotherhood sang the last verse of the psalm—"*Domine, ut scuto bonae, voluntatis meum*"[6]—I distinctively heard him respond: "*Intellige clamorem meum.*"[7] And immediately he opened his eyes, looked up to the sky, and said in a loud voice: "*Lux ultra!*"[8]

It was all over. . . . The soul, freed from the physical world, was flying up to the luminous region that the man had seen open up beyond this earthly existence! The Guardian approached the bed and mercifully closed the eyes of the dead man. The brothers filed silently out of the cell and into the lonely cloister.

Immediately afterward, the commander Zubiaga entered. He had a cigarette in his mouth and his hat was tilted sideways over one ear, in the manner of a ruffian.

"This won't take but a minute, Most Reverend Father," the villain said, tossing his cigarette aside and taking a large pair of shearing scissors out from the tail of his long coat.

"But your Excellency has arrived too late," the octogenarian Guardian answered impassively. "My brother, «who is free in Heaven», can no longer tell you what he did with the papers that he had hidden in the mattress of his bed. Look here, your Excellency," he concluded, raising the sheet and showing the commander the wide tear in the mattress.

"Devilish priests! You seem more like sorcerers. . . . Oh! We'll see each other again!" Zubiaga replied, threatening the old priest with his fist.

The Guardian looked straight at him, pointed to the door, and said in a firm voice:

"I will now pray at the side of a dead man, commander. If your Excellency does not leave, I will go tell Don José Manuel Goyeneche that the defenders of the altar have no respect for God, nor for his priests, nor for the most tremendous of all of his judges, the one who opens the doors of Heaven. Oh!" he continued, hearing the explosions and petards that announced that the procession had entered the main plaza, "there's the religion of the Spaniards!"

Zubiaga took a step forward in a threatening stance. The Guardian grabbed a cross that was on the table between two tall candles and jumped at the commander, forcing him to flee, terrified. I think that if he had not left quickly, as he did, the Father Escalera would have struck him in the head with the instrument of death of the Savior. How large and majestic the rebuilder of the Church of St. Augustine was at that moment!

I have not yet recounted to you, nor will I attempt to do so now, what I thought and felt while I was kneeling down in my corner of the cell, shedding many tears and trying to control my sobbing. It would be impossible. You already know the whole story of my humble childhood and can very easily understand my pain. . . . I do remember perfectly well, however, that when the Spanish officer threatened the Guardian, I stood up and jumped to intervene.

I planned to dive at the feet of the attacker to make him tumble forward, and I would not have stopped until I had stomped on his head, either.

But he fled, as you know, so I ran to kiss the dead man's hand, which was hanging off one side of the bed. I stayed there a long time, mechanically repeating the prayers of the venerable old man, who had kneeled down beside me, by the head of the bed.

"Listen, my son," he said to me at last, tapping me on the shoulder.

I turned to look at him, bewildered. He was already standing and was holding a luxuriously bound missal in his hand, which contained golden chants.

"Don't waste a single moment," he went on. "Brother Justo wanted you to have it. . . . Hide it carefully. . . . Go on!"

I took the missal mechanically, wrapped it up in a handkerchief that the Father gave me, kissed the dead man's hands one last time, and left.

The procession had ended. Naturally, very few people must have participated in it. I later learned that the Count of Huaqui was at the front and that he was followed by his military staff, his advisors Cañete and Berriozábal, and some ten or twelve notable members of the community—"very loyal subjects of the King" motivated by fright. The immense popular masses that usually flooded the streets and the plaza were represented by just three or four hundred wretches from the lowest and most despicable elements of the popular rabble. The Count had taken the cross, as it was his place to do. His countenance was humble and penitent . . . he prayed in a loud voice, kneeling before all the altars! There were *dragons* and *giants, lechehuairos*[9] and *tactaquis*.[10] It had not been possible to gather the *faillires*[11] together, which are the only decent and handsome group of dancers. Instead, the only dancers present were children. Luxuriously dressed like the thirteen gentlemen from Seville,[12] they sang and danced round a pole, winding ribbons of every color around it, hanging them from its very top. This pole was held by the tallest devotee, someone bulky and robust who had been especially selected for this role. When I went out to the main plaza, the three troops that I have mentioned were still entertaining a group of curious onlookers. The devils in these troops—all three of them had these devils, with horned masks, harlequin suits, and long tails—were making grotesque contortions and obscene gestures that were received with boisterous cheers and laughter. . . .

I continued on my way. But I soon stopped at the sight of an incredible scene, which seemed inconceivable at that point, even in spite of all the horrors that Goyeneche's troops had already committed. A group of soldiers was bringing a priest from the Church of the Recollect along the street with the general stores. It was a barefooted Franciscan from the order that wore gray cassocks made from plain, coarse woolen cloth. They were dragging him along at times and pushing him brusquely with the butts of their rifles at others. The priest was not resisting in any way whatsoever. It was clear that the men leading him down the street were trying to torment him. I have never seen nor heard more abuse, or more grotesque curses, directed at any other man. I also saw the deaf-mute Paulito walking some ten steps behind the group. His clothes were torn, and he was covered in blood. His guttural screams were frightening, and he kept following the priest, regardless of what cruel actions the soldiers took as they tried to get him to flee. . . .

"Aha! The Governor. . . . Death to the Governor!" I heard the *Maleso* yell. He was completely drunk, and had come forward with others of his kind.

"Death to the Governor! Long live the King!" his noble companions replied.

Everyone in the mob, including the dancers, crowded forward to the street corner. The devils from the dance troops continued doing their most grotesque contortions, their most vulgar gestures, and now prepared to direct their jeers at the victim.

The man in the cassock was, in effect, the Governor Antezana. He had taken sanctuary the day before in the monastery of the Recollect, which is located outside the city, on the other side of the Rocha River. There are no traces of it left there today, incidentally, other than the church and the hamlet, which has kept the name of the Recollect. I do not know—I was never able to discover—who turned Antezana in to Goyeneche. In any case, the latter had sent one of his closest and most devoted officers, with a group of his beloved and very loyal grenadiers from Cuzco, to seize him. The monastery having been searched with the utmost orderliness, probing into absolutely every nook and cranny, every dresser drawer, and even in the very place where the Holy Sacrament is kept, it turned out that "The main leader of the rebels" could not be found anywhere. His pursuers were just about to give up their undertaking, when the unknown Judas went to kiss the hand of one of the priests sitting at the chorus at the time and greeted by name the man he had sold out—either out of fear or for money, a fact that I have also been unable to discover.*

What a *Via Crucis*[14] awaited the first citizen of Cochabamba, the great patriot of the homeland, from the place where the mob recognized him to the seat of government, where his inexorable victor was to welcome him! It was more or less three hundred steps. But in the process of taking them, the victim suffered innu-

---

*The patriot Don José Miguel Córdova y Rivero, who was known as the *Inglés*,[13] was hiding in a rancho next to the monastery, and was miraculously saved there. It was from him, as well as from other just as reliable sources, that I obtained these details regarding the capture of Antezana.

merable blows and heard a continuous, clamorous death toll coming from mouths that he himself must have fed out of his generous hand many times, or from mouths that he had taught, by example, how to joyfully greet the name of the homeland! Oh! I saw Goyeneche's ferocious soldiers being encouraged to torture Antezana by the shouts of human beings who had been born in my beautiful land of Cochabamba, in the same place where the brave and rough soldiers of Aroma, and where Arze's active and untamable guerrillas, and where the heroic women who died next to their tin cannons on the crown of San Sebastián were also born! Mad with pain, I ran away to hide somewhere, cursing my compatriots. However, I later understood that throughout history, in every place of the world, there have been incredible aberrations such as this one, born from ignorance and misery, from fear, from selfishness, in which men are transformed into animals more repugnant than foul and poisonous reptiles!

But it was not just the popular mob that fell so low that day. Goyeneche was surrounded in his dining room by the "very loyal subjects," those ten or twelve *criollo* gentlemen who had accompanied him in the procession. It was these men, more deplorable even than the popular mob, who fed the victim the bitterest dregs of the cup from which he was forced to drink. Eyewitnesses have told me that when the Count of Huaqui stood up from his chair, smiling, to get closer and be able to better appreciate the patriot's shame and humiliation, the Governor's old friends, some of whom had praised him when he was in power, shouted as loudly as they could, each one trying to have his voice heard above the others', to better assure the survival of their own heads.

"Death to the Governor! As your Lordship knows, it was his obstinacy that led us to the brink of doom!"

I can believe this, my dear readers, because I saw the same thing happen in the case of the popular mob with my own eyes. As long as history is recorded, victims shall always be heard to wail the loudest when they remember this, their cruelest martyrdom. Besides, I have seen so many things in this world. . . !

Goyeneche was smiling, as I have said, and his inherent

wickedness induced him to mock the man whom he had unpardonably condemned to death.

"Oh, Don Mariano! I was not expecting this visit from you," he said to him. "Although it is certainly true that your Excellency does not appear to pay it so very willingly. Or could I be wrong in this? Could your Excellency be coming here to repent your mistakes and to ask me to forgive you in the name of the King, whose paternal kindness is endless? Do you think we might be able to understand each other?"

Antezana looked at him, first astonished, but then with unshakable calmness.

"I am a patriot. . . . I will not allow my name to be defamed like Rivero's," he answered. "Let's go, officer," he said to the one in charge of the soldiers, pointing to the door. "I have an appointment to appear before God very soon."

Goyeneche screamed out in anger, and he pushed the great patriot so hard that, as I have been told, he knocked him down to the floor.

"It will be done when the time is right. . . . He can confess, if he wants," he then said right away to the officer.

But that is not all. Listen to the following detail of the Count of Huaqui's clemency, which is absolutely historically accurate. The group of soldiers had already reached the corner below the wide balconies of that house, when the Count went out to the balcony, called out to get the officer's attention, and said in a loud voice so that everyone could hear him, especially Antezana:

"Tell them not to shoot at his head. . . . I need it, so that I can put it on a pike and have it displayed in the center of the plaza."

Antezana wrote a letter to his wife during the final moments of his life, before confessing and being executed by the firing squad: "After suffering insults and the greatest inconsequences from a people whom I have served honorably, the only thing left for me is to await my death. . . . May God help me, and bring you peace and harmony. . . ." I once held that document, which has now already been copied into other books, in my hands. It was a small, thick, resistant piece of paper, of the kind known back then as "parchment paper." It was written in well-formed, Spanish handwriting, with many circles. There was not a single extra line, nor one light ink blot. It must have been symmetrically folded when it was closed, and the hand that wrote and folded that letter could not have shaken even for an instant. The patriot had faced his death straight on and had only bowed his head before God!

Antezana was shot to death at three in the afternoon, on an adobe *poyo*, on the west end of the plaza—which was known as the sunny side because it received sun in the afternoon—underneath a small balcony painted green. Known as the "*lorera*,"[15] it was the only balcony in the plaza among all the one-story houses that surrounded it. By that time, Gandarillas, Ferrufino, Lozano, Azcui, Zapata, Padilla, and thirty others had already been killed in different parts of the city, most of them in the quarters of the company of soldiers. Some of these also died by firing squad, while others, who did not receive this, their sole blessing—which could be obtained from the executioners only by begging for it—were hung to death or killed by the garrote.

The bloody tribunal made up by Imas, Cañete, and Berriozábal continued to work without rest, delivering new victims to the Count. The latter had now heard an infinite number of accusations in the Cabildo. The list of patriots who were denounced as rebel leaders, or as audacious slanderers of the triumphant general, was already incredibly long. To have said at some point that he was a mestizo or a sambo, thus failing to recognize the absolute purity of his ancestry, was as serious an offense as having led a *republiqueta*. The members of the tribunal picked out the names that they believed, according to their reports, to be the main ones from the list, and posted them beside the notice of exoneration. Then they offered monetary rewards for turning in the rebels to them, dead or alive. I later had one of those lists in my hands and saw on it the name of «Alejo Nina», the poor locksmith, my uncle. On this day which I have been recounting to you, he was busy burying his loved ones so as to prevent them from being thrown into the common grave—which was no other than the old, open quarry on the west side of the historic hill—where all the victims from the hill and from the city lie today, confusedly mixed together.

This is how the Count of Huaqui celebrated the holy day of the *Corpus Christi* after his victory on "The Tall Mountain of San Sebastián." These were what Torrente calls: "The severe measures tempered by the realistic leader's future kindness, as well as by his promises to forget the dark ungratefulness forever."

XXIV

Brother Justo's Legacy

I was alone in my room, sitting at the table where I had set down the missal, lost in my sad thoughts, having exhausted all the tears that my eyes could shed, when my door opened part way, and I saw Carmencita stick her blond and disheveled head through the opening. She looked at me and put her finger on her lips, warning me to keep silent. Then she looked back carefully to make sure she had not been followed and finally came in. She closed and locked the door behind her and came running to sit on my knees, throwing her small, bare arms around my neck.

"Don't let anyone know that I came to see you," she said to me. "That yellow man, who is always so well dressed, with the beautiful laces on his shirt frill and his cuffs . . . who speaks to everyone with his lips like this, like Doña Goya Cuzcurrita . . . he scares me. When I see him come into the house from the street, I run away. . . . It looks like he wants to kiss me! But I cover my face with my skirts, Juanito! His hands are so cold and clammy! His fingers feel like snakes. . . . I touched a dead snake once, and that's what it felt like. And you should hear the things he says to my mother! 'My good lady *Marquesa*, the nobility of one's blood is expressed in one's sentiments. . . . Your Ladyship, my generous friend, is truly a pure Spaniard. Let the poor, miserable soldiers take what they can. . . . Although it's certainly true that they committed a serious sacrilege when they destroyed the images of the saints in the chapel.

Oh! His Lordship will have the infidels executed for that! And the poor Imas is crazy about the silver service. He aims to have it at all costs. But no. It's a family legacy. Couldn't we satisfy him with the two beautiful candelabra instead? Bah! What importance does silver have for you, your Excellency, my noble lady *Marquesa*, who have hundreds of pounds of it?' Oh! That Cañete is so ugly, so mean, so foul!"

I listened to her distractedly, but her voice, her amusing gestures, and her gorgeous blue eyes produced an indescribable pity in my soul.

"Stop talking about Cañete and give me a kiss," I answered, leaning forward with my lips to her forehead.

She stuck her tongue out at me and pretended that she wanted to get out of my arms, but she gave me a kiss on the cheek and broke out into a loud laughter.

Then, right away, with the natural curiosity of children, she lifted up a corner of the missal, and exclaimed:

"How pretty! Where did you get it from? Is it for me?"

"It's a holy book," I answered.

"You're so silly!" she replied. She had already unwrapped it, and was examining it with her hands. "This is not a book, no sir! It's a box, a very pretty box for me to put my toys in."

She was only too right. What I had believed to be a luxuriously bound Mass book was actually a box in the shape of a missal, which was very well painted and gilded in gold, and each one of its brass clasps ended in a lock, the key for which hung from a ribbon that looked like a book marker. I must also tell you that these kinds of boxes were very common back then. Perhaps you have seen one yourselves, stored somewhere with your grandfather's antiques. It is possible that the rarity of books at the time, and the fact that they were considered to be extravagant objects, led people at least to keep them in that manner, as they were not truly printed and bound. This did not, however, affect the indifference with which people like Doña Teresa allowed them to be destroyed or burnt them themselves supposedly for being heretical and irreverent.

I realized that the box probably contained very important papers, perhaps even the answer to the impenetrable mystery that had tormented me ever since I had first heard the word "father" and had asked that angelic woman—who, for her part, could not even refer to me as her son without letting out that painful cry that was torn from her insides—who mine was. I wanted to be alone again, to prevent at all costs that the papers be discovered by the girl. . . .

"It's true. There's no way of fooling you, is there?" I said. "It is a box for you. . . . Who else would it be for, my cajoling *gringa?*"

Right at that time, Feliciana began shouting out in the patio for the girl to come to her.

"Go on. . . . Don't make me have a fight with the lady," I added, "and if the yellow man tries to kiss you, tell him that he smells of blood, and you'll see how he doesn't try it again."

Carmencita left, resentful, making charming gestures and grimaces at me on her way out. I closed the door behind her, locked it as well as possible, and opened the box.

There were several manuscripts written by different hands on paper that was more or less yellowed depending on its age. I have them here right now, on the same table on which I write these memoirs. They were saved by the same girl who, at the time, I kept from seeing them. I shall relate to you the manner in which she did so at the appropriate time and place. Oh! I have read them on my own, or have had Merceditas read them to me, so many times! They have taught me so much, my God!

The first one that I laid my eyes on was a complete translation of *The Social Contract*, in my teacher's handwriting, with many original notes at the foot and in the margins of the pages. Another contains a miscellaneous assortment of selected sections from the works of Montesquieu, of Raynal, and of the *Encyclopedia*; some of these are signed with the initials F.P.C, and others with the full name, "Francisco Pazos Canqui." The third contains the *Declaration of Independence* and the *Constitution* of the United States of America, carefully translated and transcribed by Aniceto Padilla. This same manuscript contains, immediately afterward, Mirabeau's challenge to the Crown, before the famous oath[1]; speeches by Vergniaud[2]; the declaration of the rights of man and of the citizen, and other fragments of the writings and speeches of

the delegates, signed by different names, such as: «B. Monteagu-do,[3] Michel, Alcérreca, Rivarola, Quiroga, Carrasco, Orihuela».[4]
... Oh! These manuscripts show the intense desires of the intelligent youth of Upper Perú, of those bright souls, of those burning hearts who were able to communicate their ideas, their patriotic aspirations, at the University of San Javier! The solemn teachers had them conjugate Latin verbs all day long; or at most they allowed them to read books with carefully edited contents. But at night, when the teacher on duty fell peacefully asleep, believing that "the boys were dreaming of the cane of a Doctor of Law, or of the prebend of a canon," the forbidden book was silently brought out from between the folds of the mattress, a circle formed around it and a candle, and "the boys" would dream about assemblies and battles! "But to do that they would have had to know French and English, which were both forbidden," you might say. In which case I would reply that all of them also learned the language of Voltaire, and some that of Franklin. No one knows how they did it—it was "the work of the Devil"—although it is suspected that they first learned to decipher some of those same books word by word, with the aid of Calepino's *Octolingüe*, which the teachers themselves placed unknowingly in their hands when the students asked for it in order to translate a canto from the *Aeneid*, or one of Ovid's *Tristia*, or Horace's *Odes*.

A manuscript with some burned and blackened edges, full of ink blots and round marks, which were undoubtedly tears, drew my attention above all the others at the time. I devoured this one with my eyes, reading every single word in it. It filled my soul with bitterness, and at times I moaned from the pain as if live embers were actually being placed on my heart.

As I have made you confidants of my entire dark life, in which I have suffered so much and later found so many sweet comforts, I will now transcribe a summary of this document in the following chapter. I will try to control the emotions that it so cruelly stirs up in me even to this day as well as I can.

XXV

A Criollo *Family in the Good Times of Our Majesty the King*

I

Pedro de Alcántara Altamira was born on a small farm on the shores of the Tirón, near Logroño. Although his parents were humble peasants, they were also "Old Christians," without a single drop of Jewish or Moorish blood in them. They taught him to pray, they told him stories about ghosts and what happens to criminals, and he saw the public whippings of the last sects of the famous witches and the burning of a Molinist heretic.[1] This was the sum total of his moral education. As a child, he watched over the grazing sheep; a little later, he took care of the oxen on the farm; and, as a lad, he was at times given a hoe to brandish and at others the handle of the plow.

He was plowing his parents' land one day, when a more worldly neighbor who was passing along the path stopped, and exclaimed:

"He's a man already. . . . And what a handsome boy! If I were him, I would go by any means possible straight to the Indies of our Majesty the King, may God protect him!"

So the young man thought about it, and he decided that it would be outrageous for him to live out his entire life and then die as a farm laborer and a commoner. So he said to himself:

"No, sir! I'm going!"

And he came straight over, in the manner that he had found to do so—as part of the entourage of a Judge—to Santa María de los Buenos Aires.

Thanks to a generous act on the part of his master, he received a quintal of indigo and a box of lentils to sell in the Provinces of Upper Perú. There, he saw the marvelous hill of Potosí with his own eyes. He lived near the base of the hill, but was forced to leave it behind, with its numerous jobs but scarce maravedís, because of some quarrel having to do with vicuñas and Basques. He finally arrived in the beautiful valleys of Cochabamba, where a future awaited him that was better even than the ones he had dreamt about.

As a "handsome boy," he asked who the wealthiest of the available *criollas* was in Oropesa, and he was told that it was Doña *Chabelita*[2] Zagardua. He saw her only once, in church, from a distance and when she was completely covered in her long mantilla. He did not know the color of her eyes, nor had he heard the sound of her voice, but he asked her parents for her hand in matrimony, and received it. This, which will surely surprise my readers today, was very simple for a Peninsular Spaniard to do in those times. There were many parents who said, «the husband, the wine, and the clothes, everything must be Spanish», and Doña Isabel's parents numbered among these. In addition, they had asked for a Zagardua nephew to be sent from Vizcaya so that he could be married to their daughter. However, despite the fact that they had received news of his departure two years before, the fiancé had not arrived. They believed that he had been shipwrecked at sea, or that he had been taken prisoner from the galleon by the heretics who were constantly fighting the King of Spain for being such a good Catholic.

II

Don Pedro—he had become «Don» the moment he stepped on the shores of the New World—could have had, in Doña Isabel, a sweet and loving companion, just like the exemplary ladies of my country are to their husbands to this day, but his Peninsular pride would not allow it. He wanted her to be his most solicitous and submissive slave, without the right to make the smallest of comments to him, unworthy of his slightest confidence.

He lived idly, surrounded by wealth. He was almost always resting at the closest and most beautiful of his wife's estates, and with a respectable supply, which was constantly renewed, of the best cigarettes that could be rolled and the most exquisite chocolate made explicitly for him, and in his presence, by the humble and resigned Doña Isabel.

She had four children, whom I shall name in the order in which they were born: Pedro de Alcántara, Enrique, Teresa, and Carlos.

They were pampered by their good mother. They worshipped, foremost after God, the author of their existence, but always from a distance, without ever disturbing him with their cries, or their screams, or their pranks, and they frequently interacted with the servants. It was only on Sundays and on celebrated holy days that they were bathed and dressed formally to go before the "Great Gentleman" to kiss his hands. At this time, the latter would smile and, it is said, sometimes caress them by patting them on the cheek. If news of a more serious prank reached his ears, perchance, the most he would do is shrug his shoulders and say:

"They're *criollos*. . . . What can you expect from them?"

He was thoroughly convinced of the physical, moral, and intellectual inferiority of his children. He believed them to be irremediably condemned to being weak, sickly, and idiotic due to the misfortune of having been born so far from Logroño, and in another world. Do not be surprised, my dear readers. This is what the majority of our Spanish grandfathers felt and thought, just like Don Pedro. Each one of the characters in this, the story of my life, is nothing more than one of the different types of men who lived during my time.

III

But even with everything that Don Pedro had, having gained it just by being a Spaniard in the New World, he was not satisfied. He was not of noble birth! He was given the «Don» here by custom, for it was lavished on everyone. He heard his servants use it commonly with each other, and even his Negro slaves and his mulattos would use it, calling each other «Don» Clemente, «Doña» Feliciana! He would never be able to legitimately place an "of" in front of his surname! And it would have sounded so good, too! «Of Altamira»!!!

But luckily, a neighbor of his, a man with a title, raised some argument about the boundaries of their estates, and even this slight cloud was soon cleared from his skies.

This is how it happened.

The expert who Don Pedro named to assess the situation was a young Baccalaureate whose name was renowned throughout Oropesa. The reason for this was the noteworthy fact that his studies at the University of San Javier de Chuquisaca had been so wondrous that it was no longer possible for him to speak in anything other than in Latin. This was the case even when he said good morning to his servants or asked them for warm water with which to shave. It was said that his ingenuity was such that he had proposed to his fiancée, Doña *Goyita*, the wealthy heir of the *Cuzcurritas*, in Latin verses that no one understood—and that only his confessor suspected what they contained because of the few sacramental words included in the verses.

Having concluded the inspection of the area in dispute, drinking his cup of chocolate with Don Pedro in a passageway of the estate that faced a vast orchard, his learned Honor said more or less the following to him:

"My noble friend, if I lived here, I would say, like Flaccus[3]: *Cur velle permutem Sabina?*"[4]

Don Pedro smiled to let him know that he understood.

"And by the way," his companion continued, "has your Excellency not thought about founding a primogeniture,[5] as well?"

"Huh?" Don Pedro asked, jumping to his feet as if he had been shot out of a spring and letting the cup of chocolate fall to the floor. "Yes, certainly. . . . I have been thinking about it, as a matter of fact," he added. But, in actuality, this bright idea, which was to clear his skies, had only then entered his mind.

Two years later, the great Altamira primogeniture had been

founded. The money—was there anything that a wealthy Spaniard could not get from the Metropolis?—the money revealed that an ancestor of Don Pedro's had accompanied the Cid Campeador himself in his undertakings against the Moors. Don Pedro overcame every difficulty along the way with as many peremptory claims as necessary. The primogeniture was to be legal, conforming to the Laws of Toro; the line of succession was established like that of the Crown of the kingdom; women would have a right to it only in the absence of a male primogeniture.

From that point on the future of the children of the founder of the primogeniture became fixedly determined by him as if he were Fate himself. The oldest, Pedro de Alcántara, would inherit all the wealth and belongings and be encharged with the glorious duty of passing on the noble family name to the end of posterity. Enrique would serve our Majesty the King in the armed forces. Teresa would marry whomever would take her because of her good qualities, or would be bequeathed as a descalced nun in the Carmelite Order—which was the «aristocratic» convent of Oropesa, since the Clarist convent for the Franciscan nuns was for people who were not quite of «their» class. And Carlos, the youngest, was perfectly free to choose from whichever one of the six different monasteries in the city that best suited him. All of this would be done without Doña Isabel having the least say in the matter, because—for Heaven's sake!—what do women know about these things or about what is best for their children? In any case, the poor lady, who had languished under an unknown illness ever since the birth of her last child, died shortly thereafter. She had heroically borne her cross like a saint, without ever uttering the slightest moan or sigh. At first, her children mourned over her inconsolably. But time, which slowly sees new grass grow over the grave, also extends the veil of forgetfulness over the memories of those who survive. But she was also mourned by someone who could have made her much happier, although he too was a Peninsular Spaniard. I am referring to the nephew Zagardua, who was believed to have been lost in the depths of the ocean or at the hands of the heretics. This man, whose name was Don Anselmo, had arrived exactly on the day that his fiancée's wedding was being celebrated. Having learned to love her as his parents had wished him to, before he even knew her, he continued to love her hopelessly after he did know her. Don Pedro . . . well, it is said that he did not drink his chocolate at the usual hour the day that his wife died, but that this did not happen again the next day.

IV

God arranged matters differently than Don Pedro had planned them. The oldest son, who was born sickly and languished like his mother, was to die without fulfilling his glorious mission. Enrique did not wish to dedicate himself to the service of the armed forces. He wished to learn, and he devoured every book that he could get his hands on. The first serious book that he read was *The Life and Events of the Admiral Don Cristóbal Colón,*[6] by the Admiral's son, Don Fernando Colón, and his desire was to attend the university. After much begging and crying, he finally obtained permission to study in Chuquisaca. Teresa could not find a fiancé who was interested in her good qualities, since she had none, and she felt no inclination to become a bride to Jesus Christ. Carlos had artistic interests and a lively imagination. He learned music very easily, painted, and sculpted, all without teachers, and sought with difficulty to obtain models of scarce merit for his artistic endeavors.

In addition to these difficulties, which existed because of the physical constitution and the personal character of Don Pedro's children, there was yet another, which was indeed an insurmountable one. It was a sentiment that rises above everything else, and which only very strange souls, such as Don Pedro, for example, fail to comprehend.

The saintly martyr Doña Isabel had given sanctuary to an orphan girl and raised her as if she were almost one of her own. The girl turned out to be a wonder of goodness and beauty, which, according to the noble Altamira, was an admirable and incredible phenomenon because the girl had the blood of Calatayud in her veins, and because she was the daughter of his majordomo! All who laid eyes on her fell instantly in love with her, including women, who are always just a little bit jealous of other women. But

Teresa, whose soul was more impassioned with envy than any other woman, hated her to an extent beyond what can be described with words. She would look, pale and biting her thin lips, as people affectionately greeted that despicable «foundling waif» before they greeted her. And those who saw them for the first time would confuse the one with the other. They thought that the beautiful young woman was Altamira's daughter and that the "ungraceful one" was the little orphan girl. Just imagine how much Don Pedro's daughter—whose pride was as large as her father's—anguished every time this occurred!

Carlos was madly in love with the orphaned girl. The same was the case with Enrique, as soon as he returned from completing his studies at the university. And Teresa made sure that her brothers learned of the fact that they were rivals! Let me recount here just two incidents to serve as examples.

One day the four youths took cover from a storm in the hollow of the ceibo tree that I have referred to earlier in these pages; they used to call it "the Patriarch." Teresa and Rosa—there I go, writing her beloved name down at last—had sat down on the ground to rest. But they suddenly screamed out in fright and got right back up, trembling and looking very pale. A black snake was slivering between two rocks. Enrique jumped on it immediately. He grabbed it and killed it in his hands, but not before being painfully bitten by the reptile. Teresa went up to him and whispered in his ear:

"You fool, look at them!"

Rosa had grabbed on round Carlos' neck, and he was holding her in his arms.

On another day, a day in which Don Pedro was celebrating his birthday with his friends round the table, Teresa went to where Carlos was sitting and said to him:

"Come . . . follow me."

And she led him by the hand to the passageway that faced the orchard, pointing out to him with her hand a myrtle bank surrounded by a beautiful walnut tree. Rosa and Enrique were sitting on the bank, and the latter was picking at a wildflower that he was holding in his fingers.

"She loves me, she loves me not," Teresa whispered in Carlos' ear, and immediately ran away, laughing like a madwoman.

Shortly thereafter, the two brothers took up the issue with each other:

"She loves me," Carlos said.

"I am hopelessly in love with her," the other answered.

And this is why Don Pedro's son, the one who was supposed to serve the king in the armed forces, ended up instead being the one who chose from one of the six monasteries available in the city. And he chose the monastery of St. Augustine specifically so that he could help the Guardian Escalera in rebuilding his church, which he managed to do, and in reforming his Brothers, which turned out to be impossible to accomplish. Don Pedro did not consent to the change of which son would be the priest until he saw, with his own eyes, Carlos on the verge of taking his own life rather than take the cowled habit of the monk.

V

When the inexorable father finally learned of his son Carlos' love for Calatayud's granddaughter, his anger and indignation brought him close to making him lose his better judgment. This was not possible! His son could not be in love with that woman, who had Indian blood in her! Much less could he make her his wife! That girl must be a witch! And why not? Of course there would be more sorcerers and witches in that land than in Logroño! In vain did his son drag himself at his feet, flooding them with tears. What was the meaning of those mad displays, of those exaggerated extremes? The issue would be resolved by putting Rosa in the community house for lay sisters at St. Albert, until she could be made a nun at St. Clare.

Poor Rosa resignedly accepted her fate. She loved Carlos, but she understood that it would never be possible for them to be united together and that she had no choice in the world other than to be buried alive in a convent. But the impetuous Carlos did not think like that. He defied everything—his father's anger and even Rosa's indignation—and stole her away from her temporary lockup.

After this, Don Pedro did lose his better judgment and did not rest until he managed to separate the two lovers forever.

He complained to the authorities—Don Francisco de Viedma was unfortunately not in the city at the time, and his post was being executed by a deputy—he complained, that is, of "the evil means and spells with which the witch was corrupting the soul of his son." He was able to get the assistance of the bloodhounds of the police without much difficulty. Once their fervor was incited and their appetite whetted by large sums of money, it was only a mater of a few days before they located the lovers and brought them to the presence of Don Pedro. The latter immediately arranged to send Carlos to Buenos Aires, with a letter to the Judge, his old employer, asking him to "marry the youth there with the daughter of good parents, regardless of who it was." And as far as Rosa was concerned, he wanted to make her a nun that same day.

Don Carlos was led away by force, his hands tied for the first day of traveling. But that night he escaped. The following day they found him on a hill, sitting on a rock. He did not make any move to try to flee his pursuers when they came within view. He was staring at the rising sun without blinking, speaking to the cacti that grew between the steep, rugged rocks, and laughing out loud. . . . He had gone mad!

Neither was it possible to lock Rosa up in the convent. The heart of a new being was beating inside her. . . . So then—oh, you will not believe me, and how I wish that it were not true, my God!—then Don Pedro decided that she would die of shame, in misery. He had Teresa cut the witch's hair with her own hands and her servants throw her out on the street in the middle of the day looking like that—which, back in those days, was the mark of lost woman. Teresa took pleasure in cutting off those beautiful braids that she had envied, just as she had envied every one of the witch's charming features! And the servants dragged her to the front door and pushed her hard out into the street, screaming that she deserved to be stoned to death!

Enrique, that is, Brother Justo, extended a sanctuary for her in the small house of the locksmith Alejo and protected her as if she were his sister.

VI

On the same day that they brought the now mad Don Carlos back to him, Don Pedro lost his first-born son, the one who bore his name, the primogeniture.

Six months later, he agreed to having Doña Teresa married to Don Fernando Márquez, according to the arrangement that I already recounted near the beginning of my memoirs.

A year later, when God called him to appear before Him, Don Pedro received all the comforts that the Church could offer, and he blessed his grandson, who would be «Don Pedro de Alcántara 'Marquis' of Altamira».

He stated in his will that his daughter and her husband would receive, as Don Carlos' caretakers, all of his wealth and belongings, and that after the death of Don Carlos, the primogeniture would belong to his daughter. Don Fernando, as I have said earlier, had a kind heart. He wanted to take care of the poor madman personally, in his own house, and he also wanted to help Rosa and her son. But his wife, who was perpetually tormented by flatulence and migraines, the imaginary ailments with which she masked her fierce selfishness, would not allow anyone to speak to her about "things that were so sad that they were best forgotten." Since the poor man trembled before the stare of his wife's hard eyes, and as just one of her shouts would frighten him to death, he let her arrange the manner as she pleased, in the hope of keeping her calm and peaceful. Don Carlos was consequently handed over to the care of his uncle Don Anselmo Zagardua and his wife Doña Genoveva, giving them the use of one of the estates, which turned out to be the smallest and the one in the greatest state of disrepair. As far as Rosa and her son are concerned, you already know the extent of the noble lady *Marquesa's* generosity toward them.

This story of "A *Criollo* Family in the Good Times of our Majesty the King" was written in the manuscript from where I have summarized it. It was not organized in any particular order. At times it was written as a series of diary entries and at others in unconnected and lose fragments. There are pages that might be used by a pen that was more practiced and skillful than mine to greater advantage by developing them into a novel. But I am content with what I have said here, which is more than enough for the comprehension of the pedestrian telling of the simple story of my life. However, because I would like to give you a better idea of the thoughts and the tremendous sufferings of the main character that has appeared in these memoirs so far, I will now copy down two fragments as they appear in the manuscript.

"Father Arredondo, who keeps gaining weight as if he were a hog, said to me yesterday as I passed the door of his church:

"'It is surprising, really, how pious Christian women can be when they behave just as we would like them to, when they follow the best of our teachings.'

"And he told me a horrendous story, an act that even the wildest of beasts would never carry out, if wild beasts could speak and compromise the lives of their young by speaking, that is. A mother in Mexico denounced her son to the Inquisition as a philosophizing heretic after seeing him reading *The Social Contract* and *Candide*! The poor wretch was imprisoned, and although he has since miraculously been able to escape, he is now being pursued in the forests that he fled to as if he were a fierce animal, more dangerous than a *mixtli*.

"What would become of me if a wandering hand were to remove the mattresses from my cell? A priest who reads Rousseau and makes comments about it! . . . Would I be able to explain to them that I can see truths that derive from Christianity in this new philosophy, even when the philosophers argue against Christianity? Would they understand that it is possible for the religion of Christ to join the revolution and that this could create a harmonious brotherhood? Will it ever be possible to undo the monstrous consortium between the altar and the Crown?

"No, dear God! I would undoubtedly be condemned as a heretic!

"But what does it matter? Would it not be a sweeter martyrdom for me to be burnt to death at the hands of the Inquisition, over their slow fires, than to continue living with this fire that is constantly within me, that burns as deep as the marrow of my bones?"

"In vain have I tried to exercise my body to the point of fatigue with the hope of then being able to sleep and forget, if even for the briefest of moments.

"I ran round like a madman through the beautiful countryside where I spent so much of my childhood. Then I saw a hoe in a partially plowed field. I grabbed it and worked arduously, all day long, harder even than the poor Indian who depends for his sustenance and that of his children from it has ever been able to.

"I came back to the monastery at night. I have walked through the silent cloisters without rest until the light of dawn cast my shadow on the white walls and the bell called my brothers in for prayers.

"I came to my cell to pray by myself . . . but I was unable to! I believe I have doubted the fairness of your justice, oh eternal God!

"But is there anyone who has suffered as I have in this Vale of Tears? Is there any trial that is harder than the one with which I am condemned to live? . . .

"Oh! I have seen «her» publicly humiliated as if she were a vile whore! I wonder what people said when they saw the poor priest pick up the lost woman in his arms and carry her to the locksmith's small and humble house? What did they think at that point, dear God? . . .

"Beyond the northern Cordillera, on which I have tread a thousand times, there are immense deserts. One day I stopped there to contemplate an ocean of white clouds that stretched further than my anxious eyes could see. The veil was suddenly ripped off by the wind; it dissipated under the rays of a splendid sun that was rising in the skies; the largest and most impenetrable forests in the entire world were revealed before my eyes, with vast savannas and plentiful rivers. . . . Could we not flee there and live with the savage tribes? Or even with the wild animals, which would not be as pitiless as men are here?

"And much further north, very far away, at the very north of the continent, there are people who have been educated by the evangelical doctrines of Jesus to live in liberty, who have fought gloriously for their rights and privileges, where men are known as citizens. . . . I would be a proud republican there. I would be able to raise my head full of self-respect and gain that of everyone else! I am still young. . . . Oh, how my blood races through my veins! I feel so much strength in my arms! How my heart pounds at the mere thought of leaving this dungeon! I would wear myself out in the forests. I would make my home in a clearing that I would make with my own hands, with an ax. I would. . . . Nonsense! She would never consent to it! I have forgotten my oaths! The corpse of the secular man who is shrouded in a monk's cowled habit was stirred, incited by a sudden blaze from Hell, as if he could actually come back to life!"

XXVI

Where It Will be Seen That a Murmuring Lay Sister Can Have an Excellent Heart and Be Becoming

It took me many hours on end to read through the entire story that I have chosen to only recount very briefly in the previous chapter. The servants knocked on my door several times and yelled for me throughout the house, but I could not separate my eyes from those pages that held the answer to the mystery of my life for even an instant. Just once, when I was running out of daylight, did I myself open the door, and went to light a small candle stub in the kitchen. I found poor Paula there, and she offered me something to eat. I told her that I was not hungry, that I did not feel like eating, that I wanted to die, that I wanted to be left alone . . . and I do not know how many other things like this, all of which she listened to with her small mouth wide open in amazement.

"Jesus! What's wrong with you? You're as pale as a corpse, and your eyes are bulging out of their sockets," she said to me at once, but I did not give her an answer.

When I had finished reading it all the way through, I hid the manuscript against my chest, carefully buttoning my jacket over it.

Then I placed the others in the box, put the box in the coffer, and said to myself:

"I cannot stay a single moment longer under this roof. I know where I must go, and I must go there this very night."

The front door of the house would be bolted with lock and key, and everyone was already asleep in the house. I climbed up and out the window, and a moment later I found myself on the other side, in the neighboring house. The manner in which I left reminded me, through a natural association of thoughts, of my friend Luis.

"He's dead. . . . I will never see him again. Everyone I love dies!" I thought sadly.

I was in a long, thin, dark passageway. I felt my way along until I entered a silent patio, similar to the one in Doña Teresa's house. I saw a light coming from a wide open window in one of the rooms, and I went up to it to see if there was someone inside keeping vigil who might impede my exit out to the street through the front door of that house, which I knew quite well was only closed with a latch and a crossbar. But as soon as I looked inside the room, I let out a scream of surprise and happiness. Yes, my good readers, of happiness, despite everything I have just been telling you.

In a small bedstead similar to mine, on a soft and clean bed, with sheets and covers that were whiter than snow, lying on his back, with his blond hair spread out on the laced pillowcase, his face lit up and his eyes glassy from a high fever, was my poor friend Luis, in person! His lips were moving. Random, unconnected words reached my ears.

"Fire! Grandmother! Here I am!" he was saying in his feverish state.

At the head of the bed where the sick boy was lying, the lay sister Doña Martina was sitting in an armchair, dressed in the habit of the third order of St. Francis. She was completely asleep, with her head slumped forward on her chest. She held her golden denarius in one hand, and a white, cotton handkerchief in the other. Her beloved chihuahua, round and gleaming due to its plumpness, was also sleeping, sprawled out on its stomach at her feet with its snout resting on its front paws. But the scream that I had unintentionally let out made it lift its head. After looking round in every direction, it began to bark in that annoying manner that only those little dogs of its race can. How I wanted to strangle it at that point! I have heard that Bazán—the famous thief from my country who became an upright man and died honorably after being included in one of the exonerations decreed by General Belzu[1]—used to give the following advice to anyone who wanted to avoid being robbed: "Sleep with a light burning and raise a chihuahua." The light is to make people think that there is always someone keeping vigil, as was my case that night. And just one chihuahua, with its piercing barks, can stir up an entire neighborhood more effectively than a pack of hounds.

The lay sister started, waking up with a fright. She stood up and, because of her fear, saw an entire gang of criminals at the window instead of one harmless boy. This was very much to my advantage, because she did not have the strength nor the courage to yell for help, as I had feared.

"It's me . . . Juanito, Doña Teresa's «foundling waif». Do not be frightened, your Excellency, my lady Doña Martina," I said to her, taking the most prudent action, which was to make myself known.

"Oh, dear Jesus! What a fright you've given me, you evil vagabond!" she answered, quieting her chihuahua and running to open the door for me. "What's the matter? What's wrong with the lady *Marquesa*? Has she gotten worse from her ailments? Why are you here?" she asked me at once.

"There's nothing wrong at the house, Doña Martina. . . . I have come through the window in the passageway, just to see my friend," I answered.

"Oh, my son!" she replied, moved. "This wicked boy has brought me so much anguish! May God have mercy on him and make him a saint! I love him as if I were his mother, in spite of all his pranks and of all the bad things that he says to everyone about me without any reason to. I had been mourning and crying inconsolably for him, but this morning two charitable individuals brought him here, wrapped up in a blanket. The locksmith Alejo, who had found him still breathing among some dead that he had gone to bury, had him sent to me. I have done everything that I could for him since then, until the Reverend Aragonese Father came to treat him. He says that his wound is very serious . . . that it'll be a miracle if he lives. I have a holy candle burning over there for Our Lady of Mercy, and I have been praying for him without rest, even though I am an unworthy sinner. The *Gringo* is dead. . . . He doesn't have a father any more! I hope he was a Christian, like he said he was, so that he will be welcomed into the holy glory of our God! Poor boy!"

As she was saying this, the good, the excellent lady—I have never referred to her again in any way but this—was frequently drying her eyes with the handkerchief. I was also moved, as she was. I wanted to fall on my friend, to embrace him in my arms. But she stopped me, pulling me back by the collar of my jacket. She pushed me hard to one side, and exclaimed with an anger that was not restrained by her usual devout prudishness:

"You're going to kill him, you evil child! The Aragonese Father says that he shouldn't talk or move. . . . Get out of here!"

"I will do everything that your Excellency wishes me to, my lady," I answered. "But I am also a poor orphan, and I would like to ask you a favor."

"What do you want now?"

"To kiss your Excellency's hands. . . . I also have said a thousand things which I regret in my heart."

She looked at me, touched. Then she took my head in both of her hands and kissed me on the forehead, which did me a lot of good at the time.

Doña Martina was still a young woman, under thirty years of age, and quite becoming—like the majority of the *criollo* women in my country, of which Doña Teresa was one of the rare exceptions. The awful education of the time had made her a murmurer and a zealot, but she had a heart of gold. What can you expect? What could a girl become who was only taught to say the rosary, who was told stories about ghosts, who they refused to teach how to write, who they forced to confess with Father Arredondo, and in whom they implanted the belief that every man who did not wear the a cowled habit was an agent of the Devil? Some time later, a *Porteño* officer from Rondeau's army[2] married her. He cured her of her defects and never regretted having her as his companion.

After kissing her hands like I wanted to, I left and closed the door carefully behind me. The exit that would lead me out to the street only had—as I have said before—a latch and a crossbar. It took me only a minute to lift the first and slide the second, without making any noise. I was finally free!

XXVII

How I Came and Went Wherever I Wanted to

A deadly silence reigned throughout city. Burning lights inter-
mittently illuminated the deserted streets and the hermetically sealed houses. That night, a phenomenon that is frequently seen
from the beautiful valleys of my beloved land was once again present. A thick, grayish cloud extends over the northern Cordillera,
while others, thinner and lighter ones, cloak the rest of the sky, creating a mother-of-pearl veil through which the stars of the first
magnitude can be seen. The large gray cloud silently discharges
flashes of lightning, luminous rays in arborescent shapes. These in
turn light up the smallest of objects with a light that—to eyes that
are not expecting it in the middle of the darkness—can seem
brighter than daylight. I have heard many explanations for the
phenomenon, but most are quite absurd. I think that it must simply be the effect caused by the violent storms that break out over
the immense forests on the other side of the Cordillera.

I was already along the side of the Church of the Matriz when I
heard a sentinel shout out in the middle of the night. Turning to
look in that direction, I saw, with the light provided by a flash of
lightning, a human head on the end of a pike sticking into the
ground near the fountain. The soldier was sitting on the border of
the circular fountain, his rifle resting between his legs. With an-

other flash of lightning, I was able to immediately distinguish that the head belonged to Governor Antezana. I also saw a strange shadow slivering on the ground like a snake toward the pike.

"Stop! Who's there?" the soldier shouted and jumped to his feet. He must have then cocked the rifle, because I heard both dry sounds that the weapon makes when it is cocked.

No one answered. A third flash of lightning, brighter than the previous ones, must have allowed the soldier to see the man who was about to pounce on the pike, which I could clearly see. The shot went off. A guttural scream, like that of a wounded wild animal, resounded in the silent night, and the strange man ran off, heading down the Calle de los Ricos. By the scream, I recognized Paulito. And it was him, sure enough. I later learned that on another night, darker and better suited for his goal, he returned and was able to get away with his master's head, and that it was then buried in the cemetery at St. Francis. Reliable people, who say that they saw it with their own eyes, also assured me that the day afterward, Paulito was found lying dead on the grave, like a loyal dog that could not go on living without its master.

I bolted off in the opposite direction like a rabbit, down the Street of Santo Domingo, and did not stop until it came to an end, near the banks of the Rocha River. And I did stop only because I saw another head displayed there; it was clearly that of the patriot Agustín Azcui. The same thing would have happened to me regardless of the route I had chosen to leave the city. On that day, Don José Manuel Goyeneche had more heads than he needed to put one on each of the roads that led in and out of the city. However, the one thing that he was never able to accomplish was precisely his objective: "To teach a lesson to that city of untamable rebels."

I feared there would be another sentinel posted there, like the one in the plaza, and that he might detain me or slow me down, at the very least by forcing me to take a roundabout way to avoid being seen by him. With this in mind, I climbed up an adobe wall that surrounded an orchard and jumped over to the other side. And I kept on doing this as necessary. Once I had made it to the shores of the river, I sat on the fine sand to catch my breath. I saw a pile of logs and willow tree branches nearby. I picked out a good club to take with me and continued on my way, heading toward Quillacollo. It was already late at night. The ominous sign of the Scorpius constellation, which the peasants had taught me about, referring to it with the common name of "the scorpion," was shining in the middle of the sky, in a wide clearing without clouds.

I heard the wonderful, pure, and silvery voice of a woman who was singing somewhere in the distance, in the middle of that deadly silence. It was a *huaino* that later became very popular in all the valleys of Cochabamba:

Soncoi ppatanña kuakainii juntta . . .

Faithfully translated into Spanish, it was also later sung in salons by leading ladies who would gather round a guitar, a harp, or a clavichord—musical instruments that were played better by them than the magnificent Collard pianos, of which only a few of their more civilized granddaughters know how to put to use; it being rare, besides, that any of these know how to make their voices trill in the Italian style.*

My chest filled so that it could burst
　　With a sad cry,
That did not pour from my eyes,
　　When I was crushed.
Crying would be a welcomed comfort,
　　But never, ever
Would I want you to think, when you see my sorrow,
　　That I am tamed.

This is the last lament I heard as I left my brave Oropesa behind—my city, which was defeated by Goyeneche in an uneven battle; coldly handed over by the barbarian to the brutal passions of

---

*Editor's Note: We ask our gracious lady readers to forgive the old soldier from the Independence Movement. It is quite natural that he prefer the ladies of his time, whom he must have admired when his honest and brave heart pounded more powerfully with the passionate blood of his youth.

his hordes, the "defenders of the Crown and the altar"; and drowned in the blood of its best native sons, whose sacrifice saved the provinces of the Río de la Plata, from where redeeming crusades later arrived from Chile and from Perú, as I will very shortly recount to you, if God allows me to continue writing my memoirs.

I walked at a good pace through the populated areas of Maicas and through the outskirts of Colcapirhua. Then, at once, I ran across the plain of Carachi, where not even the most humble rancho could be seen, for it was known as an area that highwaymen frequented. No one stopped me, and I did not see a single living being, nor any from the other world.

I tripped over many sleeping pigs in the narrow and winding streets of Quillacollo and had a very hard time fighting off the countless barking dogs that came out from all the patios and all the enclosures. They jumped over the walls, surrounded me aggressively, but did not dare come within range of my club.* The light of sunrise was already dawning when I reached the cross road that I would now follow to my destination. A young mestizo man, tall and strong, was coming toward me, panting from fatigue. He was armed with a special whip made from a thick tucuma club with a ball of lead attached to its end that could serve him as much to shoo away the dogs as to strike a fellow human being. But I was not at all frightened when I saw him. Instead, I had a strange premonition, and asked him in Quechua:

"Brother, how is the ill gentleman?"

"I'm on my way to get the *tata* priest," he answered, and hurried off.

My premonition had not been wrong. I have had this same thing happen to me many times, even without having prior information, as I had then. I believe that there is such a thing as the ability of divination, which is still not understood, but which is revealed in this manner to many people who have a certain anxious nature, like mine.

---

*I have been told that this town, which is conveniently located in the middle of the valleys of Cochabamba, is already as large as the town of Cliza. Also, that its name was later changed to the Villa de Orihuela, and that its Sunday markets are attended by almost as many people as those in Cliza.

The door leading into the patio of the Old House was wide open. The patio had a white, narrow path that led to the foot of the stairs, which was overgrown with grass, just as I had seen it from beyond the wall the time that I passed by with Ventura and heard the melody from the violin. I followed the path unhesitatingly, but then stopped, alarmed. I took a step back and raised my club. There was an enormous Newfoundland dog at the foot of the stairs, but it did not make even the slightest of movements. I then noticed that it was lying on its back and realized at once that it was dead, as I quickly confirmed. I jumped over it and climbed up the stairs, taking two steps at a time. Some of these were very much ravaged by time.

The stairs ended in a narrow balcony that had a door and two latticed windows that led into the house from there. The door was open and dark, but light could be seen through the cracks and fissures of the planks of the closed windows. I went through the door and into a short corridor or antechamber where I saw a large, half-opened vestibule door with a strong movable railing that was completely opened. My heart was beating so fast and so hard that I thought it was about to burst inside my chest. I gathered all my courage before looking carefully into the room.

It measured some ten varas in length by six in width. The whitewashed walls were covered with strange drawings, some of them done with charcoal, others with colored chalk. Among the drawings there were men with heads of animals, and animals with human heads; fantastic trees; flowers with wings; and birds hanging from branches as if they were flowers. In many areas, broad leaks that came down from the ceiling had washed away the white plaster and the drawings. All along the walls, at a level where they could be reached by a man of average height, boards were nailed up, serving as shelves. These held many clay, stucco, and stone figurines that were as strange and unpredictable as the drawings. I have one of them in front of me right now; carved out of white stone, it is the figure of a woman dressed in a sheer tunic who is reclining back on one of her arms, resting against the back of a sleeping lion. Several friends of mine, who consider themselves experts on the matter, claim that the man who sculpted that small figurine with a makeshift chisel, without anything to model it after other than a simple illustration, could have been an artist. But an artist in colonial America! Oh, no, that would have been quite impossible! It would be just as likely to expect a poor bird whose wings are clipped at birth to be able to fly!

Near the railing, in the corner to the right, there was a large and solid bedstead. Within, on a humble bed, a man was lying on his back, completely motionless; I did not know if it was a corpse or someone on the verge of death. Don Anselmo Zagardua was standing at the head of the bed, leaning forward on his walking stick, carefully examining the man's face. A *criolla* woman, who looked to be about fifty years of age, robust, well kept, and very kindly, sat on a small, wooden stool at the foot of the bed.

Across from the bedstead, in the corner to the left, there was a table with a laced cloth draped over it. On it, there were two candelabra with the burnt-up candles emitting the last of their light, and a crucifix between them.

I turned all of my attention toward the man on that humble bed, the man who was suffering, or who had perhaps already died. I knew that he was young, that he was barely thirty-five years of age, but he looked like an aged man of more than eighty. He had barely a few tangled tufts of hair left on his balding head, above his ears and neck, and these had already turned very white. His forehead was furrowed with deep wrinkles. The features of his face, those that could be seen above his long, thick beard, that is, were thin and fair. That man, whose mind was not well, had spent the last thirteen years of his life in that place! At first he had tremendous outbursts of rage; afterward, he sunk submissively into a dark and silent melancholy. He could not stand to look at any human being other than Don Anselmo and his wife, Doña Genoveva, whose rooms were in the lower level of the house. His dog, *Leal*,[1] was always at his side, and he spoke to him, addressing him as if he were a human friend, and interpreting the growls and barks with which the dog responded. He spent his time making the drawings and figurines I have just mentioned. A violin on a small table near the head of his bed was another friend of his, from which he knew how to extract wonderful comfort through rushing lines of harmony. A real Stradivarius from the Peninsula, it had been obtained by Doña Isabel, despite a thousand obstacles, for her favorite son, the youngest of the four, her Benjamin.

"What a night! . . . I thought it would never end. That dog's barking was the worst, but it has finally stopped. I'm so scared that I'm starting to imagine that I'm hearing strange noises everywhere. . . . Just now I thought I heard someone walking out in the corridor," Doña Genoveva said.

Her husband raised his head. He sighed and went to comfort her affectionately.

"My poor little old woman!" he said to her. "*Leal* won't torment us with his barking any more. Just a short while ago, when I went down to send Roque to get the good priest, since I didn't want to disagree with you, I found the animal dead at the foot of the stairs."

"It's a bad omen," the lady replied.

"Yes, I can believe it," the Basque man answered, "the birds of night have also cawed many times, as they flapped against the bars of the windows with their wings. I don't believe that Carlos will come back to us from this accident. At least not until the Archangel calls us all to the Valley of Josafat."

"Don't tell me . . . Jesus Christ! How horrible it would be if he were to die just when he seemed like he was starting to get his sanity back! Didn't I tell you yesterday that he spoke to me about poor Rosa? Didn't he tell you that he wished to see his brother?"

"That's what confirms my fears, Genoveva. There's no question about it! It seems that God returns their sanity to the miserable ones who have lost it right before He calls them to His side. I tell you again: my nephew Carlos is already dead, for sure. . . . But you should get some rest in any case, my little old woman. I'll stay here, keeping vigil over him, until you come back to take my place."

"That I won't do, my dear man! I am very healthy and feel quite well, while you are an ailing old man and quite, quite sick."

"Bah! What are two or three nights like this to an old soldier like me? How many nights did I spend out in the high plateaus and in the Cordilleras during the campaign against Catari and Bartolina?"[2]

"But when you did that you were a young lad and you had both your legs. Go on! Don't talk back to me like that, Don Anselmo! Off to bed you go, you doddering old man!"

"The lady Genoveva will be the one who will take her robust self to bed. I will not allow the lady to wear the trousers in this house."

"Be quiet! Your stubborn whimsical actions—I know very well that you're Basque!—your stubbornness, as I was saying, will end up in such a way that I will be forced to keep vigil over two men instead of one. I can no longer be held accountable for my actions, and. . . . May Our Lady of Mercy have pity on whatever happens to us all!"

When I heard these last words, I entered resolutely into the room. Don Anselmo and his wife screamed out in surprise.

"What do you want?" the former asked, raising his walking stick and taking a step toward me.

"I have come, sir," I answered, "I have come to keep vigil without rest at the bed of Don Carlos Altamira."

But I had arrived too late. . . . There was nothing there for me to do other than to mercifully close his fixed, glazed eyes. Perhaps the man, who had been one of the most tortured souls in this Vale of Tears, had raised them consciously in agony toward the sky.

I must end here. My life changed completely from that moment onward, as you shall see, if you remain interested in this simple story.

Notes

CHAPTER I

1. Refers to the Iberian Peninsula, and Spain specifically. (Trans.)

2. The *yaraví* is a sweet and melancholy indigenous song. The word comes from the Quechua verb *arawi*, meaning to compose poetry. (Jesús Lara, *La literatura de los Quechuas*. Cochabamba: Canelas, 1961)

3. A *mameluco* is one-piece pajama worn by children. (Trans.)

4. An *alferazo* is an institution maintained in the Andes in which leading members of the community alternate in organizing and being responsible for a religious celebration.

5. Born in Guayaquil, Ecuador, José Joaquín Olmedo (1780–1847) is considered a classic Latin American epic poet. He is especially known for his poems "Canto a Junín" and "Al General Flores." Although his style is considered neoclassical, these poems already reveal the first shades of Latin American Romanticism.

6. *Tocuyo* is a fairly coarse cotton cloth used mostly in the Andes. (Trans.)

7. The *Ollantay* is an Inca-Hispanic play, written in Quechua in Perú during the Colonial Period, of uncertain authorship. Although it is presumed that it was written in the eighteenth century by Father Antonio Valdéz, other scholars believe it is of indigenous origin.

CHAPTER II

1. Francisco de Viedma (1737–1809) was a Spaniard who first lent his services to the Spanish Crown in Patagonia and Río Negro, in what is now Argentina. He was later the Governor of Santa Cruz de la Sierra (in what is now Bolivia) and published a descriptive and statistical treatise of this province. When British troops invaded Buenos Aires (in 1806 and 1807), he tried to organize and send

troops in defense of the Viceroyalty from Cochabamba, the city in which he later died. Upon his death, he left his estate to the Orphanage of Cochabamba. Nataniel Aguirre appears to be referring to this orphanage and this historical fact in the details of the relationship between Viedma and Juanito and his mother.

2. *Chapetones* was the name given to Spanish soldiers recently arrived in the Americas. (Trans.)

3. The hero of the city of La Paz, Pedro Domingo Murillo (1757?– 1810) was one of the rebel leaders of the uprising that occurred in that city on July 16, 1809. He was later named Commander in Arms. When Goyeneche victoriously entered La Paz after the Battle of Chacaltaya, Murillo was taken prisoner and condemned to death by hanging for high treason.

4. After taking over city hall, the leaders of the uprising in La Paz, including Murillo, followed the wishes of the populace to hold a public forum—in other words, an open Cabildo. This body in turn dismissed all Spanish officials and established the Junta Tuitiva. This Junta was organized around a plan for government that contained ten articles delineating the basic tenets of the revolution, and decreeing the existence of this same "Junta that was to represent and protect the rights of the entire populace" ("Junta representativa y tuitiva de los derechos del pueblo"). The Junta ceased to exist on October 20 of the same year, when Goyeneche bloodily suppressed the rebellion.

5. Juan Antonio Figueroa was a Spanish priest who supported the cause of the Independence Movement.

6. The prolific Catholic Latin writer Tertulian (160–220 A.C.) argued against the Roman persecution of Christians in his apologetic writings.

7. *Sanguis martirum semen christianorum*: The blood of the martyrs is the seed of Christianity. In the context here, the phrase is meant to compare the cause of Christianity, which was strengthened by the Roman persecution, with the cause of the Independence Movement, which was also strengthened by the bloody violence of the Spaniards who tried to suppress it.

8. Here and throughout the narrative, guillemets are used to indicate emphasis in the original version.

9. Bartolomé Guzmán was a collaborator and a participant in the uprising in Cochabamba in September 1810.

10. Francisco del Rivero, Esteban Arze, and Melchor Guzmán Quitón were the caudillos of the uprising in Cochabamba on September 14, 1810. Following the example of Murillo in La Paz, they attempted to depose the Governor José González de Prada. They received the support of the Cabildo at Oruro and achieved the first major victory of the Independence Movement against the Spanish Army at the Battle of Aroma, near Oruro, on November 14, 1810.

Further, after being defeated at Sipe Sipe in 1811, Esteban Arze rebuilt his army and achieved another victory in the Battle of Chayanta. He is known as the hero of Cochabamba. Francisco del Rivero, for his part, was accused of having made a pact with Goyeneche to avoid an attack on the city. This historical event is incorporated into the plot of the novel in Chapter XIII.

11. *El Overo* literally means gold-colored or golden. (Trans.)

CHAPTER III

1. The Cabildo is a Spanish community institution that was transplanted to the Americas with the Conquest. Although this body mostly administrated local and judicial matters, it was sometimes constituted as the seat of political power, especially toward the end of the Colonial period. It was constituted preferably by descendants of conquistadors and the founders of the city. See also n. 4 for *Junta Tuitiva* in Chapter II.

2. After having been a cadet in the Spanish army, José Ballivián (1804–1852) joined the forces of the Independence Movement in 1820. He was later the ninth president of Bolivia, from 1841 to 1847.

3. The phrase "Long live the homeland!" in Spanish is "¡Viva la patria!" The term "homeland," however, does not carry the exact meanings and connotations as *patria*. At the time of the Independence Movement, "¡Viva la patria!" expressed the desire for independence from Spain and the establishment of autonomous forms of government in the Americas. Before the different nation-states that are found today in Latin America were formed, *patria* could also refer to Bolívar's conception of a Gran Colombian state uniting all of the regions of South America, after they achieved their independence from Spain, into one single country, analogous to the United States of America. By the time *Juan de la Rosa* is written, however, *patria* already refers to the different national entities, such as Bolivia, Perú, Argentina, and so on. Therefore, a late nineteenth-century reader of the novel would garner the meanings of *patria* from the time of the Independence Movement, as well as the more traditional "patriotic" meanings of the word that would be implied once the nation of Bolivia had already been founded. (Trans.)

4. The Junta of Buenos Aires was the group that constituted itself in Buenos Aires on May 25, 1810, declaring the beginning of the revolution against the Spanish domination, thereby abolishing the Viceroyalty of Río de la Plata. The Junta was in charge of the administration of the region and also organized the expansion of the Independence Movement. The president of this Junta was Cornelio Saavedra (1759–1829), who was born in Potosí, in what is now Bolivia.

CHAPTER IV

1. See n. 8 in the Foreword.

2. An illustrious Carmelite priest, Fray Joseph Antonio de San Alberto (1727–1804) occupied important positions with the church in Spain, and later accepted the Archbishopric in Cordoba del Tucumán in 1780. In 1784, he was promoted to the Archbishopric of Charcas, which was the seat of the Audience of Charcas. This city, which today is called Sucre, was also known as La Plata. His pastoral letters have been collected into twenty volumes. He defended the presence and leadership of the Franciscans in the universities and also founded several orphanages.

3. See the section "Nation and Narration: A National History" in the Foreword for a brief explanation of the importance of the institution of primogeniture in Colonial Spanish America.

Chapter V

1. *Gringo* is used to refer to any foreigner. (Trans.)

2. Born in what is now Asunción, Paraguay, the jurisconsult Pedro Vicente Cañete (1751–?) was named Deputy Counsel of the Government and Intendancy of Potosí in 1783 and later became the Honorary Royal Judge (*Oidor*) of the Audiencia of Charcas. He is the author of the *Chronicle of the Intendancy of Potosí* (*Memoria de la Intendencia de Potosí*). Historians assert that when the Viceroy Elío approved the forming of the Junta of Montevideo, Cañete foresaw the awakening of the Independence Movements, and wrote in an attempt to discredit such a form of government (i.e., the Junta), although the latter was permitted under the Laws of the Indies (i.e., the laws governing Spanish America).

3. *Redondo* literally means round, or circular. (Trans.)

Chapter VI

1. *Berenguela* is a stone found in Perú and Bolivia similar to marble. (Trans.)

2. A *duende* is a mischievous spirit, such as a goblin, a fairy, or a ghost. (Trans.)

3. See the section "Nation and Narration: A National History" in the Foreword for a brief explanation of the importance of primogeniture.

4. *Accentus est, quo signatur, an sit longa, vel brevis syllaba*: Writing an accent mark can make a syllable long or short.

5. *Simillime, per omnia saecula saeculorum*: It has been the same for centuries upon centuries (i.e., It has and will always be like this).

6. *Facie ecclesiae*: Before the church, or by the church.

7. *Nunc dimittis*: Now, go.

8. In the Spanish text, Burgulla is referred to as the Licenciado Burgulla. A licenciado is someone with an academic title, probably in Law; it is also used before a person's name out of respect, much like Sir or Doctor. As there is no good equivalent in English, I have opted to use his Honor Burgulla instead of the literal the Licentiate Burgulla. (Trans.)

9. Antonio de Herrera y Tordesillas (1559–1625) wrote the *Historia general de las Indias Occidentales o de los hechos de los castellanos en las islas y tierra firme del mar océano*, which was published in Madrid in 1601. The work is characterized by the abundance of details that Herrera y Tordesillas included in the narration of the events of his time. It has been accused of being partial and exaggerating Spain's glorious events, while hiding or trying to extenuate the negative ones.

Chapter VII

1. *Huacas*, or *Guacas*, from Aymara and Quechua, are places in the Andean countryside demarcated as sacred, often containing idols and other religious items.

2. The "prince of poets" is Virgil (70–19 B.C.), the Latin poet, author of the *Aeneid*, a national epic poem in twelve books. The *Aeneid* postulates the origin of the predestination of Rome to become an Empire through the legend of Aeneas, a fugitive from Troy who founded a new family lineage and a Trojan settlement in Latium.

3. This quotation is from Book IV of the *Aeneid*, verses 181, 184, and 185. Aguirre omits verses 182 and 183, where the ellipsis is after the first verse that is quoted in the text. These verses speak of the speed of Fame, to which Dido attributes her loss of Aeneas. The actual verses 181 through 185 in Latin are:

181: *Monstrum horrendum ingens: cui, quod sunt corpore plumae*
182: *tot vigiles oculi subter (mirabile dictu)*
183: *tot linguae, totidem ora sonant, tot subriget auris*
184: *Nocte volat coeli medio terraeque, per umbram*
185: *Strident, nec dulci declinat lumina somno.*

The English equivalent to these verses is: She is a terrifying, enormous monster with as many feathers as she has sleepless eyes beneath each feather (amazingly), as many sounding tongues and mouths, and raises up as many ears. She flies at night between heaven and earth, through the shadows, and does not give in to sweet sleep. (Trans.)

4. *Quare dubitas?*: Why do you doubt?

5. *Videre et credere, sicut Thoma*: One must see to believe, according to St. Thomas.

6. *Accedo*: I am coming closer; I am going.

7. *Feminae intellectus acutus*: The intellect of women is sharp.

8. *Chicha* is a fermented liquor made from maize. (Trans.)

9. Sánchez Chávez was the Governor of Oruro, a district between La Paz and Cochabamba, during the time narrated in the novel.

10. *Chuño* is potato that has been frozen and starched through an ancient Andean technique that takes advantage of the thermal difference between day and night in the Andean Altiplano.

11. *Charqui* is dried, preserved meat, similar to jerked meat.

12. *Ichu* is a coarse highland grass used for thatching.

13. *Tola*, from the Quechua *t'ola*, is a thick shrub that grows at high altitudes.

14. *Lagua* is a heavy broth made usually from corn flour, although it can also be made from wheat or *chuño* flour.

15. A *montera* is a conical hat worn by Indians in the Andes. (Trans.)

16. *Huauque* is a Quechua term that a brother uses to refer to another brother. In this case, the plural, *Huaques*, is a hispanicized version of the Quechua word.

17. *Leque*, from the Quechua, is a wool hat. The plural, *leques*, is a hispanicized version of the Quechua word.

18. *Tata* is a respectful and affectionate term for a father or an older person. (Trans.)

19. *Huincui*, from the Quechua, is the imperative command to drop or fall to the ground.

20. *Huactai, huauque* in Quechua means "Fight, brother!"

21. *Pututus* are whistles whose sound can be heard at great distances.

22. A mammal of the Andean foothills, the guanaco is in the same family as the llama, the vicuña, and camels.

23. *Porteños* are residents of or from Buenos Aires. The term derives from the word port (*puerto*), and the fact that the city of Buenos Aires was built around its port. (Trans.)

Chapter VIII

1. A general in the Independence Movement, Antonio González Balcárcel (1774–1819) was the victor of the Battle of Suipacha in November 1810. He also fought in Maipú and in Cancha Rayada as San Martín's second in command.

2. Vicente Nieto (1769–1810) was appointed President of the Audience of Charcas by the Viceroy of Buenos Aires. He vigorously suppressed the revolutionary uprisings in Chuquisaca and Cochabamba. In 1810, he was a field marshall and fell prisoner to General Balcárcel. He was executed in Potosí along with Paula Sanz and José de Córdova in December 1810.

3. Born in Spain, Francisco de Paula Sanz (176?–1810) went to Buenos Aires in 1780, where he carried out administrative duties for the Spanish Crown. He later became Governor of Potosí and as such was categorically opposed to the Independence Movement. He was captured and ordered to be executed by Castelli (see n. 10).

4. A brigadier in the Royalist armies, José de Córdova (1778–1842) fell back to Potosí after being defeated in the Battle of Suipacha. However, he was captured by Balcárcel after Suipacha's own uprising, to be later executed by firing squad.

5. Colonel Juan Ramírez was appointed Governor of La Paz after the efforts toward Independence by Murillo and the Junta Tuitiva were suppressed. He later sent the Spanish troops from La Paz to combat the rebels from Cochabamba and Oruro; the former were defeated by Arze in the Battle of Aroma.

6. Fermín Piérola led several sections of the troops that advanced upon La Paz from Cuzco under the leadership of Goyeneche.

7. The Spanish playwright and poet Pedro Calderón de la Barca (1600–1681) is considered the last exponent of the Spanish Golden Age. His works display a special mastery in the complicated machination of their plots. His most famous works include "El Alcalde de Zalamea" and "La vida es sueño."

8. Agustín Moreto y Cabaña (1618–1669) was a prolific Spanish playwright and poet. He is known for the mastery of dialogue in his plays.

9. *Nihil novum sube sole*: Nothing new under the sun.

10. Juan José Castelli (1764–1812) was one of the leaders of the Revolution of May 25, 1810. He was a member of the Junta of Buenos Aires along with Saavedra. He went with the first expedition to Upper Perú under the leadership of General Balcárcel and participated in the first victory of the Argentine troops in Suipacha, in November 1810. The Junta of Buenos Aires then appointed him

leader of the expedition. In this position, he excelled in his eloquence in promoting the Independence Movement and in his policy of working to incorporate indigenous populations into it. In 1811, he signed the Desaguadero Armistice with Goyeneche, which the latter betrayed, to then defeat Castelli in Huaqui, thus recovering Upper Perú for the Spaniards.

11. *Anibal in Capuae*: Hannibal in Capua.

12. *Quos Deus vult perdere, primo dementat*: He who wishes to lose God, is mad from the beginning.

13. Born in Spain, Moxó (1763–1816) was appointed Archbishop of the Audience of Charcas in 1804. Since his response to the uprisings of Chuquisaca and La Paz in 1809 was one of absolute condemnation, he was removed from the diocese by the revolutionary Junta of Buenos Aires by Rondeau.

14. *Capio, intendo*: Caught, I understand.

15. The *Marseillaise* is the national anthem of France, composed by Claude Rouget de Lisle (1760–1836). It was popularized by the Marseillaise Federals in 1793 and is associated with the struggle for liberty of the French Revolution.

Chapter IX

1. Mariano Antezana (1771–1812) was a well-to-do citizen of Cochabamba. In 1810, he sided with the Independence Movement, lending his estates to the Movement's cause. As Governor of Cochabamba, he resisted the entrance of the Spaniards. For this, he was ordered to be executed by Goyeneche, who also had him beheaded and his head displayed on the end of a pike as a warning to the rebels. Nataniel Aguirre incorporates this historic episode into the novel in Chapter XXIII.

2. *Excelsior! Audite, cives!*: Grand! Listen, citizens!

3. The Spanish priest and chronicler Fray Bartolomé de las Casas (1474–1565) resigned his "encomiendas" in 1515, denouncing the abuses of colonialization. He went on to dedicate himself to the defense of the Indians in the face of the excesses of the Conquest.

4. The Inca Garcilaso de la Vega (1536–1616), whose mother was a descendent of the Incas, was the first Peruvian indigenous chronicler and historian. He traveled to Spain at a very early age, where he came in contact with all aspects of the culture of the Renaissance. He is the author of "La Florida del Inca," "Comentarios Reales," and the "Historia del Perú."

5. See notes 7 and 8 in the Foreword for an explanation of the *encomiendas*, as well as the Apportionments, the Tribute, and the *comunidades*.

6. When the Spanish government did not respond to his complaints, the indigenous cacique Túpac Amaru (José Gabriel Condorcanqui) decided to capture the Collector from Tinta in 1780. This, in conjunction with the rebellious movements of the Catari brothers in Chayanta, Potosí, went on to become the large indigenous rebellion of the eighteenth century.

7. At first, the *forasteros* were the Indians who did not belong to the *comu-*

nidades as determined by Toledo, and they were considered fugitives fleeing from their obligation to pay the Tribute. In the eighteenth century, they were made to pay the Tribute as *forasteros*; at this point, they composed a majority of the population subjected to the Tribute.

8. See the section "Nation and Narration: A National History" in the Foreword and the notes therein for a brief explanation of how the Colonial economic institutions functioned.

9. Juan Antonio Alvarez de Arenales (1770–1831), who served as a soldier in the Regiment of Burgos, Spain, arrived in the Americas in 1784. He was sent to Upper Perú, where he denounced the ill treatment of the indigenous people. This led to an antagonism between him and Governor Viedma. When the May Revolution arrived, he sided with the cause of the Independence Movement and led the retreat to Tucumán after the defeat at Sipe Sipe. Due to the disastrous losses at Vilcapugio and Ayohuma, he was isolated in Cochabamba, but was able to flee and reorganize his troops.

10. The Ruins of Tiahuanaco is an archeological site outside the city of La Paz that contains the remains of an ancient civilization that had existed in the Andean Altiplano. According to some scholars, it dates to 133 A.C.

11. *Tahuantinsuyu* is derived from the Quechua *tawa*, meaning four, and *suyu*, meaning part or section. Thus, it means the four regions united together. The term was used to refer to the Inca government that oversaw four large Andean regions.

12. The Argentine writer probably refers to Bartolomé Mitre, who was very widely read in Bolivia from the end of the nineteenth century onward, especially his *Historia de Belgrano y de la Independencia argentina*, published in Buenos Aires around 1878. Mitre is also cited by the Bolivian historian Alcides Arguedas in his *Historia General de Bolivia*, published in La Paz in 1922.

13. King Xerxes (519–465 B.C.) was a Persian King who drove away his older brothers in order to inherit the kingdom from his father, alluding that they were born before their father was King. He executed 300 Spartans in Thermopylae, and later set fire to the city of Athens.

14. *Mellizo* literally means a twin brother. (Trans.)

15. *Jorro* literally means a dragnet. (Trans.)

16. *El valiente justiciero y el rico hombre de Alcalá*, by Agustín Moreto, was published in Madrid in 1654. A comedy with a historical plot, it deals with a king who is just, but not cruel. Don Tello García, however, a wealthy gentleman from Alcalá, exercises a cruel tyranny over the king's subjects. To discover if this is indeed true, the King, Don Pedro, dresses up as an ordinary subject and ends up by admonishing the cruel Don Tello García.

CHAPTER X

1. José de Armendáriz Marqués de Castel-Fuerte was the Viceroy of Perú from 1724 to 1736, during which time the uprising of Alejo Calatayud took place in Cochabamba. His viceroyalty was characterized by his severity with the in-

digenous people, his tight control of regional commerce, and his bloody repression of the protests that were starting to arise. He was also in favor of the Inquisition, and it was considered by the Spaniards that his policies led to a blossoming of the Peruvian economy.

2. A *vinchuca* is a flying insect that nests in bedrooms, like bedbugs. It can carry the disease known as the illness from Chagas (*el mal de Chagas*), which is widely spread today.

3. The *charango* is a five-stringed bandore or guitar played by the Indians in the Andes. (Trans.)

4. *Samay* is the Quechua verb meaning to rest, or to breathe. In this case, a *sama* is a rest.

5. *Bayeta* is a thick, flannel-like material. (Trans.)

6. *Chunco, tatitoi* is an affectionate, intimate expression said to one's father. It comes from the Quechua *chunco*, meaning heart, and *tatitoi*, my father.

7. A *poyo* is a stone or adobe bench built directly against a wall. (Trans.)

8. *Habas* are known in English as haba beans, broad beans, or sweet peas.

9. *Locoto* refers to any variety of fresh, hot peppers: red, green, or yellow. They are similar to the Mexican chiles. The term is *rocoto* in Perú.

10. *Ulupica* is a very small, spicy fruit used to season soups.

11. *Loritos* literally means small parrots. The glasses have this name because *loritos* tend to be green. (Trans.)

12. An *era* is the threshing-floor where the chicha is fermented. (Trans.)

13. *Guemals* are small deer, native to South America. (Trans.)

14. *Viscachas* are burrowing rodents in the chinchilla family, native to South America. (Trans.)

15. *Yurackasa* in Quechua means the white—in other words, snowy—ravine.

16. Alcides Dessalines D'Orbigny (1802–1857) was a French naturalist who undertook an extensive scientific journey from 1826 to 1834. He traveled through Brazil, Uruguay, Argentina, Chile, Bolivia, and Perú and was awarded the annual prize by the Geographic Society. The French government then commissioned him to write a memoir of his South American travels; after thirteen years of working on the project, he published his well-known and important work in nine volumes, *Viaje a la América Meridional*.

17. *Ovejero* literally means shepherd or sheep dog. (Trans.)

18. *Harahui*, or *yaraví*, comes from the Quechua verb *awai*, meaning to compose poetry. It is a sweet and melancholy indigenous song.

19. Ollanta is the main character in the *Ollantay* drama (see n. 7 in Chapter I). He was a brave warrior in the times of the Inca Pachacutec, but did not belong to the same class level as the Inca.

20. Cusi Coyllur is another main character in the *Ollantay* drama. The daughter of the Inca Pachacutec, she falls in love with Ollanta even though he does not belong to her class level.

21. The Inca Pachacutec, in the *Ollantay* drama, is the father of Túpac Amaru as well as Cusi Coyllur. The drama begins as his kingship is coming to an end.

CHAPTER XI

1. General Joaquín de la Pezuela (1761–1856) was the military officer who replaced Goyeneche after the latter retired. He achieved victory for the Spaniards in several battles, including the Battle of Viluma against General Belgrano, for which he received the title of Marquis.

2. The quotation is from the *Historia General de la Revolución Hispanoamericana*, published in Madrid in 1829, by the Spaniard Mariano Torrente (1792–1856), who conducted research for this work in France and England. Torrente is cited by several historians in their writings on the Wars of Independence, including Bartolomé Mitre and Alcides Arguedas.

3. The character of *Sganarelle* appears in several of French playwright Moliére's (1622–1673) comedies as the unfortunate, cuckolded husband who believes he was betrayed even before he was married.

4. Eustaquio Díaz Vélez (1790–1856) was a captain when the Revolution of May broke out in Buenos Aires. In 1811, he left for Upper Perú with the revolutionary army. He participated in the Battles of Sipe Sipe, Vilcapujio, and Ayohuma, and in the victories of Salta and Tucumán. In 1813, he was appointed Governor of Salta; that same year, he took possession of Potosí, a very important stronghold during the Wars of Independence, for it contained the Mint from which the Spanish armies, and later the revolutionary ones, drew heavy resources.

5. The Spanish painter Francisco de Goya y Lucientes (1746–1828) is well known, in part, for the realism depicted in his paintings of local people and landscapes.

6. A *valluno* is a native from a valley. (Trans.)

7. Tristán, an officer in the Royalist armies, was Goyeneche's cousin and a close and reliable relation of his.

8. *Consuelo* literally means consolation or comfort. (Trans.)

CHAPTER XII

1. Claudio Pinilla was a Bolivian politician and statesman, member of the Liberal Party. He was the Secretary of the Bolivian Legation to Asunción in 1906.

2. *Mistela* is a drink made from grape juice and alcohol. (Trans.)

3. *Tostón* was a small, silver coin from Mexico worth fifty cents. It was originally called *testón* from the Latin *testa*, meaning head, because of the image of a head that is engraved on it.

4. See n. 2 in Chapter XI for more information on the writer Mariano Torrente and his work *Historia General de la Revolución Hispanoamericana*.

5. *Huainos*, or *huayños*, is a traditional Andean rhythm used in songs and dances.

6. *Sacaqueñas* is music from the region of Sacaca.

7. *Chicherías* are taverns where chicha is served. (Trans.)

8. *Quenas* are Indian reed flutes. (Trans.)

9. See n. 3 and n. 4 in Chapter II on Pedro Domingo Murillo and on the Junta Tuitiva for a brief explanation of these events.

10. The *Te Deum* is the Catholic Mass and ceremony giving thanks to God. It comes from the Latin, meaning "To you, God."

11. Literally, *el Católico* means "the Catholic." (Trans.)

12. *Chunco*, from the Quechua meaning heart, is an affectionate appellative.

13. *Cholo* is an appellative generally used to refer to a mestizo and which carries a derogatory connotation. *Mocontullo* comes from the Quechua *moqo*, meaning encumbrance or protruding, and *tullu*, meaning bone. Here, it is used to mean hunchbacked.

14. Teodor Hahenke (or Tadeo Hanke) (1751–1817) was a naturalist from Bohemia who undertook a trip around the world, and later settled in Cochabamba, where he built a botanical garden and established a magnificent herbarium. A description of the latter, *Raeliquia Haenkeanae*, was published by Prest in Prague in 1830.

15. *Invictus Caesar:* Triumphant (unconquered) Caesar.

16. The reference is to the episode in which the mythical hero Ulysses, along with a group of other Greek warriors, are able to enter the city of Troy hidden inside a large wooden horse, which the Trojans had accepted as a gift from the Greeks. The episode is briefly recounted in Homer's *Odyssey* (Books IV and XI), and then expanded in great detail in Virgil's *Aeneid* (Canto II).

Chapter XIII

1. This chapter of the novel deals with the historical event to which we alluded in n. 10 on Esteban Arze and Francisco del Rivero in Chapter II. Juan Martín de Pueyrredón (1777–1850) was a harbinger and an officer in the Independence Movement. The Junta of Buenos Aires first appointed him Governor of Córdoba; then, in 1811, he was appointed Governor, Intendant, and President of the Audience of Charcas.

2. By defeating the troops of the Viceroy of Serna in the Battle of Ayacucho in 1824, Grand Marshal Sucre garnered the definitive independence of Perú and Bolivia from Spain (see Map 1).

3. The Inisterio was a water fountain near the University of San Francisco Javier in the city of Sucre (or La Plata), the site of the Audiencia of Charcas during the Colonial period. Because of the proximity of the fountain to the university, it was said that one would acquire great knowledge if one drank from its waters.

4. Elio Antonio Nebrija (1444–1522) was a Spanish humanist and grammarian born in Seville. His work *Arte de la lengua castellana* was the first book on grammar to be published in a common language in Spain (i.e., in a language other than Latin). He also wrote several studies on Latin, and a Spanish-Latin, Latin-Spanish dictionary. Due to his broad knowledge of classical languages, and for revealing the scientific and political meanings of the Spanish language, he is considered

the most brilliant Spanish literary figure from the period of the reign of Ferdi-
nand and Isabel.

5. Marcus Tullius Cicero (106–43 B.C.) was a great Roman orator and statesman, and a prolific, classical Latin writer.

6. Guerrero and Lamar were officers who fought in the last battles of the Independence Movement. The former served under General San Martín, and the
latter under Grand Marshal Antonio José de Sucre.

7. The Centaurs of the Argentine pampas refers to the soldiers of the Argentine armies who, until 1816, reached Upper Perú to fight the Spaniards as part of
the Independence Movement.

8. Born in Salta (in what is now Argentina), Martín de Güemes (1785–1821)
joined the revolutionary armies in 1810. He was then dispatched to Upper Perú,
where he participated in the Battle of Suipacha. He is especially known for the resistance he later led in Salta in a war for resources with mounted troops, which lasted five years, from 1815 to 1820. He turned the inhabitants of Salta and Jujuy into
soldiers, who came to be known as "*los gauchos de Güemes*" (Güemes' gauchos).

9. José Antonio Páez (1790–1873) was a celebrated Venezuelan officer in the
Wars of Independence. He came from a family of Indians who had converted to
Catholicism. Known for his military genius, he was one of the men who designed
the strategy leading to the triumph of the Battle of Carabobo in 1821 (See Map 1).
After Bolívar's death in 1830, Páez approved and carried out the disintegration of
the Grand Colombian state and founded the Republic of Venezuela. Nataniel
Aguirre compares Páez, as a founding father, with Esteban Arze.

10. The writer and politician Eufronio Viscarra (1857–1911) was a contemporary of Nataniel Aguirre. The two of them together founded the Liberal Party. He
is the author of *Apuntes para la historia de Cochabamba*, a *Biografía de Esteban Arze*,
and *La rebelión de Alejo Calatayud de 1730*, among others. Viscarra also wrote the
Prologue to the second edition of *Juan de la Rosa*, published in 1909.

11. The Venezuelan General and politician Francisco Antonio Miranda
(1756–1816) was an early supporter of the Independence Movement. In England,
he promoted the cause of the emancipation of Spanish America, and he also participated in one of the first uprisings of the Independence Movement in
Venezuela in July 1811. He was then named Commander in Chief of the land and
sea forces, but in 1812 he surrendered to the Spanish General Monteverde. This
led to the complete loss of his prestige, and even Bolívar turned against him.
Nataniel Aguirre compares Miranda's fate with Monteverde with that of Francisco del Rivero, as Governor of Cochabamba, with Goyeneche.

12. *Aillos*, or *ayllu*, from the Aymara and the Quechua, refers to social and geographic organizations of Andean peoples and their agricultural production, kinship ties, and regional relationships.

13. *Chuquiaguru* is the Aymara indigenous name for the city of La Paz.

14. Choqueguanca was an indigenous cacique.

15. Mateo Pumacagua was an indigenous cacique from Cuzco who collabo-
rated with the Spaniards during the rebellions of Túpac Amaru and of Túpac

Katari and who later joined the Independence Movement in 1814.

16. Huisi was an indigenous cacique who fought in the Wars of Independence.

CHAPTER XIV

1. *Per istam*: Therefore.

2. Jacobins took on radical democratic positions during the French Revolution. A Jacobin, therefore, is used to refer to anyone with radical political beliefs.

3. A city in French Guyana, Cayenne was the site of an infamous prison.

CHAPTER XV

1. The treasures of *Tangatanga*, a colloquialism, is an imaginary kingdom that a child might dream about. The word *Tanga* suggests an African origin.

2. In the drama of the *Ollantay*, the maidens of Ollanta, who is the mother of Cusi Coyllur, sing yaravís as a chorus (See n. 7 in Chapter I and n. 19 to n. 21 in Chapter X).

3. *Chasca* comes from the Quechua word *chaska*, meaning star.

4. The older name given to recently arrived Spanish soldiers, *guampos* has the same meaning as *chapetones*. (Trans.)

5. *Paloma* means dove in Spanish; hence, *Palomita* is a little dove. Further, this affectionate appellative has a second derivation from the Quechua, in which *paloma (urpi)* means honey. The appellative *Paloma* also appears in the *Ollantay*. (Trans.)

6. Born in Buenos Aires, Bartolomé Mitre (1821–1902) undertook his military education and training in Argentina and went on to participate in that country's civil wars. He later traveled to Bolivia, where he gained the command of this country's military academy. During his time there, he wrote a small novel entitled *Soledad* (*Loneliness*), which was considered Bolivia's first novel. He also spent time in Perú and in Chile, where he practiced journalism. As a historian, Mitre is the founder of Argentina's erudite historiographic tradition. His *Historia de Belgrano*, mentioned here, was published in Buenos Aires in 1877. He was elected President of Argentina in 1861.

CHAPTER XVI

1. According to legends, the Gran Paititi was a rich kingdom, found somewhere in the Andean region, which had survived the Inca Empire. Many explorers set out to try to find it, believing it to be full of gold. Its legend is similar to that of El Dorado.

2. This quotation is from Moreto's comedy *El valiente justiciero*. See note 16 in Chapter IX.

3. *Choco* is a colloquialism meaning blond, or fair. In this case, it refers to the color of the dog's fur.

4. *Maleso*, from *malo*, meaning bad, is a nickname given to troublemakers. (Trans.)

5. *Pallacos*, from the Quechua *pallay*, meaning to grab or pick up, are people who pick up or gather things from the street.

6. Juan Espinoza published the *Diccionario Republicano* in 1852. He wrote other articles in newspapers and periodicals in Lima, but under the pseudonym of *El Soldado de los Andes* (The Andean Soldier). He took part in the Wars of Independence, first in the Battles of Chacabuco (1817) and Maipú (1818), and then in the Battles of Junín (1824) and Ayacucho (1824).

7. Arriaga, Vidal, and Cabrera participated in the uprising of Cocha-bamba of 1812.

8. Vélez and Salinas participated in the uprising of Cochabamba of 1812.

9. *Ut supra*: Formalism meaning "as stated herein."

CHAPTER XVII

1. *Pilluelos* (as well as *carachupas* and *gamins*) means street urchins. (Trans.)

2. *Soltero* is a side dish made with tomatoes, onions, *locoto* (a pepper found in Bolivia), and *quesillo* (a fresh white cheese) and seasoned with *quilquiña* (an herb).

3. *Humita*, from the Quechua *umint'a*, is an Andean dish made from fresh corn paste, with cheese and peppers. It is wrapped in a corn husk and then cooked.

4. The ecclesiastical Spanish writer Juan de Torquemeda (1388–1460) was a vigorous defender of church dogma, and as such became a symbol of the Spanish Inquisition. He contributed to the condemnation of the doctrines of John Wiclef (an early exponent of the Reformation) and of the Hussites (followers of John Huss, a fifteenth-century religious reformer). He also maintained the dogma of the Immaculate Conception of the Virgin Mary and wrote *Summa de Eclesia*.

5. Fernando VII of Aragón (1452–1516) and Isabel I of Castille (1451–1504) are known as the *Reyes Católicos* (the Catholic Kings). Their reign witnessed the expulsion of the Moors from the south of Spain with the completion of the Reconquest and the taking of Granada, as well as the discovery of America. The support of Isabel for Christopher Columbus was a determining factor in the latter's accomplishment. Fernando and Isabel also formed a modern state, reforming many institutions, and subjecting nobles who had held excessive power.

6. *Oportet semper orare*: It is always opportune to pray.

7. *Majestatem tuam laudant Angeli, adorant dominationes*: The angels praise your majesty and adore your power.

8. *Prima via veritatis est humilitas; secunda, humilitas; tertia, humilitas*: The first path to the truth is humility, the second is humility, and the third is also humility.

9. The prayer *Flos Sanctorum* literally means "Flower of the Saints."

10. The City of Kings refers to Lima, Perú. (Trans.)

11. The principal director of the *Encyclopedia* was French writer and philosopher Denis Diderot (1713–1784). Father Arredondo shows his ignorance—or con-

tempt, or both—in confusing Diderot's name. The objective of the massive *En-cyclopedia*, which consisted of thirty-three volumes, was to compile the totality of human knowledge, including the fields of science, the arts, and all the professions.

12. A Franciscan priest and a censor appointed by the Inquisition, Antonio Arbiol wrote numerous religious and moral works. His best known include the *Desengaños místicos a las almas detenidas o engañadas en el camino de la perfección* (1713) mentioned in the novel, and *La religiosa instruida* (1717).

13. Saracens refers to Muslim Arabs.

CHAPTER XVIII

1. Known also as Pepe Botellas, Joseph Bonaparte (1768–1844) was Napoleon's brother. He led the invasion of Spain, and dethroned King Fernando VII during the French occupation of Spain, from 1808 to 1813. He was also the King of Naples.

2. Carlota Joaquina del Brasil (1775–1830) was the Princess and Queen of Portugal when France invaded Spain. It is said that once Fernando VII left Spain, she used the argument that there was now no king to rule over Spain's colonies in order to try to extend her rights and expand her kingdom in the Americas to include the Spanish possessions.

3. Lombera was an officer in the Spanish armies under the command of Goyeneche.

4. On his way back from Spain under the order of the Junta of Seville to defend the cause of Fernando VII—the exiled Spanish king—in the Americas, Goyeneche met with Princess Carlota Joaquina del Brasil. The Carlotist schemes refer to the supposed agreement that Goyeneche reached with Carlota to support the aspirations and ambitions that the Portuguese Queen held over Spanish America.

5. See n. 13 on Archbishop Moxó in Chapter VIII.

6. *Les chanoines vermeils, et brillants de santé*: The bright red, and wonderfully healthy, canons.

7. *D'abord pole et muet, de colére inmobile*: At first pale and mute, and without rage.

8. Nicolàs Boileau-Despreaux (1636–1711) was a neoclassical French poet and rhetorician and a friend of Molière and Racine.

9. A hispanicized way of saying zambo, or sambo, *zambillo* is meant to sound at once derogatory and ridiculous. (Trans.)

10. Juan Imas was an officer in the Spanish armies under the command of Goyeneche. He was feared for the violence with which he suppressed the rebels.

11. *Republiquetas* is the name given to the different isolated regional groups in Upper Perú that fought against the Spaniards from 1816 to 1825 under the leadership of separate caudillos.

12. *Montoneros* are guerrilla soldiers who fight from, or in, the mountains.

13. *Hayopaya*, or Ayopaya, is a province in the District of Cochabamba, bor-

dering the District of La Paz to the west (see Map 2).

14. *Chapín de la Reina* literally means the queen's shoe or clog. (Trans.)

CHAPTER XIX

1. See n. 2 in Chapter V for a brief explanation of the personage Cañete.

2. *Ingeneratur hominibus mores a stirpe, generis*: Men's habits are created by their family lineage.

3. *Excelsior*: The highest, the most.

4. *Odi profanum vulgus, et arceo*: I hate the irreverent masses, and leave them behind.

5. *Nullam, vare, sacra vite*: There is no sacred ceremony for life.

6. *Justum, et tenacem prositi virum*: Justice and tenacity are what make men.

7. *Haud flectes illum, ne si sanguine quidem fleveris*: Do not subject yourself to them, even when they cry tears of blood.

8. *Nunc est bibendum, nunc pede libero*: Now he is drinking, now he is strolling.

9. *Excelsior! Feminae intellectus acutus*: The highest, woman's intellect is sharp.

10. Lozano, Ferrufino, Ascui, Zapata, Padilla, Luján, and Gandarillas were citizens in favor of the Independence Movement who participated in an outstanding manner in the defense of Cochabamba on May 27, 1812.

11. Corrales was a citizen in favor of the Independence Movement who participated in an outstanding manner in the defense of Cochabamba on May 27, 1812.

CHAPTER XX

1. An invention of the Grandmother's, she crosses *guampo* (the old name of the Royalist soldiers) with *chapetones* (the name used at the time of the current scene) to get *guampones*. (Trans.)

2. *Cuzqueño* is a nickname for someone from Cuzco. (Trans.)

3. Pepe Botellas is the nickname of Napoleon's brother, José Bonaparte. See nn. 1, 2, and 4 in Chapter XVIII for brief explanations of why he, as well as the Junta of Seville and Carlota, are important to the novel in relation to Goyeneche.

4. *Non, sacré Dieu! Non, par la culotte de mon père!*: No, Holy God! By my father's undergarments, no!

5. The Spanish version of Louis-Aime Martin's (1786–1847) *Education des meres de famille*, which first appeared in French in 1834, was published in Mexico around 1857 as *La educación de las madres*.

6. Théophile La Tour D'Auvergne (1743–1800) was a celebrated French officer.

CHAPTER XXI

1. The Cid Campeador, Rodrigo Díaz de Vivar (1043–1099) was a Spanish knight who fought and triumphed in many battles against the Moors on the

Spanish Peninsula. He is the hero of the well-known, anonymous epic poem *El Cantar de Mío Cid*, the oldest known Spanish epic.

2. The *Tizona* was the Cid's legendary sword, from the Spanish epic *El Cantar de Mío Cid*. Colloquially, it is used to mean a powerful and deadly sword. (Trans.)

3. Calleja, Bobes, and Morales were Spaniards who fought for Spain in the Americas.

CHAPTER XXII

1. The Spanish King Carlos III (1716–1788) carried out a series of reforms in the eighteenth century that led to economic and material progress in Spain. The reforms also extended to the Colonial institutions in the Americas.

2. *Delicta majorum inmeritus lues, Romane*: Major offenses, unjust calamity, Roman!

3. See n. 2 on Vicente Cañete in Chapter V. The "Advice Regarding the Situation of the Spanish Colonies" ("Dictamen sobre la situación de las colonias españolas") is one of his works.

4. The first official Argentine newspaper, the *Gaceta de Buenos Aires* was created by the Junta of Buenos Aires to inform and disseminate the Junta's decrees and measures. According to Bartolomé Mitre, it inaugurated the freedom of the press in South America.

5. *Divis orte bonis, optime Romulae*: The beginning of an abundance of goods, most perfect for Romulus. (A quotation from an ode by Horace.)

6. Themistocles (c. 514–450 B.C.) was a celebrated Greek commander and statesman from Athens. He defeated the Persians in the victory of Salamis.

7. The *Pacha mama* is the Mother Earth, the beginning of life, and the center of all Andean agrarian rituals.

CHAPTER XXIII

1. *Corpus Christi*: Body of Christ. The *Corpus Christi* is an important Catholic celebration of the Eucharist. In the Americas, the celebrations also incorporate indigenous rituals. Characteristically, the ones in the Andean region juxtapose the image of the Eucharist with the image of the sun, or Inti, the most important of the Inca gods.

2. Alexander von Baron de Humboldt (1769–1859) was a German naturalist and explorer. He explored several large regions of South America with the support of the Spanish government, gathering extensive information that he then published in the 30 volumes of his *Viaje a las regiones equinocciales del Nuevo Continente*. He is attributed with numerous geographic, geologic, and botanical discoveries, and he was also the one who introduced guano from the Pacific coast to Europeans.

3. *Miserere*: Have mercy. The religious song *Miserere* is based on Psalm 51 of

the Bible, which begins with *Miserere mei Deus* (Have mercy upon me, oh God).

4. *Ecce enim in inquitatibus conceptus sum*: (From the *Miserere*) Behold, I was shapen in iniquity, and in sin did my mother conceive me.

5. *Ecce enim veritatem dilexisti*: (From the *Miserere*) Behold, thou desirest truth in the inward parts.

6. *Domine, ut scuto bonae, voluntatis meum*: (From the *Miserere*) God, in the hidden part thou shalt make me to know wisdom.

7. *Intellige clamorem meum*: (From the *Miserere*) Hear my cry.

8. *Lux ultra*! Higher light!

9. *Lechehuairos* is a group of dancers dressed in white.

10. *Tactaquis*, from the Quechua *tactaqeay*, meaning to crow or cackle, is a group of dancers that imitate birds.

11. *Faillires* is another kind of group of dancers.

12. "The thirteen gentlemen from Seville" refers to how the dance group is dressed, comparing it with the thirteen gentlemen from Santiago.

13. The *Inglés* literally means the Englishman. It is also an appellative for someone who speaks English. (Trans.)

14. *Via Crucis*: The Way of the Cross. A devout Catholic exercise that consists of walking a path marked by crosses representing the fourteen Stations of the Cross.

15. *Lorera* probably comes from *loro*, which is a parrot. (Trans.)

Chapter XXIV

1. Although a nobleman, Honoré Gabriel Riqueti Mirabeau (1749–1791) was elected as a delegate to the National Assembly during the French Revolution. He then presided over the National Assembly and argued in favor of a constitutional monarchy in the famous challenge to the Crown. His taking this position made both the delegates and the king suspicious of him.

2. Vergniaud (1753–1793) was a politician during the French Revolution, from the Girondist Party. He delivered the famous speech denouncing the king.

3. Bernardo Monteagudo (1791–1825) was one of the architects of the May Revolution of 1809, plotted from the Universidad de San Francisco Javier in Charcas, Chuquisaca. Monteagudo was educated at this university; he was a very important and highly articulate defender of the ideas of the Independence Movement, as expressed through his speeches and writings, to which Brother Justo refers in the novel. He also contributed to the writing of the Act of Independence of Chile, in 1818. After his death, Perú, Bolivia, and Argentina argued over this forefather's birthplace, until it was finally established that he had been born in Tucumán, in what is now Argentina.

4. Although they did not produce major texts, the other men listed in the novel—Michel, Alcérreca, Rivarola, Quiroga, Carrasco, and Orihuela—all played active roles in the Independence Movement, presenting speeches in various Congresses, and participating in the uprising of La Paz in July 1809, as well as the one in Buenos Aires in 1810.

CHAPTER XXV

1. Molinists followed the teachings of Miguel de Molinos (1628–1696), who held the heterodox belief that the union of holy souls with God could be reached without the external practices of religion. Molinos was expelled and condemned by the Inquisition.

2. *Chabelita* is a nickname for Isabel. (Trans.)

3. Flaccus refers to the classical Latin poet Horace (65–8 B.C.), whose name in Latin is Quintus Horātius Flaccus.

4. *Cur velle permutem Sabina?*: Why would it be fine to change Sabina? (Referring to his wife.)

5. See the section "Nation and Narration: A National History" in the Foreword for a brief explanation of the importance of the institution of primogeniture in Colonial Spanish America.

6. *La vida y hechos del Admirante don Cristóbal Colón.* (Trans.)

CHAPTER XXVI

1. General Manuel Isidoro Belzu (1811–1871) was president of Bolivia from 1848 to 1855. During his term in office, he received the broad support of small businesses and artisans from the urban areas because his policies tended to favor these groups. He also utilized the press to disseminate his actions.

2. José Rondeau (1773–1844) was the commander of the army fighting for Independence in the Banda Oriental del Uruguay (in what is today the country of Uruguay). He was named General of the United Provinces of Montevideo and Commander in Chief of the army of the Alto Perú for his actions in the Battle of Cerrito (1814).

CHAPTER XXVII

1. *Leal* literally means loyal or faithful. (Trans.)

2. Túpac Catari was the head of an indigenous uprising against the local Spanish government in 1780. After unsuccessfully presenting their demands to the Viceroyalty of Buenos Aires, the rebels, led by Catari, laid siege to the city of La Paz. The Spaniards mobilized all their forces and eventually defeated the indigenous group. Bartolina Sisa was Túpac Catari's wife.